INTERNATIONAL LAW IN ACTION

This book provides an indispensable source for understanding Korean economic and political views. It compiles select news commentaries on the impact of international law on Korean domestic markets and politics from 2010 to 2020.

Each section of the book begins with an original essay by the author discussing core issues covered by the news commentaries. Articles then follow, providing at-the-time analysis of the interactions between international law and international relations, as well as the interaction between domestic and international law. Many of the issues, such as China-US relations and refugee policy, are of global relevance, and the thematic clusters will give the readers and students a picture of:

- how international law actually operates in the field,
- how international law and international relations interact, and
- how legal discourse is taking place in the global and domestic community in this process.

Written with a colloquial tone and colorful idioms, this supplementary reading is perfect for students looking to enrich their understanding of how law lies behind newspaper headlines. It will also be of interest to scholars and instructors of international economic law, Korean studies, and international relations.

Jaemin Lee is Dean and Professor of Law at School of Law, Seoul National University in Seoul, Korea. He served as President of the Korean Society of International Economic Law (2020–2021).

INTERNATIONAL LAW IN ACTION

Domestic and Global Legal Affairs Viewed through a Legal Prism

Jaemin Lee

Routledge
Taylor & Francis Group
LONDON AND NEW YORK

Designed cover image: Getty Images

First published 2026
by Routledge
4 Park Square, Milton Park, Abingdon, Oxon OX14 4RN

and by Routledge
605 Third Avenue, New York, NY 10158

Routledge is an imprint of the Taylor & Francis Group, an informa business

British Library Cataloguing-in-Publication Data
A catalogue record for this book is available from the British Library

ISBN: 978-1-032-81859-7 (hbk)
ISBN: 978-1-032-81857-3 (pbk)
ISBN: 978-1-003-50174-9 (ebk)

DOI: 10.4324/9781003501749

Typeset in Times New Roman
by Apex CoVantage, LLC

BRIEF CONTENTS

CONTENTS

ABOUT THE AUTHOR

Jaemin Lee is currently Dean and Professor of Law at School of Law, Seoul National University in Seoul, Korea. He obtained his LLB, LLM, and PhD from Seoul National University; LLM from Georgetown University Law Center; and JD from Boston College Law School. He served as President of the Korean Society of International Economic Law (2020–2021). His book entitled *Artificial Intelligence and International Law* was published by Springer in May 2022, and *East Asia in a New Legal Landscape: FTAs and Dispute Settlement* was published by Seoul National University Press in September 2022. He can be reached at jaemin@snu.ac.kr.

I

INTRODUCTION

I have had the privilege of submitting columns to major newspapers in Korea and abroad to cover issues of international law and international relations. In particular, I have contributed columns to the Korea Herald, the flagship English newspaper in Korea, on a regular basis for ten years. The contribution to the Korea Herald started on November 9, 2009, and ceased on July 14, 2019. The total number of columns to the Korea Herald was 250. When I first started, I did not realize that this contribution would continue for the next ten years. As my columns ran every other week, finding timely subjects, conducting related research, and writing the columns were sometimes quite challenging. The pressure when the deadline was approaching was immense. Despite all these difficulties, however, writing columns regularly for the nation's major English newspaper was my privilege, and I enjoyed every bit of it. I would like to thank Mr. Nam-hyon Choi, the editor in chief, for all the time and effort he took to run the columns on time and deal with logistical issues.

I have also contributed my columns to foreign newspapers, such as the South China Morning Post of Hong Kong and the Straits Times of Singapore. They are all major English newspapers in Southeast Asia. Needless to say, it was my great honor to share my views with foreign audiences on topics of international law and international relations. I am still contributing to these newspapers as issues of global concern arise.

Over the years, I have realized that I have to look back on my columns for reference from time to time. Some colleagues of mine have also mentioned my columns in one way or another. They have even cited them in their own academic writings as well. Oftentimes, I have wanted to ask my students to refer to the columns I have written for their own research and thinking. More importantly, I thought that a compilation of the commentaries would help the general public obtain a comprehensive view of various issues that surround Korea and the global community

DOI: 10.4324/9781003501749-1

from the legal perspective. Law is usually regarded as something both aloof and distant. I have tried to show the general public that law is near us, and international law is among us. The collection of the commentaries will thus help bring the point across more effectively for audiences in Korea and abroad. Each column was my best effort at that time to pinpoint legal issues and provide my own assessment, so collecting them may help readers get the message that I wanted to deliver more efficiently and systematically.

As with any other newspaper commentary, all such commentaries are separate and independent. I then realized that they can be organized into different categories to present them in a more structured way. They are (i) Law as a Critical Component in Domestic Society—Stipulating Norms and Resolving Disputes; (ii) Law as a Critical Component for the Global Community—Achievements and Challenges for a Rules-Based System; (iii) International Organizations and NGOs—Contributions and Limitations in Various Sectors; (iv) International Law in the Field—Disputes, Treaties, and International Courts; and (v) Outer Parameters of Law—Limitations of Legal Discourse.

As the columns target ordinary readers, their tone may be rather different from that of my professional writing. Perhaps more colloquial terms are used, and more colorful idioms are inserted. Difficult concepts were explained in daily language. That said, the contents of each column are the core of my observations as a legal scholar studying international law and international disputes. Sometimes, I am startled to realize that the themes of my academic articles are closely interrelated with previous columns. This should be inevitable because all these writings represent who I am and what I think as a legal scholar.

Since the second semester of 2018, I have been teaching an international law liberal arts course for undergraduate students at Seoul National University. The title of this course is *Sovereign States and International Courts.* Teaching international law and international disputes to students from various majors, spanning both humanities and sciences, has been a challenging endeavor. I constantly pondered how to make the material more accessible and engaging. I often wondered how to connect with Generation MZ students, who are 30 years younger than me, and capture their interest. I experimented with various methods to systematically explain the extensive scope of international law in a way that would resonate with students. The students had diverse ages, majors, interests, and career aspirations. Most were encountering not only international law but also the field of law for the first time.

Over the course of five years of lectures, the biggest challenge was the lack of a dedicated textbook, which caused inconvenience for students. The demand for a textbook tailored to liberal arts courses grew increasingly significant. Handouts and PowerPoint slides alone had their limitations. Encouraged by this situation, I decided to compile my lecture materials and course content into a book. This book is the result of that effort. First and foremost, I extend my gratitude to the students from various majors who actively participated in the course over the past five years.

I hope that this book will serve as a useful resource not only for undergraduate students taking international law as a liberal arts subject but also for those new to international law or seeking an overview of the system as a whole.

The international community is currently in crisis. The US-China conflict continues on multiple fronts, with the possibility of military clashes in the South China Sea and the Taiwan Strait keeping the world on edge. The Russia-Ukraine war, which began with Russia's invasion, has persisted into its second year, and now the Israel-Hamas war has erupted. Azerbaijan and Armenia have resumed armed conflict. Tensions are rising as US and Russian fighter jets engage in close-call maneuvers over the Black and Baltic Seas. Climate change has reached a critical stage. The world has experienced an unprecedented pandemic with COVID-19, and it is difficult to predict when a new virus might again paralyze the globe. Space exploration is intensifying, with nations competing fiercely, and private companies taking the lead in space development, marking a new phenomenon. Competition is also heating up in the rapidly melting Arctic Ocean. Despite facing complex crises, the United Nations (UN), which is supposed to manage and control these issues, seems to be largely absent. The UN system, established in 1945, appears to be faltering at its very foundation.

In addition, the advent of the digital age has transformed our daily lives. The rapid spread of artificial intelligence (AI) has raised global concerns. As significant societal activities and decision-making occur without human involvement, nations are grappling with how to understand and manage this reality. In this context, the international economic system is also undergoing significant changes. The fundamental framework and principles that have sustained the international economic order, centered on free trade and expanded investment, are rapidly shifting. Calls for substantial reforms to the World Trade Organization (WTO) system and the International Centre for Settlement of Investment Disputes (ICSID) system are growing louder.

At the heart of all these issues lies "international legal norms" and "legal reasoning based on international law." Whether in war or peace, analog or digital, Earth or outer space, human beings or AI, the United States or China, current discussions revolve around and rely on international law as a tool. This era demands greater interest in and understanding of international law. Without knowledge of international law, it is difficult to protect our interests or guide the international community in the right direction. I sincerely hope this book will contribute to spreading awareness of the importance of international law and disseminating its core content in an accessible way.

II

LAW AS A CRITICAL COMPONENT OF DOMESTIC SOCIETY—STIPULATING NORMS AND RESOLVING DISPUTES

How is Korea perceived by our foreign friends? What are the unique characteristics of Korean society? There are aspects of our society that foreigners admire. At the same time, there are certain aspects that elicit unfavorable perceptions among our foreign friends. Occasionally, the latter misunderstand Korea by seeing only a partial picture. I find it intriguing to observe the divergent perspectives held by my Korean colleagues in comparison to foreign colleagues from other countries on the same issue. This does not revolve around matters of what is right or wrong, but rather it focuses on notable disparities in these modes of thought. Through the columns for the English newspaper that primarily caters to a readership composed of foreigners, I attempted to gain a foreign perspective on Korean society. I also endeavored to touch upon how ordinary Koreans perceive foreign cultures or foreign countries. This has been one of the core themes of numerous columns I've written. It was fascinating to acknowledge these differences and write columns discussing them. These differences do not merely serve as subjects of cross-cultural interest or comparison. They may also give rise to significant misunderstandings and sometimes develop into legal disputes. The comprehension of how Korea is perceived by foreign friends and colleagues does not aim to alter our existing state or identity. If there is any room for improvement, we can and should make adjustments. Otherwise, it is imperative to preserve the fundamental essence of Korean society. In any event, this realization serves as the initial stage toward facilitating the integration of Korea into the global community, as well as fostering mutual awareness between the global community and Korea. The potential benefits of this approach include promoting the achievement of true globalization.

According to the Organisation for Economic Co-operation and Development (OECD), Korea was ranked as one of the hardest working countries in 2022 among 34 member countries with working hours of 1,901 hours per year—149 hours

DOI: 10.4324/9781003501749-2

above the OECD average. Korea had been at the top of this category since 2000, a year when the country put in 2,512 hours, exceeding the average by 668 hours. Korea's dominance in this category has gradually become diluted since 2000 with the phased introduction of the no-work-Saturday system. Although Korea seems to be slowly moving away from this status, long working hours and a rigid work ethic still largely define the country. Anyone who knows Korean society may say that the official reduction of working hours does not necessarily lessen the intensity and pressure in the workplace as long as the hard-working environment persists. Hard-working people, the educated workforce, and innovative businesspeople have worked a Korean miracle. Over the past several decades, Korea has undergone a drastic transformation across various sectors. The ongoing process of change is still taking place. Indeed, the pace of change appears to be accelerating each year. In the 1980s, it would have been highly improbable for individuals to anticipate the rise and impact of cultural phenomena such as BTS or the film *Parasite*. At the same time, some facets of our contemporary society remain firmly entrenched in our historical or cultural heritage. Contemporary Korean society continues to be characterized by monoethnicity, Confucianism, and paternalism, which serve to elucidate the prevailing dynamics and phenomena observed within this context.

The United Nations (UN) defines a society as an "aged society" when the population of 65 and older accounts for 14 percent of the total population. The society becomes "super-aged" when the percentage reaches 20. Korea is experiencing a rapid increase in the proportion of elderly people, while its overall population started to decrease last year due to persistently low birth rates. Korea became an aged society in 2017, and it is widely anticipated that the country will transition into a super-aged society by 2025. The social ramifications of rapid aging are widely recognized, including the decline in economic productivity, the shrinking labor force, the emergence of intergenerational conflicts regarding employment opportunities, the rise in health care costs and medical expenditures, and the depletion of the national pension fund. It is important to note that these challenges related to an aging population are not exclusive to Korea. Several other countries are also undergoing swift demographic shifts along the same trajectory. However, Korea faces a distinct issue: the prevalence of elderly poverty. Experts warn that the current working generation in Korea will encounter more severe poverty during their retirement. Parents are allocating a substantial proportion of their income toward their children's education. Engrossed in expenditures for their offspring, the majority of middle-class parents lack the financial ability to adequately plan for life beyond age 65. This situation highlights that Korea's persistent issue with private education is a fundamental cause of numerous social challenges, both present and future.

As of now, Korea is facing a variety of challenges on many fronts. The nation is struggling to manage these challenges and contain their consequences. These challenges stem from both domestic and international planes. One of the critical challenges is the rapidly dwindling population of the country. It has become a major issue for other developed countries as well, but in Korea's case the pace of the falling birth rate is startling. Realizing the damaging consequences, the Korean government is now mobilizing all kinds of policies to turn around the downward spiral of the country's birth rates. It has indeed appointed a new ministerial post dedicated to the issue. The consensus is that the birth rate is the outcome of many different social issues and factors, so to change the trend all government agencies need to cooperate and coordinate. At any rate, one good thing for the recent development is that (i) finally the government has realized that this is a national emergency issue; (ii) that it has realized the importance of systemic effort on the part of the government as opposed to the effort of particular, individual ministries as before; and (iii) that both government and private sectors are joining forces, as such coordination was lacking in this field, and companies' efforts have not been able to fully bloom because of government regulation (unintended and due to other policy objectives), or the government's efforts have not been able to prosper because of companies' lack of cooperation (again unintended but it turned out this way).

In that regard, many issues are being evaluated from the perspective of boosting birth rates. For instance, the newly opened GTX-A, which is a high-speed commuter train for the larger metropolitan area of Seoul, is now regarded as a tool for more people to find affordable houses with a good living environment far away from Seoul. The areas that are now connected by the GTX-A used to be a one-and-a-half-hour train ride away from Seoul. Now it has been reduced to 20 minutes. So, the expectation is that people, particularly young couples, may find those areas more appealing for the location of their homes. With a more family-friendly environment and facilities in those new metropolitan areas, the expectation is that the opening of the new high-speed train will help boost birth rates for the country. Korea's experience shows one negative consequence of a highly competitive and efficiency-driven society. The young generation tends to focus on its own survival and success, breaking away from the traditional formula of raising a family. It is now affecting almost all segments of the national agenda, whether real estate, education, economy, military, immigration, or culture. Other countries are facing the same or similar challenges, but the Korean situation offers a drastic example of a fast-changing society in the modern world. These days, the threats to a society or a country do not just come from abroad. They also emerge from domestic factors and internal development.

Law is not able to address all the problems, nor can it offer solutions to all the challenges. And yet, it is still critical to understand the legal issues embedded in many of the societal problems and challenges that we face domestically and globally. Understanding these legal issues helps us clarify the situation, sort out options, and guide discussions in the right direction. In short, law provides a framework for the debates and discussion of social issues. The early reaction to COVID-19 is telling in this regard. Mindful of the fact that China was the origin of the virus and that its failure to contain the virus in the early stage of the disease caused the pandemic, some countries and opinion leaders were vocal in placing responsibility on China. This early reaction is understandable emotionally, but whether the early reaction could be supported legally was a different story. Customary international law imposes legal obligations on each state to manage its territory with due diligence and notify neighboring states of transboundary harm when such is suspected. This jurisprudence was frequently referred to as a basis or establishing China's legal responsibility. These customary law obligations, however, presuppose a physical flow of moving particles or something similar to it, which does not necessarily exist in the context of a pandemic, which is in fact caused by human beings carrying a virus in their respiratory system arguably without meeting the traditional criteria involving a physical flow of particles. As such, a more thorough analysis should be conducted to confirm the responsibility for the COVID-19 spread under international law, going beyond simply pinpointing China as the originating country and as the country with loose initial responses. A more thorough legal analysis is required to determine the responsibility of a particular state. This type of legal discourse has been frequently lacking, and emotional reaction caused by domestic politics and diplomatic consideration has instead taken center stage.

Misunderstandings of legal issues are common. Many people tend to believe that actions taken by local governments are beyond the reach of international agreements or international disputes. As a result, when local governments participate in international activities and address international affairs they hardly contemplate legal obligations arising from international agreements or prospective legal proceedings. The actions of local governments are equated with those of a central government and thus become fair game for treaty violation debates. Consider the following example. In a dispute involving local governments' measures to impose a bi-weekly close-down requirement for large-size retail shops, the Korean Supreme Court basically held for the local governments, the defendants in the dispute.[1] Regardless of the conclusion, this case shows how local governments' actions implicate treaties that Korea has concluded. This case was brought by owners of large retailers, called Super Supermarket (SSM),[2] who were subject to the bi-weekly mandatory close-down requirement of the local governments at issue. Under the requirement, these stipulated SSMs were ordered to close down their businesses twice a month. The measure at issue was an implementation, on the level of respective local governments, of the enabling act (*Act on the Development of Distribution Service Business of 2013*) and its Enforcement Decree.

The plaintiff SSMs, including Lotte Shopping, E-Mart, and Home Plus, argued that the ordinances of the local governments pronounced under the Act and the Enforcement Decree violate Korean Administrative Law principles (i.e., abuse of

1 *Case Concerning Revocation of Limitation of Operating Hours for Certain Retailers*, Supreme Court of the Republic of Korea, 2015DU295, Nov. 10, 2015, available at www.scourt.go.kr/supreme/news/NewsViewAction2.work?currentPage=5&searchWord=&searchOption=&seqnum=5035&gubun=4 (last visited Jan. 10, 2016) (in Korean) (hereinafter Judgment), at 18.

2 Retailers with the Size of 3,000 square meters or larger. *See* Judgment, at 4.

discretion and disproportionate regulation) and the WTO's *General Agreement on Trade in Services* (GATS) and the *Free Trade Agreement between the Republic of Korea and the European Union* (Korea-EU FTA).[3] As the measure attempts to regulate retail distribution service providers operating in the Korean market, and as one of the plaintiffs is owned by an EU corporation (Home Plus), the dispute referred to the relevant provisions of the treaties at issue, that is the GATS and the Korea-EU FTA. The local governments at issue, the defendants, are various district offices of the Seoul Metropolitan City Government. The defendants issued respective ordinances following the enactment of the Act and the Enforcement Decree in 2013. The purpose of the Act and the Enforcement Decree was to maintain "good order in the distribution service industry," the "health right of the employees working in the distributions service industry," and "the co-prosperity of the large corporation and Small and Medium Enterprises (SMEs)," to name a few.[4] In particular, the Act authorizes the heads of respective local governments to impose a close-down requirement not exceeding twice a month.[5] The local governments thus adopted their respective ordinances mandating two close-downs per month for SSMs operating within their jurisdictions.

In a nutshell, the objective of the Act, Enforcement Decree, and the ordinances was to protect the small retailers who stand to lose their sales due to the penetration and expansion of the large retail shops, some of which were Korean and others foreign. Thus, the legal scheme aimed to protect the interest of the SMEs in the retail industry from the fierce competition caused by large retailers. It was argued that the new scheme would ensure an even distribution of wealth in the society. Arguably, no one would challenge the noble cause of equality in society, but the issue was whether such a measure was compatible with the Korean Administrative Law and international agreements that Korea had concluded. In the proceeding of the Seoul Appeals Court, the plaintiffs prevailed: the court decided that the ordinances of the local governments constituted a violation of Korean Administrative Law principles because they constituted an abuse of discretion on the part of the agency and a disproportionate burden on certain corporations in the industry. In addition, the court also found that the measure constituted a violation of the GATS and the Korea-EU FTA because of a deviation from the provisions in those international agreements.

In its decision of November 10, 2015, however, the Supreme Court of Korea, reversed the decision of the Seoul Appeals Court on both counts, remanded the case back to the lower for reconsideration: the Seoul Appeals Court then issued a new judgment following the jurisprudence clarified by the Supreme Court. Further, the Supreme Court held that the challenged ordinances were within the discretion

3 *See* Judgment, at 3–5, 6, 8.
4 The Act, at Article 12-2.
5 *See ibid.*

of the local governments as empowered by the Act and the Enforcement Decree,[6] and that they managed to maintain the conflicting interests of those regulated and of the society at large.[7] Thus, the Supreme Court found them to be compatible with the Administrative Law principles requiring "reasonable regulation" by a governmental agency.

With regard to the issue of the possible violation of international trade agreements, the Supreme Court basically held that as international agreements these cited trade agreements create rights and obligations *only* for the contracting parties (i.e., governments of the contracting parties).[8] As such, according to the Court, the plaintiffs, as corporations, do not possess the right to bring a legal action before the Korean domestic court based on the trade agreements at issue.[9] The Court thus essentially dismissed the claim of the plaintiffs to the extent that it referred to trade agreements without reaching the merit, that is, whether or not said measure constituted a violation of schedules of specific commitments. So, in a sense, in this high-profile dispute attracting attention from the European Union and the United States, the Supreme Court managed to avoid addressing the difficult issue of evaluating the measures from the perspective of trade agreement obligation. Based on this decision, the Supreme Court remanded the case back to the lower court for further consideration.

All in all, the finding of the Supreme Court may arguably have been a correct interpretation of the Korean Administrative Law principles. It was not entirely clear, however, whether the judgment could also be found to be consistent with the general understanding of treaty obligations imposed on Korea. The plaintiffs were likely not attempting to exercise their rights under the trade agreements, a situation that the Supreme Court referred to in its judgment. Rather, it seems that the plaintiffs were invoking the GATS and the Korea-EU FTA in an effort to point out that the legislation and enforcement decrees should be interpreted in a way that is consistent with obligations under international agreements. If that was the case, it may not have been entirely appropriate to dismiss the issue simply because the plaintiffs were alluding to or relying upon treaties. In any event, the case shows that local government actions are reviewed by Korean domestic law, but they are also reviewable by international agreements.

Another recent example in this regard is economic security. Economic security has become a term of art both domestically and internationally. Many governments adopt a wide range of measures to protect their geopolitical and geoeconomic interests and refer to economic security as their rationale. In some instances, obvious violations of existing treaties and international agreements are brushed off as

6 *See* Judgment, at 14–15.
7 *See* Judgment, at 15–17.
8 *See* Judgment, at 17.
9 *See ibid.*

relying on "national security" exceptions of those international instruments. Economic security does cover a broad range of national policies and strategies of many countries. And yet, few have considered carefully the meaning and scope of economic security from the legal perspectives. Legally speaking, economic security as we understand it today still falls under the purview of the national security jurisprudence of international law. As such, national security exceptions contained in recent treaties or necessity defense under customary international law should apply to the economic security dialogue. This realization of the legal parameter will help the global community align economic security debates in a more predictable and reliable manner, which will then pave the way for a new governance regime of international economic law that is on the table at the moment.

This understanding also sheds important light on the current debate on the global supply chain, one of the core issues of the economic security dialogue. In some critical areas and as regards some critical products, global supply chains are currently being reformulated and restructured. The most vivid examples include semiconductors, quantum computing, and artificial intelligence. Arguably, the current discussion of supply chains is mainly being driven by the geopolitical and geoeconomic considerations of key stakeholders. In the meantime, however, few analyses have been conducted from the perspective of international law. This obvious absence of legal discourse seems to be problematic because supply chain debates would apparently implicate key provisions of various treaties and agreements one way or another. One of the main reasons for a legal discussion vacuum at present seems to lie in the notion that any measure relating to supply chains may well be justified by national security exceptions included in treaties and agreements. It may be true that national security exceptions can cover some aspects of supply chain-related issues. But it may not be the case that any and all aspects of supply chain-related measures are covered and justified by national security exceptions. Such being the case, supply chain measures need to be examined from the prism of international law, most notably national security exceptions, to see whether and to what extent they are justified by the exceptions and remain compatible with current international norms. If not, serious discussions should begin as soon as possible at relevant global forums as to new elements and contours of national security exceptions relating to economic interests to reflect the changing circumstances and concerns of states. These examples show the importance of understanding legal issues, both under the domestic and international planes, when important measures are adopted and implemented. We are indeed living in a tightly knit web of legal norms.

1. Stay Vigilant When Exports Hit Record

Korea's annual exports set a new record of $466.4 billion last year and semiconductors did it again. Statistics just released by the Korean Customs Service listed semiconductors as the country's No. 1 export in 2010 at $51.5 billion. Second and third on the export list were chemical products at $47.5 billion and commercial vessels at $47.1 billion. Automobiles took the sixth place with $31.8 billion, but actual sales figures of Korean automobiles could be much higher than that when those manufactured by Hyundai's Alabama plants and sold directly in the US market are added. Overall, a very positive outcome.

The strong performance of semiconductors was mainly boosted by the surge in demand for new IT products such as iPhones and iPads, which require a wide range of semiconductors. Apple makes iPads, and Korean companies sell semiconductors to Apple. It is no wonder that semiconductors are called the "rice of modern industries." Riding the wave, Korean semiconductor manufacturers continued to increase their shares in the global market last year. In the DRAM global market—the most popular type of semiconductors—Korean companies occupy more than 55 percent of global supply with Samsung taking up 33.8 percent and Hynix 21.4 percent. As consumer demand for new IT products is expected to continue to grow, semiconductors will probably remain near the top of the export list for the time being.

Not surprisingly, Korea's dominance in the semiconductor market also forces foreign competitors to explore new ways to survive and compete. One of the common strategies is to increase in size either through acquisition or alliance. Just a couple of days ago, Elpida of Japan, the third-largest manufacturer with 17 percent global market share, announced its plan to purchase sixth-ranked Powerchip of Taiwan to find a breakthrough in the ever-solidifying market dominance of Korean producers.

Another conventional strategy employed by foreign semiconductor manufacturers to keep Korean competitors at bay in the global market is to seek to introduce trade restrictions. As a matter of fact, Korean companies have been under constant surveillance from competing companies and their governments, and have been slapped with trade restrictions when market shares surged. Forms of restrictions have changed depending on the circumstances at a particular point in time. Antidumping investigations and duties occupied much of the 1990s, followed by countervailing duty investigations and duties in the first half of the 2000s. Antitrust investigations and hefty fines haunted Korean companies in the second half of the 2000s. These investigations and restrictions were not confined to a single trading partner, but sometimes occurred in multiple jurisdictions simultaneously or in succession.

The robust performance of Korean semiconductor exports since the 2008 global economic recession fully deserves encouragement and compliments. But past experience also reminds us that strong performance is sometimes a precursor for trade restriction of all sorts. It is true that some restrictions were legitimate and warranted under the circumstances, but there were also instances where reasonable questions could be raised about the rationale of restrictions.

In some instances, trade restriction measures by one country are greeted by counter restriction measures by the other country. The numerous bilateral tit-for-tat maneuvers among the United States, the European Union, and China provide examples. Unfortunately, Korea is inherently vulnerable in this game because its reliance on the foreign export market is much higher than that of foreign competitors on the Korean market due to the relatively smaller size of the domestic Korean market. As such, Korea can rarely conduct similar investigations against and impose restrictions on major foreign export items to Korea which can be comparable to Korea's semiconductors.

At the same time, another important lesson from the previous experience is that these trade restrictions can be either preempted or effectively contained when proper preparation is implemented. All these trade restrictions do not come out of the blue; they at least require triggering events to justify investigations at issue. If these events are somehow avoided, frivolous investigations could be checked in advance.

The report of another record-breaking year of exports with continued strong performance of major export items including semiconductors is quite encouraging. But at the same time, the surge of exports in the midst of the continued economic recession for other trading partners may require us to stay alert and vigilant for the possibility of unexpected trade restrictions, as seen in the past.

[The Korea Herald, February 9, 2011]

2. Entitlement to a Perfect Vacation?

Koreans work long hours. In the eyes of foreigners, Korea is a country of hard-working people, and the epitome of work ethic. A recent OECD survey says that Koreans work 2,193 hours a year, while the OECD average is only 1,749 hours. As "dynamic" as the country is in many different ways, there is simply too much work to be done with a streamlined workforce. On top of that, the general unwritten rule of the office is that people stay in the office at least until the boss of the section calls it a day and walks out the door.

Having realized the toll taken on ordinary family lives and the importance of work–life balance from a socio-economic perspective, the government has been keen to change this part of the Korean culture. The 2004 introduction of a five-day workweek for schools and companies with more than 1,000 employees was a turning point.

Some agencies even adopt "Family Wednesdays," when people are forced to go home on time, at least on certain designated Wednesdays, to spend more time with their families. Despite all this, long working hours and common overtime followed by after-work gatherings are deeply engrained in the Korean corporate and office culture.

Long working hours have traditionally shrunk vacation time to an absolute minimum. It is not uncommon that workers take only two to three days off during summer for a quick trip to a crammed beach. Although the average vacation time is now being extended to almost a week, one is still supposed to be discreet in planning and requesting a vacation.

These Korean workers may find that they have been shortchanged when they hear about a widely touted decision of last Thursday from the Court of Justice of the European Union, the highest court of the EU located in Luxembourg. After hearing a labor dispute between Spanish trade unions and employers, the highest court of Europe ruled on June 21 that a person should be entitled to more vacation days if he or she becomes sick during vacation.

The decision describes the purpose of a vacation as "to enable the worker to rest and enjoy a period of relaxation and leisure." So, based on this rationale, if one was prevented from enjoying a vacation due to an illness, extra days should be given. In other words, an employee should be able to redo a vacation if the previous one was ruined. As a decision from the highest court, this decision will bind all 27 member states.

Now, an interesting thing is to see how far this rationale of a perfect vacation can go. For instance, could the logic also apply, mutatis mutandis, to a situation where one's rental car breaks down during vacation? Perhaps an argument could be made that as much as the vacation has been ruined, one should get extra vacation days to make up for it. What if you fall ill again during your second vacation? Should you have another vacation for a third time? The basic rationale of the decision seems to indicate that you may claim a third one (and a fourth one, if necessary) until you have achieved full "relaxation and leisure."

This perfectionist approach of vacation in one part of the world and the minimalist approach of vacation in this country imply that there may be night-and-day differences when people talk about the same issue. Imagine the embarrassment managers from one region may feel when they discuss these mundane (but critical) topics with employees from another region in a global corporation. This may be another version of Martian-Venusian talking.

Well, you might want to put this well-timed decision on the table of your frowning boss when you discuss your summer vacation schedule. Brave, but the risk is all yours.

[The Korea Herald, June 27, 2012]

3. No Rest for a Busy Country

In the heat of the welfare-enhancing policy exploration, at the earliest starting from next year, workers may have one more day off if a public holiday falls on Saturday or Sunday. There are 15 official public holidays in Korea at the moment, and each year three to four days on average fall on weekends with no compensatory day offs given.

Under this system of "letting the chips fall where they may," the actual number of holidays changes every year, and having the full benefit of 15 holidays becomes quite unlikely. Finally, a new bill to address this situation is being seriously contemplated under the name of "alternative holidays," as promised by one of the presidential platforms of the last election. Under this proposal, if the overlap happens on Saturday, the preceding Friday will be a holiday. If Sunday, then the following Monday will. Similar systems are adopted in many other countries.

As the opposition to this new system has been also strong since the idea was first floated in 2009, particularly from some business sectors fearing likely increases in the cost of production, the proposal is now taking a cautious, step-by-step approach. So, the new scheme will first apply only to Lunar New Year and Chuseok holidays as opposed to all national holidays. Also, it applies only to governmental agencies whose working days can be changed by a presidential decree without amending the underlying statute itself.

While private entities will have the discretion to follow the new rule or not, the expectation is that many of them will end up subscribing to it because oftentimes labor agreements and employment contracts incorporates the government's holiday mutatis mutandis.

Obviously, the idea behind this proposal is to guarantee more rest for the hard-working people of Korea, in the hopes that a well-rested, refreshed workforce yields higher productivity. In fact, a 2011 International Labour Organization (ILO)-commissioned research paper on the effects of working hours on productivity concludes that longer working hours tend to decrease manufacturing productivity. Not only that, but the government is also expecting the new scheme to stimulate domestic economy through increased consumer spending.

According to the OECD, Korea was ranked as the hardest working nation in 2010 among 34 member countries with working hours of 2,193 hours per year—444 hours above the OECD average. In 2011, Korea took the second place with 2,090 hours after Mexico, but still 312 hours more than average. Korea had been at the top of this category since 2000, a year when the country put in 2,512 hours exceeding the average by 668 hours.

Korea's dominance in this category has been gradually diluted since 2000 with the phased introduction of the no-work Saturday system, and in 2011 it was edged out to second place. Although Korea seems to be slowly moving away from this status, still the long working hours and rigid work ethic are those that define Korea. So, the proposed change will bring Korea closer to the average, at least statistically.

Anyone who knows Korean society, however, may say that the official reduction of working days does not necessarily lessen the intensity and pressure in the workplace as long as the hard-working environment persists.

Where overtime and weekend work are commonplace, the effect of the official reduction of working days may well be a drop in the bucket. To have a glimpse of the intensity of work during working hours, visit any bank in Korea. You can tell that the tellers have the fastest hands in the world, but they work until late into the evening even though the bank's official closing time is 4 p.m.

As the proponents of the bill argue, rest does facilitate creative thinking—but only if one is indeed free from work and shrill orders of the boss. To many of us who still have to work even on many weekends and answer office calls on holiday mornings, the new system would not mean that much. At the same time, in many occupations, new digital equipment has made physical presence in the office not so material anyway.

[The Korea Herald, August 21, 2013]

4. A High Bar for Political Asylum in Korea

Korea's low acceptance rate of foreign nationals' political asylum draws our attention. Between January 1994 and October 2017, 30,082 applications were submitted by foreigners for the recognition of their status as refugees in Korea. Among these, only 767 applications were approved. This is just a 2.5 percent acceptance rate. It stands out compared to the global average of 37 percent reported by United Nations High Commissioner for Refugees.

The Refugee Act of 2013 is the governing law here, which was enacted to implement the UN Refugee Convention to which Korea acceded in 1993. The legal requirement under the act for the recognition of refugee status is rather simple: whether an applicant shows well-founded fear of being persecuted for reasons of race, religion, nationality, membership of a particular social group, or political opinion.

The simple legal requirement becomes tricky in practice, though. It is the applicant who should prove possible persecution back in the home country, but carrying this burden is anything but easy. Note that here we are talking about people who fled their countries. More often than not, those seeking shelter in this far corner of Asia have left their hometowns and countries hurriedly and in secret. Perhaps the last thing they could think of in the moment of terror and physical harm would be some documentation or certification that they can attach to their future applications in foreign countries for the status of refugee. So, it is not uncommon pieces of evidence and materials are either elusive or unreachable when their application is pending before Korean agencies or courts. Unfortunately, the agency and the judiciary apparently demand "concrete evidence" in their refugee status review proceedings. Mere circumstantial evidence is likely to lead to rejection of the application.

Situations get more complicated when an applicant's statements during interviews and hearings are inconsistent. Absence of solid consistency sows suspicion in the minds of agency officials and judges, also leading to ultimate rejection of the application. But here also it should not be forgotten that interviews, at least initial ones, are sometimes done within the confinement of limited resources of translation and interpretation. These applicants' early encounters in a foreign country tend to proceed in a completely different environment and culture. Expecting them to come up with watertight explanations may be setting the bar too high for them.

Presumably, the high thresholds explain the substantially low acceptance rate of refugee status. A high-profile decision from the Korean Supreme Court in the past July prompts us to contemplate on these practical aspects. On July 11, 2017, the Korean Supreme Court overturned a lower court (Seoul High Court) decision granting political asylum to an Egyptian national for fear of persecution in his home country due to his sexual orientation. The case was then remanded to the lower court for further review.

In the judgment, the Supreme Court focused on the preceding legal criterion whether the applicant proved possible persecution in his home country. In the view of the nation's highest court, the applicant failed to provide concrete evidence in this regard, other than the applicant's own assertion and some circumstantial evidence. Inconsistent statements from the applicant also caused the Supreme Court to reject the applicant's petition. The core part of the judgment covering the two issues reads, in my own translation: "The plaintiff's statements show a lack of consistency and persuasiveness . . . and there does not exist sufficient material to prove whether the statements are compatible with the objective circumstances of the country at issue." The highest court then reversed the lower court's judgment for the applicant.

The overturning decision of the highest court attracted attention because the lower court did find the associated evidence sufficient, citing widespread discriminatory environment in his home country. The case is still pending, so we do not know the final outcome yet. But it does show that the issue of sufficiency in the refugee status context can be elusive and debatable.

High legal thresholds will certainly help identify and deter fraudulent applications. Nonetheless, the increasing gap between the global refugee acceptance rate and Korea's indicates that the thresholds are not reflective of the reality refugee applicants face.

[The Korea Herald, November 28, 2017]

5. Oops, Korea Labeled as Tax Haven

It was in 2013 that the EU designated Korea as an illegal, unreported, and unregulated (IUU) fishing country along with 11 other states, indicating a possible EU-wide sanction on Korean ships and fisheries products. The alerted government mobilized a year-long campaign to persuade Brussels to delist Korea, and it was eventually taken off the list. Korea had its own problems of IUU fishing at that time, but so did many other countries. So, it was odd to see Korea on the list, the only industrialized state in the group. It is one thing to warn Korea to do better, but another to include the country in the worst group of the global fishing universe.

Now the EU has surprised Korea with another "list." Brussels designated Korea on Dec. 5 as a tax haven—a non-cooperative jurisdiction, to be precise—together with 17 other states such as Barbados, Grenada, and Panama. This latest categorization means Korea is allowing itself to be used by global businessmen and corporations as a tax avoidance conduit—bad enough behavior to be condemned by other countries. Interestingly, this time again, Seoul is an odd member of the group. Korea is the only country of meaningful economic size on the list: in fact, it is the only one that is a member of the Organization for Economic Cooperation and

Development states and has concluded tax treaties with EU member states. It is all the more embarrassing that the EU itself has concluded a free trade agreement with a country it now regards as a bad actor in the global finance system.

It all started with South Korea's administration of tax exemption and reduction law for foreign investors in the free economic zones. As the EU explains, preferential tax treatment in the zone is a magnet for possible tax evaders, so much so that the country should be included in the category of global tax havens. I have no desire to defend the government—much less its tax law—but this is a perplexing rationale, because this type of exemption is adopted by and available in many other states, including some of the EU member states. If a tax exemption measure is branded as a tax avoidance facilitator, it should be so regardless of whether both foreigners and nationals receive it or only foreigners do—the same incentive for foreign corporations. So, hard to fathom the logic.

The government, though belatedly, is now putting full-court press in Brussels to reverse the decision. Well, Korea may be taken off the list one way or another. But the damage has been done. As the tax system and larger economic policies are implicated here, the damage is far worse than the IUU wrangling several years ago. From a wider perspective, it is a repetition of the IUU fishing listing and delisting. In both incidents, the government is to blame for clumsy handling of important matters. More active engagement with decision makers in Brussels should have taken place in advance. That said, speculation is that Korea has been inserted as an easy target to send a signal that new regulations do not necessarily target certain easily identifiable, developing states. South Korea is the "right size" of economy for such purposes, so goes the speculation. I believe the speculation is wrong. But proving it to be so would require some more plausible explanations from the listing authorities.

The EU's general objective here is legitimate by any standard. Illegal tax avoidance in the global community is now calculated as $32 trillion per year. Combating it is one of the top priorities of any responsible government. Korea should be warned if it does not abide by its international obligations. Absolutely. Failure to live up to a global standard should render any listing all the more deserving. Elements of mistrust or opaqueness in the tax laws and regulations should be addressed quickly. Certainly. If, on the other hand, Korea has been made an example of to dilute an image that only vulnerable, small states are captured on the list, it is a different story.

[The Korea Herald, December 26, 2017]

6. Time to Play It Cool

Nobody knows for sure what GM's plan is. Maybe the US automaker is just adjusting its business in Korea by closing an underperforming manufacturing plant in Gunsan City, or perhaps it is taking a first step to fold its Korean business entirely. Rumors and conjectures have swirled around the country since the automaker's latest decision to shut down the Gunsan factory, but there is no knowing the exact reason of the decision or future plans of the multinational corporation. The government is trying to talk to GM to address the automaker's concern and is eager to hear reassurance of its commitment to the Korean market. Hopefully, the discussion works, and the US corporation decides to stay in Korea.

Thus far national reactions have been rather emotional. As surprising and embarrassing as it may be, this is no time for panic. It is time to play it cool. Prevalent in media reports are two aspects of what may be called "anachronistic" sentiments.

First of all, when a foreign investor contemplates and then decides to close its business and depart, there is little a host county can do. Such a decision must be based on dozens of reasons and scores of considerations. Maybe the foreign market has lost its appeal. Maybe a better option has emerged elsewhere. Or the foreign investor just wants to scale down its offshore subsidiaries. If the foreign investor believes departure makes sense in terms of its business, it will pack up no matter what the host government does. At this point, fretting and begging won't help. Presenting calm business calculation will.

In today's global business environment, no assumption could be farther from the reality than the one that a foreign corporation can or should stay in another country for eternity. How hardly do we believe that Samsung will stay in Vietnam or LG will reside in Mexico forever. And even Korean corporations leave the country and go abroad for better business packages. GM's decision—whatever it may be—should be viewed from the same perspective. Criticizing a foreign corporation's departure as some sort of a betrayal does not fit with today's globalized world.

Certainly, efforts should be made to explain why staying in Korea is a win-win situation. Earnest persuasion should be exhausted. But at the end of the day, the decision is for the foreign corporation.

Secondly, and more importantly, criticizing a foreign investor for making significant revenues, in and of itself, through its business operation is also out of tune with the reality of the global business environment. Unless illegal activities are implicated, corporations are supposed to pursue the objective to maximize their business interest. Local newspapers are already reporting, in a critical tone, that the US corporation has made a return of several times its original investment. Even if the calculation is accurate, this should not be something to be criticized, supposing all activities and transactions have taken place within the bounds of applicable laws and regulations. Again, imagine similar situations against Korean companies in foreign countries.

This business-as-usual, cool-head approach will help us see it through and make a wise decision at this juncture. In the meantime, whatever outcome comes out of this negotiation with GM, Korea should contemplate on how to improve its business environment for foreign corporations. Imperative in this respect is the self-assessment whether this latest development is the reflection of the observation of foreign corporations operating in Korea that Seoul's business environment has deteriorated over the years while that of other countries has improved. If so, a remedial action needs to be taken, to stay competitive.

Providing hurried financial incentive packages in return for a promise to stay, without addressing core issues on both sides, will not solve the problem. It will only postpone the problem. When the money runs out, mentions of departure will re-emerge.

[The Korea Herald, February 20, 2018]

7. Despite 20-Year Deregulation Drive, Businesses Still Concerned over Red Tape

After a roller coaster year on the trade front, we are now well-versed in other countries' trade barriers restraining Korean products and businesses. We, however, tend to forget how we are viewed in the eyes of other nations. The latest observation came from the Nov. 30 joint statement by five chambers of commerce operating in Seoul: the American, European, British, French, and German Chambers of Commerce. The joint statement was the first of its kind.

What was mentioned in the statement is their shared concern over regulatory barriers in Korea for foreign business entities. Some may refute the descriptions offered by the five chambers, but when it comes to regulatory barriers, foreign entities are not alone: domestic companies are also pleading with agencies to ease regulation in various sectors. A rare joint statement of this sort raises a red flag. Our regulations need a close look in order to prevent the attractiveness of the Korean market for foreign investors from being compromised. What is wrong here? What is the problem?

From the joint statement and other documents released by these chambers, here is a summary of the concerns.

You figure it out yourself. Vague regulations and agency discretion undermine predictability, argues the joint statement. It is difficult for foreign business entities to know relevant situations in advance. Officials are typically cautious, defensive and risk averse. A thick book of regulations is dumped on the lap of foreign entities. And yet, clarity in regulations is scarce. Basically, one is told to figure it out himself or herself. When something goes wrong, regulation—all of a sudden—comes forward. Agencies pinpoint the regulation and explain why a breach has taken place together with consequences. This is portrayed as a "due process" concern in the joint statement and other documents.

We are the same yet different. Foreign business entities complain about the lack of coordination and consistency among different agencies. Decisions are fragmentary and dispersed sometimes. One agency's determination does not dovetail with another agency's views. You are in a double bind.

Again, let's put aside for a moment whether such descriptions are entirely accurate or whether they stem from misunderstanding. What also counts here is the perception. If the shared perception of foreign business entities can be summarized as just described, this in itself sends a critical message that should be taken seriously. The chambers of commerce need to be assured that their voices are being heard.

We need a liaison officer in the government. There has got to be a person who is in charge of communicating with these foreign business entities and representatives and listening to their concerns. Outstanding issues can then be sorted out and sent to agencies in charge of the matter quickly. Misunderstandings, if any, can be dispelled. Something like a chief liaison officer or chief listening officer for foreign business entities in the government. The joint statement by the chambers of commerce tells us that we need such a post in the government. Deregulation was made a priority in the nation exactly 20 years ago. In 1998, the Regulatory Reform Committee was established, co-chaired by none other than the prime minister and a respected senior expert from the private sector. The committee is still in operation. It was also that year when then-President Kim Dae-jung instructed his ministers to slash 50 percent of all government regulations by year's end. Twenty years onward, regulation still continues to be a source of debate and concern. Sadly, foreign business entities still express concern over regulatory red tape in Seoul.

"Korea-only" regulation and "Galapagos-type" regulation, as mentioned by the chambers, hardly match up with the national image we strive to build—a dynamic Korea. The homepage address of the Regulatory Reform Committee is quite telling and symbolic. It is www.better.go.kr. That is so right. Dealing with regulatory red tape would help make the country better.

[The Korea Herald, December 11, 2018]

8. Defining "Cyberattacks"

Two spats of cyberattacks shut down, though momentarily, websites of major bank and broadcasters of the country, reminding people of the similar attacks in 2009 and 2011. The source of the attack is not clear yet, but they showed that the information infrastructure remains quite vulnerable to outside attacks.

As Korea is one of the most wired countries in the world with almost all sorts of social services provided over the internet, any disruption of the information network is particularly detrimental—it could be the country's Achilles' heel. In fact, this is not only Korea's problem as many countries face a similar threat. The US government recently announced a plan to impose trade restrictions for products to be used for or related to hacking activities overseas.

The core problem that many countries encounter in coping with cyberattacks is how to define them. Is it a law enforcement issue dealing with criminal activity or is it a national security issue dealing with invasion of a territory? Maybe a little bit of both.

This question, however, is critical because an answer to it ultimately determines who is responsible for a cyberattack, and, more importantly, what kind of action is permitted or appropriate in response to such an attack.

More practically, a definition for a particular cyber threat is important because it determines which agency should be in charge. In the absence of such a definition, any agency related to cyber issues—which, by the way, is almost every agency—appears on the scene with its own task force or something, causing too much confusion for a prompt, coordinated initial response.

In the recent attacks on March 20, Korea's police, other law enforcement agencies, military units, intelligence agencies, financial supervisory agencies, information technology agencies, and even government-funded research institutions all hurriedly scrambled to the common threat, without knowing who was actually in charge. The less-than-optimal coordination seems to be to blame for the misidentification of the sources of the attack.

A definition of a given situation early on can identify which agency should play the lead to ensure coordination among domestic agencies. Everybody's problem can be nobody's problem.

If a given cyberattack is categorized as a transboundary criminal activity, a key to solving this problem is to enhance the cooperation among law enforcement agencies of different countries involved—an issue generally dealt with by mutual legal assistance networks including joint investigations and extradition.

It is a transnational crime, but just occurs in the new territory known as cyberspace. If, however, a cyberattack is categorized as a national security threat, a different rule applies. Under these circumstances, the issue is whether the victim country's right of self-defense can apply, with a focus shifting to the possibility of a unilateral response as opposed to the cooperation with other countries.

The traditional concept of self-defense has been applied to the invasion of physical territory, but apparent consensus has been building that an attack on the new territory of cyberspace could trigger a similar invocation of self-defense on the part of a victim state.

As the response mode and legal tools are different depending upon how a particular cyberattack situation is understood, it is imperative to make an effort to determine, as early as possible, which of the two categories a given cyberattack falls under.

More importantly, depending upon this critical determination, there is a significant difference in what a government can or cannot do vis-à-vis foreign entities.

Thus, it is not sufficient to simply call it a "cyberattack," but rather it is necessary to determine which category of cyberattack is suspected.

The omnipresence and intricacy of cyberspace do not fit into the traditional profile of governmental work manuals. Cyber threats seem to be located at the confluence of both rivers—law enforcement and national security.

Nonetheless, an analysis and a decision should be made for an efficient and prompt response to this new threat. The point is, someone or some agency should coordinate a pan-governmental response. Otherwise, people will keep seeing ten different agencies scramble to fix downed computer servers only, as opposed to formulating a concerted counter-response on a national level.

[The Korea Herald, April 3, 2013]

9. Shifting into Reverse Gear?

For those who remember the long-held criticism of the (alleged) close relationship between the government and banks in Korea and a series of disputes emanating from it, recent developments certainly raise a red flag. What is presumably unfolding threatens to undermine the effort Korea has made for the past decade.

Interestingly, the names of the Korean banks and financial watchdogs are relatively well known in other countries, partly due to the seven-year legal disputes between Korea and the United States, Korea and the EU, and finally Korea and Japan concerning the relationship between the Korean financial regulatory authorities and the financial institutions. It is only recently—April 2009—that these disputes were finally wrapped up with some victories and some losses. In case one wonders, these decisions are all public documents and thus readily available.

These controversial disputes related to the assertion, based on various pieces of circumstantial evidence, that the banks in Korea (both commercial and policy banks) were under the influence of the financial authorities. One of the key pieces of evidence cited against Korea here was the authorities' alleged intervention in the selection and appointment of the CEOs of major banks.

In particular, the other countries pointed out that former government officials were appointed to lead the banks in a certain direction. Thousands of materials and reports were submitted by these countries to substantiate the alleged relationship, and, unfortunately, core elements of such arguments were generally accepted, though the details of each dispute somewhat vary.

It is now June 2013 and here is a surreal sense of déjà vu. For reasons known and unknown, presidents and other high-ranking officials of key financial institutions are being reshuffled—some are silently leaving and others with traces of a muffled protest. Preferred candidates are then almost openly being discussed. It turns out that many of the new candidates are former government officials.

It is undisputable that these officials possess the necessary expertise in the relevant field. But it misses the point. These selections may revive the unsavory impression that the government still attempts to exert influence, albeit indirectly, in the financial sector. What is being suggested at the moment bears striking resemblance what forced Korea to participate in the seven-year legal ordeal. It seems that perhaps what we have learned has already sunk into oblivion in just four years.

Experiences tell us that developments like this tend to be monitored and followed by foreign governments and entities. These examples may be formulated in a way that produces a rationale to put Korea in an awkward and difficult position when another wave of "government-controlled financial sector" claims arises. It may not come for a year or two, but the possibility is always there as financial sector regulation has become one of the critical topics for many countries: note that recent developments were timed to coincide with the just-released announcement that Korea has decided to participate in the 21-country Trade in Services Agreement, aiming to further liberalize services trade among the participating countries.

Believing that these developments will not be flagged by others is arguably complacent, if not self-deceptive.

Yet again, the real concern here is that it is not the financial regulatory authorities or the financial institutions that may end up paying the price at the end of the day. It is those manufacturers and service providers that use or participate in the financial sector because of possible regulation and trade restrictions. Korea has learned this hard way. These recent lessons should be digested and reflected on, to avoid a future trap.

[The Korea Herald, June 12, 2013]

10. Uber Battle Moves to Seoul

To many, Seoul has been known as a paradise of public transportation. Its clean and fast subway system gets you to anywhere you want in virtually every corner of the city. The bus stops are equipped with digital signboards that tell you the estimated time of arrival of all buses using exclusive bus lanes. Taxis are cheap and readily available at the curbside. One transportation card works everywhere. The Passenger Transport Service Act and Urban Railroad Act enshrine the sanctity of public transportation in the lives of Seoulites.

The remaining hole of public transportation in Seoul is filled by a unique system of "paid surrogate drivers." A common scene toward the end of a dinner gathering in Seoul is people taking out their smartphones to call surrogate driving companies. In just a couple of minutes, a designated driver calls back and the meeting location is then explained. In another ten minutes, the driver arrives at the location. He then drives your car home with you sitting in the backseat. In Seoul, the average fee is merely between 10,000 won to 15,000 won, sometimes cheaper than the taxi fare.

The solid public transportation fortress in Seoul has just encountered the first wave of "Uber" penetration, a digitalized ridesharing service provider using smartphone applications. The San Francisco-based venture company's business model has opened up a can of worms of legal issues throughout the world since its inception in 2010. Taxi drivers are claiming that Uber is illegally taking away passengers from them, to which Uber counters that all it does is connect people—someone willing to purchase transport service and someone willing to provide it—via smartphone apps. For the last two years controversies and regulatory sanctions have consumed many municipalities and taxi trade associations in the United States and Europe. Decisions of these municipalities all vary with their distinct situations.

The regulatory battle over Uber has finally arrived in this country. The venture corporation started its service in Seoul in August 2013, and the business has been taking off recently. Having seen the increasing presence of the unheard-of business, ten days ago the City Government of Seoul issued a stern warning to the corporation's Korean branch with a series of possible regulatory sanctions. The City Government views the service as violating said Passenger Transport Service Act, which prohibits any unauthorized person from engaging in paying transport service activities. Uber is certainly not authorized under the act.

In its July 21 press release, the City Government refers to "consumer protection" as its main rationale for blocking the service in the city. Needless to say, as far as a municipality such as the Seoul City Government is concerned, none could top the importance of ensuring consumer protection. Considering the widespread and very popular business of surrogate driving in Seoul, which is authorized by the city, one might find the consumer protection rationale somewhat overreacting, though. If someone is willing to let a stranger drive his car home while he himself is sleeping in the backseat at night, he may find it less worrisome to purchase a ride service in broad daylight through a smartphone where the location of the vehicle and information of the driver are fully disclosed. If the new service raises a new concern, perhaps one would expect a more persuasive pitch backed by a more thorough evaluation that overrides the obvious market demand.

In many countries, this has become a symbolic confrontation between traditional business entities and new business models made possible through the application of new technologies. Quite often, new business models using emerging technologies are not clearly covered by the provisions of the existing statutes. The absence of applicable provisions, however, does not necessarily provide a sufficient reason to ban a new business model. What can be explored at the same time is whether a new regulation is necessary—instead of a total ban.

[The Korea Herald, August 6, 2014]

11. Here Come the Hearings Again

Based on various interviews and stories, this is what generally happens when candidates for high-ranking government positions are notified of their selection. The bliss brought by the offer of a lifetime is short-lived, and thoughts of the dreadful confirmation hearings soon enter their minds.

Having seen all the grilling and televised dissection of nominees' lives, they face sleepless nights, agonizing over whether to accept the nomination.

Objection from spouses and children, who are also fair game in confirmation hearings, are said to be a major factor. Quite a few candidates turn down the offer simply because of the hearings and their ugly consequences.

Confirmation hearings these days do not simply check nominees' competence. They have become a national ritual to check whether the person has led an impeccable life in all respects—and I do mean all. It is like a political version of a medical CT scan. No stone is left unturned.

Records of military service, tax payments, personal relationships, bank accounts, health insurance, academic degrees, and financial transactions are just a few of the items scrutinized at a parliamentary hearing.

Unconfirmed facts and hearsays from hidden sources are then added to the mix, at which point the distinction between truth and rumor is blurred and political mudslinging starts.

This is also when the three most common themes appear: the opposition's threat to pronounce the candidate "dead on arrival," the ruling camp's accusation that the opposition is "the pot calling the kettle black," and the voice of reason stressing that filling a cabinet position is not an occasion to find someone "as clean as a priest."

Don't forget the media, a critical player in the whole process.

During this white-knuckle ride of several weeks, nominees sometimes quit, and even if they emerge from the process successfully, they do so with political scars and their leadership weakened, arriving in office exhausted. Knowing this, those who receive the call of a lifetime often decline the offer, so they say.

Confirmation hearings were introduced in 2000, and the coverage has steadily expanded through two amendments of the enabling statute, so that now almost all key positions are subject to one.

Not all hearings are the same, though. Some positions require confirmation hearings followed by a vote of approval by the National Assembly, while others do not require parliamentary approval. In the latter category, the president may consider the views of the Assembly detailed in the final report, but does not have to act accordingly.

For instance, the prime minister's appointment requires the approval of the National Assembly, but the appointment of Cabinet ministers does not. The president is not mandated to follow the contents of the report, but its political weight has been immense.

The process represents a positive development for Korean society. There is a consensus that only those with the highest ethical standards can be chosen for key positions in government. Those harboring a desire to assume higher posts have become aware of the close societal monitoring and are now more cautious in managing their career, while "condoned irregularities" have gradually disappeared.

On the other hand, confirmation hearings have become a political point-scoring session. Many times, policy issues become blurred and personal attacks take over. If the process has scared off many able candidates, the burden falls into the lap of the organization in question and ultimately the people.

As the possibility of cabinet reshuffle is now being mentioned, there may be some people somewhere sitting by the phone who will begin to agonize once the call does come. Yes, a grilling is what it is, once a confirmation hearing starts.

[The Korea Herald, February 11, 2015]

12. Ending 18 Years of Controversy

The 1997 indictment of a doctor was the turning point of how the medical fraternity and hospitals treat patients who are terminally ill and in a coma with no prospect of recovery.

The doctor involved agreed to release a patient from the hospital at the request of family members wishing for a peaceful final moment. When the patient subsequently died, the doctor was indicted and found guilty of aiding a murder.

What followed (naturally) was a strictly defensive reaction from doctors and hospitals. They refused to release patients even in their dying hours and continued to treat them in hospitals until the final moment came. It would clear them of any legal problem, and the medical cost will be covered by the well-funded national medical insurance and the patients' families anyway. The choice of patients and family members was no longer a prime determinant.

Then came a 2008 case where family members of a terminally ill patient brought legal action against one of the major hospitals in Seoul that had refused to disconnect life-prolonging equipment despite the family's request. In a legal suit leading all the way to the Supreme Court, the family members prevailed, and the life-sustaining equipment was taken off. The 1997 and 2008 incidents have since galvanized national debates over the need to legislate a law that regulates this sensitive issue.

Another factor that has played a part here is the deeply rooted Confucian culture in the country where filial duty to parents has been taught as being of utmost importance. Traditionally, filial sons and daughters are supposed to do whatever it takes to ensure that their parents live longer. What the traditional teaching did not envision was the technological innovation that can prolong life even if there is no chance of getting cured or recovering.

So, the fuzzy legal parameters and the cultural tradition have apparently forced family members and doctors to apply the palliative treatment even if it may be presumed that the patients themselves might think otherwise. In the meantime, according to 2014 statistics, 81 percent of Koreans aged 65 years or over end up dying at hospitals while 57 percent of the adults actually wish to stay at home in their final moments.

One of the new laws that passed the legislature in early January aims to address this uneasy situation. The new legislation, colloquially called the Well-Dying Law, aims to address this uncertainty of 18 years. Now, with a prior written statement from a patient, life-extending treatment for a patient with a terminal, incurable illness can be terminated. Written consent can be provided by a patient before hospitalization or, in the absence of such consent, all family members can attest to the patient's statement to that effect based on prior discussion in the family followed by certification from two doctors that the patient has entered the dying process. So, once this law goes into effect in January 2018 after a two-year grace period, terminally ill patients and their family members can choose to discontinue life-sustaining treatment for incurable diseases.

This law is the first attempt in the country to define the outer legal parameters of death with dignity. What is concerning is that the two-year grace period will likely see confusion on the part of hospitals and families, since it is not clear how hospitals and medical staffs will (or will have to) respond in the interim until the law finally enters effect two years from now. Also, under the law only four types of treatment are to be covered by a patient's own choice: CPR, mechanical ventilation, hemodialysis, and anti-cancer drug administration. So, when a new medical treatment is developed, which is quite likely, the law apparently will not apply to it. That is another question mark.

How you live is important. But how you die is becoming equally important in this fast-aging society.

[The Korea Herald, January 27, 2016]

13. No More Gifts and No More Lunches

Come Sept. 28, Korea will see a drastic change (for the first time) in how people socialize and interact with government officials. Having survived the most recent challenge at the Constitutional Court, the controversial Kim Young-ran Law is set to enter into force on that day. This anti-corruption law is an ambitious legislation, ready to impose criminal punishment on government officials who respond to outside requests for favors or receive gifts or monetary equivalents from others.

Unlike the previous bribery punishment provision, now the new law does not require any quid pro quo pledge. Mere provision of a certain amount of financial resources to officials will be punishable. The threshold is set at 1 million won per occasion, and 3 million won from the same person annually. Furthermore, government officials are not supposed to take invitations for lunch or dinner exceeding 30,000 won. Nor is an official allowed to accept a gift whose price exceeds 50,000 won.

Importantly and interestingly, this law is not merely confined to penalizing government officials taking money or gifts. It in fact aims to cover a wider group of people. Here are four unique elements of the law.

The term used in the law is "public official" and is defined to cover not only those working for government agencies per se but also those employed in other government-related entities—such as state-run corporations. The number of these government-related entities reaches almost 100. In other words, people who are not conventionally considered government officials are treated as such for the purpose of this law.

And then, the law applies to two specific groups of the private sector—journalists and educators. Noting the two occupations' public function, those employed in the two private sectors are treated as the same as government officials.

And now, the spouses. This law applies to "spouses" of the aforementioned groups. In other words, wives and husbands of public officials, journalists, and educators also fall under the scope of the law. If the spouse receives a gift but the official fails to return it or report the incident, the official (not the spouse) will be punished.

Finally, the law also punishes "anyone" who solicits favors from or offer gifts to the aforementioned three groups of people. Any private citizen initiating regulated contacts or providing monetary equivalents is to face the same criminal sanction. As the number of people falling under the three designated categories reaches roughly three million, anyone who contacts or interacts with any of these three million people are potentially implicated by the new law.

As there is no nationality requirement attached, the final category of "anyone" also includes foreigners and foreign corporations operating in Korea. So, they all fall under the ambit of the new legislation. As a matter of fact, the law does not stipulate any territorial confinement—it will apply activity that has taken place both within and outside the Korean territory.

Thus, it may also apply to business dinners in Paris and personal presents and a golf invitation in Dubai. This law is expected to significantly impact foreign corporations and businessmen dealing with a wide group of Korean counterparts either in Korea or abroad.

Despite the good intention of the law to wipe out corruption in Korea, there still remain ambiguities for key operating terms of Kim Young-ran Law. These ambiguities were the main reason for the recent constitutional challenge. Now that the law is ready to enter into force just one month later, individuals and corporations are bracing for the drastic changes to stem from the new legislation.

Some business entities consider ceasing to issue periodic publications such as newsletters as doing so might lead them to fall under the category of media publishers. Not surprisingly, some restaurants are preparing a dinner set menu of 29,000 won. Gift sets are priced at 49,000 won. As it currently stands, at least in the initial stage of implementation, confusion and controversy seems inevitable. Some provisions are just still unclear.

[The Korea Herald, August 10, 2016]

14. Responsible Parliamentary Audit

September is the busiest month for governmental agencies. An annual parliamentary audit and inspection of the government takes place for about a month. Ministers and other high-ranking officials attend audit sessions and respond to questions and comments from National Assembly Members. This year's session was officially scheduled to begin Sept. 26 and run until Oct. 19.

As regards the National Assembly overseeing governmental affairs, none would be a more effective and influential tool than the audit authority.

It is here that national policies are examined, adjusted, and changed and illegalities are unearthed and corrected. Some lawmakers shine in the national spotlight with thorough preparation and tough questions.

The parliamentary audit does not stop at governmental agencies. Under the law any entity where government funds or tax money is injected is subject to the audit requirement. At present, as many as 600-plus entities are covered. This year's audit will look into 154 agencies among them.

This type of a monthlong, pan-governmental, general inspection is not commonly seen in other countries. The current audit system was introduced in March 1988 through an amendment to the nation's Constitution in late 1987.

Understandably, questions and comments from the lawmakers are usually harsh and rough. So much so that rumors sometimes swirl that heads of agencies or witnesses schedule overseas business trips as excuses not to attend. During an audit session last week, a head of an agency whispered a complaint during a break, which was overheard by a lawmaker. You can imagine what happened when the session resumed.

Here is the twist. The reach of the law in fact goes beyond the listed 600 entities. The law allows the National Assembly to call anyone to appear as a witness in one of the audit sessions. Thus, officials from noncovered entities are also required to appear if they are called. This explains why sometimes businessmen from the private sector and even CEOs from foreign corporations stationed in Seoul appear in audit sessions of the National Assembly. There are grounds to refuse to attend, but they are very narrow such national security concerns. More than anything, those summoned are afraid of the political repercussions from a non-appearance, as there are many strings for the National Assembly to pull.

From the perspective of inspected entities, the logistical burdens are anything but trivial. Document preparation and prep sessions occupy prior weeks before the actual audit. On the day of the audit, a head of an agency is accompanied by a large entourage: from vice ministers to director generals, to directors, and to working level associate directors. In principle, it is the only the head of an agency that is supposed to respond. When a question outside a prep session is presented, staff members are busy scribbling down answers and pass a note to the head. The logistical burden has worsened since governmental agencies and government-related institutions have been relocated to Sejong City and other parts of the country.

After all these efforts, a national audit has a short memory. Remarkably, few follow-up investigations or subsequent measures are taken or, if taken, shared. There is a website of the National Assembly summarizing an annual audit with corrective action from agencies involved, but the information there is too skeletal, at least too scant to justify all the fuss and logistical burden for about two months in the fall. As a matter of fact, only few remember what happened during a national audit, except for some high-profile political debates.

For the conduct of a proper audit, a post-audit evaluation is a must. Detailed records should be prepared, even if some of them are not disclosed for sensitive nature, as to what questions were asked, why they were asked, and how the questions were responded to. People know about this only from news clips. And, most importantly, a lawmaker who raised a particular issue should be responsible for following it up including remedial action from an agency and any misperception on his or her part, if any. They should be placed on record.

[The Korea Herald, October 5, 2016]

15. Divided and Adrift

So many of us have heard too many times for so long that it's the politics that is a drag on Korea's future. Hard-working people, the educated workforce, and innovative businesspeople have worked a Korean miracle, but at the end of the day, the failing politics will be what holds Korea back. While we have known this for some time, we never imagined that the sub-average politics could actually ruin the country this fast.

Ever since the presidential scandal engulfed the country, political leaders, both in the ruling and opposition camps, have made it no secret that they will take advantage of the national turmoil to drive their political agendas—amass the political clout and take over (or maintain) the national helm at the Blue House. What is best for the country is not necessarily in the calculation mix, where provoking outrage brings votes but the echoing voice of reason kills them.

Thanks to this outrage escalation leadership of the politicians, the nation is now deeply divided. So much so that the demonstration duel last weekend raises a fair question whether the pro- and anti-impeachment groups are from the same country. Nonetheless, there is no wise man to calm them down or broker a compromise. Really, "outrage is easy; strategy is hard," as Tony Blair quipped recently,

> Now the final turning point is coming this week. Before we knew it, three months have passed and the impeachment trial is about to end soon. The Constitutional Court is scheduled to issue the verdict by later this week. An impeachment ruling will remove the president for good, and an election will take place within 60 days.[10]

Unless a dramatic rapprochement is somehow brought about before the final ruling, no matter what the outcome post-impeachment Korea will remain deeply divided. Not just divided but fractured and splintered. Add some fake news and conspiracy theories in the mix. A fireball will be thrown in the oil mist. Possibly, a disaster that no one can handle.

In theory, the decision of the Constitutional Court should close the chapter on this saga. We call it rule of law. But both pro- and anti-impeachment groups are now ratcheting up pressure on the Constitutional Court by threatening non-obedience if the decision is adverse. This is simply unacceptable: with the rule of law replaced with street anger, we simply stop being a democratic society.

At this critical juncture, leading politicians remain silent. No one pledges to respect the court's decision yet. Come to think of it, rule of law does not serve the leading politicians' interest. Rule of law means people listening to voice of reason as opposed to an outcry of anger. They know that voice of reason may be good for the country but is inefficient in generating popular votes. Instead, galvanizing people with a constant supply of anger is much more efficient. The past three

10 Korean Constitution, Art. 68(2) ("If the presidency becomes vacant or the President-elect is disqualified, the successor shall be elected within sixty days."), translated by Korea Legislation Research Institute.

months have laid bare the true face of the political circle of the country: be it ruling or opposition, they are unable to lead and unable to think for the nation's future.

We can only blame ourselves. We looked at politics and politicians with cynicism but did not do much to have young, reliable, and visionary leaders to join the force and prosper. Cynicism in us becomes parochialism and factionalism at each election time, only to see the bad drive out the good. One leader is gone, and a neck-and-neck next one comes along. There is no big difference between the conservative group and the liberal group—a chronic dearth of talents in the political sector. Only big egos and presidential hopefuls are the last men standing. Come next election, poor people then are forced to pick the lesser of the two evils. More cynicism settles in, and a new cycle begins.

At stake in the coming months after the Constitutional Court ruling is the future of the nation. If political leaders cannot lead, we can only yearn for voice of reason from people on the street. The court issues a decision. Everyone accepts. The country moves on. Simple three steps expected of any responsible democratic society.

[The Korea Herald, March 7, 2017]

16. Detail National Issues for the Record

In Seoul, how a person goes about his business in a given day is now easily reconstructed. CCTVs are everywhere; payment terminals at buses, subways, and convenience stores record all transactions; and black boxes in vehicles scan streets and alleys 24 hours a day. Pedestrians are ready to pull out their smartphones to take pictures or start videorecording upon unexpected encounters.

Ironically, such reconstruction becomes a serious challenge when it comes to a government decision-making process for key national policies. The point is, the entire process is hardly traceable. Oftentimes, documents detailing a deliberation process are usually not created or maintained. What is put on the record is usually just a short summary of the discussion and deliberation together with a final conclusion along with official seals or signatures. So, even a key national decision tends to leave only a several-page document. The Real Name Financial Transaction policy of 1993, a reform measure that brought a significant change to the Korean financial market, is reduced to an eight-page report. As has been pointed out by many, only scant records exist inside the government regarding the chronology for the 1997 financial crisis in Seoul.

Likewise, more often than not, important meetings tend not to produce detailed minutes. Minutes, even if called that way, contain a short summary of discussions and a final decision. Minutes hardly reveal what actually happened and who spoke what. Some meetings even do not leave a written record, prompting speculation. So, during the probe into the scandal surrounding President Park Geun-hye recently, it was the diaries and schedulers of officials, rather than official government records, that helped reconstruct what happened when and where.

Even if records and documents exist, not all of them are fully shared. Aides of the former President Kim Young-sam once mentioned that they had found empty cabinets when they entered the Blue House in February 1993. Same complaints were lodged by the aides of the former President Kim Dae-jung five years later. Similar problems were again raised during the recent transition of administrations.

What apparently prompted this "record minimalism" seems to be the (wrong) perception that a detailed record, if left, may haunt those who have participated in the decision-making process. So, the belief goes, it is better to leave as little record as possible: detailed records may provide plenty to criticize afterward, but a lack or even absence thereof rarely does.

Unfortunately, this systemic lack of records sows doubts in the minds of outsiders from countries where detailed record-creating and -keeping are an important virtue and sometimes obligation. In some countries, it is not unusual that even phone conversations are recorded in documents, if they relate to important issues. To them, absence of documents only raises questions as to the purpose of a meeting and appropriateness of a decision.

Our ancestors were much better record keepers. The Joseon Dynasty was obsessive about making and leaving a detailed record of the daily activities of kings. The Annals of Joseon Dynasty (Joseon-wangjo-silok) recorded in 1,707 volumes 472 years of daily conversations, debates, and events of 25 kings. Two royal history officials followed a king in his every move to record virtually everything. One wrote down conversations and the other described the king's outer appearance and complexion. The arrival of a results-oriented, fast-growing industrialized society has suddenly washed away this good practice. And we now know much more about a conversation in the Chosun court several hundred years ago than a recent cabinet meeting. Detailed records should be made of debates and deliberations on key national businesses, so that the next generation knows exactly what happened and learns from it. Of course, some highly confidential information may not be disclosed to the public for a certain period of time, but at least it should be kept in the national archives for the next generation. Many times, we start empty-handed and create the wheels again.

The story of memoranda prepared by a former FBI director and other US officials after important meetings and conversations, even after one-on-one meetings, spotlights the record minimalism in our government's business. In retrospect, a lot of political controversies and national confusion would have been averted if we had a system of leaving detailed records.

[The Korea Herald, May 30, 2017]

17. Will Minimum Wage Hike Step Up Automation?

As heralded, the minimum wage is being increased substantially by the Minimum Wage Commission.

The commission is raising the minimum wage from 6,470 won ($5.80) per hour this year to 7,530 won next year, a 16.4 percent increase and the largest increase since 2001. The rise will continue until the minimum payment reaches 10,000 won. As of now, Korea's per hour minimum wage is roughly in the upper middle among Organization for Economic Cooperation and Development countries, when per capita gross national product and gross national income are factored in.

The increase is part of the government's effort to narrow the gap between the haves and have-nots in Korean society, as the widening gap is now threatening social cohesiveness. It is one way to alleviate the problem by providing real benefits to low-wage workers and their families.

On top of that, the increased wage will lead to fewer people quitting and stable employment, ensuring a productive workforce. More importantly, it will result in increased consumer spending, spreading positive effects in the economy. Low-wage workers from other countries will also become important beneficiaries of this new change. This is a good development, as they will receive a fair share of their contribution to the national economy. Overall, it's indeed a step in the right direction. However, the minimum wage hike is also shaking the Korean labor market, with small businesses and shop owners voicing concern over the increase in labor costs.

They say that higher labor costs will drive them out of business gradually if the minimum wage reaches the 10,000 won mark over several short intervals, eventually hurting the Korean economy and welfare of low-income earners.

Only time will tell how this latest policy will turn out.

At any rate, a predictable change in the era of higher minimum wage will be the more widespread use of automated machines at shops and restaurants.

Compared to its peers, Korea has been relatively slow when it comes to automation in small shops and restaurants. Self-check-in kiosks are still hardly seen at Korean airports, despite the trend at other major airports these days. Self-ordering kiosks at restaurants are still a relative rarity in Korea compared to neighboring Japan.

While "food court" style self-service eateries are on the rise, full-service restaurants—even for small mom and pop shops with cheap prices—are more common in Korea.

There has notably been a slow pace of automation for a country known as the most wired with the fastest internet connection.

Given Korea's potential, the hikes in the minimum wage will make automation more appealing to owners and employers.

In the global workplace, kiosks and automated machines are increasingly replacing human labor. Last November, upon the increase of the minimum wage in certain jurisdictions, the first response from fast-food eateries such as McDonald's and Wendy's was the expanded installation of ordering kiosks. Touch-screen service machines and ordering kiosks are nothing compared to self-driving cars at the doorstep of commercialization or artificial intelligence's deep learning capability displayed by AlphaGo. Certainly, more automation will define our future labor market.

Automation means the reduced hiring of workers. Even a simple, self-service assistance machines threaten routinized low-wage jobs. So, if owners in Korea turn to automated machines in response to increased wages, we will see rather unintended consequences at least in the short run: job losses for certain people in certain segments of the economy. The very group of people to be protected by the new policy may bear the brunt of the change, at least in the initial stage.

Consider what happened with the government's plan to reform the part-time lecturer system at universities to improve their working environment.

Seemingly enhanced protection for part-time lecturers on campus mandated by the legislation of 2011 has been met by reduced hiring by universities.

Since the inception of the legislation, part-time lecturers themselves have opposed its implementation, which has ultimately forced the National Assembly to push back the implementation as many as three times since 2011, with the new date now set for Jan. 1, 2018.

Again, over time we will know the final balance of pros and cons for the increase in minimum wage. But the real effect will be more complex than it seems.

[The Korea Herald, July 25, 2017]

18. In the National Assembly We Trust

The same scenes are repeated each fall. Angry faces, shouting matches, and group boycotts, and all these in front of national TV cameras. The National Assembly started this year's plenary national audit on Oct. 12. It will run for 20 days until Oct. 31. The first four days of the audit indicate that we can expect the same this year as well.

To governmental agencies and entities with state funding, the annual audit is one of the most critical moments of the year for leaders and organizations alike. Not only that, but any entity can be subject to the legislative audit under the law if deemed necessary by the National Assembly. So, CEOs of private corporations and even foreign corporations are thus summoned for questioning. A lot of pressure for them indeed.

In a democratic society, the legislative body's inspection of the national business cannot be emphasized too much. It is the hallmark of the modern democracy. But the National Assembly's almost limitless authority of the inspection and ineffective conduct of the audits have long been criticized in the country. Here are the most common disappointing scenes in my view. One: long lines and endless waiting. You can see dozens of officials sitting behind a person responding to questions from lawmakers. They are directors, director generals, and assistant ministers. The protocol is that only the minister is supposed to answer, so all other officials are mobilized and seated behind the minister to assist him or her. They shuffle through thick documents and files and pass on notes to the minister. They are not all accounted for. Other working level officials are not even able to enter the room and instead crouching in hallways. With every key official in the National Assembly, the daily wheel of national business comes to a halt. For 20 days, some wheels somewhere stop spinning or slowly moving. Two: long paper trails and extensive information. Before the session, lawmakers (and their aides) send requests to target entities seeking information and documents in preparation for the national audit. Tables, charts, and forms are sent to be filled out. Some requests demand an extraordinary amount of information—a dragnet fishing expedition as opposed to targeted pinpointing. A month or two before the audit is the busiest moment for officials and employees to collect information and organize documents in response to seemingly endless requests from the National Assembly. Three: one-way communication. Conversations at the national audit are far from two-way, interactive communication. National assemblymen spend a long time to admonish or rebuke a head of an agency with stern faces, and only a short time is given for the person to respond. Sometimes questions end with "you don't have to answer," and answers are interrupted with "your answer is not necessary." People would expect serious and professional two-way interaction between ministers and lawmakers. Four: politicization. National audit is abused by some lawmakers as their PR occasion or as an opportunity to score political points. Ruling and opposition party members engage in fierce verbal battles with fingers pointing in all directions. Harsh words are exchanged. Those words are beeped in news coverage. After that, one group retires from the room in protest. The other remaining half then continues to carry on. Serious discussion based on a bi-partisan spirit is a rare item in this environment.

Legislative scrutiny of national affairs is the final line of defense for a democratic society. National Assembly's audits have dug up blunders, mishandling, and mistreatment by government agencies. No one would countenance suppression of the authority of the National Assembly as a national watch dog. But there's got to be a way to fix the aforementioned four scenes. As long as the four scenes are the first image of the audit, the National Assembly only undermines its own authority. Will this fall be the first step for a change?

[The Korea Herald, October 17, 2017]

19. Unique Problem of Graying Korea

In traditional Korea, the age 60 marked an important occasion. It is the year when one's life makes a full circle according to the sexagenary (60-year) cycle of the lunar calendar. It was the point in time when one was considered to have lived a healthy and long life, so it was certainly a time for a big celebration among family members and also a memorable festivity for the entire village. However, 60 years old is now considered young in today's Korea, as the country's average life expectancy has risen dramatically over the years, reaching mid-80s and counting. Nowadays in Korea, a man "officially" becomes elderly at the age of 65: a special card is issued by the government, subway rides become free, and elderly pension is provided. Sixty-five is also the standard adopted by the international community. The UN officially defines a society as an "aging society" when the population of people 65 and older accounts for 7 percent of the total population. The society becomes an "aged society" when the percentage reaches 14 percent. It then turns into a "super-aged" one if the number rises to 20 percent.

Here is how Korea is doing. Korea passed the first two marks in 2000 and 2017, respectively. This 17-year run is the fastest in this category. The previous record was Japan's 24 years (1970–1994). Statistics predict that Korea will reach the final mark of 20 percent in 2025. And of course the number will continue to rise afterward. It was just 5 percent in 1990. By any account, Korea is aging and aging very fast.

Rapid aging's social problems are well-known: weakening economic vitality, a dwindling workforce, and intergenerational tension over jobs, just to name a few. Rising health care costs, increasing medical expenditures, and a drying national pension fund—you bet. Mind you these problems of a greying society are not just Korea's. Many other countries are also experiencing rapid demographic changes in the same direction. But there is one unique problem for Korea: elderly poverty.

Korea's elderly poverty rate—those who live with less than half of the national household median income—stands at 49 percent, the highest among 34 Organization for Economic Cooperation and Development countries. This means half of us are going to end up living in poverty when we reach 65 and above. Sadly, some say this widespread poverty is one of the main reasons for another category in which Korea marks the highest in OECD statistics: the elderly suicide rate.

Long gone is the traditional Korean virtue of fulfilling the filial duty to support parents financially and emotionally. As the holiday season nears, we will soon see charity drives for the underprivileged. Those charity drives and related media reports feature the perilously inhumane living conditions of poor senior citizens who live in solitude. Some of them make a living by collecting cardboard on the streets. You may see fragile elderly men and women pulling small carts full of cardboard.

Each December, I used to accompany students in my school when they carry out charity in winter. We bought and delivered coal briquettes to the elderly who live in poverty around the campus. Their small homes are clustered along narrow alleyways where one person can barely walk through. These briquettes are an absolute minimum that can warm them during the cold winter. Elderly poverty is widespread in our own neighborhood.

Experts warn that today's working generation in Korea will face harsher poverty in their retirement years. Parents are spending a significant portion of their earnings on their children's education at private teaching institutions and on private tutoring. Caught up in spending on their children, most middle-class parents do not have the luxury of worrying about their lives after 65.

By the time parents retire, their savings may well have dried up. It again tells us that Korea's chronic private education problem lies at the core of many other social challenges, present and future. The national college entrance exam falls on Thursday. Before and after the exam, parents will again line up at (well-known) private teaching institutions.

[The Korea Herald, November 14, 2017]

20. Not a Good Time for Divisive Politics

Korea in 1987 and Korea in 2018 are like day and night. The sharp difference means the current Constitution adopted in 1987 does not accurately reflect the reality of Korea today and the minds of the people at present. The intervening three decades have seen the emergence of national practices that have outgrown the clothes of the provisions of the Constitution. Some wordings turned out to be inadvertent loopholes. Add recent political developments, most notably the presidential impeachment of 2017. It showed how far off track the currently "omnipotent" presidential system could go.

This is the logic, quite persuasive by the way, that has prompted current discussions of constitutional amendment. A plausible suggestion is to put a constitutional amendment proposal to a national referendum on the occasion of the upcoming local government election slated for June 13. One stone, two birds. Korean efficiency.

Who would oppose updates and improvements? But the only problem is "politicization." Even with whispers of constitutional amendment, national politics is already boiling hot. What is being said about constitutional amendment in the political arena these days foreshadows a major clash between the political camps: an otherwise "one-point" technical amendment process is now morphing into another occasion to show how divided our society is. Different political camps are now shooting up test balloons to check on the wind currents, and digging their heels in. What is good for their respective political camps and what is best for the nation are all thrown into the mix together, so each side questions the real intent of the other side with respect to any proposal of the amendment.

Come to think of it, to political parties striving to rally their supporting groups, none would be more appealing than the topic of constitutional amendment. It has the potential to become a political detonator of everything. Ideological differences of all sorts can come roaring back to life as political camps galvanize and mobilize their core supporting groups.

The question is, can we afford to have such an acrimonious row at this time of increasingly unforgiving surroundings of the country? The next several months will be a critical period. This is the time when even a deeply divided country would try to find a reason to stand together and speak together. Sensible and responsible political leaders would try to bury the hatchet.

Back to the Constitution. The Constitution is outdated, and an amendment is long overdue. Undoubtedly, there are obvious benefits from updates and improvements. But if they mean months of national rallies and further national division, again at this time, we had better be cautious. There is no reason to check how deeply divided we are and advertise it to others. It is time to boost the sense of togetherness and try to do something cohesive, time to smooth things over. With apologies to the Constitution waiting for an overhaul, this is probably the worst timing for ideological division and political infighting. Once the situation stabilizes a bit, we then can promptly initiate the national debates and conclude the project.

After the first month of 2018, we know that we are looking at a pivotal year. Everybody is eager to see the tide turn in the coming months for a peaceful resolution of the current Korean situation. Who knows what will happen: maybe there will be a magical breakthrough sometime this year, perhaps after the Winter Olympic Games. But for the luck to fall in our favor, we should stand (or at least look and sound) united.

The next several months is not a good time for political infighting. This is not the time for a deepening national split. Rather, a time for boosting national spirit.

[The Korea Herald, February 6, 2018]

21. Jeju a Testing Ground for Refugee Policy

Jeju Island has become a hot potato inside the Korean government. On the same day the Ministry of Justice listed Yemen as a state whose nationals are not permitted to enter the sub-tropical island without a visa, the National Human Rights Commission issued a strong statement urging agencies in charge to take more active measures to protect the basic rights of the refugees from Yemen staying on the island. Both happened on June 1.

It all started with a recent surge of Yemeni refugees entering the island. Originally, before the latest Justice Ministry's decision on June 1, Yemeni nationals could enter South Korea's southernmost island without a visa under the island's no-visa entry policy. Once on the island, they could then apply for refugee status. As a party to 1951 Refugee Convention and under 2013 Refugee Act, the Immigration Service should review applications and accord refugee status to those who satisfy the requirements.

As arrival means entry, application for refugee status through Jeju has been made relatively easier than other entry points such as Incheon Airport, where visas are required in the first place to enter Korea. And as a result, Yemeni refugees arriving in the island seeking asylum has increased fast. As of May 24 a total of 869 refugee applications are pending in Jeju, 479 of which have been filed by Yemeni nationals. Most of them cite the possibility of persecution in their home country due to the civil war. By way of comparison, there were only 10 and 52 Yemeni applications in 2016 and 2017.

So, now after June 1, newly arriving refugees from Yemen can only apply for asylum in Korea through a much-tougher regular entry procedure.

In its June 1 recommendation statement, the NHRC does not take issue with the government's decision to list Yemen as a visa-requiring state for Jeju entry (by the way, only 12 states including Yemen are now listed). Rather, the commission underscores the importance of ensuring an expedited review process for applications, citing the hardships that applicants have to go through during the pendency. It also recommends increasing the immigration agency's capacity to hear the claims and make decisions swiftly, in order to "fulfill Korea's obligation under the Refuge Convention and the domestic statute."

The current situation on Jeju is of course rather peculiar, stemming from the island's unique status as a liberal entry point of the nation. But the problems that Jeju government and Immigration Service Jeju branch office encounter at the moment mirror the challenges we are facing nationally—a chronic shortage of resources and manpower to handle and process refugee applications. With a continuing surge of applications the whole system is overburdened. In 2017 alone, 9,942 applications were filed.

Korea has been one of the most rigid countries in terms of granting refugee status to foreigners. Among 32,733 applicants during the 1994–2017 period, only 792 received the status. As each case is different, it would be difficult to provide a one-size-fits-all answer. But a meager 2.4 percent acceptance rate implies that our refugee review system needs its own reviewing. A lack of skilled manpower and logistical resources should be one of the reasons, undoubtedly. The commission's recommendation therefore is not just directed at the Jeju situation as an aberration, but nudges the government to contemplate a structural reform.

Korea has a legal obligation to protect refugees from other countries. We are now entering a new phase where adequate infrastructure is established so as to fulfill our obligation.

By coincidence, the Constitutional Court issued a ruling on May 31 that a foreign national who has applied for refugee status upon arrival at a Korean airport has the "right to counsel" under the Korean Constitution. This is a ruling in response to a petition filed by a Sudanese national claiming his right to counsel was denied at Incheon Airport in 2013. It is not just international instruments. Our own judiciary mandates a more thorough process in refugee reviews and protection.

[The Korea Herald, June 12, 2018]

22. How Many Hours Do You Work?

What is work and what is leisure? This long-standing philosophical question has suddenly become a legal question as a new labor law (Labor Standards Act) is entering into force on July 1 to cap the maximum weekly working hours at 52, together with a penalty provision for noncomplying employers.

Having realized the unclear dividing line between work and nonwork and the fear of imminent confusion in the field, the Ministry of Employment and Labor announced at the last minute a six-month grace period for the new law. In other words, the law will not be enforced until Jan. 1, 2019. It is a wise decision: clear guidelines and codes of conduct can now be prepared for businesses and workers before the new year.

To comply with the new law, businesses have already started to scramble. Some companies adopt a "PC Off" system where employee's computers are shut off at 6 p.m. unless authorized for extended work beforehand. "Family days" are introduced for a mandatory early closure. A very positive sign for a country with the world's longest working hours.

The only challenge is, the six-month grace period may still leave a critical question unresolved: i.e., what is "working hours"? Sometimes, it is difficult to keep track of time spent for work. Questions arise in many different varieties.

Interestingly, working hours is not defined in the law. It is to be determined "on a case-by-case basis, taking all circumstances into consideration." That is what the Korean Supreme Court stated in its 2014 judgment. At the core in this "totality" consideration lies the analysis whether an employee is subjected to the "direction and supervision of an employer." If so, then it is working hours even if you are relaxing or having downtime, or in a different location. If not, the time is not working hours, even if you fret over the unfinished work at the office.

MOEL follows this guidance from the court. Startled by flooding questions, MOEL disseminated booklets on May 18 to answer them. Here are some examples. A team seminar for effective work coordination is counted as working hours. But a seminar or workshop for collegiality or friendship enhancement is not. Quite confusing, indeed. What about work-related dinners? If you are officially requested by your boss to attend a dinner for a business partner, that is work. But if you have a business pitch dinner looking for a referral, then it is not.

If you hang around with your colleagues and boss after work, that is not work. That is an easy one. But consider this. When you attend a team dinner at the request from your boss even if you would rather go home, what would that be? MOEL booklet says it is not work. It says a team leader's request for dinner attendance, in and of itself, is not sufficient to make the dinner into working hours. Well, enigmatic indeed.

As you can tell, gray areas abound in real life. As the Supreme Court itself says, and MOEL acknowledges, this very issue is not amenable to a clear-cut decision. You can't tell which is which, and many times it's both.

And yet, this new law comes with a stringent penalty provision (maximum two years imprisonment or a 20 million won fine). It may take time, cases, and prosecution before we know for sure in borderline situations. Learning by doing is a good approach in many areas, but probably not in the law enforcement sector. This "you-go-figure-it-out" approach has been observed in some of the recent legislative endeavors. Of course, they all have good intentions and pursue legitimate public objectives. But from the law administration standpoint, they are a little far from a textbook model legislation where you know in advance what is prohibited and what is not.

MOEL can prepare detailed guidelines and a practical handbook before the law starts to be enforced six months later. The current booklets posted on its website raise more questions and conjure up counterfactuals.

[The Korea Herald, June 26, 2018]

23. Still Torn between Two Cities

Recent price hikes for housing in Seoul have fanned deep frustration among those living outside Seoul. While prices in Seoul are going through the roof, real estate markets elsewhere are struggling with too many vacancies. Local money is flocking to the Seoul real estate market in droves. As ever, people and money keep coming to Seoul.

Seoul's status as a powerful magnet for people and national resources is a chronic problem for Korea. The Seoul Metropolitan Area accounted for 49.5 percent of the national GDP and (coincidentally) 49.5 percent of the country's population in 2017. Which is why the government's plan in 2005 to disperse governmental agencies and public institutions across the nation was not only proper but essential. Relocation started in 2007, and 153 agencies have since found new homes in ten cities. The culmination of this plan occurred in 2012, when the Sejong Administrative Capital first appeared on the map. Stay tuned: the government is now contemplating a second wave of relocation, one where 122 additional institutions will be asked to leave Seoul.

After 11 years, the relocation is still unfinished business. Every relocated institution has its own story of staff loss, hiring difficulties, and an infrastructure vacuum. A recent article in the Wall Street Journal about the National Pension Service in North Jeolla Province typifies these struggles. Hopefully, logistical difficulties will get better with time. Construction of buildings and roads is proceeding fast. Social and cultural infrastructure is catching up.

The real question, though, is how to handle the structural problem. After the move, the agencies and institutions had to leave one foot in Seoul. Events, meetings, and conferences have not followed them to their new locations. They still take place in Seoul, and officials and employees are expected to attend. Under the circumstances, it is hard to harness the benefits of relocation. Efficiency is an easy victim when an institution is essentially forced to maintain two offices.

Perhaps what is most to blame is a detached and divided decision-making process. For any given institution, important decisions must still be made in the capital. Which means the heads of the agencies and ministries are forced to travel to Seoul on a regular basis. Their time and presence are split between Seoul and their official headquarters. A great deal of work has to be done on the KTX bullet train and over messenger programs.

If we are truly serious about decentralization, decision-making processes should be localized as much as possible. Leaders and CEOs should spend more of their time at their official headquarters, instead of at liaison or branch offices in Seoul. To achieve that, cooperation from powerful agencies in Seoul—such as the National Assembly, the Board of Audit, and the Blue House—is an absolute must. That is the only way to achieve the intended objective of decentralization as we mark the 11th anniversary of the move.

This year's National Assembly audit starts Oct. 10. Dozens of government officials and company representatives will be called to testify, as usual. They will have to travel to Seoul and stay here. By way of example, the National Policy Committee alone—one of the most prominent of the national Assembly's 18 standing committees—has called as many as 217 witnesses to testify during its two-week session. On my count, about half are from local offices. Much of their time in

October will be spent on the road. When the second wave of relocation is complete, the majority of witnesses at future audits will be chosen from local towns.

Truly, decentralization is an important solution to one of the nation's oldest conundrums. But its success can only be achieved if it is done right. As we mark the 11th anniversary of the national policy and contemplate the next step in this massive move, it is time to evaluate the past 11 years and see what can be done better.

[The Korea Herald, October 2, 2018]

24. New Technology, the New Economy, and Overregulation

Korea is a "fast" country. Everything is quick and speedy, with one exception: the regulatory framework. By and large, laws and regulations fall way behind technological development in the market. Startup companies' first encounter is regulatory red tape. How ill matched for a country that excels in information and communication technology.

The tricky part is these regulations have legitimate objectives. In particular, they are intended to mitigate risks, known and unknown. The default answer is usually no, instead of yes, to be on the safe side. Naturally, this is an uphill battle for new ideas and new endeavors. Concerns over safety and risk management are part of the job for any responsible government. But if pushed to the extreme, concern becomes overconcern. That is the point where regulation turns into overregulation.

Some recent examples. First, the drone regulations. Under the current regulations, even small, hobby drones (including toys) need flight permits to fly in the "flight regulation zone," which takes up a significant portion of the Seoul Metropolitan Area. So hobbyists flock to the banks of the Han River to fly them. In response to calls for change, the government proposed new rules in early October. After the necessary hearings and other procedures, the new rules should go into effect early next year.

The new rules are more practical. Toys are OK now. More specifically, drones weighing 250 grams or less (that is, toys and leisure drones) are exempt from regulation. Core aspects of the regulations remain in place, while adjustments have been made according to the weight and capabilities of the particular drone model in question. For instance, flying a drone beyond one's sight range is still prohibited. So is flying a drone higher than 150 meters without prior permission. Risks to pedestrians and security threats are cited as the main reasons.

Let's look at another example. Three years after UberX withdrew from the Korean market, protests from taxi companies have flared up again. This time the target is a Korean company launching a web-based carpooling service. Many reasons are cited—one of which, again, concerns the potential risks. Namely, unregistered or unregulated drivers might engage in illegal activities; more cars on the road during rush hour would mean traffic jams and other problems.

What we see now is just the beginning. With new technology and a new digital economy, many new ideas and business models are being tried for the first time, mostly in the twilight zone of regulation. As we proceed, similar questions will continue to arise. Of course, it remains necessary to ensure that existing industries are not marginalized in a way that threatens the welfare and livelihood of conventional workers. This is a matter that requires extensive national debate.

That said, overconcern as a blanket justification to maintain existing regulations or reject new regulations should be carefully scrutinized. Again, these are all valid concerns. More so considering this country's unique situation, where so many people live in densely populated residential neighborhoods in the Seoul Metropolitan Area. Add to that the constant national security factor. The real question is not whether there are risks, but whether the risks can be managed and, if so, how. In other words, regulations should be carefully tailored and crafted to balance competing goals. Consider a textbook example of overregulation. In the early days of automobiles in the late 19th century, a UK law required that a man holding a red flag walk ahead of each vehicle. His job was to prevent the car from speeding and wave a red flag to warn the pedestrians and horse carriages nearby.

Reasonable regulations, undertaken to protect public safety, are always welcome and enforcing them is a task that all responsible governments must undertake. Too much concern and the resulting overregulation, however, only stifle innovation. The victims are companies and individuals with new ideas and technologies.

[The Korea Herald, November 13, 2018]

25. Debates, Sufficient Deliberations Key to Legislative Process

Usually, society changes first. Laws then follow. Which means a gap between the two. The norm-reality gap has become more evident these days: the speed of social changes is unprecedented, and laws are lagging behind, panting.

The narrower the gap, the more likely society benefits from harmony and stability. A gap left unattended grows into a gulf, fostering social discord and instability. It all depends on the quality of the legislative institution. The legislature fails us either by overregulation, under-regulation, or sometimes no regulation. Finding the right balance at the right time helps the society move forward. Otherwise, the legislature becomes a stumbling block.

Well, we know the track record of our National Assembly is far from optimal. Important legislations are being held up amid political bickering. Key bills are withering on the vine. Sadly, all this is happening while the society is changing at lightning speed.

Sometimes quite the opposite happens for certain enactments: hastily processed for political motives or as proof of something being done, before the consequences are fully understood and digested.

That said, we also find instances where the National Assembly carries out the legislative task in a way that is responsive to new social controversies, in an effort to find common ground. New legislative endeavors then put an end to long-lasting controversies, or at least are able to manage them reasonably.

A common thread for these "responsive" or "gap-narrowing" legislations is thorough debates and sufficient deliberations. Even better if detached from partisan politics. Here, the National Assembly listens to competing views, consults experts, holds conferences, studies examples of other countries, and then seeks the least common denominator.

Consider, for example, the legislation that has just passed its first anniversary—euphemistically called "well-dying law" instead of its long, official title.

The law permits, under strict conditions and with proper consent, patients and their family members to refuse life-sustaining treatment for enumerated incurable diseases during the terminal stage. It came into effect in February 2018, and one year on, philosophical, ethical, and legal debates are still continuing. They will probably never end given the fundamental nature of the issues involved.

Contents of the act aside, its enactment process chronicles the history of debates and deliberations at many different levels spanning over two decades. Experts' views and professional opinions have been solicited and juxtaposed. At the core was the direct clash between two values: deeply rooted Confucian culture in the country versus changing society and medical technologies. In the clash, family-hospital disputes, medical staff indictments, and intra-family disagreement ensued.

There is no right or wrong answer to this fundamental question. But the deep social contemplation with proper inputs has at least produced a legislation that is responsive to long-lasting social controversies.

Check the statistics from the Ministry of Health and Welfare. Since its enactment to February this year, prior consents submitted by ordinary citizens under the act reached 115,259. In the same 12 months, 36,224 treatment-suspension applications were made at hospitals. This accounts for 12.1 percent of total deaths in 2018.

The first-year statistics indicate that the new legislative framework offers guidance for the society and families for this difficult subject. Again, we'll have to see how ongoing debates on this very fundamental issue will evolve in our society. Experience tells us the importance of debates and deliberations for a legislative process. Different aspects and diverse views should be kept in sobering perspective and in mature contemplation. For a controversial issue, this is critical.

Certainly, sometimes exigent circumstances demand quick action. Think about the fine dust legislation that passed the National Assembly last week. Time is of essence here. Even so, full debates are still indispensable, even conducted in an intense and condensed manner.

Unfortunately, we often observe debates and deliberations to be replaced with intense confrontation among interest groups. Legislative projects are used for political gains. These laws, even when enacted, hardly address a social problem. They may only exacerbate it.

[The Korea Herald, March 19, 2019]

26. Supreme Court Is Swamped

"Best out of three" runs deep in settling grievances in the Korean culture. This tradition apparently explains the exploding dockets of the Korean Supreme Court. Almost regardless of merits, many litigants like to have a day in the Supreme Court after adverse decisions in the District Court and High Court. An appeal to the nation's highest court has been acknowledged as a right of every individual.

The inevitable outcome of this stance is the exploding caseloads at the Supreme Court. The numbers are stunning. Just last year, the Korean Supreme Court handled as many as 38,141 cases. As there are 12 justices at the court who participate in hearing ordinary disputes (excluding the chief justice and a justice who assumes the role of the Head of the Court Administration), this translates into 3,178 cases for each justice, which again means 8.7 cases for each judge each day. As access to the nation's highest court is regarded as a right, there is no way to control the caseload. It is dreaded that this year will see 40,000 cases brought.

What about other countries? Quite a few countries have adopted a "judicial discretion" system as opposed to a system granting such a right, due to this very problem of managing the docket of the highest courts. For instance, the US Supreme Court hears only 70–80 cases out of 10,000 petitions submitted each year. Only those with important national policy implications are received, while others are dismissed. The resources of the court are not mobilized to determine erroneous factual findings or misapplication of law.

As the management of cases swirls out of control, a serious discussion is currently underway in Korea to reform the Supreme Court appellate mechanism. An idea to create a new appellate court between the High Court and the Supreme Court to handle ordinary three-level appeal cases while leaving the highest court to deal with only cases with national implication or those of imperative public importance has been floated for some time now. The Supreme Court itself has been busy advocating the proposal to introduce a new appellate court. Its public relations activity has been noticeable recently. A bill implementing this new idea is being tabled at the regular session of the National Assembly this fall.

As with other judicial reforms, the discussion has not always been as merry and consensual as one would hope. The practical demand notwithstanding, the controversy continues. There is strong opposition in the legal community including the Korean Bar Association. Critics argue that this idea is unconstitutional as the Korean Constitution guarantees the right to review by the nation's highest court, not by some other substitutes. The best way to deal with the exploding dockets, they argue, is to increase the number of Supreme Court justices. Yet another lingering question is how to divide the role between the Supreme Court under the new system and the existing Korean Constitutional Court which has the authority to hear and determine issues of national importance within the ambit of the Constitution.

All these legal issues and questions do merit careful attention, of course. There are certainly many associated issues that need to be clarified or discussed beforehand.

But, in any event, handling 40,000 cases a year is simply a practical impossibility. A new appellate court seems to be the only way to ensure a three-level judicial process and at the same time save the Supreme Court from the swamp.

The reform, if approved and implemented, would mark a major change of the substantive variety in the Korean judicial system. This fall we will see an intense debate over the merit of this new proposal, both inside and outside the National Assembly.

[The Korea Herald, October 7, 2015]

27. Checks and Balances Key to "Prosecution-Police" Debate

Should police be permitted to terminate a criminal investigation on their own? This question is at the core of a long-standing debate between the prosecution and police over the adjustment of investigative power.

There are many other issues, but this one has become very symbolic. The prosecution opposes it, while the police treat it as the lynchpin of the whole debate. National Assembly deliberation this fall will finalize the adjustment. As expected, it was also a hot topic at the confirmation hearing of the new prosecutor general on Monday. Korean criminal investigations center on the prosecution. Only a prosecutor can terminate an investigation and indict a person as a result of an investigation. Furthermore, only a prosecutor can seek an arrest warrant.

However, the reality is that police conduct most actual investigations. Once the investigation is over, police then transfer the case to the prosecution for either indictment or termination of the case. The reform being considered now is whether to permit police to end a case of their own volition.

Concerns have been raised. What if the police close a case inappropriately? Recent high-profile scandals implicating police officers have fanned such concerns. True, the police have a long way to go to earn the public's trust. The power balance will shift toward the police if they can initiate and terminate an investigation. The question is how much of a shift we are looking at.

What has been missing in this debate—and what should come up in this fall's deliberation—is what is a better model for the country? The benchmark, in short, should be how to ensure checks and balances between these two powerful law enforcement agencies. They are cut from the same cloth—aren't they?—so checks and balances would be critical. The dominance of one agency may not work in today's Korean society. The current system was structured as long ago as in 1962. Viewed from that perspective, it is not entirely clear whether the proposed "police termination" option would have such large negative effects. I am thinking of a couple of things.

First, the prosecution can still request the reinvestigation of a case closed by the police. If misconduct is suspected, the prosecution can still reopen the investigation. Besides, the prosecution will still monopolize the indictment authority, which means it can decide not to press criminal charges after a police investigation. So, a rough balance between the two agencies seems to be there. Let's see how this scheme shapes up in the final package.

To dispel worries, another safeguard can be put in place. For instance, a police officer in charge should remain and be held responsible in case of investigation termination. Administrative penalties and criminal sanctions for police misconduct can provide yet another layer of protection.

Also, come to think of it, the other party of the investigation, once termination is decided, will probably submit a petition to the prosecution for reinvestigation. The prosecution will be alerted and prodded anyway, which could serve as a counterweight to termination by police.

Therefore, the termination of investigation by police will still be self-censored, party-monitored, and prosecution-examined. Incidents of misconduct may not arise as argued by the prosecution.

Of course, irregularities and controversies may appear here and there. However, it may not be an indication of a systematic problem as a result of the proposed overhaul.

On the other hand, the benefits arguably look tangible: checks and balances between the prosecution and police could be better ensured that way. A police termination model is presumably something that we can explore, with proper conditions in place.

The two agencies have been engaged in fierce debate for several years now. With proper consensus in the fall, it is about time to make a decision and move on.

[The Korea Herald, July 9, 2019]

28. Global Games of Chicken

You can make a lot of money in the boom cycle. With the stockpiled cash, you can then hope to ride out the bust cycle, waiting for the next boom cycle. The cycle alternates between the two and in this business timing determines everything. In the boom cycle the price of the product is high, but when the market turns around, the price then plummets, many times becoming one-tenth of the original price. The weak or the unlucky go out of business in the interim and the survivors stand to reap tremendous profits when the next wave comes. The survivors then start another round of competition. Through this global game of chicken, only five companies are supplying the ever-growing global demand. The venue for this cutthroat competition is the global semiconductor industry.

There are two types of memory chips on the market: those used for PCs and laptops (called DRAM), and those for smartphones and digital gadgets (called NAND Flash). The former market is supplied by Samsung (Korea), Hynix (Korea), Micron (US), and Nanya (Taiwan) in the order of market share. Demand in the latter market is met by Samsung, Toshiba (Japan), Micron, and Hynix. So, the five companies produce virtually all the chips that go into everything digital. And in this market the performance of the two Korean chipmakers has been particularly strong recently. According to recent industry surveys, the combined market share of the two companies in the DRAM market has exceeded 70 percent for the first time. The number for the NAND Flash market has reached 40 percent and is rising.

Samsung has been the dominant player in the semiconductor market for a long time, and is now further distancing itself from the pack. What really changed the dynamics of the industry was the recent upward surge of another Korean chipmaker, SK Hynix. In 2014, the company registered record-high profits of 5 trillion won, solidifying the second place in the global market after Samsung.

Perhaps the term "sea change" can describes the fate of Hynix. The company almost faced bankruptcy after the 1998 Asian financial crisis and the continuing bust cycle of the global semiconductor industry. The share price for the company nosedived to a meager 136 won at the lowest point (compare this to today's 47,600 won).

Knowing the company's technological potential and the cyclical nature of the semiconductor market, creditor banks agreed upon debt restructurings in 2001 and 2002 instead of liquidation. During the next decade of global competition, the company managed to survive while better-positioned competitors left the market one by one. Among the dozens of Korean companies that went through similar debt restructuring processes after the financial crisis, Hynix has been one of the most successful.

The revival of the company is living proof that it is technological edge and timely investment that count at the end of the day in the fierce competition of the global market. While it was the creditors who decided to keep the chip manufacturer as a "going concern," it was the technological innovation through wise investment that enabled the company to survive in the global competition.

One may also realize the importance of sound domestic competition between well-meaning rivals, which has obviously facilitated their collective strong performance in the global market as well. Now, the competition in this winner-takes-all market is getting fiercer as, finally, China has just rolled up its sleeves, opened its wallet, and is putting its own horse in the race. The next round is shaping up, with more at stake.

[The Korea Herald, February 25, 2015]

29. Supreme Court's Pivotal Decision

Picture the following: a treaty is negotiated and concluded by a duly authorized government representative. The treaty is then applied and implemented for the next five decades. In the interim, the government maintains a shared understanding and expresses a settled position about the meaning of the provision of the treaty. Diplomacy is conducted and policies formulated therefrom. Five decades later, the judicial branch enters the scene and declares that the government's interpretation is in fact wrong and replaces it with a new one. What next, then? Should the government press the rewind button to go back to day 1 and start the diplomatic business all over again? Of course this is theoretically possible, but it is practically infeasible.

Now put the following into the frame. In the now well-known decision of May 2012, the Supreme Court declared that individual claimants are still entitled to compensation from Nippon Steel Corporation and Mitsubishi Heavy Industries for forced labor during the World War II period. Unfortunately, this decision contradicts the government's long-held stance that this particular issue was resolved by the 1965 Korea-Japan Claims Settlement Agreement. To paraphrase the 2005 report of the Government Task Force on this point: the forced labor issue was covered by the 1965 agreement. Those left out in the agreement were only "comfort women" victims, Sakhakin draftees, and atomic bomb victims. The decision of the nation's highest court does discuss the government's position as such but then disregards it as erroneous.

The judicial branch's replacing the government's official interpretation with its own is so rare, if not unprecedented incident. Obviously, doubts may be raised as to the wisdom of the court's active intervention in a fundamentally diplomatic issue. In many jurisdictions, when the judicial branch confronts diplomatic issues. It is not uncommon to observe courts in many jurisdictions refrain from rendering decisions on diplomatic issues by dubbing them political questions or something along those lines. Regarding the case at hand, questions are raised as to whether the judicial branch can declare what the underlying intent of a treaty was in the face of the government's position.

After all, was the government that negotiated and implemented the treaty for half of a century. Should it be a legal issue, the judicial branch can and should declare what the law is in the country. Since the core question concerns the intent of the government in a highly complex diplomatic issue, perhaps the executive branch's position is entitled to high judicial deference.

On a procedural note, the judicial review here has not been completed yet. After the May 2012 decision, the cases were then remanded to the High Courts (Appeals Court) for new analyses. On remand, the Seoul High Court and the Busan High Court ruled for the plaintiff last July in their respective cases. Mitsubishi and Nippon Steel appealed the High Court's decisions and the cases are now back in the Supreme Court docket again, awaiting a final disposition by the court.

Since the original decision was rendered, it has become one of the most frequently discussed topics among practitioners and academics in this field. In fact, the decision is partly attributable to the government's inaction. While the government's intent and positions were being discussed in proceedings, submission of an opinion statement or other documentation by the government, which is usually expected in this kind of context, did not take place.

Attention is now turned toward the Supreme Court's disposition of the issue in its second deliberation. How this issue will be dealt with is not entirely clear. Before the court reaffirms its decision in the second review and issues treaty interpretation that is not compatible with the government's long-held position, a through discussion of the government records and documents should take place. At least a more detailed and refined analysis than the first one is in order so as to avoid unintended repercussions.

[The Korea Herald, February 19, 2014]

30. Remember-Me-Not and Korea

People are set to forget. German psychologist Hermann Ebbinghaus' (1850–1909) famous research shows that we start to forget ten minutes after the study, losing 50 percent after an hour, 70 percent after one day, and 80 percent after one month. This human forgetfulness is sometimes a blessing. During his lecture trip to Korea in 2013, Eran Katz, an Israeli record holder in "memory" in the Guinness Book of World Records, praised "forgetting" as good for a healthy mind by releasing one's brain space to store new necessary information.

In fact, forgetting is how we overcome our failures, reset our minds, and reformat our lives. This natural medicine of healing and emotional well-being now has limited effect. All pieces of information are now scattered to the farthest corners of the internet and etched in the cloud hard drives of the search engines. With a search click, the information pops up on the screen.

Attending academic conferences these days, I am surprised by the level of details in the information organizers or fellow participants have collected about me. It has now become simply a matter of time to compile a dossier on a person through a quick search using search engines. Come to think of it, requests for submission of my resumes have become relatively rare these days: perhaps they don't have to as everything is on the internet. Then I realize that some information over the net fails to provide a full picture of an event or an issue surrounding me—sometimes it is taken out of context or includes mis-summarized or outdated information.

Some people just can't bear the discrepancy, and the question then is whether they can force the search engines to change or delete certain search results. This question underpins the May 13 decision from the European Court of Justice, the EU's highest court, wherein the "right to be forgotten" has been examined and ultimately recognized. This dispute was brought by a Spanish national in 2010 who did not like the Google search outcome which showed outdated information on a property attachment proceeding involving him. Since the decision was rendered, individual requests for deletion of information from search results have been flooding the Google website.

The same rationale would force newspapers to redact or black out certain information contained in old newspapers if a person registered a protest citing changed circumstances. But is it something achievable? The ECJ decision tried to distinguish search engines from newspapers in that the former undertake "processing" of information at the request of a searcher.

Contrary to the wide media coverage around the world as a decision championing the "right to be forgotten," this decision is actually specific and limited in scope. Obviously, it is only confined to EU countries, so unpleasant information can still remain over the net somewhere else which may be accessible by re-routing.

The rule also does not apply to a person living a "public life" or a situation warranting "public interest." So, every decision will be individual and case specific. In any event, this latest decision signals that the individuals' right-to-be-forgotten and the society's right-to-know will continue to clash in the digital age.

To some extent, our societal system has evolved based on the notion that something (though with some exceptions) will be and should preferably be forgotten at some point in time and everybody has the ability to start anew. Consider some financial regulations, juvenile criminal law or statutes of limitation. The advent of the digital age is now changing this conventional notion as well.

Korea is one of the most wired and SNS-saturated societies in the world. Even at restaurants, young people go through the ritual of taking pictures and posting them on their SNS accounts before starting to eat. In this post-everything, regret-later society, perhaps the new digital conflict will become more acute. Time to stay tuned to a public hearing of the Korea Communications Commission on June 16 on this very issue.

[The Korea Herald, June 11, 2014]

31. South Korea's Birth Rate Has Become a National Emergency

South Korea has beaten its own record once again. The country has registered a new low in its already faltering birth rate. The rate for 2023 was just 0.72. This is an unprecedented number in the global community (the average for OECD countries was 1.58 in 2021).

At the current pace, the South Korean population will be halved by 2100 to just 24 million. In 2022, 249,000 babies were born. For the country's labor market to function, South Korea needs 500,000 babies a year at a minimum. It is operating at half that figure.

And don't forget that this is the scorecard after the injection of around $247 billion by the government since 2006. A host of childcare vouchers and direct grants have not had the desired impact.

It was as long ago as 2005 that the birth rate of 1.2 first startled South Korea, causing the government to realize the extent of the problem and begin working on it. The Presidential Committee on Ageing Society and Population Policy was established. It is still at the helm of national policy. But despite these efforts, South Korea has reached a point where the problem is becoming more of a national emergency.

The short-sighted, small-family campaigns of the 1970s and 1980s played a role in the current predicament—"One child per family is still too many for Korea" was the slogan then. But experts agree that there are two outstanding culprits today: the exorbitant cost of education and housing. Fearful of these twin expenses, young couples have not dared to have and raise children.

The government may be able to find a way to deal with the housing issue. Agencies can control housing prices through taxation and construction permits, and offer preferential packages to families with young children through special laws and regulation. It is difficult and costly, of course, but doable.

When it comes to schooling, however, things are different. A huge number of South Korean children attend private teaching institutions, regardless of whether they also go to public schools. In 2022, South Korea registered its highest tuition expenditure for private education yet, spending almost $20 billion. This number does not even show the full picture; there are myriad associated costs, such as those of books, materials, counselling fees, and food.

It is therefore not uncommon for families in Seoul to spend a significant portion of their monthly household income on private education. According to a December 2023 report released by the Federation of Korean Industries, 26 percent of the drastic drop-in birth rates between 2015 and 2022 was attributed to the prohibitive cost of private education for potential parents.

This problem is difficult to fix because it is so intertwined with the country's culture. South Korean society is deeply competitive. This will take time to change. In the meantime, artificial intelligence and digitalization may have a role to play in reducing the cost of private education.

AI-enabled education programs could replace conventional, late-night in-person cramming at teaching institutions. Digitalization could help make private education more accessible for poorer families. Of course, both moves have their own perils—the possibility that they might engender further competition between children is an important concern. But with planning, these side-effects can be curbed.

Many countries are witnessing a decline in birth rates. Earlier this month, France, alarmed by the lowest birth rate in almost three decades in 2023—at 1.68 compared with South Korea's 0.72—announced a major reform to its parental leave system. But while South Korea may not be unique in facing this problem, or in attempting to tackle its causes, it stands alone in just how bad things have become.

[Financial Times, January 30, 2024]

III

LAW AS A CRITICAL COMPONENT FOR THE GLOBAL COMMUNITY—ACHIEVEMENTS AND CHALLENGES FOR A RULES-BASED SYSTEM

Korea has always been deeply engaged with the global community. As the world's sixth largest exporting country and eighth largest trading country, Korea is inevitably inclined to pay keen attention to the development of the global community. In that regard, the protectionist trend surging in many places of the world is an alarming wake-up call to Korea. In particular, the inward-looking trade policy of the United States has been having a direct impact on Korea.

Over the past several years, Korea has been diligent in monitoring US trade policy. It has been quick to examine trade and investment measures that appear to contain protectionist elements of various sorts. Korea has been concerned about the new trend of utilizing (in fact sometimes abusing) a "national security" rationale to justify otherwise applicable trade and investment agreements. As this trend has been visible not only during the Trump administration but also in the Biden administration, many countries including Korea are now seeing this phenomenon as the emergence of a new trade policy on the part of the United States regardless of the political platform. As a matter of fact, other countries are also showing a similar pattern of national security-oriented protectionism or unilateralism. Consider recent developments in the European Union (EU), China, Japan, etc. They also seem to be as willing as ever to utilize various national security grounds to justify their own regulation and restrictive measures for foreign trade and investment. Korea is also stepping onto this new bandwagon. Seoul is increasingly geared toward national security considerations in various sectors of national business. In trade and investment sectors, Seoul is now willing and ready to turn to national security factors in making decisions and implementing policies. The Korean government is also under increasing domestic pressure to pursue more protectionist measures and national security-related decisions similar to those appearing in other countries. Many people wonder at this juncture whether the global community will

DOI: 10.4324/9781003501749-3

maintain its current trajectory or shift in response to future contingencies, such as depending on development of US-China rivalry, the return of the Trump administration, or the conclusion or continuation of multiple wars at the moment. In other words, whether the current situation in the global community as regards trade policy and investment schemes is ad hoc or aberrational in nature or whether it represents a structural or more permanent change in the world is a critical question that many people currently ask.

Amidst the fast spread of "polycrisis" in the global community, "national security" has become one of the most important topics for many states. National security has also occupied center stage in treaties, whether in negotiations, conclusion, interpretation, and implementation. Over the years, national security has also turned into a key item raised in dispute settlement proceedings. The intensifying confrontation between the United States and China, the lingering tensions between the European Union and China, and the worsening relationship between the EU and Russia offer vivid examples of national security considerations in many segments of national policy. The fast permeation of digital society and the unexpected advent of artificial intelligence (AI) have also added yet another layer of national security considerations when it comes to protecting core national interests and securing hegemony in a new global competition. Not only major countries but also other countries (both developed and developing) are orienting their respective national policies toward the direction of national security.

Accordingly, over the past several years, national security considerations have taken center stage in shaping national policy in various sectors, be it military, diplomacy, human rights, labor, environment, economy, science, technology, and the like. Such considerations have reached the point where key provisions of existing treaties are now being viewed from a new angle with national security as a driving force in the minds of many governments. In particular, treaty clauses containing "national security exceptions" are being invoked actively so as to justify the otherwise treaty violating policies and measures of a country. Governments and companies are colliding over the legitimacy of invoking these exceptions in which the question of whether national security threats have been properly pinpointed is critical. All in all, discussions on and disputes over the interpretation and application of various national security-related provisions in treaties have been intensifying steadily. In any event, a clearly emerging phenomenon in the global community at the moment is the broadening meaning and expanding scope of national security provisions. Under the traditional concept, they used to be understood to cover situations involving military establishment, military activity, or military conflict. Now they are moving out of the traditional military confinement and are beginning to cover a wide range of national policies. As such, states are widely invoking national security provisions of various sorts to address their existential concerns over many issues such as diplomacy, technology, economy, and politics. Accordingly, major countries are beginning to accommodate this new "expansive" concept of national security into their respective national policies. Other countries are following suit as well.

As regards Korea, while treaties that it has concluded are going through changes at the moment, whether in the form of the interpretation of existing treaties or in the form of negotiations of new ones, domestic laws and regulations of Korea have remained almost intact when it comes to national security. They still remain within the boundaries of the traditional concept of national security, which is anchored to its "military" underpinnings. The continuation of the traditional concept despite the rapid evolution in this field indicates a growing gap between the provisions in domestic laws and regulations of Korea on the one hand, and the demand from the government and industries on the other. This growing gap constitutes a critical hurdle to government agencies in addressing pressing national security matters in many sectors. As the legal norms are not updated or fine-tuned in light of the advent of new types of national security, government agencies' hands are sometimes tied and their discretion is meaningfully restricted. This phenomenon would mean that Korea will not be able to cope with the emergence of new national security threats in an efficient and systematic manner. These provisions need to be amended, and new provisions should be introduced as soon as possible so as to deal with the new national security matters that Korea confronts. In particular, the implementation of various policies and measures in the area of economic security and global supply chain reformulation requires the systemization and alignment of national security-related provisions in domestic laws and regulations scattered across many different areas of Korean legislation. The national discussions on the economic security and global supply chain reformulation for the past couple of years have lacked the necessary systematic consideration under the overall legislative scheme of Korea relating to national security.

At the same time, national security provisions in various domestic laws and regulations of Korea have been introduced in a piecemeal manner within the specific confinement of individual laws and regulations. Thus, they all appear to vary both in form and substance. While they all purport to address national security, the terms used are not consistent, the procedures adopted are not uniform, and the conditions stipulated are not compatible. In other words, the national security provisions in domestic laws and regulations seem to be fragmented and splintered. Such being the case, the current norms in Korean domestic laws and regulations may be said to lack systemization and alignment. Korea should initiate a legislative endeavor to address this emerging problem as soon as possible. Other countries have embarked on these projects recently and Korea should keep up with the global trend to overcome various challenges in the global community.

Diplomacy holds significant importance for every country. It is all the more important for Korea, surrounded as it is by the four major powers: the United States, China, Russia, and Japan. Korea's recent history attests to this claim with ample evidence. The survival and prosperity of Korea hinge on its ability to navigate and handle its relationships with these countries. The preceding decade has demonstrated the inherent volatility of this particular state of affairs. The intensifying US-China confrontation has constantly placed Korea in awkward situations: the United States is Korea's closest ally while China is Korea's largest trading partner.

Any decision made by Korea has the potential to cause a ripple effect one way or another. There are arduous challenges and intense pressures that Korea must confront economically and militarily in the treacherous context of the Sino-US confrontation. Korea has the potential to effectively navigate the narrow passage of conflicting interests between the two countries and find a solution that satisfies both. Yet, there are other concerns that completely negate any possibility of flexibility, and thus a definitive choice must be made in either direction. Adopting a resolute position on a specific matter, grounded in a meticulous evaluation of the long-term national interest, might have led to uncomfortable deliberations and consequences. However, it would have prevented and will continue to prevent a lot of trouble down the road. Judged from a standpoint of national interest, the answers to these questions are arguably obvious from the start. Ambiguity is indeed indispensable and occasionally the optimal approach. Strategic ambiguity should be a deliberate decision rather than a random occurrence. It is no substitute for indecisiveness and procrastination. Committing an error is catastrophic. Choosing to refrain from making a decision due to the fear of committing an error is even more disastrous.

The diplomatic ties with Japan have reached an unprecedented low point in recent decades, primarily due to the enduring repercussions of Japanese colonial rule over the Korean peninsula in the first half of the 20th century. The two countries are proximate neighbors experiencing a growing interchange of cultural influences. There is both potential and the need to further enhance the bilateral relationship, which includes the ongoing discussions regarding a free trade agreement. However, as long as Tokyo persists in rejecting Korean sovereignty over the islets such prospects and needs would remain merely illusory, evoking painful recollections of the past. Japan is renowned for its meticulous planning and execution, with virtually every aspect being carefully organized and carried out according to predetermined plans. Genuine camaraderie with its closest neighbor can only be achieved by temporarily setting aside preconceived notions and embracing open-mindedness for the future. Russia is also endeavoring to reclaim its status as a regional stakeholder. Its military exercises in the East Sea have witnessed an increase in activity, occasionally conducted jointly with China. This development appears to be a deliberate indication of opposition toward the United States and Japan.

Relations with North Korea have always been one of the top priorities for Korea. All administrations pay significant attention to the inter-Korea issue during their tenures. Embedded in the national psyche, inter-Korea issues and the unification agenda have absorbed public attention regularly, sometimes leading to acute standoffs between different domestic political factions. Typically, Koreans have a tendency to divide along ideological lines when it comes to North Korean matters. Conservatives generally have a skeptical and cautious attitude toward the liberals' endorsement of improving relations with Pyongyang. It is widely believed that Koreans have endured a prolonged period of vulnerability to the constant threat from the North since the end of the Korean War in 1953, and it is unfair for their children to live in even greater fear of a nuclear attack. Against this backdrop, numerous columns address a range of issues pertaining to the diplomacy of Korea. These columns are intended to maintain impartiality and refrain from favoring Korea or any other country, aiming solely to elucidate the circumstances and present an objective perspective. As such, some of them criticize neighboring countries while others criticize Korea. Interestingly, numerous issues relating to diplomacy exhibit a strong interconnection with legal issues. A considerable portion of diplomatic topics manifest themselves in the guise of legal issues at some point. This observation underscores the importance of adopting a legal framework in comprehending diplomatic interactions with neighboring countries. The columns address these legal issues in a lay person's language.

We are now living in an age of polycrisis. Numerous issues of global concern are taking place in many parts of the world. They are being reported by newspapers, magazines, TV news programs, and YouTube postings. These reports contain errors and mistakes in terms of legal perspectives, in particular in terms of international law. If one believes in the notion that accuracy is the most important trait for any news report, legal correctness should also take center stage in preparing, releasing, and distributing the report. Legal loopholes then tend to produce discussions and debates heading in the wrong direction. They also tend to stoke unnecessary confusion and conflicts. For instance, amidst the Israel-Hamas war, the statehood of Palestine has also emerged as one such touchy subject. Some states such as Spain and Sweden recognized the statehood of Palestine as a form of protest against Israeli conduct in its war against the civilian population. The United States, the United Kingdom, and other Group of Seven countries have not recognized a Palestinian state. However, France has pledged to formally recognize the State of Palestine during the United Nations General Assembly in September 2025, and the United Kingdom has also announced its intention to do so unless Israel takes concrete steps toward peace. This trend will continue as more countries seek to "distance themselves" from the Israeli military campaign in Gaza.

Although this is a legal issue, few reports consider it from a legal perspective. Under international law (1933 Montevideo Convention), statehood requires a defined territory, a permanent population, a government, and an ability to enter into international relations. If one entity satisfies the four elements, it becomes a state under international law. Other states do not have a legal obligation to recognize the existence of a new state. So, the question is whether a new state in question—Palestine—indeed satisfies the four elements. This is the critical question to be asked. If the requirements are found to have been met, the new state exists under international law. Other states' recognition or nonrecognition does not change the result. On the other hand, other states also have their own legal rights to refuse to recognize the existence of a new state as a state. If this confrontation takes place, it usually stems from the absence of diplomatic relationship as seen in the context of the United States–North Korea relationship. These are two states legally speaking, but each of them does not recognize the other as a state. The Palestine statehood debate does not look at the legal aspect of the issue and instead portrays it as a political and diplomatic matter. It of course includes political and diplomatic components but deep down it is anchored in key jurisprudence of international law and is related to many branches of international law. The insufficient attention paid to the legal aspect of global issues should be changed in the future, so that states and international organizations can initiate and carry on meaningful discussions on these issues. In that regard, the lack of attention to and the resulting errors of international law in the media pose a challenge for the global community.

After all, incentives move everything. Many fancy modifiers are attached—from political, historic, cultural, to moral ones—to reasons behind any behavior or institution, but the rule is simple: you choose to do the good and avoid the bad. It is the basic nature (although we often assume this as a strong condition of being "rational") of all human beings and the very same rule applies to state behaviors as well. When a certain number of entities gather together, be it individual or state, interaction is inevitable thus leading to a demand for a set of common rules. Without a governing norm that commonly regulates the players, it is rather bothersome to anticipate the other's action while also preparing your own. The core question of this circumstance could then be boiled down to the problem of allocating limited resources: it is about how you distribute scarce resources to the better deserved causes. Similar to how national law came into operation in history, the advent of international law also springs from the need of mediating the co-existing and sometimes conflicting incentives over a limited pie. International law differs a lot from domestic laws, one of which is the legitimacy of the binding power. The legitimacy of a domestic law in liberal democracies resides with the sovereign power of the people. Legislation is implemented by the representatives who are elected by the people, and it is also governed by the highest law in order, the Constitution. On the contrary, international law basically operates upon the consent of the participants. Since it is almost impossible to formulate an absolute authority or a universal government that enforces law to sovereign states, consent is the necessary condition for the existence of international law. So, in principle, a state is free to choose whether or not to join a treaty, convention, etc.

When individuals confront legal disputes, it is often a one-shot game. The purpose of suing the other and defending the case is to defeat the opponent and settle the dispute in a favorable manner. Once you step out of the court, you do not have to worry about being troubled with arguing a similar issue with the same counterparty. In addition, judgments from domestic courts create a legally binding force (res judicata) almost identical to that of written law. On the other hand, legal disputes between sovereign states can be described as repeated games as discussed earlier. Even if there is no absolute authority to make a state forcibly comply with the judgments of the court, and though Article 59 of the Statute of the International Court of Justice limits the general applicability of res judicata, the way it responds to the judgment not only affects the legal relations but also influences other sectors of the complicated international relations. Therefore, the legally binding force of international law has been commonly explained by the trust that states owe to the international community.

Let us take a further step to analyze the legally binding force of international law. When Korea negotiated with the United States to conclude the FTA, why did both countries frantically struggle to argue over the Investor-State Dispute provision? Why was Japan desperately trying to defend the case in *Whaling in the Antarctic* by purchasing expensive lawyers abroad? If we roughly separate countries into two categories, there are weak nations in terms of economic, military aspects, and strong nations (or the traditional developing and developed nations grouping). Weak nations have an incentive to win the legal dispute to overcome their relatively disadvantaged status. It gives them a supporting power to stand shoulder to shoulder with strong nations, which is otherwise almost impossible. International law can be a powerful means of leverage for weak countries to access the larger dividends of the world pie. Meanwhile, strong nations have an incentive to earn additional justification for their expansion of influence in the international arena. The behaviors of strong nations often face criticisms that it is based on selfish motivations to widen the gap between the two groups of nations rather than contributing to global prosperity. However, as more and more winning cases accumulate, strong nations can display an image that their actions are within legitimate boundaries and further enhance their influence. But more importantly, the incentive analysis is not only about external relations among states, but it is also about the internal relations within the country between the people and the government. The action of a sovereign state in the international arena represents the whole people of their country. We discuss the violation of international law at state level, but in real life the consequence of state behaviors comes down to the respective nationals.

International legal disputes bring nationals together and make people strongly expect the government to win, as we can see in many territorial disputes such as over Dokdo Island and Diaoyudao/Senkaku Islands. When the government unfortunately loses the case, people still expect it to abide by international norms—whether through a formal countermeasure or direct compliance with the ruling. This is because modern society is undeniably governed by law in almost all aspects and the sense of legal obligation is deeply rooted in an individual's mind as well. Hence, people are unlikely to support a government that ignores the norms of international law, for it is the very entity that prescribes and enforces domestic law over themselves. If the support and trust relation is broken between the people and a government, the government will experience hardships while managing state affairs and even fail to consolidate its political foundation in future elections. Such a backlash would be more severe than merely risking national status in the international community or being recorded as the losing party in textbooks forever.

The Terminal High Altitude Area Defense (THAAD) System continues to this day. China has strongly opposed the deployment of the THAAD system in South Korea, citing the radar included in the system as being capable of detecting and monitoring mainland China. After the South Korea-US FTA went into effect in

July 2016, the South Korean and US governments decided to deploy THAAD in the Korean Peninsula. Nine months later, on April 28, 2017, the deployment of two THAAD units in South Korea was carried out. Since then, China has taken retaliatory measures against South Korea in various areas. If we look into the various aspects of China's retaliatory measures in this process, we can easily understand the situation in which the Korea-China FTA has been nullified. China has effectively restricted or banned its own tourists from traveling to Korea in various ways. Due to the decrease in Chinese tourists, with the loss of approximately 7 trillion won in 2017 alone, it has been estimated that Korea suffered damages amounting to 15 trillion won. In addition, performances by Korean entertainers and artists in China were restricted or canceled for various reasons. Customs procedures for Korean products also became more complicated than ever, which hindered exports. A boycott of Korean products by Chinese consumers also began. This was followed by concentrated sanctions against Lotte, which had provided the site for the THAAD deployment.

As soon as China began its retaliatory measures, the issue of violations of the WTO agreement was immediately raised, and our government considered filing a complaint through the WTO dispute settlement procedure if necessary, but ultimately failed to file such a complaint. Regarding these various restrictive measures, China has denied the existence of such restrictions themselves, stating that they are the result of voluntary decisions by private companies or consumer groups. If this is a voluntary decision by a private company or consumer group, it is not a government measure, and it is not subject to the application of trade agreements, whether it is the WTO agreement or the Korea-China FTA. What China is saying precisely points out a blind spot in the current trade agreement. In a situation where foreign governments do not take full action, it may be difficult for the government of a trading partner (Korea) to raise the issue of violation of trade agreements. This is because it is difficult to prove the involvement of a foreign government. In this situation, either the WTO agreement or the FTA agreement becomes meaningless. In the end, our government ended up considering whether to file a complaint with the WTO, but it ended up being hushed up. It is very unusual that our country has not followed the WTO dispute settlement procedure even though it has suffered damages of up to 7 trillion won. As of July 2020, our country has referred to other countries' violations of agreements to the WTO dispute settlement procedure 21 times. In comparison, it is worth considering how China's retaliatory measures due to the THAAD deployment were not brought to the WTO.

THAAD also has several discriminatory measures against our companies in the Chinese market. It has become prominent since its deployment. For example, the Chinese government is trying to promote this industry by providing significant government subsidies to domestically produced electric vehicles. However, it did not provide such subsidies to domestic vehicles that use batteries produced by Korean companies. Ultimately, this is putting a significant burden on the sales of our battery manufacturing companies that have advanced into China. This is because the scale of the subsidy is quite large. The government is providing subsidies of up to 50 percent of the actual total sales price. Therefore, companies that do not receive subsidies are in a situation where they cannot manufacture electric vehicles. As a result, these electric vehicle manufacturers have no choice but to use Chinese batteries regardless of quality and price. As a result, our companies that have advanced into China, LG Chem and Samsung SDI, have suffered significant blows.

There is something noteworthy about the logic behind the Chinese government's refusal to provide subsidies to electric vehicles using Korean batteries. Because it directly addresses safety issues. The Chinese government excluded electric buses equipped with "ternary batteries" from subsidies in January 2016, citing electric vehicle fires that occurred in January 2016. However, in fact, the ternary battery is a relatively high-quality battery that uses nickel, cobalt, and manganese as its main ingredients and is mainly produced by Korean and Japanese companies. However, by excluding these high-quality batteries from subsidies, the effect is ultimately to restrict these companies' activities in China and support the activities of domestic companies. In the context of discriminating against foreign investors, it is one of the typical violations of the investment chapter of the Korea-China FTA. It is not easy to argue that this measure constitutes a violation of the agreement, as it is ostensibly a consumer safety issue. This is one of the representative workarounds we looked at previously. The implication of this case is that, regardless of how the agreement text defines it, various circumvention measures ultimately render the rights under the agreement virtually ineffective. Therefore, future agreement texts must include specific provisions on how to identify and respond to circumvention measures. Even when problems arose, these agreements played no special role. Based on this, future agreements need to include mechanisms to accurately check circumvention measures.

1. The Price for a Korean Peace Treaty

The end of the armistice agreement could lead to the unraveling of defense arrangements involving the US and its allies, and must be approached with great care.

Like his predecessors, United States Army General Vincent K. Brooks wears three hats: one as commander of US Armed Forces in Korea; another as commander of US-Korea Combined Forces Command; and the third, which is rarely known, as commander of the United Nations Command (UNC). One man wearing multiple hats signifies how the Korean War started and concluded, but never quite ended.

The UNC that Gen Brooks commands with his last hat was established by the United Nations Security Council Resolution 84 of July 7, 1950, 12 days after the outbreak of the Korean War. This UN-facilitated military organization represents the armistice regime and, sadly, the continuation of hostilities on the Korean peninsula.

Troops from the 16 states that came to South Korea's rescue were put under the command of the UNC. It still operates today and is ready to exercise its command should hostilities ever resume on the peninsula. In other words, Gen Brooks' third hat is a symbolic but important one for legal and military reasons. Now, most likely, the US general is about to lose his 68-year-old UNC hat.

In a dramatic reversal of tides, at the inter-Korea summit meeting last Friday, South Korean President Moon Jae In and North Korean leader Kim Jong Un declared that they would pursue official termination of the Korean War within the year and replace the present armistice regime with a peace treaty.

The same issue will also be tabled at the summit meeting between US President Donald Trump and Mr. Kim likely to be held within two months, possibly in Singapore or at the truce village of Panmunjom, which was also the site of the inter-Korea summit.

While a demand for the withdrawal of US troops from South Korea may not be in North Korea's game plan for now, assuming North Korea has finally changed its stance as reported, the introduction of a peace treaty inevitably forces significant changes in the structure of the multilateral cooperation system that has been in place for the past seven decades.

People still hold their breath to figure out what this is all about: perhaps this is another attempt by the North to sell the same horse again; or perhaps this time the young North Korean leader is really into it and ready to sit down with the US and others for serious negotiations. The mood is positive, but the outcome is still too early to tell.

In any event, for now, let's assume a face-to-face meeting in good faith is held between Mr. Trump and Mr. Kim. One highly plausible scenario at the meeting is an exchange of mutual covenants involving an agreement from Pyongyang to Washington to scrap all its nuclear warheads and an acceptance of complete, verifiable, and irreversible denuclearization. In return, Washington is to offer Pyongyang a guarantee of non-aggression, which the North sees as necessary for the continued stability of its regime.

It is noteworthy that North Korea at this stage seems open to the continued presence of US armed forces on the peninsula. By all accounts, these two covenants, if ever agreed, could be the first step toward the conclusion of a peace treaty, followed by normalization of diplomatic relations.

Whatever the specific title the treaty may bear, the essence is the same: it will officially conclude the 1950–1953 Korean War and replace the present Armistice Agreement, effective since July 27, 1953, with a new legal regime on the peninsula. The deconstruction of the armistice regime, however, entails potential far-reaching consequences.

The regime underpins a tightly knit network of military strategic operations involving the US, South Korea, and other allies. Its disappearance would call for an overhaul of the existing system and network.

For instance, most immediately, a peace treaty challenges the existence of the UNC. With the official termination of the hostilities on the Korean peninsula, the

UN-facilitated command specifically targeting North Korea as an enemy would lose its raison d'etre. North Korea has long argued for dismantling the command upon the advent of a peace regime. Thus, chances are, a peace treaty with the North means General Brooks will lose his UNC hat.

Furthermore, the dissolution of the UNC is rather tricky because it has been the linchpin of the logistics support from US forces in Japan for US forces in South Korea.

Even today, the UNC Rear Command is located at Yokota Air Base in Japan, comprising small detachments from some of the 16 Korean War-participants, such as Australia.

In addition, several military bases in Japan are marked as UNC facilities. At present, in the unlikely situation of the resumption of hostilities on the Korean peninsula, this UNC Rear Command and bases in Japan are supposed to provide platforms for military support for the troops (made up almost entirely of US forces) to be sent to South Korea. Japan concluded a Status of Forces Agreement (SOFA) with the UNC in 1954 to permit the presence of UNC forces in Japan, which is still effective today. In short, the UNC is small and skeletal, but still up and running.

To quote General Brooks at the change of command ceremony held on Jan. 29 this year at Yokota Air Base in Japan: the participation in the ceremony of representatives of UNC constituent countries "says an awful lot about the importance" of the UNC. One of his priorities is "to keep the UNC vital and relevant." So, quite possibly, the dismantling of the UNC and its Rear Command means this critical linkage is now going to be missing.

A new trilateral treaty (or similar arrangement) between the United States, South Korea, and Japan may fill the gap, but a treaty embodying military cooperation between South Korea and Japan will likely be too difficult to achieve due to the historical scars.

While a demand for the withdrawal of US troops from South Korea may not be in North Korea's game plan for now, assuming North Korea has finally changed its stance as reported, the introduction of a peace treaty inevitably forces significant changes in the structure of the multilateral cooperation system that has been in place for the past seven decades. These changes, once made, may in turn have further, broader consequences.

The knock-on effects are another reason great vigilance is needed in poring over the details before any final agreement is reached to dismantle the existing legal regime and start anew.

The hope is that the latest rounds of summitry may finally bring peace to the Korean peninsula. To accomplish this, a peace treaty is a must to terminate hostilities. But, at the same time, there is a lot of homework to be done with many legal questions to be tackled before the deal can be signed off. Coming to grips with dealing with the many questions that will arise will be immensely complicated, if not impossible.

[The Straits Times, May 2, 2018]

2. Searching for Effective Countermeasure

It is reported that within this week the government is planning to officially release the results of the two-month investigation into the cause of the Cheonan incident. At the Korea-China-Japan trilateral ministerial meeting in Gyeongju over the weekend, South Korea reportedly made efforts to secure support from Beijing leading up to the official announcement this week. At this stage, it does not seem that difficult to predict the contents of the upcoming announcement. The question is what to do next.

Some people advocate exercising the right to self-defense. However, under the prevailing jurisprudence of international law (including Article 51 of the UN Charter), it is not so clear whether Korea can exercise that right since the attack was two months ago.

The concept is premised on the notion that a state should sometimes be allowed to respond to an imminent or present attack. As such, the concept does not support ex post facto punishment. Timeliness and temporal vicinity are of essence in this concept, so reference to self-defense at this stage may not necessarily help Korea resolve the problem.

Another difficulty is that no matter what Korea says, North Korea will most likely disregard it as a complete fabrication—note that all pieces of evidence turned up so far are reportedly circumstantial in nature. When controversies heat up regarding the evidence, the right to self-defense option may face yet another legal obstacle.

Likewise, any attempt to resort to the right to self-defense by South Korea on its own accord may undermine its subsequent efforts to resolve the issue through a legal proceeding. Legal action against North Korea is hard to imagine, but that option has been floated by some experts since the incident. The risk of choosing the option of exercising the right to self-defense does not only lie in the outbreak of military conflict through the escalation of cross-retaliation; it also carries important legal implication.

What South Korea can adopt instead is a countermeasure which is permitted under international law under this kind of situation. Economic or diplomatic sanctions are the most common examples of countermeasures. The problem for these ordinary countermeasures is that North Korea would hardly blink an eye: its economy and diplomatic status are at a nadir anyway—it is difficult to think what could make the North Korea's situation worse.

Even if China cooperates, it may be the case that there is just one more UN Security Council resolution condemning North Korea, accompanied by further trade restrictions. An otherwise effective countermeasure for any other country would not work in the same way for North Korea. Getting the coveted support of Beijing and having everyone on side could give us mental assurance that our anger is shared and our position vindicated, but that would not necessarily translate into an effective countermeasure, if that is what we are looking for.

So, the task for Korea now seems to be how to break out of this straight jacket of legal and practical constraints. With regard to the legal constraint, if the tragedy has made Korea more vigilant and willing than before, any future attack by North Korea could be immediately responded to with the same level of military force, which may easily satisfy the legal requirements for a claim of self-defense.

Regarding other responses, South Korea may ponder over various atypical measures that may deliver the North Korean leadership the message that military provocation actually causes it more trouble. The recent resumption of anti-North Korean regime broadcasting along the Demilitarized Zone could be one example. South Korea must know better than anyone else about the sorest spots of the North Korean leadership. Countermeasures relating to such spots will certainly turn out to be effective and force North Korea to think hard before future endeavors.

Winning the diplomatic war vis-à-vis North Korea on this issue and having China on our side will not alone provide the countermeasures that we are looking for, unless these diplomatic efforts lead to international cooperation to collectively touch these sore spots. One more sanction, one more resolution, or one more forced return to the six-party talks would hardly become an effective countermeasure against North Korea, nor will it provide a sufficient deterrence for future recurrences.

It is also reported that once all investigations are completed the government will prepare a report to record what went wrong in this incident. Getting the record straight is always important to elicit future lessons from past mistakes. What is more important, however, is to prepare a contingency plan for if and when similar attacks occur in the future.

This may include a list of possible countermeasure options available and the priority of their application with their merits and demerits outlined, based on thorough legal and practical analyses. Once an incident occurs, it is simply too late to think about the scope of the right to self-defense under international law, and to scramble to find an effective retaliation measure. A standard operating procedure is necessary not only for military operations, but also for all of us. The ultimate solution lies in us, not in recruiting China.

[The Korea Herald, May 19, 2010]

3. Treaty of Ganghwa of 1876

Rallies and marches erupted throughout the country this past Aug. 29 as Korea marked the 100th anniversary of one of the most tragic moments in its history: the conclusion of the Korea-Japan Annexation Treaty of 1910. Compared to the wave of self-reflection on this "day of national disgrace" when Korea surrendered its sovereignty to imperial Japan, however, another treaty between the two countries receives little attention: the Joseon-Japan Treaty of Amity of 1876 concluded on Ganghwa Island, 34 years before the annexation treaty. If the 1910 treaty was the final chapter of the imperial Japan's invasion of Korea, the 1876 treaty was the preamble. As much as we remember the final chapter of the saddest moment of Korean history, we should not forget the preamble and how it all began.

The 1876 treaty was the outcome of Japan's careful and thorough preparation to set its colonial foot in Joseon. Ostensibly, the treaty was to address the aftermath of the military conflict between Joseon and Japan when a Japanese warship named Unyo Maru had intruded Ganghwa Island the previous year. The skirmish was a mere excuse, and Japan was determined to take advantage of this rare opportunity to force Korea to accept an unequal treaty. The Japanese delegation for the treaty negotiation, headed by General Kuroda Kiyotaka, came to Ganghwa Island on Feb. 10, 1876, with the support of cannons (eight warships and soldiers) and a new weapon of choice: international law.

In fact, Japan was quick to understand the importance of international law in international relations through its reluctant prior dealings with Western countries. Japan's negotiation with the United States for its 1858 Treaty of Amity were even conducted in Dutch because of ties between Japan and the Netherlands. The 1858 treaty ended up having three authentic texts made in English, Japanese, and Dutch, which indicates the legal sophistication of Japan. When American Henry Wheaton's famous book, *Elements of International Law*, was published in Japan in 1864, it became one of the must-read books in the then upper echelon of Japan. Furthermore, Minister Enomoto Takeaki, who was apparently the de facto advisor to General Kuroda during the course of 1876 Ganghwa Treaty, spent a long time in the Netherlands studying international law.

So, when Feb. 10, 1876, came and the negotiation between Joseon and Japan started on Ganghwa Island, Japan was fully equipped with knowledge of international law from its 20-year study and experience of it. Not surprisingly, the record shows that the negotiations proceeded at Japan's pace and demand. Joseon's delegation head, General Sin Hon, was not able to overcome the obvious disparity in knowledge and skill. The negotiations ended in two weeks and Joseon was forced to accept the 12-article treaty with Japan. This treaty was the initiation of Japan's invasion of Joseon and paved the road for the 1910 annexation treaty 34 years later.

On the occasion of the centennial anniversary of "the day of national disgrace," it is noteworthy that the first wave of Japanese imperialism came to Korea with international law as well as with sheer military power. The final closure in 1910 was not that different with the combination of the two elements tying Korea's hands. It is also telling how much effort Japan made in studying and mobilizing international law to drive its national interest during this period.

The rallies and marches to mark "the day of disgrace" showed that what happened 100 years ago is still a vivid memory for many Koreans. All possible lessons should be extracted, and this tragic chapter of Korean history should never be repeated. In this regard, one of the important tasks is to thoroughly analyze how it all began. Thus, the Treaty of 1876 merits an equal amount of attention as the treaty of 1910. It is sad that international law was behind Japan's orchestration and implementation of its imperialism in the Korean peninsula. But at the same time it reminds us of the importance of cultivating the national pool of expertise in the field of international law to survive in this treacherous world. International law alone will not defend the country. But it is an essential element for the defense of the country. What happened 134 years ago is exhibit A of this.

[The Korea Herald, September 9, 2010]

4. Settlement of Comfort Women Issue

"Much as we may feel for the plight of the (comfort women), the court of the United States simply is not authorized to hear their case."

That was the final sentence of the judgment of the US Court of Appeals for the D.C. Circuit in Hwang Geum Joo et al. v. Japan issued in June 2005, which was one of the several litigations pursued in the US courts by former "comfort women" victims from Korea, Taiwan, the Philippines, and China. The case was dismissed as the court decided that it did not have jurisdiction to issue a judgment against a foreign country based on the concept called "sovereign immunity." The US court did not exonerate Japan's wartime atrocities but ruled that a proper forum to address this issue was the state-to-state discussion between Korea and Japan.

The state-to-state discussion has become the newest topic in the Korea-Japan bilateral agenda. On Aug. 30, the Korean Constitutional Court declared it unconstitutional for the government to have failed to pursue the compensation from Japan on behalf of the former comfort women because such inaction had amounted to violation of the constitutional rights of these victims. Pursuant to the mandate from the nation's highest court, Seoul requested initiation of consultation with Japan on Sept. 15 in accordance with Article 3 of the Claims Settlement Agreement attached to the 1965 Korea-Japan Basic Relations Treaty. The request, however, was promptly rejected by Tokyo.

The request and refusal last week in fact raised a complex legal issue: whether the 1965 Korea-Japan Claims Settlement Agreement settled all claims between the two countries including those held by individual private persons. In fact, Article 2 of the agreement provides that "the problems concerning property, rights and interest of the two Contracting Parties and their nationals . . . and concerning claims between the Contracting Parties and between their nationals . . . are settled completely and finally." Korea takes the position that private persons' rights were not settled by the agreement, so they can pursue their claims on their own subsequently. Japan's position is exactly opposite.

The provision is indeed vague in terms of the scope of the settlement. A plausible interpretation, however, seems that both countries agreed to give up state-owned properties and rights in the other's territory, and the states' right to seek redress on behalf of their nationals. But the settlement did not include the claims individuals may have possessed vis-à-vis the other's government.

As a government's property and right and an individual's property and right are conceptually distinct, one cannot contract away the other's property or right without clear consensus or language to that end. Arguably, consensus can hardly be found because this issue of giving up individuals' rights was not on the negotiating table during the 1965 negotiations. Nor was a clear wording to that effect inserted to the treaty: for instance, the two countries could have said that individuals' own rights were waived or relinquished.

The limited scope of Article 2 of the Korea-Japan agreement is conspicuous when compared to Article 14(b) of the 1951 San Francisco Peace Treaty between Japan and the Allied Powers, which provides that "the Allied Powers waive all reparations claims of the Allied Powers, other claims of the Allied Powers and their nationals arising out of any action taken by Japan and its nationals in the course of the prosecution of the war." Here, arguably the waiver of individuals' own rights through the treaty is expressly mentioned.

This is further evidenced by Japan's position in other treaties. As regards a similar claims settlement issue between Japan and Russia, Japan has taken the position that individual Japanese rights have not been renounced because of the 1956 Japan-USSR Joint Declarations, which contains a similar provision.

As the cardinal rule of treaty interpretation accords a significant weight to the parties' intention when terms of a treaty are ambiguous, both Korea's and Japan's positions should be carefully examined to elicit and confirm the intention of the two countries in 1965. Taken as a whole, at least it is not clear whether both countries at that time relinquished the rights of individuals on behalf of them. In the absent of clear language, the presumption should be that the rights of the individuals were not liquidated by the governmental action.

Furthermore, the argument that comfort women's right to compensation was "completely and finally settled" back in 1965 seems too detached from reality. The factual record itself cries out that "complete and final settlement" has not been achieved yet, at least to the extent this very issue is concerned. The situation where victims going to all levels of courts in Korea, Japan, and third countries for help is no way near to "complete and final settlement." As people say: "It ain't over till it's over." Confronting this issue head on appears to be the only viable way to attain complete and final settlement.

[The Korea Herald, September 21, 2011]

5. Why Do We Keep Losing This Game?

In Seoul, a somber reflection on the past 20 years imbues the minds of the people. To many here, the third nuclear test by North Korea on Feb. 12 was an official proclamation that the strategies of Washington and Seoul for the past two decades to deter the Pyongyang regime from acquiring a nuclear weapons capability had failed.

Unlike the previous two nuclear tests by the North in 2006 and 2009, in which the effectiveness and appropriateness of the two competing sets of policies (i.e., a big stick policy versus an appeasement one) were being extensively debated, this nuclear test of February, coupled with Pyongyang's increased military threat in the past couple of weeks, has made Seoulites admit the cold, hard truth: it has been two decades of remarkable deceit. The "wasted twenty years" has since become a key theme of press reports and talking heads here in Seoul. Which means the North has fully taken advantage of the 20 years—every minute of it.

Many people ask a fundamental question: why do we keep losing this game vis-à-vis the North, despite the fact that virtually the entire international community has fallen in line with us and that a web of tight sanctions has been in place? At its core, the current disaster has stemmed from the unfortunate misperception that the North Korean nuclear program can be bought out. As it turns out, to them this program is way too precious to put a price tag on it. As one would say, there is something that money can't buy. The US and South Korean policy makers have failed to be apprised of the depth of North's desire for nuclear arsenal. Maybe they were, but only superficially.

The situation has reached the point where whatever the North says now, the United States and South Korea will not believe it. The almost complete loss of faith makes it more difficult or unrealistic for Washington and Seoul to engage Pyongyang to find a breakthrough.

As the level of frustration goes up, so does a demand from the general public for more positive action. Although neither practical nor realistic, the taboo discussion of Seoul's own nuclear armament, citing the example of Israel and others, is being touted by some opinion leaders and groups in Korea. In fact, one of the recent polls conducted by Gallup Korea showed 66 percent of those surveyed were in favor of Seoul's nuclear armament for its own self-defense. Anyone who knows the gravity and consequence such a course of action would entail would readily know that it is not a viable option for South Korea, at least under the current circumstances. The almost obvious economic sanction, the domino effect on nuclear armament in the region, and more important, the weakening of the US-Korea alliance would leave Seoul shortchanged in the end. So, this option of a conventional response, as seen in Israel or Pakistan, would not work in this part of the world.

Upon the sudden appearance of nuclear armament arguments in Korea, apparently frightened Washington immediately issued a "don't-even-think-about-it" warning and keeps reaffirming its commitment for the nuclear umbrella for the South. But given that the whole point of Pyongyang's nuclear weapons development is to stop the US from abiding by its promise to extend its umbrella for South Korea, the auto-play statements of commitments, without explaining the durability of the umbrella under any circumstances, do not seem to offer an effective solution.

All in all, the current situation surrounding the North Korean nuclear program and the recent development between the two Koreas has rendered the conventional framework of discourse inoperative and ineffective. Pretending that there is a solution nearby is hypocritical and self-deceitful. Such false pretense has enabled North Korea to play its own game—through thin and thick—for the past 20 years. It is time for a new game plan, a plan to turn around the losing streak. Perhaps one thing to consider in this regard is how to make Beijing fully aware that unbridled, nuclear-armed North Korea would undermine its national interest. In light of this, it is interesting to watch the reportedly growing complaints in China against North Korea after its nuclear test.

On the surface, everything remains the same in Seoul—as calm and stable as ever. But a lot is going on in the minds of the people in Seoul. Nothing has changed, but a lot has changed since Feb. 12.

[The Korea Herald, March 20, 2013]

6. Strategic Ambiguity and Paralysis

Kicking the can down the road does not solve the problem. It may buy some time but the moment of truth will come soon. Through the recent AIIB and THAAD issues, we are now learning it the hard way. Delaying a decision or even making no decision at all has been described as a deliberate choice of "strategic ambiguity." While we kept dodging reality, the once quiet courtship has turned into a direct request, and the direct request is now almost becoming diplomatic pressure.

Strategic ambiguity only works if one country remains noncommittal on a particular issue so that it can have a wide choice of policy options. The art is to keep others guessing your real intent. The moment others know what the county thinks, its strategy value just fizzles out.

Regarding AIIB and THAAD, Korea's procrastination and pronounced indecisiveness are already telling others what we have in mind—being at a loss, torn between the two key players in the region—and there is nothing ambiguous about it. Since Korea's position is evident to others, including the Americans and Chinese, the purported strategic ambiguity has apparently failed to deliver.

While we are agonizing over the two difficult issues, high-ranking diplomats from Washington and Beijing visited Seoul to make their affirmative cases. Now, whatever decision is made, the smoldering discontent of both countries is likely to remain.

Splitting the prize may be an easy way out—one for the United States and the other for China. After all, it seems that the two issues are now being finally aligned in that direction: Korea is leaning toward joining the new China-led bank, while accommodating the THAAD battery in Korea. But again, despite the split, both countries will not be happy.

The two issues wise us up to the difficult challenges and pressure, both economically and militarily, that Korea has to face in the treacherous landscape of the Sino-US confrontation. On some issues, Korea may be able to successfully navigate through the narrow passage of the two countries' competing interest and satisfy both. But there are also other issues that simply deny such leeway and a decision must be made one way or another.

These hard questions simply do not offer a box of "I do not know" or "none of the above." While Korea keeps checking these boxes over and over again, the time is suddenly up and quick choices have to be made while the proctor is approaching. A firm stance on a particular issue based on a careful assessment of the long-term national interest may have caused some uncomfortable discussions and consequences, but would have saved and will save a lot of trouble down the road. Judged from a standpoint of national interest, answers to these two questions are arguably obvious from the beginning.

A big steel safe is before us, and we need to open it. The lock of the safe has two wheels—a US wheel and a China wheel. The door will open only with the correct alignment of these two wheels with accurate turns of the dial stopping at precise numbers. What we need is such accuracy and precision as opposed to "being nice" to all partners at all times.

Ambiguity is indeed necessary and sometimes the best strategy. A choice of strategic ambiguity, however, must be deliberate rather than accidental. Strategic ambiguity is no substitute for indecisiveness and procrastination. Making a mistake is disastrous. Taking no decision for fear of making a mistake is even more disastrous.

[The Korea Herald, March 25, 2015]

7. A Warm Breeze from Cuba

Out of 196 states in the world, there are four that Korea does not have diplomatic relations with—Macedonia, Syria, Kosovo, and Cuba. It seems that the number will go down to three soon: re-establishing Seoul-Havana diplomatic ties is steadily becoming a reality.

It was in 1905 that the first ship of immigrants sailed from Incheon to Mexico with 1,033 Koreans on board looking for a new life, 200 of whom were soldiers from the disbanded army of Joseon. What waited for them in the Central American state was hard labor at sugar cane plantations for 35 cents per day.

"Henequen," as the poor laborers were called, were just desperate to find a way to survive at the turn of the century. When their initial contracts were up, some of the early settlers in Mexico then moved to a nearby Caribbean state in search of better working condition. So, in 1921, 280 people came to a small port of Manati in Cuba, starting the lives of "Coreanos en Cuba."

Records show these Korean-Cubans financially supported the independence movement in Korea until 1945. The Korea-Cuba relations after the 1948 establishment of the Republic of Korea had also been largely amicable until the severance of the diplomatic ties in 1960 after the Cuban Revolution. Cuba even provided $3 million to South Korea during the Korean War.

Since the severance of the diplomatic ties in 1960, however, Cuba has been one of the closest allies of North Korea. Through ups and downs including the disintegration of the former Soviet Union in the early 1990s, Pyongyang and Havana have remained close at a time when each side had few friends.

The news that the United States and Cuba have just agreed to restore relations by opening official diplomatic missions each other's capitals on July 20 is also raising the possibility of re-establishing the diplomatic ties between Korea and Cuba.

In fact, de facto rapprochement between Cuba and South Korea has been there for some time. South Korean exports to Cuba currently stand at around $70 million annually, and South Korea is now Cuba's third-largest trading partner in Asia after China and Vietnam.

Not surprisingly, Korean dramas have become popular items in this Caribbean island state, and the interest in Korean culture has been rising. The growing interest is mutual: just last year 5,000 Korean tourists visited Cuba through various routes, and Cuban volleyball players have dominated the Korean professional volleyball league. While the Korean Embassy in Mexico deals with consular issues for Koreans in Cuba and the Korean Trade-Investment Promotion Agency has been promoting business ties between the corporations of the two countries since 2005, the absence of official ties has been inherent limitations.

While the close relationship with North Korea has certainly made Havana hesitant to accelerate the pace of normalization of ties with South Korea, now Seoul and Havana have reached the point where the increasing economic and cultural exchanges require that the bilateral relationship is finally made official.

The unexpected US-Cuba reconciliation is setting the stage for Korea and Cuba to achieve this long-delayed goal. Hopes are indeed high that the two countries will be able to announce the re-establishment of diplomatic relations sometime soon.

This will make these two countries, nearly 13,000 kilometers apart, close friends again after 53 years, with more exchanges and visits to come. The time has finally upon us.

[The Korea Herald, July 15, 2015]

8. A Peace Treaty—More Complex Than It Seems

A peace treaty is being mentioned in the course of exploring an ultimate solution to the military confrontation on the Korean Peninsula.

It has been suggested that a peace treaty would tame North Korea by replacing the current armistice agreement and officially ending hostilities in the region.

China supports the idea of pursuing denuclearization and a peace treaty in parallel. The US position has been that denuclearization should be a prerequisite for any meaningful discussion of a peace treaty, but it apparently does not explicitly rule out the possibility that the two issues can be discussed together. So, while the US and China adopt different tones, both signal that a peace treaty is one of the options on the table in dealing with North Korea.

From a legal perspective, a peace treaty is necessary to officially end a war. This is the legal instrument that brings the warring nations or parties back to normalcy. Remaining claims and compensation, if there are any, are also settled through a peace treaty. Diplomacy is restored and envoys are exchanged. So, in the absence of such a treaty, the two Koreas are still technically at war, and thus any renewed full-scale hostilities are not an initiation of a war but a resumption of the existing war.

It is indeed unprecedented in modern history for an armistice agreement to regulate warring parties for more than 60 years. Every confrontation under the Korean armistice agreement is like walking on a tightrope. A peace treaty will presumably eliminate these uncertainties.

That said, the term "peace treaty" has prompted an allergic reaction in South Korea since it was first proposed by the North in 1974. This reaction stems from the reflection that the replacement of the armistice with a peace treaty would raise a complex set of issues. Of course, a peace treaty would officially declare the end of the Korean War and the establishment of diplomatic relations. Nevertheless, a prospective treaty does not stop there. It will also have to deal with other transitional measures and situations stemming from the Korean War and the armistice regime.

Once the war is officially terminated, the legal status of the United Nations Command will have to be discussed. A possible dissolution or adjustment of the UNC will have a ripple effect on the role of the US commanding general, who also serves as commander of the UNC and the mobilization of US forces in Japan in the case of a Korean contingency, in which the UNC is to play a linking role. More importantly, with the dismantling of the armistice, the scale and presence of US forces in Korea will also be subject to continuing discussions. All these complexities have made South Korea wary of a peace treaty whenever there is a proposal from the North.

Recent development in Washington and Beijing indicates that there is some flexibility on this issue depending on how North Korea responds to the conditions set by these two countries. Discussion of a peace treaty, however, should not forget the structural changes that will stem from the dismantling of the existing framework. There should be a guarantee that any new framework is indeed better and safer than the existing one in terms of deterring hostilities and maintaining peace on the Korean Peninsula.

The worst-case scenario would be for North Korea to get its long-coveted peace treaty with the United States because of its nuclear weapons development program. It may be a crucially improper reward for the regime's two-decade nuclear effort.

[The Korea Herald, March 23, 2016]

9. Struggling in China

It was a subdued celebration of the Trade Day on Dec. 5. For the first time since 1957–1958, the nation is expected to register a decline in exports for two consecutive years. After an 8 percent decrease last year, we will see a 5.6 percent decline with total exports reaching $500 billion by the year's end. Last month there were small signs of recovery, but whether this ember in the ashes is a signal of a sustainable recovery is anyone's guess.

At this juncture, the last thing South Korea would expect from its largest trading partner is trade restrictions of various sorts. But the situation for Korean exporters is not that friendly in China. Fears are spreading now that retaliatory actions against Korean products and services are being taken since Korea decided to deploy a Terminal High Altitude Area Defense system here. Of course, there is no hard evidence, just speculation.

Complaints from Korean exporters include an extended amount of time for customs clearance at ports and an "enhanced" scrutiny of imports by the Chinese authorities. More-than-usual safety and sanitary inspections of Korean products and facilities inside China are also being reported. Korean entertainment events are being delayed or canceled for different reasons. What is clear at least is that a more rigorous application of regulations is taking place at the border and beyond.

A fundamental difficulty with rigorous enforcement of the law lies in the almost impossible task of proving the underlying intent. When authorities counter that they are only applying the law as written down, the conversation usually stops there. There are many ways that a governmental agency can give business entities a hard time entirely within the bounds of law. Perhaps that is why CEOs of Korean corporations succumbed to the demand from the higher echelon in the recent scandal.

This reality applies to international trade. At the border and in the home market, an importing state has many options available to give a hard time to foreign exporters and their products. Provisions are contained in trade agreements and investment agreements, but oftentimes there are issues that are not directly regulated by those provisions and unfortunately left for the discretion of the authorities. When such discretion is exercised, it is quite difficult, if not entirely impossible, to pinpoint any particular violation.

To make the situation more complicated, certain regulatory measures take the form of a legitimate law enforcement activity to conduct criminal investigation and consumer protection. Take tax evasion investigations and product safety inspections for example. They are done by any government on a regular or an ad hoc basis upon receipt of relevant information. So, the mere fact that investigations and inspections are pushed forward, in and of itself, does not necessarily mean that it somehow constitutes a violation of these treaties.

Coming back to the difficulties Korean exporters are facing in the Chinese market at the moment, it is still too early to tell whether these irregularities somehow implicate promises and covenants made in these treaties. Complaints from the field are mainly pieces of anecdotal experience and have not been filtered for a more meaningful discussion.

We tend to believe that difficulties in a foreign market directly amount to a violation of trade agreements with that foreign country. They do sometimes. But that is not necessarily the case. Anecdotal evidence should be accumulated to see if a pattern is found to show bad faith. Until then, a mere rigorous enforcement of the law falls short of pinpointing violations of particular elements of trade agreements.

Hopefully recent difficulties for Korean exporters in China are mere individual aberrations, and the benefit of the Korea-China FTA is enjoyed by all Korean and Chinese traders. The first anniversary of the agreement is next week.

[The Korea Herald, December 13, 2016]

10. A Rough Start to the New Year

When it rains, it pours. And it pours heavily. As if not to be sidelined by domestic disarray, foreign woes are flooding the first week of the new year. Diplomatic friction with neighboring countries is now biting us where it hurts most: the faltering economy.

THAAD-angered Beijing continues to ratchet up its economic retaliation against Seoul. As the THAAD deployment has now become a signature issue of the Korea-US alliance, Seoul is simply unable to undo its official decision. For its part, China will continue to draw from its playbook different cards of economic bashing—at least for the time being.

The economic sanction from Tokyo at the start of the new year could not have come at a more painful time. Tokyo has suspended the currency swap negotiation with Seoul. Bilateral economic meetings have also been called off. And more will be on the way, depending upon how Seoul responds.

Tokyo complains that Seoul has failed to honor what was agreed in the Comfort Women Settlement agreement in December 2015 by not taking necessary action on a new statue in front of the Japanese Consulate General in Busan. Seoul counters with its own complaints. Japan seems to be determined to play its economic pressure card—also at least for the time being.

The double bashing from the two neighbors is not good news for the already battered Korean economy struggling to emerge from an economic recession. It's quite symbolic too: do we ever recall an instance where Korea faced economic squeezing from both sides of the peninsula at the same time? The neighbors must know that economic sanctions are a particularly effective way to drive their diplomatic agenda at this juncture. The two countries seem ready to dial up the level of sanctions when pending diplomatic issues do not proceed as they desire—a sad reality for Korea, which has to rely upon them for many aspects of its economy.

The problem is many of these retaliatory sanctions do not lend themselves to an easy challenge by Korea. They are mainly refusals to cooperate or to extend favorable consideration. Consider China's recent refusal to provide charter flight permissions to Korean carriers. Look at Japan's termination of negotiations for a foreign exchange swap. Refusing to cooperate is usually a permissible policy option for a sovereign state unless there is a treaty or something that dictates otherwise. Other countries can complain, but it pretty much depends upon a state's own decision.

It is an illusion to believe that Korea is entitled to a cordial friendship from other countries. The only leverage would be to have those other countries realize that economic retaliation does not necessarily work vis-à-vis Korea, and that economic sanctions could harm their own interests as well. This is where diplomacy comes in.

In an ideal world, the machine of diplomacy would work diligently by now. National leadership would take this development as a serious issue and mobilize all leverage available. Since national leadership is an item that is temporarily out of stock, perhaps Korea can only repeat what is already stated and ask other countries to refrain from resorting to economic retaliatory measures. In the face of the two-way squeeze, and at the time a key national decision is most needed, the next several months of sheer uncertainty could be an eternity for Korea.

Likewise, in an ideal situation, the two neighbors would not have taken such an aggressive approach even if there were issues of disagreement with Korea. Sensitive issues would have been dealt with quietly and deliberately. Any pretense of such subtlety seems to be gone now. That is more concerning, and it bodes ill for managing future relations.

The year 2016 was one of the worst years in Korea's modern history. If 2017 continues at its current pace, this year may beat it.

[The Korea Herald, January 10, 2017]

11. Forgotten Procedural Checkboxes

Much has been written and spoken about the Korea-US Free Trade Agreement, but very little of it has been directed at the procedural "homework" scattered throughout the text. Some even regard it as a set of cosmetic provisions or say that it is of a hortatory nature. On the contrary, one unique aspect of the FTA is the specific legal obligation to guarantee procedural due process in agency investigations and determinations. Interested parties' right to be heard and right to defend themselves are underscored in the text of the agreement.

Compared to other heavyweight issues in the FTA, these small, nicely worded provisions do not stand out. However to the agencies concerned, they pose a real logistical burden because sometimes it may mean an overhaul in administering their daily operations. They would find it embarrassing to learn that a small procedural defect could render an otherwise legitimate agency determination problematic.

The Competition Chapter of the Korea-US FTA offers an example. It is one of the shortest chapters with nine provisions, mainly underscoring cooperation between competition authorities of the two countries and recognizing the authority to apply competition policies according to respective domestic laws. At the same time, the chapter sets forth procedural steps to be taken in the course of investigations and hearings, citing procedural due process. This is not surprising at all, as similar procedural provisions appear in other parts as well.

For the first time in five years since the agreement went into effect, these procedural provisions are now being mentioned. In response to the Korea Fair Trade Commission's decision in late December last year to impose a 1.03 trillion won ($854 million) fine for anti-competitive business practices, Qualcomm, among others, referred to its procedural rights under the Korea-US FTA.

According to the press release of the San Diego-based company, here are the highlights of its assertions: its fundamental procedural safeguards, such as access to case files and right to cross-examine, guaranteed under the Korea-US FTA were breached. Again, this development marks the first instance in which a US corporation has referred to, in an actual investigation, largely forgotten procedural provisions of the FTA.

As the Korean FTC has dealt with many high-profile antitrust cases recently amid heightened scrutiny and as the agency has been particularly keen to the requirements of the Korea-US FTA, it remains to be seen how much of Qualcomm's assertion would actually prevail. Nonetheless, the company's immediate response is a meaningful refresher in our minds of the procedural elements of the FTA.

Given the enormity of the proposed fine, lengthy legal battles seem inevitable, as with the Korean FTC's 2009 determination against the same company. So, most probably, a final agency determination, once officially issued, will be challenged to the Seoul High Court, and possibly again to the Supreme Court. The judicial proceeding will determine whether the company's business practices constitute a violation of the competition law of Korea.

Regardless of the domestic judicial proceedings, if Qualcomm holds on to its claim of procedural defects, the matter will register itself in the long list of outstanding bilateral trade issues. As the company has been subject to similar probes in other jurisdictions for several years—for instance, in China in 2015, it settled a similar investigation by agreeing to pay a $975 million fine—the KFTC's decision would not stand out. If anything, it seems to represent a natural flow of investigation on the part of Korea. But the timing of the decision could still be sensitive as the new US administration may try to find every reason to bring attention back to the Korea-US FTA in one way or another.

[The Korea Herald, January 25, 2017]

12. Will This Dose of Sanctions Work?

North Korea's missile tests on July 4 and 28 were met with one of the most stringent sanctions adopted by the UN Security Council over the weekend. A new sanction of the Security Council, known as Resolution 2371, is now going to slash North Korea's export of coal, iron, and seafood by $1 billion, roughly one third of its total annual exports. Will the measure exert more pain on North Korea? Of course, it will. Losing one third of the export revenue should be a significant blow to any country. Undoubtedly, the new sanction will further choke North Korea's economy. Will the new sanction then force North Korea to think differently and come to the negotiating table finally? Unlikely.

North Korea has managed to survive previous sanctions. These sanctions would have easily toppled any normal government with an ordinary sense of responsibility. North Korea has been different all along. Presumably, an economic sanction has an inherent limitation for a country that has virtually given up on the development of its economy, for a country whose leadership stands to gain more politically by facing ever stronger outside pressure. Over time, incremental doses of sanctions have increased the North Korean regime's immunity to outside economic pressure. An additional slap on the wrist, however hard it is, would not change the basic thinking of the North. Only if a sanction leads to a direct threat to the regime, might it has that effect.

One way to get there is to control oil imports to North Korea. This may push the reclusive regime's economy to the brink of collapse, probably a threatening the leadership. Despite its effectiveness, or rather because of it, oil import restrictions are again left out of the new sanctions. With these elements omitted, the new sanctions will impose more difficulties, but will not be able to push North Korea to seriously reconsider its course of action. With more rattles and clunks, the car will continue to run, as it has done before.

Frustrating and unfortunate, but at the same time, there is really nothing else that can be done. All in all, at this time this is the most that can be achieved with the cooperation from China and Russia. So, we can only hope that the new sanctions will do something this time. Perhaps other countries will be more vigilant in implementing this resolution because of the likelihood of US trade sanctions against lapses and loopholes in enforcement.

And the new sanction specifically prohibits economic cooperation schemes with North Korea. It bans "the opening of new joint ventures or cooperative entities with" North Korea. As long as this resolution is in place, a suggestion or proposal of reinitiating economic exchange programs with the North including reopening Kaesong Industrial Complex will be directly affected. South Korea's effort to explore some minimal economic exchange programs with the North, even if there is a positive response from the North in an unlikely breakthrough, will now hit a legal stone wall. An approval for an exception should be sought from the Security Council on a case-by-case basis.

Previous experiences tell us that economic penalties would hardly make North Korea budge. Nonetheless, if this is the only option and if this much is the most that can be achieved, then our only wish is that the new sanction will be fully enforced this time, such that Pyongyang will have to change its strategy and come to the negotiating table. Unanimous adoption of the resolution with the support from China and Russia with strong vows to enforce them, having observed the startling strides in the North's ICBM technologies and capabilities, throws a flimsy hope that maybe this time the sanction will work somehow. It should, because the alternative is so disastrous.

[The Korea Herald, August 8, 2017]

13. Red Line? NK's Sixth Nuclear Test

The otherwise blue and crispy Sunday afternoon was juxtaposed against the shocking news from the North. The now familiar veteran lady newsreader appeared on the North's state television channel to announce the successful blast testing of a hydrogen bomb. The latest test has brought North Korea one step closer to the completion of its nuclear program and military deployment of nuclear arsenal.

With the sixth nuclear test, North Korea again thumbed its nose at the international community. This latest one is more startling because it was just one month ago that the UN Security Council imposed the strongest ever sanction (Resolution 2371) against North Korea after the regime's consecutive missile launches on July 3rd and 28th. North Korea is almost asking, what is your next red line?

Even in the face of imminent military conflict, North Korea defies any notion of predictability and self-restraint. It is going its own way, no matter what, refusing to heed anyone's advice, even China's. It is not wavering a bit.

Come to think of it, for the North Korean regime, there is no reason to stop its nuclear program at this stage, as it is just one step away from the full operability of the weapon. In two or three years, with this armament it will seize military and diplomatic hegemony on the peninsula. So, it must be ready to endure any warning, threat or economic sanction in the interim. If it is a North Korean version of a dream come true, there is no reason to balk at this crucial time.

South Korea's gross domestic product is 45 times bigger than the North's. The South's military spending is ten times larger than North's. All the economic success and military superiority of South Korea have now been upended at a single stroke. In retrospect, North Korea's nuclear armament and companion missile development programs were the last straw of the regime on the verge of collapse. The last straw turns out a silver bullet for economic assistance and now for military superiority.

It was March 1993 that North Korea declared its withdrawal from the NPT. North Korea was faltering at the time, after the collapse of the east bloc and the continuing, devastating famine. Militarily and economically, North Korea was not a match for South Korea. The German-style absorption unification seemed within reach and almost a matter of time. In 24 years, the table is turned around and North Korea is now going to dictate the terms for peace or otherwise on the Korean Peninsula. Continuing on this path, it will be North Korea that will be in the driver's seat of the car.

The 24-year chronology gives us belated enlightenment that it was a myth that North Korea would give up its nuclear ambition in exchange for economic incentives or mere assurance for the survival of the regime. Facing this, nobody takes the responsibility. There is no acknowledgment that the 24-year North Korean policy, through both conservative and liberal governments, has failed. While President Trump made a statement the other day that the US's North Korean policy has failed for the past 24 years, a similar acknowledgment has not been made by anyone in South Korea, yet. As with anything, the first step is to acknowledge the failure and confront the reality. Only then can we explore future options.

It seems that unfortunately the only option now is to acknowledge the North Korean regime as a nuclear power and then find a way to respond or contain. Public views in Korea are fast changing in favor of bringing back US tactical nuclear weapons as a first step to restore the broken military balance. Dangerously, continuing provocation of the North will trigger a nuclear armament domino in this region.

The Sept. 3 test blasting marked a new turning point for the North Korean nuclear issue. Before we know it, we will encounter a completely new paradigm of confronting this issue.

[The Korea Herald, September 5, 2017]

14. Two Koreas Finally Recognize Two Koreas

"Betwixt and between" is the term that best describes South Korea when it comes to determining the legal status of North Korea. In the South's legal system, North Korea is not regarded as an independent, separate state. Our Constitution describes "the whole Korean Peninsula and adjacent islands" as the territory of the Republic of Korea; hence its northern part is simply considered an unrecovered territory under the temporary rule of a rebellious entity. And yet, Seoul has had to deal with Pyongyang as a counterpart, a very effective one indeed, over the past seven decades.

We all see the mile-wide gap between the official description and the reality, but it has been one of the cardinal rules of the constitutional regime. When faced with specific legal questions, the Korean Supreme Court and the Constitutional Court repeatedly confirmed this constitutional principle. South Korea in the North's legal regime has been no different.

Here is the practical consequence of this firm position: the possibility of concluding legally binding documents between the two sides, as between two sovereign states, has been systematically precluded. Check all inter-Korea documents signed so far. They are not even called "agreements" (as the term is used to mean treaties) but instead called "arrangements." Under the Korean law, they have been treated as aspirational "gentlemen's agreements"—meaning not legally binding. So, when the relations soured, these documents were rendered virtually meaningless. Neither side bothered to refer to them.

In my view, the "unsettled" nature of these documents stemming from the "unsettled" nature of the legal status of the two Koreas in the other's eyes and system is one of the many reasons that these documents have not been taken seriously or fully implemented.

Well, a prospective Korean peace treaty may finally handle the dichotomy between the reality and the legal fiction. A peace treaty does not just mean the end of the hostilities. Its conclusion also automatically means that the two Koreas will now recognize each other as legitimate states, and as sovereign counterparts. Which in turn would mean that they are now ready to conclude "agreements" that are legally binding on both.

Assuming that the June 12th summit meeting in Singapore goes well, as it seems now, a peace treaty will be within reach sometime soon. As soon as the treaty is inked, massive economic assistance and cooperative programs will head to the North. As it pledges, South Korea will be quick in resuming and expanding the suspended economic cooperation projects with North Korea. South Korean corporations may test the water a little bit, reflecting their bitter experience from the Kaesong Industrial Complex investment and hurried exit. But as soon as they confirm that this time is different, they will be happy to make robust investment in projects in the North.

Emerging projects and new investment will all have to entail various documents, both at individual entities' and the two governments' levels. How these documents are now going to be treated will become ever more important. That the two Koreas recognize each other legally as well as practically is an important first stride for a stable and sustainable cooperative framework. In terms of managing the economic cooperation projects with the North, the most important change in the post-peace regime is this mutual recognition, done officially and legally.

Once a new framework is adopted, within the domestic legal regime there are many places that need corresponding changes. There are certain provisions in the Constitution and statutes that will be out of sync with the new development. When and how to make these changes will be controversial. From abroad, other countries will demand the two Koreas follow in their dealings key principles applicable to, say, two sovereign states, trying to keep at bay two Koreas' preferential treatment toward each other. A lot of homework is waiting for us in the uncharted territory after June 12th.

[The Korea Herald, May 15, 2018]

15. To Make Peace, Declaring the War Is Over Is an Important First Step

"We declare that the war is finally over and that interested parties will seek to establish a peace regime on the peninsula" or something along the line will be the gist of an official "declaration" to terminate the Korean War. As encapsulated in the title, it is just a declaration—a political, diplomatic statement without binding legal effect. Even if adopted, it itself does not change the present Armistice Agreement. So, it is an easy target. At least so it seemed. After the sluggish meetings in July, however, such a declaration is still an elusive target. With the first milestone left up in the air, US-North Korea negotiations are losing momentum.

Hopes are still alive that one can be announced during the UN General Assembly session in New York in September, or sometime in the fall, or at least by the end of the year. Under the circumstances, it seems critical to clear this milestone—adopting a declaration to officially terminate the Korean War—in due course.

A declaration does not solve the problem, nor does it guarantee peace. Nonetheless, under the unique situations of Korea, a declaration of that nature is absolutely essential to initiating a peace discussion seriously. More than anything else, its symbolic weight will be immense. They say what we have here on the peninsula is the longest armistice regime in modern history. Declaring "officially" to the world that the regime is coming to an end is a prerequisite first step to wrap up the old regime and explore a future one. Were it not for the closure of an old chapter, a new one could not be opened. That is why an official declaration to terminate the hostilities, even still maintaining the armistice regime during the pendency of the peace regime discussion, is important and critical. It is a way station between an armistice regime and a peace regime.

We feel that the euphoria in May and June is subsiding as US-North Korea negotiations and inter-Korean meetings are raising more questions and doubts. This is the moment when eagle eyes and sharp ears are needed to spot any loophole, caveat or trick. It is also true that an official declaration may well be taken advantage of by North Korea. That said, a declaration is still necessary if we are serious about giving peace a chance, because without it we cannot even start the discussion on peace. Perhaps we can view a declaration as the "starting point" of peace negotiations, which may or may not succeed.

It may be prudent to decouple the two: a declaration on the one hand and a peace treaty on the other. A peace treaty entails a more complex and complicated process: this is a legal framework to lay out rights and obligations for all the interested parties. Naturally, this is something that requires thorough calibration and careful preparation. If anything, it may take a lengthy process. In addition, it is still possible that, unfortunately, a declaration may fail to lead to a peace treaty. It is also possible that, again unfortunately, hostilities may re-emerge when the two sides lose patience during the prospective peace regime discussion. Nonetheless, it is worth a try.

A declaration of termination of war is a political statement to initiate that long process. No stones must be left unturned at this crucial moment. But at the same time, there does not seem to be a plausible reason to treat a declaration as a peace treaty or part of a peace regime, which is more complex and sensitive. Viewed from this perspective, a declaration of the termination of hostilities on the Korean Peninsula can be done relatively quickly, as long as there is agreement in principle and as long as there is a reliable (even if not full) level of trust.

This Friday marks the 65th anniversary of the Korean Armistice Agreement.

[The Korea Herald, July 24, 2018]

16. With Progress on Denuclearization, Economic Cooperation Projects Ready to Roll

The names and faces of government officials and business leaders in the presidential entourage for this week's third inter-Korean summit in Pyongyang send a clear message as to how serious we are about the two Koreas' economic cooperation projects. To start with, it includes eight minister-level officials. Also joining are corporate leaders from Samsung, LG, SK, Hyundai, and Posco, among others. Not only that, the CEOs of KDB, Korail, and Kepco are flying North as well. With entourage members of this caliber—the real decision makers where corporate investment and infrastructure projects are concerned—the stage is set for serious discussions about inter-Korean economic exchange programs.

Unquestionably, economic cooperation projects cannot move an inch forward as long as UN sanctions are in place. And any easing of those sanctions hinges upon a promise of, or at least some concrete action toward, denuclearization from the North. Whether that can happen this week in Pyongyang is anybody's guess. All we can do now is hope for the best. The world and everyone here in Seoul will be all ears, hoping to hear the D-word (denuclearization) or at least the R-word (reporting) from the North Korean leader's mouth. A meaningful promise will be able to soften the sanctions, and then tap the South's funds and resources for mutual projects. For its part, South Korea has been anxious to initiate economic cooperation programs. In South Korea's mind, it is the best way—the only way—to engage North Korea and usher in a peace regime once and for all. From a business perspective, it has been said that the "Northern passage" will allow for a breakthrough in the sagging domestic economy. No wonder the topic has been the top priority for the government. But Seoul's desire can become reality only if the North responds in kind with its schedule for denuclearization.

At any rate, while many things remain unclear, the heavyweight pan-South Korean economic entourage will likely exert critical influence on North Korean decision makers. They will hear, see, and feel economic assistance packages and cooperation projects at their doorstep. The list of programs and projects waiting for the go-ahead signal will probably whet their appetites for concrete action on the denuclearization front. If nothing else, this visit could be a three-day "roadshow" for the North—a showcase for future economic exchange packages for Pyongyang to see and feel. Those will serve as tangible incentives to entice Pyongyang to accept the offer on the table.

Assuming a long-awaited breakthrough is made this time or sometime soon, what will then follow are various categories of investments from public and private entities from the South. This raises the critical question of how to protect them. Last time, the basic framework was not carefully contemplated, and no effective system of protection was put in place. And we all know what happened afterward. The mistakes of the South-North Investment Protection Arrangement in 2000 should not be repeated. That instrument did not set forth the necessary provisions usually found in similar documents, but instead relied too much upon goodwill and handshakes. In particular, South Korean investors lacked access to an effective dispute-settlement process. This time, too much is at stake to go down the same path.

To our surprise, North Korea also has investment protection treaties with as many as 24 countries—the most recent having been signed with Singapore in 2008. There is no reason that key elements of those treaties could not also be incorporated into a new instrument between the two Koreas.

The pivotal three-day summit will be a turning point for the North Korean denuclearization issue, the stalled US-North Korea negotiations and inter-Korean relations. If strides are made toward denuclearization, economic cooperation projects and assistance programs will soon be in full swing. Whatever comes out of the

Pyongyang meeting will be the subject of much discussion at Chuseok holiday dinner tables when families gather next week.

[The Korea Herald, September 18, 2018]

17. South Korea's Thaad Trilemma, a Tricky Balancing Act

In the joint statement released after the first summit between US President Donald Trump and South Korean leader Moon Jae In, there were visible efforts to iron out differences between the two sides and put positive spins on them.

What is most noteworthy from last week's summit is the glaring omission of THAAD, or Terminal High Altitude Area Defense anti-missile system, from their statement.

Seoul and Washington, in order to present their leaders' first meeting in the best light, decided to sweep their differences over THAAD under the rug. The issue is so controversial and delicate that the two sides agreed to keep it out of the summit agenda (at least officially), apparently fearing the grave consequences that could arise from any public display of differences.

Since the first batch of the anti-missile system was deployed—under the cover of darkness—in late April, less than two weeks before the South Korean presidential election, THAAD has become the lynchpin of the United States countermeasure against the threat of North Korean missiles.

All of a sudden, THAAD has become representative of the backbone of the US-Korea military alliance, but it has also presented the Moon administration with its thorniest foreign policy issue.

While a slight majority of people in South Korea view the anti-missile system as a necessary measure to counter escalating North Korean military adventurism, THAAD's deployment on Korean soil has also resulted in Seoul being wedged between its security guarantor the US and next-door giant China. Beijing opposes THAAD because of its radar's potent detection capability, possibly well into Chinese territory.

South Korea is now struggling with a trilemma over THAAD, having to send all three messages at the same time:

It has to tell domestic constituents that "a lot has changed" since the previous conservative administration;
It has to tell American counterparts "nothing has changed";
It has to tell China "something has changed."

By doing so, it will inevitably sow more confusion in its foreign policy direction. In the message to the domestic audience, the government must convince its people that "a lot has changed" within the past year.

South Korea's new administration feels it has the political obligation to fulfill its campaign promises that it will take correctional measures with respect to

THAAD. Apparently, the new administration is unable to accept as a fait accompli the deployment decision made by the previous administration. Mr. Moon and his party, formerly the main opposition, had earlier vehemently opposed the decision in July last year to deploy THAAD. Mr. Moon has since moderated his position on THAAD.

The "a lot has changed" message to South Koreans and the ruling party's core support groups will serve to justify THAAD without the Moon government being seen as backtracking on its position. In the message to Washington, Seoul must vow that "nothing has changed and nothing will."

The ultimate decision to omit the topic from the official US-South Korea summit agenda only underscores South Korea's THAAD predicament. As long as Seoul purports to satisfy all three parties at the same time, it will have to present ambiguous words and positions that keep shifting along the spectrum of "changes." It has to accommodate the US demand: Washington has made clear that the deployment of the anti-missile system is the only option in its game plan. Indicating changes in the face of this specific demand will lead to a diplomatic disaster that may test the bilateral military alliance—a consequence that South Korea can ill afford.

When the US referred to the deployment as a measure to protect the lives of its soldiers in South Korea, it clearly showed it would tolerate no changes to the THAAD deal as agreed upon by the previous administration. So, toward Washington, Seoul must continue to send out the "no change" signal. In its message to China, South Korea has to show that it has done something to accommodate Beijing's demand. In retaliation for the THAAD deployment, China has imposed various bilateral sanctions against South Korea for several months.

Chinese retaliation is real and intrusive: statistics put South Korea's economic loss during this period at US$15 billion (S$20.7 billion). China also makes clear that the sanctions will continue unless South Korea scraps its original plan and reverses deployment and returns the batteries to the US. Signaling that "something has changed" in its exchanges with Beijing is critical to keep the Chinese retaliation at bay, at least for the time being.

Now, caught in the bind of this trilemma, South Korea's only viable option is to slow down the deployment process without scrapping the plan entirely. A recent decision to check if all statutory procedures have been satisfactorily completed, including an environmental assessment, will delay the process.

South Koreans, the US, and China can then interpret the delay in ways that suit their respective agendas. But the problem with this option is that it will not solve the trilemma. It simply kicks the can down the road. Given the heightened tensions on the Korean peninsula, South Korea will face constant calls from all sides for a clear position on THAAD. As the three competing demands cannot be met at the same time, one (or two) will have to be ultimately chosen over the other.

The price to be paid for the lack of clarity on the issue of THAAD will increase proportionally to the amount of time thus bought.

The ultimate decision to omit the topic from the official US-South Korea summit agenda only underscores South Korea's Thaad predicament. As long as Seoul purports to satisfy all three parties at the same time, it will have to present ambiguous words and positions that keep shifting along the spectrum of "changes" as discussed in this piece. It will be a situation that satisfies no one.

While Seoul is agonizing over its choices in the trilemma, Pyongyang yesterday ratcheted up its missile threat a few notches by claiming that it had succeeded test-firing an intercontinental ballistic missile. If the claim is confirmed, the vice of the trilemma will further tighten around South Korea.

South Korea must have more clarity, not less, on its final stance on Thaad.

[The Straits Times, July 5, 2017]

18. TPP, a Victim of Its Own Success?

Has the Trans-Pacific Partnership (TPP) scheme hit a stumbling block? Questions are lingering as the ministerial-level talks in Singapore in late February ended without a final deal. This outcome raises a red flag as it is the second failure to meet the deadline in as many months. Nor has there been any mention of a new deadline, for that matter.

Of course, the issue is not simply about deadlines: after all, deadlines can be missed and adjusted. What grabs outsiders' attention, however, is that the Singapore meetings have apparently underscored a wide gap in positions among the key players.

In particular, the United States and Japan showed that there's still a long way to go to reach a compromise on the issue of market access for agricultural products and automobiles. Can they resolve all these differences in the next few months? It's anyone's guess. Will President Obama secure the fast-track authority to complete the TPP deal? Things are getting more complicated.

Some speculate that a breakthrough will be sought when President Obama comes to Asia in late April. But that is just one month away. It is doable but the stars would have to be aligned for a mega-FTA scheduled to cover almost 40 percent of the global GDP to be inked. Since last November when it registered its "interest" in the pan-Pacific agreement, Korea has fretted about when the final deal will be struck. The unexpected delays may now make it possible for Seoul to join the negotiations before they close.

Like most negotiations, very little is known about what is on the negotiating table. It has been speculated that the agreement aims to cover a wide range of issues including digital commerce, state-owned enterprise, labor and the environment, beyond the standard points of tariff reductions and market access. The only public glimpse into the agreement was provided by the documents posted by WikiLeaks in January. Although the source was not disclosed, the website has posted the environmental chapter of the TPP being discussed as of November 2013.

The draft environmental chapter shows that "new" issues are being discussed at the negotiating table. A perusal of the environmental chapter further indicates that the TPP is being used as a platform for issues that have stayed out of the reach of trade agreements thus far—such as fisheries subsidies and binding dispute settlement for environmental measures. Again, this is just one chapter and the full spectrum of new issues being discussed for the agreement is not known to outsiders. For example, some in the United States are calling for the agreement to address foreign-currency manipulation—another "hot button" issue for a trade pact.

These pieces of the puzzle tell us that many issues being discussed at the TPP are from a menu different from those of previous agreements. By all accounts, the TPP will not follow the usual playbook, which brings up many questions for countries like Korea that are sitting on the fence. To be precise, Korea is not sitting on the fence, but is now apparently ready to step down into the field, but not knowing exactly what is going on creates hesitation and concern.

Against this backdrop, preliminary discussions with other participating countries have become more important for Korea in making an official decision to join. This week, preliminary talks with Japan, the last one among the 12 participating countries, are taking place in Tokyo.

Once the preliminary talks are over, a clearer picture will be available. The critical question then is what the administration would or should do with all the novel issues in the new playbook. There is no textbook precedent to turn to, as we have never dealt with these issues before.

[The Korea Herald, March 5, 2014]

19. Iran Deal's Implications for Korea

The news of a grand settlement of the Iranian nuclear issue from Lausanne has vindicated the importance and efficacy of an international economic sanction targeting financial institutions. Once the operation of financial institutions of Iran and those dealing with Iran was restricted, trade flow was slowly disrupted. In terms of achieving the stated goal, the UN-authorized and US-led economic sanction of 2010 knew where the Achilles heel is in a modern trading nation. An intensive international sanction has evidently forced Tehran to consider other options.

Now, a downside of an economic sanction is that sometimes it can cause a sanctioning state to hemorrhage as well due to the increasingly interdependent nature of the global economy.

Korea can present its own firsthand account here. The closure of the Seoul branch office of Bank Mellat in 2010, in tandem with international sanctions, was a painful decision for Korean companies that had relied upon the Iranian bank for the settlement of their business transactions with Iranian counterparts. Korea's robust exports to and imports from Iran were all cleared through the bank. So its closure has since choked bilateral trade and the vacuum left by Korea's departure has been largely filled by Chinese exports and construction companies.

As the news of the grand settlement in Lausanne spreads, hopes are high among traders and businesspeople in Korea that a restored economic relationship with this country of 80 million people will open up a new market of goods and services in the Middle East. Before the sanction, Iran was Korea's fourth largest provider of crude oil with annual imports worth $7 billion.

Korea's export of manufactured goods, mostly electronic products, household appliances, and automobiles, reached $4.5 billion annually. That market is now coming back. On top of that, the lifting of the economic sanction would mean more construction projects in the region and a further fall of oil prices. Not bad news for Korean companies.

The emerging thaw in Iran in fact fits nicely with the "second Middle East boom," which has been the talk of the town recently as the region becomes a hallmark of the successful economic diplomacy of the current administration. The elimination of the biggest uncertainty in the region is certainly a tailwind at a right timing.

In retrospect, Tehran was an iconic symbol of the first Middle East boom in the 1970s: now bustling Tehran Boulevard in the Gangnam district is the only street in Seoul that carries the name of a foreign city. Iran reciprocated by naming one the main arteries of Tehran as "Seoul Street." "Korea Plaza" and "Seoul Park" were also opened in Tehran in 2002 and 2003, respectively.

Korean dramas have been very popular in the country. The TV series "Jewel in the Palace (Daejanggeum)" still remains one of the biggest hits in Iran, and just two weeks ago the Iranian embassy in Seoul invited the main actress of the drama to its national reception of Nowruz New Year celebration—the first of its kind.

Tehran's coming back to the global economic regime is arguably yet another catalyst for the recovery of the global economy. With the lifting of the economic sanction, Korean businesses are also in a sweet dream of new opportunities in the region. The pieces are falling into places one-by-one to herald a second Middle East boom.

[The Korea Herald, April 8, 2015]

20. Spirit and Violation of Bilateral Pacts

It is indeed rare, if not entirely against protocol, for foreign ambassadors to visit the chairman of the judiciary committee of the legislature of a receiving state regarding a pending legislation. Ordinarily, one would expect foreign envoys to deliver their views and comments through the diplomatic channels or through other counterparts in the executive branch.

This rare incident happened last Friday when the ambassadors of the United States and a few members of the European Union paid a visit to the chairman of the Legislation and Judiciary Committee of the National Assembly to raise their concerns over the proposed amendment of the Foreign Legal Consultant Act—which seeks to implement Korea's commitment under its free trade agreements with the US and the EU, among others.

After the visit, the chairman suspended the remaining process at the committee, asking for a further review of the compatibility of the new legislation with the two FTAs.

Under the proposed amendment prepared by the Justice Ministry, new requirements will be imposed on joint venture law firms involving overseas companies. Examples of the new requirements include restriction of a foreign law firm's ownership of a JV at 49 percent and a requirement of "good standing" practice record of more than three years in respective jurisdictions.

It has been pointed out that these restrictions tend to create a favorable business environment for Korean law firms and put their foreign counterparts in a disadvantageous position. And reportedly, that was the main point raised during the ambassadors' meeting with the Judiciary Committee chairman on Jan. 8.

Treaty interpretation is always complex and complicated. To make it simple, one cardinal rule to interpret a treaty provision is to read and apply it as it is written down. The texts are presumed to reflect the parties' true intent when they are negotiated, and so the texts should overrule unless and until the parties amend the treaty provisions.

So, whether Korea can adopt such restrictive measures as envisioned in the FLC Act should be determined by what the relevant provisions actually state. How a particular measure would now affect the market or the players in the market is an important factor, but it is usually unable to overcome the text of a treaty.

In plain reading, the two treaties stipulate, in pertinent part, that Korea preserves the right to adopt specific regulation of joint law firms. They are arguably phrased as open-ended provisions, which are then interpreted to mean that the authorities of contracting parties are accorded the right to adopt specific ways of regulation. As long as the texts are straightforward, it is difficult to sustain a claim that exercising the right under a treaty leads to its violation merely because of favorable or unfavorable business conditions.

To be blunt, an FTA is a package deal: the purpose of any free trade deal is to find an equilibrium of the entire interests of the contracting parties, which would mean that give-and-take has inevitably taken place in individual sectors. Viewed under this general scheme of an FTA, the fact that one particular sector can be favorable or unfavorable to a party, even if true, does not necessarily mean that a particular provision should be interpreted one way or another, or that any violation has taken place. Only the terms of the text should control.

Points raised so far refer to the "spirit" of the FTAs rather than "provisions" of the agreements. In a sense, the reference to the spirit may indicate that the texts themselves do not necessarily support such points. The spirit of the agreement is important and meaningful, but it cannot replace the specific language in the texts. The ongoing debates on the FLC Act are an important precursor of sometimes different understanding of FTA contracting parties and of how such differences can be resolved.

[The Korea Herald, January 13, 2016]

21. Bringing Chorus Back to KORUS

Since the inauguration of the Trump administration, South Korea has been holding its breath. The fate of the five-year-old Korea-United States Free Trade Agreement (once termed as "KORUS" FTA hinting at chorus) has suddenly become uncertain. The dreaded term "termination" finally surfaced during President Trump's interview on April 28, where he described the trade pact as "a horrible deal that should've never been made," vowing renegotiation and possible termination. This has set South Korea scrambling to prepare for the first encounter of the two governments to discuss this issue: the summit meeting between President Trump and President Moon to be held in Washington, DC, later this month.

A trade agreement can survive only if, and as long as, it can ensure a win-win situation for both parties. If one party believes it is being shortchanged, no words of friendship or good will could save it. At the end of the day, in a trade deal money talks. An aggrieved party has the option of triggering the kill switch (called a termination clause) embedded in a trade pact. The KORUS FTA is no exception.

So, it is important and critical to read the balance sheet of the KORUS FTA carefully and accurately when this issue is put on the table this coming June. If the balance sheet does indicate one side stands to gain more systematically, then the playing field should be leveled. Otherwise, it would be simply a matter of time or a matter of patience before the "losing" party invokes termination. In light of this, the upcoming negotiation provides a good occasion for candid discussions between the two major trading partners.

Reading the KORUS balance sheet, however, requires understanding of some unique aspects of the trade pact. First is how to account for a time gap between goods trade and services trade in terms of "market opening" effect. The effect of goods trade liberalization (i.e., tariff cuts) is usually immediate: you just don't pay extra tax anymore at the border. Meanwhile, services trade commonly demands prior planning and a time-sequential process: in a foreign country you need to rent an office, hire staff, undergo registration and run advertisements. So, here market penetration takes more time.

Between the two countries, the United States has a competitive edge in services trade. And the five years' time may not be sufficient yet for full penetration into the Korean market by competitive US service providers. USTR's own assessment in the National Trade Estimate of March 31, 2017, regards KORUS as "provid[ing] meaningful market access commitments across virtually all major services sectors" of Korea. While Washington has registered concerns over implementation of the services market opening in certain sectors of Korea, this time lag in services trade is a factor to be reflected in the KORUS assessment.

Reading the balance sheet properly also requires recognition that the pact is not just about market liberalization and tariff reduction. It is (at least intended to be) much more than that. The almost 1,000-page treaty texts cover virtually the entire spectrum of economic activities. For instance, facilitation and protection of foreign investment is a core concept. At least on the part of Korea, the KORUS

FTA has induced more Korean investment in the US, totaling 51 billion dollars during the five-year period, more than double the US investment in Korea during the same period. Transparency and due process in the regulatory regime are another examples. Again at least on the part of Korea, the FTA has played a pivotal role in attaining these objectives. The USTR's 2017 NTE attributes "improvements in the transparency of Korea's regulatory system" to KORUS. We know that there is still a long way to go, but it seems to be working, albeit slowly.

A final score sheet of KORUS will only be available when all these multiple facets of the agreement are fully taken into account. And yet, quite a few people in the two countries tend to look at only the tip of the iceberg such as trade surplus or deficit in a given year. One needs to look at what is below the water at the same time.

Once the two counties sit together sometime soon, they will have to see to it that the trade pact reflects long-term trade interests of the two countries in a balanced manner. If not, adjustment should be made, and a compromising ground should be found.

Korea and the United States have sung many songs together in chorus, and most of the time very successfully. It is time to bring this chorus back to KORUS. Disbanding the choir just because of some miscues and missed tunes would be like throwing the baby out with the bathwater.

[The Korea Herald, June 13, 2017]

22. Start Small, Think Big on Cooperation with NK

Maybe it was just an honest mistake. A typical "rules of origin" confusion or infraction. Origin faking or laundering is not new to customs officials at the border, so importers may have believed that the coal shipments really originated from Russia. The low price and unusual loading port (Kholmsk, Sakhalin) may not have been sufficient to raise a red flag for the importers and the government.

Coal arrived at Korean ports and was put into the stream of commerce. This took place last October.

What happened afterward, however, raises a question. It was as early as Jan. 26 that major foreign newspapers started to report the source of the coal as North Korea. Seven months after the reports and ten months after the transshipments, a government investigation is still ongoing. A rather unusually long investigation for such technical issues as rules of origin confirmation and infraction.

More so given the gravity of the issue: a potential violation of the UN Security Council resolutions—if confirmed, these incidents contravene UNSC resolutions 2371 and 2397 of last year—and possibly a unilateral sanction of entities involved by other states. Of utmost relevance is criticism over South Korea possibly breaking ranks with other countries on the UN sanctions front.

One can only guess why it is taking such a long time. There may have been unknown technical difficulties, or perhaps Seoul has been fearing it would ruin the party—the Winter Olympics and the mood of detente.

In any event, putting this into perspective, there is an important lesson to learn from the incident. It reminds us how easy it is to be implicated in North Korean trade and suddenly in violation of UNSC resolutions. The coal scandal has brought up an elephant in the room: South-North economic cooperation is pivotal in engaging the North, but, sadly, inter-Korean economic cooperation projects can barely move forward under the present UN sanctions.

Indeed, exceptions can be secured. But they have been so far issued for one-time, specific-purpose encounters, such as military hotline recovery or inter-Korea delegation visits. Exceptions for general and broad economic interaction will be in a different league altogether.

Which again brings us to the importance of the "one step at a time" approach. Whether we like it or not, the peace process will be a long process. Economic cooperation will be no different. There are rules to be followed and procedures to be cleared. Of course, our national enthusiasm for peace and unification is unquestionable and unwavering. Unfortunately, enthusiasm is not a panacea to all the problems and challenges ahead. Persuasion is necessary. But preaching to other states about our enthusiasm, even in violation of the agreed rules, may only complicate the problem.

Peace can take root and continue only if denuclearization is guaranteed. At least that is what we have believed so far and that is what Korea has explained its official position to be. If so, the UNSC resolutions play a critical role to quicken the process. Cooperating with other countries is important, and maintaining their trust is ever more important.

Yes, it is time to shake things up and try something new. We are in need of a turnaround. But that does not mean that UNSC resolutions are a cumbrance to inter-Korea economic cooperation, or that sanctions should cease instantly. We should view this as a process—the first part of a long process. For instance, to maintain the momentum, some pilot programs may be developed with specific exceptions approved from the UNSC. Commensurate with the progress of denuclearization, exceptions can be diversified and expanded.

As I wrote last time, an official announcement of the "termination" of the Korean War would be meaningful as the starting point of a long process to explore and negotiate a peace regime. In the interim, the present regime can remain intact. For economic cooperation, it is also a process: going forward one step at a time under the consensus of the international community is critical to ultimate success. As they say, let's start small, and think big.

[The Korea Herald, August 7, 2018]

23. Korea Caught in the Middle Again

The intensifying US-China confrontation has just taken a new twist. Reportedly, Washington is asking Seoul to join its anti-Huawei alliance. The reason is security concerns posed by the Chinese IT giant.

This latest development puts South Korea in a difficult spot again. Korea is confronted with what it dreads most: choosing sides in a decisive manner.

It is one thing to worry about the G2 confrontation and its overall economic impact. It is quite another to be forced to choose sides openly and officially. Whatever choice is made will not satisfy both trading partners. Worse yet, it may displease both.

To put it bluntly, the real concern is retaliation. It is a deja vu moment from the still-unending THAAD drama. One estimate puts Korea's overall loss from China's retaliatory moves at 15 trillion won and counting.

Yes, the situation is way different now—but mostly for the worse, as the mood is more confrontational and divisive than it was several years ago. The confrontation between the US and China has intensified to an unprecedented level. It was not this contentious when the missile defense system was an issue several years back. Further thickening the plot is the fact that if Korea sides with either country and the other retaliates, it is Korean IT companies that stand to feel the sting. Any restrictions in the sector will hit Korea in a sore spot.

So, how do we handle this catch-22 situation? A modest Plan B is to take a principled stance, or at least something resembling one. As in dealings with personal friends, you cannot please everyone all the time. But at least you can try to embrace your own principles and stick to them as much as possible. Angry moments are inevitable at first, but over time you can loosen the vise grip.

Well, let's come back to the question again. One way to handle this latest problem is to underscore the private nature of the transactions. The sales and purchasing decisions of IT companies and telecommunication service providers are their own. There is little, if anything, the government can do about private business affairs. Perhaps, at most, it can engage in discussions or offer suggestions or recommendations. But the ultimate decisions fall outside the purview of the government.

To add a little bit more flavor and flesh to a principled approach, legal explanations may lend a helping hand. Government requests directed to private entities either to do or refrain from doing business with a particular entity may entail their own legal consequences. Just look no further than recent domestic legal proceedings—powerful people who intervened in private decision-making processes have found themselves criminally implicated or charged. Direct intervention may also have implications for trade agreements and investment agreements. So there are reasons here for the government to be cautious in taking action.

Granted, issues surrounding the G2 trade war extend well beyond the legal realm. No question about it. But if Korea is called upon to explain its decision—whatever that might be—offering some sort of rationale will help make the other states more receptive and understanding. Here is one way to arrive at a principled approach on the Huawei issue: when pressed, the government can listen to requests from the two states but should explain that the ultimate decisions are to be made by companies. And then it should let the companies make the best decisions possible under the circumstances. Regrettably, this will not solve the problem nor erase the dilemma Korea faces. And inevitably, there will be negative consequences as well. But at least this approach could reduce or minimize such consequences. If you cannot please both sides, an alternative is to try to anger both sides less. A prolonged G2 confrontation is Korea's worst nightmare. Unfortunately, this nightmare is becoming a reality.

[The Korea Herald, May 28, 2019]

24. What Went Wrong? It's Time to Look at the Military's Security Posture

The poor police officer who got the call may have scoffed, thinking it was a prank. Imagine the caller saying something like this: "I have just talked to four people claiming to have come from the North. They are standing on the quay."

Then imagine the startled police officers rushing to the scene. Recent media photos of South Korean police officers talking to the crew of a North Korean boat that apparently strayed into South Korean waters captured exactly this bizarre encounter.

The story of a North Korean boat, just 10 meters long, crisscrossing South Korea's territorial waters for several days in the East Sea, then approaching a major port and finally docking at its quay without ever being detected or stopped, is almost surreal. In the photos, the four men on board seem to be on a day trip, looking relaxed, hands in their pockets. Here is the funny part: one even asked a passerby for a cellphone to make a call.

This is what happened ten days ago in Samcheok, a port city on the east coast. An investigation is underway to find out just what happened and how it happened.

Sometimes accidents do happen. Things fall through the cracks. It may be the case that a string of coincidences led to the boat's arrival at the port city.

It may also be the case that this incident is telling evidence of a structural problem. Does it reflect a lax security posture in the aftermath of the inter-Korean rapprochement since last year? Opposition parties are homing in on this possibility. Probably, it's a combination of the two. The investigation will tell.

Whichever story we hear at the end of the day, at least one thing is clear. Thankfully, there is a common thread running through all the statements from government and political leaders about the incident, making this a rare occasion when we are hearing one national voice. To paraphrase: the rapprochement policy and the peace process have no business affecting the military's alertness and preparedness.

Very true. It is such a basic principle that it does not need repeating. But now seems like a good time to reaffirm the obvious with one voice.

If its aftermath is handled properly and the right lessons are learned, the boat incident could be a bitter but effective antidote. It could serve as a cautionary tale about the security posture of the armed forces. It could offer an opportunity to turn over every stone to ensure vigilance.

Consider another incident that took place during the same week, on June 20. Two Russian bombers entered South Korea's air defense identification zone over the

East Sea, prompting Air Force fighters to scramble. Over the past couple of years there has been a trend toward more and more foreign military aircraft encroaching on this space—yet another reason to maintain sharpened discipline and a vigilant security posture.

That said, we should be careful not to exaggerate or overplay the boat incident for political gain. Similarly, downplaying it or even covering it up for fear of political consequences would be equally disastrous. Either way, politicization of an incident like this would be wrong and harmful. It would inevitably amount to politicization of the military—absolutely the last thing we would want at this juncture. It is worrying to see the incident snowball into a political scandal, rather than a serious effort to find the problems and fix them.

There is no room for political considerations in military operations. Permitting them to intrude would be a grave mistake, given where this country stands now. If the wooden vessel incident reminds us of this basic principle and forces us to adjust our stance accordingly, then it will have served as a valuable lesson. Full transparency and a thorough investigation are essential.

[The Korea Herald, June 25, 2019]

25. Peaceful, but Not Peaceful March

The June 24 incident should have never happened. This is the type of thing that wouldn't happen in a country of law and order—much less in a globalized metropolitan city like Seoul. Roughly 3,000 demonstrators "encircled" the US embassy in downtown Seoul marching with shouts and fist-raising, cutting off passage from the diplomatic compound to main streets. Demonstrations are part of daily life in Seoul, but such encircling (with the euphemism of "Human Belt") has never happened in Seoul. Nor has it been tried in other major cities in peaceful times. That incident was startling, to say the least.

More startling was the fact that the encircling plan was approved by the court. The Seoul Administrative Court overruled the police's initial banning of the encircling march, citing freedom of assembly and freedom of speech, and permitted it with some conditions—only 20 minutes, and one time only.

Peaceful picketing and chanting in front of foreign embassies for political or diplomatic cause are common in any country, but thousands of people surrounding a foreign embassy is a different story. As much as such encircling is unprecedented, imposing a time limit does not alter the essence of the incident. Freedom of assembly and freedom of speech can be achieved by dozens of other means: there is simply no reason to surround a foreign embassy to exercise this right.

Here, we are not merely talking about diplomatic courtesy. Protecting foreign embassies and their staff is one of the core tenets of international law. As a matter of fact, modern international law started, after the Thirty-Year War in 1648, by protecting foreign emissaries. These norms are codified in the 1961 Vienna Convention on Diplomatic Relations, which imposes "a special duty" on states "to protect the premises of the (embassy)" and "to prevent any disturbance of the peace" or "the impairment of (the) dignity" of the embassy. Korea has been party to this convention since December 1970.

The June 24 demonstration was peaceful, in the sense that it did not employ any physical violence. Only shouts, slogans, and chants with banners, flags, and pickets. But at the same time, if "peaceful" in a strict sense means the absence of any pressure, threat or intimidation, it was not. By any account, thousands of people surrounding, hand in hand, a small compound had to be intimidating and imposing to those inside the enclave. It sounds like "disturbance of peace" or "impairment of dignity" as the terms are used in the said convention. In issuing the June 24 decision, the court stated that encircling should not pose a threat to a foreign embassy. This is a rationale hard to fathom.

Just imagine how we would feel if the same thing happened to a Korean embassy in another country. It will easily be one of the top stories of the 9 o'clock KBS News. Why should we not expect the same level of sensitivity and reaction from other countries?

In light of this, the decision of the Seoul Administrative Court on Aug. 14 to refuse permission of the same "Human Belt" plan during the Aug. 15 demonstration to surround the American and Japanese embassies in Seoul is all the more welcoming. This time, the court rejected the request referring to the Vienna Convention (finally) and other geopolitical developments, including the importance of alliance in the face of the mounting North Korean threat. The judicial branch's attempt to explain geopolitical implications sounds rather bizarre, but its reference to the convention is accurate and appropriate. The Aug. 15 demonstration took place in the main streets before the US embassy but did not encircle the mission this time. Demonstrators' messages were as effectively delivered. Which again raises the question of why not on June 24?

In a country where law and order are respected and upheld, things like foreign embassy encircling (let alone pointing a laser at the premise, which happened this past January) are almost unthinkable. Demonstrations will and should continue in Seoul in the future. But they should never be used or permitted to inflict pressure on foreign missions or their emissaries.

[The Korea Herald, August 22, 2017]

IV

INTERNATIONAL ORGANIZATIONS AND NGOS—CONTRIBUTIONS AND LIMITATIONS IN VARIOUS SECTORS

Korea is progressively assuming important roles in the global community. In particular, its participation in international organizations has become increasingly proactive and robust. Korea has contributed to the international community through individuals who have held prestigious position such as the Secretary General of the United Nations and the Chief Justice of the International Criminal Court. Korean professionals have also attained prominent positions within international organizations. In addition, Korea is home to up to four international organizations where permanent representatives are stationed in their Seoul headquarters. Columns delve into these issues of Korea and its interactions with international organizations. Sometimes, previously unresolved issues resurface while fresh issues come to the forefront. In particular, the columns address legal issues associated with a range of activities and circumstances concerning Korea.

The unique position of Korea occasionally confers significance on its voice in the deliberation process of international organizations. It has undergone a substantial socio-economic transformation, progressing from a state of poverty to that of a developed nation. As such, it possesses a comprehensive understanding of the perspectives held by both developing and developed states. It is thus capable of fulfilling the function of a moderator in relation to contentious issues. Korea has been elected to a non-permanent seat of the United Nations Security Council (UNSC), first in the 1995 election, again in the 2012 election, and most recently in the 2023 election. When confronted with critical issues, members of the council occasionally express divergent perspectives, and Korea could play a role in bridging those gaps in such situations. In many respects, Korea is positioned to play a supportive role in global discussions as shown in its active participation in other fora. As a member of the UNSC, Korea is expected to be more actively engaged in making and enforcing the decisions of the UNSC.

DOI: 10.4324/9781003501749-4

Multilateralism refers to multiple countries coordinating national policies with common goals. There are various theories regarding the origins of multilateralism, but in principle, it can be said that multilateralism came about after World War II when countries united. The trend of changing from bilateralism to multilateralism accelerated in the 20th century, and after World War II, countries actively participated in various multilateral organizations including the UN and formed alliances. Since then, the system has been strengthened as newly independent countries and NGOs emerged as important actors of multilateralism. There is criticism that national interests are becoming more complex and traditional multilateral organizations are not responding effectively to transnational issues. Major powers tend to favor unilateralism or bilateralism. In particular, nationalism, which emphasizes a common national ideology, plays an important role in forming national policies in modern society. There is continued concern about the crisis of multilateralism, as it can cause various problems that transcend national borders (transborder global risks).

Crises in multilateralism manifest themselves in a variety of areas, but the essential reason for their occurrence is virtually the same: it is more advantageous for states to act alone, driven by national interests, than to cooperate. This characteristic stems from the anarchic nature of the international community, where no one can enforce or regulate agreements against a particular state.[1] Scholars such as Waltz and Keohane argue that because of this anarchic nature, we have become accustomed to conflict rather than cooperation, especially in the military and economic spheres.[2] While there has not been a history of cooperation between states, it appears that most forms of cooperation have been formed at the initiative of great powers, or when there is a hegemony that states should not cooperate.[3,4] States also appear to cooperate only when they have a relative advantage over other states or when there is an absolute incentive to do so.[5] States weigh the comparative advantage of joining a multilateral agreement by considering both the benefits of joining

1 Lechner, S., 2022, *Anarchy in international relations*. Oxford Research Encyclopedia of International Studies.

2 Realists and neo-realist argue "International anarchy is unmitigated (Waltz, Keohane). States have little or no incentive to work together to solve joint problems, and their attitudes towards each other have been conditioned by a history of international conflict, not one of international cooperation. They are motivated primarily by rivalry and the pursuit of relative power, most particularly power in military or economic terms."; O'Neill, K., 2017, *The environment and international relations*. Cambridge University Press, p. 14 (emphasis supplied).

3 One example is the free trade agreement between the United States, the sole superpower in World War II, see *ibid*.

4 Another example is that the current Artemis agreement was also created at the initiative of the United States, a space technology power.

5 This reflects key assumptions in structural realism and neoliberal institutionalism. See: Waltz, Kenneth N. (1979). Theory of International Politics. Reading, MA: Addison-Wesley; Keohane, Robert O. (1984). After Hegemony: Cooperation and Discord in the World Political Economy. Princeton, NJ: Princeton University Press; Mearsheimer, John J. (1994/95). "The False Promise of International Institutions." International Security, 19(3).

and the costs of not joining or deviating from the agreement.[6] In other words, before cooperating, states consider collectively whether (i) the benefits of implementing the treaty are large; (ii) they will have to exert little effort; (iii) the state leading the cooperation will exert a lot of effort; and (iv) the lead state will make good on its commitments.[7] Taken together, then, in order to promote cooperation among states and realize multilateralism, there needs to be a strong initiative and implementation by a great power, either through the shaming strategy just mentioned, which creates an atmosphere that cooperation should not be done, or, as in the current Artemis Agreement, there needs to be a strong benefit to cooperation, as in the Artemis Agreement, where countries are able to mine resources, which was not possible under the Outer Space Treaty, but is now possible under this agreement.

Multilateralism, on the other hand, is a pattern of countries trying to maintain their power superiority in the international community, which sometimes thrives and sometimes falls into crisis. Currently, China and the United States are designing their own multilateral cooperation system to maintain their superiority in the hegemonic war, but if one side becomes dominant and becomes the single power in the international community, a country can always take a single line for its national interests. To solve this problem, it is necessary to try to balance[8] between countries, which is one of the main roles of multilateralism. In the case of South Korea, for example, it will need to develop its own technology while working with its allies in a space supremacy war.

The operation of international organizations also presents a variety of legal issues. In fact, most of the decisions made at the United Nations carry legal implications. Consider the resolution passed by the Security Council against North Korea or Iran. The United Nations' human rights bodies engage in the adoption of reports and the conduct of investigations, which encompass a multitude of legal implications. The ILO is responsible for the adoption and promotion of fundamental principles of international labor standards, as well as the examination of how individual states adhere to and implement these standards. The WTO oversees the administration of the multilateral trade regime where many legal issues proceed to its dispute settlement proceedings. Korea actively participates in all these

6 Espinola-Arredondo, A., & Munoz-Garcia, F., 2011, Free-riding in international environmental agreements: A signaling approach to non-enforceable treaties, *Journal of Theoretical Politics* 23(1) 111–134.

7 (i) the higher the return from the improved environmental quality resulting from the treaty; (ii) lower the commitment level that the agreement specifies to the follower; (iii) higher the commitment level that the leading country signs in the agreement; (iv) higher the probability that the leading country implements most of the commitments agreed to in the treaty; *ibid.* (investigator's underlining provided).

8 Milani, Carlos R.S., & Klein, M., 2021, Cooperative counter-hegemony, interregionalism and 'diminished multilateralism': The Belt and Road Initiative and China's relations with Latin America and the Caribbean, *Third World Quarterly* 42 2820.

organizations and engages in a diverse range of activities, resulting in an inevitable encounter with various legal issues.

Since 2020, the World Health Organization has emerged as the focal point for the global response to the COVID-19 pandemic. Its primary emphasis has been on verifying cases and gathering data, as well as providing governments with statistics and health recommendations. While these are undoubtedly crucial, they do not fully meet the requirements for assuming a prominent position in a global undertaking that entails complex legal and policy aspects. There has been a lack of a readily available comprehensive manual for governments to consult during a global health crisis. The absence of a systematic approach implies that each government operates independently, leading to varying levels of success among them. In an interconnected world, the consequences of misguided decisions made by a single government are likely to be felt by the entire community. Indeed, the responsibility for ensuring health protection lies inherently with the national health authorities of each respective country. However, a crisis of such severity and magnitude cannot be resolved without close coordination and cooperation among states in a systematic and multidimensional manner.

Combatting IUU fishing has emerged as one of the top priorities of the international community for the past decade, spearheaded by UN's FAO and relevant NGOs. Regulating and punishing illegal fishing activities and corruption are indeed critical. They serve the public good. However, they have been pursued using the domestic laws of the territorial country, not the laws of another country. These new legislations by the EU and the US are targeting those in a foreign country for the conduct taking place in Korea, a classic instance of the extraterritorial application of domestic law. They can justify their domestic law referring to the minimal contact between them and the Korean entities and the conveyance of effect through such contact. It is not entirely clear, however, whether such a low level of effect is sufficient to mobilize the conventional effect doctrine. It is another legal question being triggered by deeper globalization. Recognized as a major contributor to the global depletion of fish stocks, IUU fishing has prompted a substantial international endeavor. The global community's sense of urgency motivated them to include this specific issue in the WTO's DDA negotiations as a key negotiation topic under the category of fisheries subsidies. The ISS has consistently been the focal point of these discussions and negotiations. It is particularly concerning to recall that Korea has been actively engaged in the fisheries subsidies' negotiations, expressing strong disapproval of IUU fishing. In light of the adverse publicity and humiliation associated with IUU fishing activities, the Korean Ministry of Oceans and Fisheries has made efforts to promptly address the issue. Setting aside the negative publicity, it can also lead to a serious trade ban or other types of restriction. More importantly, other vigilant countries will also take similar measures unless Korea takes quick remedial action. While the effort to deter the IUU activities should be enhanced, one country's adoption and enforcement of unilateral legislation against other countries together with significant economic sanctions based on its own judgment raises the issue of the extraterritorial application of domestic law, which may be in contravention of international law principles.

Laws of another country are sometimes applied to those living in Korea. This is called the extraterritorial application of domestic law, and usually creates diplomatic tensions. When certain conditions are met, this kind of extraterritorial application of one country's domestic law to corporations and individuals residing in a foreign country is permitted. The legal standard is whether the applying country has a sufficient legal nexus with those foreign corporations and individuals such that application of domestic law beyond the territorial limit and into the foreign territory is justified. The legal nexus here means the existence of "effect." This concept thus is called the "effect doctrine." The conduct of the foreign corporation and individual should have exerted an effect on the law applying country. The problem is that effect is now almost omnipresent—few activities would have no effect on other countries because we are now living in a closely linked global community. This means that the effect doctrine would give nexus in many instances, which in turn means that countries can more easily exercise the extraterritorial application of domestic law than before. Tensions are bound to increase. So are disputes.

When the international community is in chaos as conflicts between nations grow, the importance of norms that regulate them becomes more evident. Though we are in the aftermath of World War II, we are facing the most serious international crisis. Wars are raging in Europe and the Middle East, and the possibility of new wars breaking out elsewhere is growing. Camps are centered around the US, EU, and Japan, and Russia. The camps centered around China have split into separate factions, entering a new Cold War era. The conflict between developed and developing countries shows no signs of abating. Even among developing countries, the positions of those countries that exert international influence and the least developed countries are gradually diverging.

Global warming due to climate change is accelerating, causing unprecedented natural disasters and environmental changes all over the world. I am experiencing it. In addition, as global warming progresses, the North and South Poles are providing new opportunities and challenges, and competition between countries surrounding them has entered a new phase. The international economic system has also entered a phase of readjustment. International trade, which was centered around the WTO and ICSID, the international investment regime is undergoing a review of its fundamental principles. A pandemic unprecedented in modern times has swept the world. It's been four years, but the after-effects still remain. It is difficult to predict when a new form of pandemic will emerge in the future and have a similar impact. AI is rapidly penetrating our lives, creating new industries, new forms of exchange, a new basis for conflict, new society. A new armed conflict is unfolding all around us. In the area where AI is operated, there are many questions surrounding who is responsible. Since a system, not a "human" system, is taking over the decisions and activities that were originally made by "humans," the issue of legal responsibility is bound to continue. Climate change due to global warming has emerged as the greatest threat to humanity. Natural disasters are already occurring in many parts of the world due to various weather changes brought about by climate change. Our country is also experiencing heavy rain and seasonal changes. Pacific island nations and Caribbean countries are facing threats to their very existence from rising sea levels. If the international community fails to properly implement its plan to achieve carbon neutrality by 2050, the international community will face a truly great crisis.

The private space industry started by Elon Musk has finally led countries to take action, and now space is changing from an unknown object of exploration to an object of development. As economic interests and national interests are at stake, competition among countries surrounding this issue is also becoming more intense. A new player has emerged in the armed conflict. Private military organizations, such as the Wagner Group in Russia, are directly participating in armed conflicts on behalf of or in alliance with states in many places through the outsourcing of military power, which is the core of national sovereignty. Such commercialization is a phenomenon that was unthinkable in the past. It is not simply a matter of hiring mercenaries, but if the core of state power can be delegated to the private sector, it raises fundamental questions about what the boundary between the state and non-state actors is and how state and non-state actions are distinguished. The essence of international law as a norm applicable to the actions of states is being questioned.

However, international norms applicable to these various new phenomena are inadequate in many ways. There are existing norms, but they are already outdated or contain content that is disconnected from reality. Even in newly developing areas, norms themselves do not yet exist. Cars appeared before roads were built. In a situation where road traffic laws and traffic lights were not prepared, cars were driving at higher speeds. The potential for contact and conflict is growing. Despite this reality, the work of upgrading existing international norms and forming new norms is progressing slowly. It is difficult to form a consensus among countries, and international organizations that should lead this are only eager to maintain the status quo and are lack the drive and motivation to overcome these difficult situations. The limitations and problems of international organizations were evident in the WHO during the pandemic, and in the WTO during the trade dispute. I came to realize the role of the UN through my experience of armed conflict. Even when the international community is in crisis, it is difficult to expect international organizations to play a meaningful role. This has become an opportunity to reexamine the rights and obligations of the 197 sovereign states that make up the international community and the various international organizations they constitute.

As international norms have not been established, international courts and arbitration procedures that apply them to resolve disputes are also facing significant difficulties. In a situation where the norm is ambiguous, the process of applying it and drawing a conclusion is also bound to be difficult in many ways. It is only natural that if the legislative process is not properly implemented, it will be difficult for the judicial process to operate smoothly. Recently, there have been cases where existing judicial procedures have been virtually paralyzed, and various proposals to introduce new judicial procedures are being discussed. Judicial procedures are also being re-evaluated. It has entered the readjustment phase. As such, the international community is now facing a great crisis. Both the substantive and procedural norms applicable to this situation face difficult situations. In order to overcome the current difficulties and avoid a return to the period of large-scale armed conflicts of the past, the international community must once again recall the principle of the "rule of law" and restore it in various areas. The principle of the rule of law, which has been developed over the past 78 years since the launch of the UN system, is now facing a major challenge. If we can successfully overcome the current challenges and demonstrate the resilience of the rule of law, confidence in it among many countries will be strengthened. After the rain, the ground will become harder. Conversely, if this work is not carried out properly, the experience of the past 78 years will become an exceptional phenomenon in human history. It will be clearly established that the international community is a society ruled by the law of the jungle. If that is the case, the future of the international community cannot be anything but bleak.

It is for this very reason, paradoxically, that the present difficulties and confusion are actually a reflection of the importance of international law and the peaceful resolution of international disputes. It once again demonstrates the importance of the rule of law in offering leadership. In the context of understanding international legal norms accurately and the practical application cases, it is more important than ever to clearly recognize its contributions and limitations at this point. Only by knowing the present can you compare it to the past and plan for the future. We must continue to develop and continue the achievements of the existing international legal norms, while at the same time we must identify the causes of the problems and limitations that have been identified and seek new attempts to improve them. In this respect, the study of international law is now more necessary and important than ever. This is especially true for our country, which has achieved growth and prosperity through the multilateral system and peace in the international community. I hope that the younger generations of our country will recognize the importance of international law and devote themselves to studying it, realizing that international law is a living legal norm that is always at work in our daily lives. And through this, we sincerely hope that our young generation, equipped with international legal skills and insight, will participate in international activities and competitions in various fields.

1. Law on the Return of Artifacts

One of the current issues that arouses a heated emotional response from the people involved is the repatriation of cultural properties to their countries of origin. The issue attracted global attention when the Metropolitan Museum of Art in New York decided to return to Turkey, after a lengthy legal battle, the so-called Lydian Hoard, which comprises 363 jewels and artifacts from the 7th century B.C. Presently, there are many pending disputes between the originating states and museums and states that own artifacts. Originating countries make such strenuous efforts because cultural artifacts are considered to represent the formation of national or ethnical identity.

If cultural artifacts represent national identity, each and every item is important and perhaps needs to be returned. In fact, however, there are two distinct groups of cultural properties located outside the originating states: those forcefully or illegally removed from the place of origination, sometimes by colonial powers or private looters, and those removed through legitimate transactions. Regarding the latter category, the only way to bring the cultural property back home is by repurchase, lease, rent or donation by the owner. Obviously, all of these options are decisions to be made by the owner.

The biggest problem is the first category of illegal removal. This usually involves forceful removal by colonial powers or illegal excavation by looters, followed by sale in the international black market. This category has been the subject of international discussions (the Lydian Hoard also falls under this category) and led to the adoption of relevant international conventions. They are the 1970 UNESCO Convention and 1995 UNIDROIT Convention.

These international conventions, however, have their own inherent limitations. As with any other convention, they are only applicable prospectively—only activities or transactions which took place after 1970 or 1995 respectively are covered. As Korea's own experience shows, most forceful transfers and illegal smuggling predate those dates. Also, as with any other convention, they are binding only on those countries that have acceded to them. So, this means that the remedy for the first category of cultural artifacts is not so effective either and that consequently the solution or repatriation also depends on voluntary cooperation from the owner or owning country.

So, from a practical perspective, there is almost no legal way of prying open the treasure box of cultural artifacts in countless countries, regardless of the circumstances that brought the artifacts in question there. Maybe this could explain why it is so difficult and time-consuming to bring lost Korean cultural artifacts back to Korea.

Given this reality, a more effective approach for the country trying to retrieve its cultural artifacts would be to convince the owning countries or entities (such as museums) of why the artifacts constitute the underpinnings of the national identity and why, more importantly, it would benefit them to help return the artifacts back to the original owner. The first explanation would be relatively easy, but the second would not. The originating country would have to develop a persuasive logic. Maybe it could explain that the returning country would benefit long-term benefit from the enhanced friendship fostered by the symbolic transfer. In fact, this is what happened to the countries and museums that have returned artifacts to originating countries recently.

The originating state could also discuss other mundane benefits. Examples would include cultural exchange programs, joint exhibition projects, joint research projects, or joint rental and lease programs between the museums or academic institutions of the two countries. As foreign museums have their own interest as institutes, it seems important to have them realize the actual benefits of returning artifacts.

Cultural property repatriation has been one of the controversial issues in the global community, sometimes inviting a great deal of national attention and emotion. This is also an area where one can observe a significant gap in opinion between the owning country and the originating country. As the legal norms are not sufficiently detailed enough in this area to adequately address the embarrassment of peoples whose national treasures were rooted out and are being displayed in foreign countries, a lot depends on voluntary cooperation from the owning countries and entities. The key then is how to introduce an international scheme to facilitate such cooperation. This seems to be the next critical project for the UNESCO.

[The Korea Herald, October 5, 2010]

2. Fast and Steady Wins the Race

On my recent trip overseas, I conducted a small experiment. I timed my entire time spent at the Incheon International Airport. As for the outbound trip, it took roughly 30 minutes from arrival at the airport to standing in front of the departing gate. The processing time for that segment of the inbound trip was even shorter: it was approximately 25 minutes from the airplane to the waiting line for the bus for downtown Seoul.

My personal experience virtually corresponds to the average time for the processing at Incheon Airport, as reported in a recent survey conducted by Airport Council International, which in May 2010 crowned the airport as the best of its kind in the world for the fifth consecutive year. This is almost a half of the average time spent at major airports in the world. ICN, the international code for the airport, is indeed another way of saying efficiency and speed.

Arguably this outstanding achievement for the nine-year-old airport reflects the two unique traits of Korea: the "hurry-up" spirit and the information technology infrastructure. As is well known, the hurry-up spirit represents the Korean mentality and is apparently deeply rooted in our national genes. Everything is fast and quick in Korea. We Koreans cannot stand slow processing in any context. At the same time, the IT infrastructure has seeped into every alley of this densely populated country.

These traits have led to Korea having the fastest and widest broadband internet connection rates, as praised by the OECD reports each year. According to the 2009 OECD statistics, 95 percent of Koreans have high-speed internet connections, compared to 65 percent in the United States. Viewed from this angle, no wonder Incheon airport is destined to lead the world in all categories of processing time.

Interestingly, the success of Incheon International Airport is exactly what the international community has been trying to achieve through reforms and adjustment of respective countries' import and export administration. In the eyes of the international community, streamlined processing is not simply a matter of mental satisfaction, it means lowering invisible barriers for the global transaction of goods and services. According to the 2002 OECD report, delays at the border for customs processing lead to as much as 15 percent additional cost for the ultimate transaction. Put differently, the same product may have a 15 percent more expensive depending on the processing system that is in place in a particular country. Indeed, time is money in the global economic regime. Prompted by this awareness, some countries started to lodge complaints about the slow pace of the customs processing of their trading partners, which in turn has put this very issue in the discussion or negotiating tables of all major international economic entities, such as the OECD, APEC, and the WTO in the name of "trade facilitation."

If trade facilitation is such an important issue, the ICN experience may be used as a beacon to streamline and expedite relevant import and export proceedings in other areas. If anything, the success of Incheon International Airport may offer the glimpse of Korea's potential in expediting the import and export procedures. If properly done, this effort may solidify, in a more visible manner, Korea's commitment to free trade and abolishment of trade barriers. "Slow and steady wins the race" may be a good maxim for teaching the virtue of patience. But it is "fast and steady" that wins the race in the global economic competition.

In a couple of days, the ICN will be crowded with the delegations from the G20. Rough calculation estimates that almost 1,000 VIPs are arriving and departing through the airport during the event. Arguably, this offers a rare opportunity to let these important visitors experience the airport firsthand and to form their own judgment on the airport as the face of Korea. Hopefully, the positive experience at the gate will also lead them to take another look at the potential that Korea possesses in the area of trade facilitation in particular, and its commitment to free trade in general.

[The Korea Herald, November 8, 2010]

3. A New Paradigm for Effective Aid

Ronald Reagan once quipped that the most terrifying words in the English language are "I'm from the government and I'm here to help." Indeed, well-intended but disorganized, bureaucratic help that does not fully take into account the real needs of a recipient may actually do more harm than good. Providing what the recipient badly needs is the key to helping someone in its truest sense. "Knowledge donations" that we see more often in Korea these days, where professionals and experts share their knowledge and experience with children from needy families, is one of such way to provide what the recipients actually want and what can actually change them. An international version of this effort has been garnering increasing attention.

The Knowledge Sharing Program is a project initiated by the Korean government in 2004, in response to the increasing demand from developing countries for Korea's unique experience of economic development in a short timeframe. Developing countries standing at the doorstep of economic development covet the trial and error of Korea in the course of planning and implementing its economic development projects. What they want is some tangible advice that can be adapted to their destitute situations instead of noble preaching on economic development theories. The experience from well-to-do, developed countries, although certainly helpful, may have sounded too remote to them. Since 2004, 25 countries have participated in the KSP projects and the reactions from the recipient countries have been largely positive. Korea's provision of financial support in official development assistance, or ODA, has also been increasing over the years, expected to reach $3 billion by 2015, but the most popular item in Korea's ODA list has always been "experience sharing."

From the perspective of the recipient countries, another area in which they are anxious to see some positive movement is the engagement of private entities in the global ODA architecture. The sets of skills and knowhow from the governmental sector of donor countries are no match for those available from the private entities. At the same time, we now live in a world where sometimes multinational corporations exert more influence in the international community than states do. It is against this backdrop that the United Nations has made efforts, since 2000, to engage private entities under the initiative called the UN Global Compact. In the setting of the ODA, the developing countries look forward to seeing the global private sector scale up its engagement by forming, for instance, public-private partnerships. The remaining question is what incentives should be given to the private entities for their participation.

These are one of the main topics on the agenda of the Fourth High Level Forum on Aid Effectiveness, currently taking place at BEXCO in Busan between Nov. 29 and Dec. 1, with the attendance of 2,000 high-level representatives from 160 countries. The HLF-4, as is widely called, succeeds the three previous meetings in Rome (2003), Paris (2005), and Accra, Ghana (2008). In 2010, the global ODA reached a record-setting $129 billion, but it is still questionable whether the ODA is indeed meeting the needs of the developing countries in an effective manner. This is the issue presented to the participants of the HLF-4 in Busan.

Genuine and probably the best ODA may come from ensuring a meaningful opportunity for developing countries to climb up the ladder of economic development. "Kicking away the ladder" by those who are already at the roof (to borrow the title of the book by Professor Ha-Joon Chang) would deprive those on the ground of any chance of reaching the top or anywhere near it. Without addressing this problem, merely handing out some charity items to those on the ground would have limited impact only. In the face of continuing economic slowdown, the relatively well-to-do countries would feel persistent temptation to kick away the ladder in the form of protectionism and other selfish measures.

At this juncture, the HLF-4 is a timely global gathering to tap into collective wisdom to adopt a new global paradigm for aid effectiveness. Hopefully, the new Busan paradigm will ensure to push the developing countries up the ladder while those at the top hold the upper end of the ladder for the new climbers.

[The Korea Herald, December 1, 2011]

4. A Bumpy Road for the GGGI

Few Seoulites are aware that the city hosts an intergovernmental "international organization." The International Vaccine Institute under the United Nations Development Programme, situated near Seoul National University since May 1997, is the first and the only international organization headquartered in Korea. Now, it is time for a second one—the Global Green Growth Institute.

Since its founding in June 2010 by the strong initiative of Korea, the GGGI has been a nonprofit think tank located in Seoul (in Jeongdong, more precisely), whose mandate is to do everything "green," by promoting an economic model of green growth as a pathway to sustainable development.

The think tank is now on the verge of becoming the second international organization headquartered in Korea as Kiribati deposited its instrument of ratification. According to the constituent treaty, the Agreement on the Establishment of the GGGI signed in June 2012 by 17 countries, this coming Oct. 18 will be the birth date of this new international organization.

Everything is right on schedule, except that it is not clear when the hosting country Korea can complete its domestic ratification procedure at the National Assembly and submit its own instrument of ratification. Embarrassing would be the only word to describe the situation where nobody knows for sure when Korea is officially joining this global body of its own making, which already exists on its own soil.

It is all bad timing. As the race for the December presidential election heats up each day, and the confrontation between political factions intensifies, a critical mass seems to be hard to form in the National Assembly to finalize one of the signature projects of the current administration. But this global initiative is too important to be put into the domestic political mix.

With just two weeks to go before the creation of the international organization and with every country watching, we simply don't have the luxury of putting this on the back burner. Ratification should be completed as soon as possible, and the entity should be left to run its business.

The fact of the matter is a long "to-do" list is waiting for Korea as a host country of an international organization. A follow-up bilateral agreement between the new international organization and Korea may be necessary to deal with such issues as the legal status of the entity in Korea and extension of diplomatic immunities and privileges to the staff. All these follow-up steps will be delayed until Korea completes its domestic procedure. The longer the delay is, the higher the level of embarrassment is. Seoul would have to watch hard-won leadership in this particular area since June 2010 slip through its fingers.

There are treaties which may carry political implications and stoke domestic debates. Ratification of these treaties should inevitably take a long time. However, there are also treaties for which national consensus is already there. It is this latter category that green growth belongs to.

More important, if the launch of the international organization in October is somehow less than optimal, Seoul's chances of becoming a serious contender for a future international organization will be virtually gone. On the other hand, given the mounting global attention to green growth, a successful launch of this particular entity in Seoul will perhaps become the first step to make the city the hub of green endeavors of the future.

Establishing the GGGI as an international organization is the culmination of the three years' hard work. Barring compelling reasons, the ratification should be done promptly, so that Korea can live up to its promises made to the international community.

[The Korea Herald, October 3, 2012]

5. Time to Eradicate IUU Fishing

While largely unnoticed under the stack of North Korea-related news, an alarming and embarrassing report has been released. The National Oceanic and Atmospheric Administration of the US Department of Commerce submitted its 2013 report to US Congress, in which it had designated ten countries as having engaged in IUU fishing activities: Colombia, Ecuador, Ghana, Italy, Mexico, Panama, Spain, Tanzania, Venezuela, and South Korea.

IUU is an acronym for Illegal, Unreported, and Unregulated fishing activities that occur in contravention of the domestic laws and regulation and international guidelines. In other words, the ten countries in the report are identified as those that are not sufficiently regulating illegal fishing activities conducted by their own nationals and vessels. A potential trade ban against fish stocks from these countries is also being mentioned in the report unless concrete measures are taken by these countries within the next two years.

The fact that Korea is the only country in the list from East Asia further embarrasses us—neither China nor Taiwan nor Japan is included in the list although they largely share similar fishing patterns and maritime policies. Likewise, the EU has also registered its concern over Korea's IUU fishing. So have various NGOs.

As a matter of fact, in the global fisheries community, nothing could carry a more negative connotation than the term "IUU." It has been one of the top priorities of the UN's FAO, and a significant global effort has been mobilized recently because it has been found to be one of the major culprits of the global depletion of fish stocks: the FAO statistics show that almost 30 percent of global fish catch is done through IUU fishing.

Now, the depletion of fish stocks has become an urgent global issue. Under the current pace of global fishing, the FAO warns that quite a few fish stocks will disappear in the next couple of decades: as of 2008, one out of three fish stocks are regarded as over-exploited, meaning that they are going down the path of depletion.

This sense of urgency also led the global community to include this very issue in the WTO's DDA negotiations as one of the key negotiation topics, under the theme of fisheries subsidies. And, again, the IUU has been at the center of all these discussions and negotiations. It is all the more troubling to remember that Korea has been one of the most active participants in the fisheries subsidies' negotiations, with its vocal criticism of IUU fishing.

Furthermore, IUU fishing has been criticized in terms of the "development" aspect as well. Foreign vessels' destructive fishing activities with drag nets along the coastal seas of small island states or impoverished countries have been regarded as taking away a critical means of livelihood from them. No wonder least-developed countries have long complained about the IUU vessels flocking their coastal waters to pillage marine resources.

Having realized the negative publicity and embarrassment associated with the IUU fishing activities, the Ministry of Oceans and Fisheries, one of the new ministries created under the new administration, has attempted to respond promptly. It has just issued several policy plans, including proposals to amend relevant statutes to increase penalties for violators. Explanatory materials are also being circulated by the ministry.

Upon careful reading of the report, however, one would realize that the foreign criticism of Korea does not lie in the laws and regulations. Rather, the core problem raised by the foreign watchers relates to the lack of "effective" enforcement of the laws and regulations in force.

As with anything, this can only be achieved through strong willingness of the agency in charge and its officials, with clear policy determination to enforce the laws and regulations as best as they can, so as to eradicate the IUU. One of the best justifications for the resurrection of the new maritime ministry will be to take a serious first step in this direction.

Korea's inclusion in the US list of countries conducting illegal fishing activities with nine other states is both embarrassing and alarming. Negative publicity aside, it can also lead to a serious trade ban or other types of restriction. More importantly, other watchful countries may follow suit, unless quick remedial action is taken by Korea.

[The Korea Herald, April 17, 2013]

6. Greenpeace's "Nuclear Emergency" Campaign in Seoul

The summer has just begun, but many people are dreading the thought of surviving the heat of July and August. In the face of the worst-ever electricity shortages, the government is imposing a nationwide electricity usage reduction regulation. Air-conditioners are turned off while coolbiz clothing is being praised everywhere.

The painful summer of 2013 is the outcome of the unexpected suspension of operation of several nuclear power generators in Korea because of various untoward reasons. In a country where at least one-third of the national power comes from nuclear generators, disruption of nuclear electricity generation delivers a critical blow to the national economy.

A national "blackout" has become a constant threat this summer. In the country's long-term scheme for the stable supply of electricity, nuclear power plants play an important role.

Well, according to Greenpeace Korea, this is going in the wrong direction. It says it is high time that the country considered phasing out its reliance on nuclear power. The Rainbow Warrior of Greenpeace is now visiting Korean ports for the first time in an effort to mount a campaign called "Nuclear Emergency," in which nuclear energy is replaced by other renewable energy such as wind or solar power. Its policy recommendation suggests that Korea shut down all nuclear power plants by 2030.

Given the plea of manufacturing industries for a more stable supply of electricity to sustain their business activities, any recommendation to move to a new source of energy would only be plausible when this new source is confirmed to be able to meet the demand.

While there has been significant development in the renewable energy sector, it is still an open question whether and when renewable energy can indeed replace the current sources of electricity. While some countries have announced an end to their nuclear energy program (such as Germany in 2011), few of them seem to experience chronic shortages of electricity like Korea.

In response to the difficulty of changing to renewable energy sources, it is being argued that countries with technological capabilities have an obligation to spend more time and resources to develop new types of energy. Greenpeace submits that more research and development support from the government would enable Korea to reach the point where it can ditch the nuclear power option.

While these are all valid points in principle, again it still remains anyone's guess when such efforts will lead to commercially viable alternatives. Suggestions to spend more time and money by the government are also oblivious of the global legal framework which stringently regulates government-initiated research and development activities.

Several countries' effort to support renewable energy development has already produced a series of legal disputes in many fronts. The mere suggestion to spend more time and money for this noble cause without being apprised of the full spectrum of implications may not be able to provide a viable solution, although it will certainly raise the level of the global awareness.

The advice and policy suggestions of Greenpeace are both crucial and important for Korea at this juncture. It is also timely considering the growing concern over the long-term safety of the nuclear power. But merely recommending the suspension of nuclear energy in the absence of a concrete and reliable alternative will sound hollow to those who have to turn off half of the lights in the office, pull the plug on the air conditioners, and reduce the operating hours of production facilities in summer 2013.

[The Korea Herald, July 10, 2013]

7. Korea and Illegal Fishing

The European Union's preliminary designation of Korea as a country failing to meet its international obligation to fight illegal, unreported, and unregulated (IUU) fishing is an embarrassing development. Although at this time this is meant to be a warning signal only from the EU to push Korea to take remedial action as quickly as possible, it is also probable that the warning turns into an official designation in the future, which may lead to the import ban by the EU of the fisheries products from Korea. Given the global stigma associated with IUU fishing, the EU's recent designation of Korea as such raises a flag that a serious action needs to be taken domestically.

This is yet another dent to the image of the country, after the United States' similar designation of Korea in January this year. With "yellow cards" from the two major countries, Korea's position in the international forums discussing this issue will become more precarious: combatting IUU has been one of the top priorities of the international community for the past decade, spearheaded by FAO and relevant NGOs. As previously noted in this column after the US designation, the IUU fishing has been criticized by the world community for a long time because of its devastating effect on global fish stocks. It is indeed alarming that both countries, in the same year, have designated Korea as an IUU-prone country.

Korea hurriedly amended its law (Ocean Industries Development Act) in July as a preemptive measure against a likely EU designation, but it apparently did not work. The core criticism from the EU is that Korea has not fulfilled the international obligation to require its vessels to install a device called a vessel monitoring system, which tracks the location and activity of vessels engaging in fishing activities in the high seas. The amendment becomes effective as of Jan. 31, but the mandatory installment of the VMS has been deferred until July 30, 2014. Reportedly, this deferral has been the main reason that prompted the EU's inclusion of Korea on the IUU country list.

Korea's slow implementation of VMS requirements is indeed noteworthy considering the intensity of international attention to this very matter. The nature of the equipment being discussed makes the slow implementation more perplexing. VMS is a readily available electronic tracking device costing $3,000 to $5,000 per ship. Foreign observers who know Korea as a country saturated and obsessed with information technology would find it puzzling that the country is dragging its foot in installing this particular type of maritime electronic device. Korea's slow implementation of this simple requirement can hardly find good excuses.

The IUU activity is a global problem. It is taking place in many countries—that is why a global undertaking is called for in the first place. Questions are thus being raised if "singling out" Korea has been somehow motivated by an ulterior motive. Competition is intense between Korean vessels and European fishermen in seas off West Africa, where illegal fishing poses a peculiar problem because of its massive scale. Critics argue that the EU's specific interest as well as an environmental concern may have been reflected in blacklisting Korea.

In any event, just how much emphasis some countries put on this particular issue when they deal with Korea is evidenced by the report that the United States is going to raise fishery subsidies—of which IUU is the core component—as one of the key outstanding issues to be discussed with Korea in advance in the context of Korea's participation in the TPP negotiations. To Korea, then, addressing this issue almost becomes a membership fee for the mega-FTA. This means that this issue will stay with us next year and perhaps for many more years.

As many of us know, the best way to save Korea from any further embarrassment and to avoid other countries' using this as a card against Korea is to implement these international obligations as promptly as possible. Korea is already paying a high price.

[The Korea Herald, December 26, 2013]

8. Korea Exits Fishing Blacklist

One sticky issue that has haunted Korea for the past two years is now being put to rest. Almost simultaneously, Washington and Brussels are scratching off Korea from the list of illegal, unreported, and unregulated fishing countries.

Since the designation was made in 2013, a pan-governmental scramble has been on to delist Korea. And these frantic efforts are now paying off. Remaining on the list would have meant import restrictions for fisheries products and port visit restrictions for Korean-flagged vessels, both of which would be an unbearable penalty for the country.

Even more damaging would have been the tarnished image as a country condoning illegal fishing, by far a No. 1 culprit for global fishing stock depletion.

In accordance with the requests from the two countries, Korea's Ocean Industries Development Act has been amended twice so that strong penalties are now imposed on fishermen who break the rules.

The Vessel Monitoring System has become mandatory, and fisheries monitoring centers have been set up. Starting from July this year, criminal sanction will become hasher for violators—punishable with imprisonment of up to five years or a minimum fine of 500 million won ($450,000).

In exchange for this statutory change, Korea is now being taken off the list.

The fault, of course, is Korea's own. Korea has been slow to respond to the growing demands of the international community to regulate illegal fishing activities. Loose statutes had loopholes. Its vessels were caught fishing illegal off the coast of West Africa. It was only after Korea was put on the list of illegal fishing countries that it realized the seismic consequences of the designation.

To cut a long story short, the two countries' joint push has herded Korea in the right direction. Good medicine is always bitter.

On a separate note, it is unfortunate that import restrictions and port visit prohibitions—actions themselves arguably in contravention of obligations under various international treaties—have been proposed by these countries to pile on the pressure.

Unilateral sanction, if imposed, would hardly survive the tightly knit web of treaties these days, including free trade agreements. But the legalese has been overshadowed by the mounting consensus on the need to do whatever it takes to curb illegal fishing. At any rate, the problem has been resolved and everybody is happy now.

In retrospect, the warning signs had been there for some time. If actions to counter illegal fishing had been taken earlier, Korea would not have found itself on the list in the first place. Efforts and political capital could have been spared. Taking action only in the face of sanctions was poor behavior.

This hard-earned lesson should guide Korea to take a more active approach on the issue of sustainable fishing. Illegal fishing is not the end of the story, but just one of the many pending issues of the global discourse of sustainable fishing. The illegal fishing regulation was the easiest target of all these. Many more will be brought up soon in different forms through different forums. Not only enhanced criminal sanctions but also termination of governmental support for the fishing industry and fishermen is seriously being contemplated.

The global fishing regulations are going through a big change and require governments to carry out many new tasks. In light of this, the two-year saga was a shot in the arm. This should be the first step for Korea to spend more time and resources to ensure responsible fishing activities within its jurisdiction.

Sustainable fishing is needed for our benefit and for that of our fishermen. Over the Lunar New Year holiday, KBS broadcast a documentary showing the efforts of Korean fishermen in coastal villages to detect and deter illegal fishing on their own to preserve the fish stocks in their waters. They do not know the scientific, diplomatic, or legal discussions surrounding illegal fishing activities, but they do know that this is the only way to preserve the fish stocks for themselves and for the next generation.

[The Korea Herald, March 11, 2015]

9. Our Ocean, Our Future

While not well known in South Korea, the Our Ocean conference was held on Thursday and Friday in Washington where representatives from almost 90 counties presented a vivid account of the current status of the global marine environment.

This was the largest meeting aimed at discussing conservation of the marine environment and the depleting fish stocks. It showed why global action is needed immediately.

For the past several decades, numerous suggestions have been made and projects undertaken in order to conserve the marine environment and ensure sustainable fisheries. Unfortunately, none of them have worked to our satisfaction.

The increasing water temperature from global warming is taking a direct toll on our oceans—last month Korea suffered from its first cholera outbreak in 15 years due to the hot water temperature.

Business entities are keen not to miss out on profit-making opportunities through offshore drilling and seabed excavation. Governments are providing harmful subsidies to their fishing industries as robustly as ever.

As a consequence, the marine environment has been steadily deteriorating for the past several decades, and there is hardly any sign of it turning around. The most recent data from the UN Food and Agriculture Organization predicts that 29 percent of the global fish species are on the verge of disappearing if the current pace of fishing is maintained. In other words, the next generation will not see one out of three fish species that we see and eat today.

Having seen a dismal failure of all the previous efforts, we may find the newest alternative approach to deal with the urgency of the problem both creative and innovative. This new alternative is to designate a certain marine area as a conservation block and prohibit human activities in the area, whether drilling, excavation, or fishing. This is just like a national park in the mountains that we have now, where development and exploitation are prohibited.

The idea behind the proposal is that sea life can find a haven in the protected area, so that various species can maintain their reproductive cycle and thrive. This is an ocean version of wildlife conservation zones in Africa, so to speak.

This new alternative approach was proposed and adopted by the United States. At Our Ocean conference last week, President Obama designated certain areas of the Atlantic Ocean off the New England coast consisting of some 12,700 square kilometers within the US Exclusive Economic Zone as "marine monument." This designation prohibits commercial fishing and oil and gas excavation projects in the area.

Granted, some countries have designated coastal conservation areas with various titles, but these are mainly to preserve the scenic beauty of the marine landscapes along the coastlines. They are more geared toward tourism and local economy as opposed to conserving marine species or underwater environment per se. To the contrary, the newest proposal purports to designate a maritime pocket in the middle of the ocean for conservation purposes only. So, it can be said to be the first attempt of this kind.

The key question now is whether other countries will follow suit. If other countries adopt this initiative and issue similar designations within their respective maritime jurisdiction, we will have multiple conservation pockets in the global oceans.

These sanctuaries will provide a new thriving ground for the endangered marine species. If we can get to that point, this new scheme may turn out to be one of the most effective ways to stop depletion and pencil in the first meaningful victory in the battle in several decades. Perhaps we will not be able to save all of the species for the next generation—it's already too late. But, with this, at least we can slow down the pace of depletion and reduce the number of species being made extinct.

[The Korea Herald, September 21, 2016]

10. The UN-Condemned Mandatory Medical Testing

Only her initials appear in the UN document, but we know she is a citizen of New Zealand. Her petition with a UN human rights body led to a finding of racial discrimination by Korea. She was one of the native English-speaking teachers working at a school in Korea.

Each year, about 30,000 foreigners enter Korea to teach English on an E-2 visa. According to Korean laws, regulations, and practices, these visa holders are required to take a medical examination, which includes a HIV/AIDS test, at a hospital designated by the government. The results are then submitted to the authorities before they are hired or renew their contract. The mandatory testing was introduced in December 2007.

As their contracts are usually one year, this means they have to undergo a medical examination each year. Interestingly, this requirement is applicable only to foreign nationals. Korean nationals and foreign nationals of Korean ethnicity are not subject to the medical examination. This issue has been criticized given the increasing rate of home-grown HIV contraction.

The testing scheme is twofold. Teachers employed by private study institutions are required to submit testing results according to laws and regulations. Those employed by the Ministry of Education and Local Education Administrations are not subject to laws and regulations, but they are still subject to "manuals" of these governmental agencies which demand submission of the same testing results.

Let's come back to the New Zealand teacher. She also taught English at a school in Ulsan under a contract with the Ulsan Metropolitan Office of Education since 2008. When her contract was up for renewal in 2009, she refused to comply with HIV/AIDS testing requirements. She said it was discrimination based on national origin and race because the testing is only required for foreign nationals. Her contract was not renewed.

She filed a petition with the National Human Rights Commission of Korea, which dismissed the complaint six months later for lack of specificity. The arbitration proceeding at the Korean Commercial Arbitration Board didn't fare well either. In December 2012, she filed a petition with the UN Committee on the Elimination of Racial Discrimination against Korea under the UN Convention on the Elimination of All Forms of Racial Discrimination to which Korea is a state party.

She claimed that she was a victim of racial discrimination and that her right to work and right to public health had been breached by Korea.

The UN deliberation is not a judicial proceeding, but its repercussion is not insignificant at all. Decisions are published and widely available through UN documents. The decision for this particular petition came in May 2015, where the UN committee found that the mandatory testing requirement discriminates against the petitioner's fundamental right and recommended Korea to repeal laws, regulations, and practices relating to the measure. The recommended remedial action has not taken place yet. So, even today those applying for an E-2 visa still have to get tested for HIV/AIDS. This past September, apparently dismayed by the government's inaction, the National Human Rights Commission issued its own recommendation to the government to bring the measure into conformity with the UN recommendation.

More than anything else, the decision of the UN committee shows how this test requirement is viewed outside Korea. The decision noted that the testing is carried out "on the basis of ethnic origin." It also found that the mandatory testing requirement is "in contradiction of international standards" and that it is "ineffective for public health purposes, discriminatory, and harmful to the enjoyment of fundamental rights." Stereotyping, profiling, and stigmatizing are the three words that are repeated throughout the decision. It concluded that the measure constitutes racial discrimination. The committee required Korea to publicize the decision with a Korean translation.

By any measure, the recommendation is clear and straightforward. It is sad that Korea has been dragging its feet in amending this anachronistic law and practice.

[The Korea Herald, November 29, 2016]

11. Money Is Fungible

As a professor teaching international law I receive questions from people from time to time asking me whether UN Security Council resolutions are binding, that is whether they are "legally" binding. The answer to that question is yes. I figure that those questions and perhaps the misperception of UNSC resolutions partly come from the title itself—"resolution." In fact, many a resolution adopted domestically or internationally is not legally binding (unlike statutes or treaties), albeit politically and diplomatically important. In fact, many times they contain recommendations rather than legal obligations. But UNSC resolutions are not mere recommendations: they become legally binding on all members with the operation of specific obligation provisions contained in the UN Charter.

There are seven UNSC resolutions codifying sanctions against North Korea, with the most recent one adopted on June 2 this year (Resolution 2356). So, all UN members, South Korea included, are bound to abide by them. In particular, they prohibit financing for trade, technical cooperation, and maintenance of banking or insurance accounts with North Korea, which was one of the main reasons that prompted Seoul to close the Kaesong industrial complex in February 2016. The rather sudden closure reflected the success of the complex. At the height of the complex, both sides benefited from it: 124 SMEs from the South located in the complex enjoyed the supply of reliable, cheap labor and North Korea found a stable supply of hard currency.

Through 13 years of operation, $500 million was transferred to North Korea as compensation for North Korean labor and $1 billion as investment in the complex. With the steady increase of the level of sanctions, the logic that inter-Korea economic exchange projects should be an exception has gradually lost support from countries participating in the sanctions, ultimately leading to the complex's closure.

As the new administration seeks a policy change toward the North, the re-opening of Kaesong complex is slowly coming back to the national agenda. While the resurrection of the complex will certainly help diffuse tension in the peninsula, the first and foremost question is how to reconcile the plan with the specific legal obligation under a series of UNSC resolutions.

Several ideas are floated to find a way where direct provision of hard currency to North Korea, the core target of the sanctions, can be avoided: some suggest providing compensation directly to North Korean workers; others suggest provision of goods in kind to North Korean workers. First of all, these suggestions may not be feasible in the first place: it is hard to expect that the North Korean authorities will now permit its workers to receive money or goods directly from the South Korean employers, given its tight control over the employees in the past.

More fundamentally, even if direct payment is somehow made, if the payment or part of it ends up in the coffer of the North Korean government in whatever form, be it taxation or contribution or fund, chances are the provisions of the resolutions will be still implicated. The idea behind these economic sanctions is that "money is fungible."

It seems that one way to introduce a resolution-consistent economic exchange project is to accrue the wages in an escrow account and restrict its usage only to livelihood or humanitarian purposes of North Korea. A trustworthy guarantee needs to be ensured that hard currency or its variation is not available to the North Korean government, so as to be compatible with UN resolutions.

Perhaps in the new atmosphere of the renewed inter-Korea economic cooperation projects, the only logic seems to be again the old one, that South Korea is different. It may have worked in the past, but believing that others will still accept the Korea-exception may be much too speculative. It is not like Korea continuing with its existing cooperative projects as in the past; rather, the issue now is whether to permit South Korea to fall out of line in the North Korean sanctions.

Inter-Korea dialogue is important. There is no question about it. Economic cooperative projects constitute a critical component of such dialogue. But the UNSC resolutions specifically restrict many types of economic exchange activities, which also binds South Korea as a member of the UN.

[The Korea Herald, June 27, 2017]

12. A Whale of a Departure

It was 1986 when the international community agreed on a ban on "commercial whaling." Depleting whale stocks urged states to adopt an extraordinary measure. Except for the two states (Norway and Iceland), all whaling countries got on board. So started the ban and has been quite effective for 32 years. While controversy has persisted concerning what is "commercial whaling," which is banned, and what is "scientific whaling," which is not, overall the ban has successfully herded states in one direction. It has helped restore whale stocks.

The legal vehicle for this global regime is the International Convention for the Regulation of Whaling (ICRW), and the organization in charge is the International Whaling Commission (IWC). It is ICRW that created the IWC, so the two are integrally linked. There have been ups and downs, handshakes, and accusations, but the regime itself has been largely stable.

The global whaling regime suffered a major dent at the close of last year. A major whaling country, Japan, adopted on Dec. 26 a cabinet decision to withdraw from the ICRW (so, automatically from the IWC too). The withdrawal simply means Japan is now going to resume commercial whaling, freed from legal hindrance. Commercial whaling can start as early as the beginning of July 2019.

A key whaling country's departure from the ICRW is sending waves of concern across the globe. It is one thing to have different views and battle in an international organization, but another to quit it. The immediate concern is the impact on the conservation of whale species as a result of the resumption of commercial whaling. Very possibly, it will have a negative impact, to put it mildly, on the three decades of global efforts for restoration.

What is more concerning is a possible domino effect. The "broken window" theory would equally apply here. It is feared that other countries may follow suit, or at least they may be emboldened by the precedent. They may now have to face increasing demand from their domestic industries. Among those being mentioned as weak links are Russia and Korea, once active whaling countries. Dominos will then fall and knock over other countries and so on and so forth, opening a critical loophole in the ICRW/IWC regime. Utmost care and prudence should be taken by the global community lest it happens.

Japan's departure is major news for Korea too. Korea's once prosperous whaling industry along the southeastern port cities has since become extinct under the 1986 moratorium, which has been implemented by municipal law (Fisheries Act and Fisheries Resources Management Act). Japan's withdrawal and weakening the cohesiveness of the global consensus may well rekindle domestic debates on whaling, albeit cautiously. This should not be the case. Korea's long-term interest is only to be served, be it from the fisheries perspective or national image perspective, when Korea stays firm with the consensus-based global cause. And there is a strong global consensus for whale conservation.

Let's look back at 2012. At that time, following Japan, Korea proposed to conduct scientific whaling, only to withdraw the plan amid international criticism.

Let's also remember the continuing criticism and scrutiny from the NGOs about the high rate of whale bycatch in Korea. Bycatch whales are those caught during regular fishing of other fisheries products. They are exempt from the regulation of ICRW and thus from the Korean law. Each year the number of whales reported as caught this way is around 80–100 whales, a number higher than other countries. The suspicion from NGOs is that bycatch may have been purposeful, not accidental. In the absence of hard evidence, there is no knowing the causes of each bycatch. But, in any event, the truth is, Korea is already feeling a hard stare from the international community.

So, prudence is required at this crucial juncture of the global whaling regime. To Korea, what is absolutely necessary is the full and effective enforcement of the domestic law prohibiting commercial whaling, as mandated by ICRW. The experience of 2012 still resonates.

[The Korea Herald, January 8, 2019]

13. Greater Role as UNSC Member

Pointed statements were exchanged between Soviet Ambassador Andrei Gromyko and US Secretary of State James Byrnes at the first UN General Assembly meeting of Jan. 12, 1946. The touchy topic on the agenda was how to select six non-permanent members of the Security Council in compliance with the principle of "equitable geographical distribution" as agreed upon in the San Francisco Conference.

New Zealand was particularly vocal, fearing that the region of the South Pacific would not be adequately represented in any of the geographical segments, and suggested Australia be included in the mix. Australia, however, had to go through intense competition with Canada (three rounds of voting), a fellow British Commonwealth country, to grab the final seat. Brazil, Poland, Egypt, Mexico, the Netherlands, and Australia were those elected that afternoon to the Security Council as non-permanent members.

Ever since, the competition among countries to join the Security Council as non-permanent members with a two-year term has always been intense. Six non-permanent members together with the five fixture permanent members (possessing veto power) constituted the UN's executive body, so to speak. The membership subsequently increased to the current 15 in December 1963. For the ten seats, five countries are elected each year.

This year's competition in the Asia-Pacific Group to replace India, whose term expires at the end of the year, was among Korea, Bhutan, and Cambodia, with Korea prevailing after the second round of voting. Those elected with Korea on Oct. 19 at the UN General Assembly were Australia, Argentina, Rwanda, and Luxembourg. Korea's election to the UN body was for the second time after its participation in 1996–1997.

By all accounts, Korea's election this time around is all the more important than its first tour 17 years ago. Korea was still a newcomer: that was only five years after

Korea's accession to the UN in 1991. The situation in the world community was relatively stable after the Cold War. Seventeen intervening years have brought sea changes. Compared to the situation in 1996–1997, this time Korea is well-known and in a position to be able to contribute more to the cause of the Security Council.

For the next two years, it is quite likely that the Security Council will have to deal with a long list of controversial issues and volatile situations. In the face of the critical issues, different views are sometimes expressed by members of the council, and Korea could play a role to bridge the gap in these instances. In many respects, Korea is positioned to play such a "supportive role" in the discussions of global issues as shown in its participation in other fora.

Korea's prospective participation in the discussions on issues relating to North Korea is yet another reason the last week's election is meaningful. More so, given that the next two years will be a decisive period for the future inter-Korea relations under the new leaderships of the two Koreas.

Korea's joining of the Security Council also means a lot of homework to be done. As a member of the Security Council, Korea is expected to be more actively engaged in making and enforcing the decisions of the Security Council. It reminds us of the difficult juggling Korea has managed since 2011 with respect to the Security Council sanctions on Iran, a significant trade partner of Korea. More and more similar issues will come Korea's way. Seoul will also be put in a tight spot in the case of US-China confrontation on the council, say over the Syria issue. Korea should also more actively consider increasing its still lukewarm ODA package. Of course, more active participation in peacekeeping operations cannot be forgotten either. The news that the government is planning to increase the staff at its mission in New York is a welcoming beacon at the moment.

[The Korea Herald, November 5, 2012]

14. Cooperation from Bali to Bali

The problem of multilateral trade negotiations is that, increasingly, negotiators are confined to the mandates and directives of their governments, with little leeway at the negotiating tables. That is just natural: what they say will be transcribed into official documents and what they agree to will be put into treaty texts, which will remain legally binding until terminated. Under these circumstances, everything said and delivered should be tightly controlled.

To the contrary, a forum designed to discuss without producing any legally binding document or expecting any quid pro quo can facilitate more candid assessments and exchanges of views. That is exactly what the Asia-Pacific Economic Cooperation is all about. And it has worked.

The 21-member cooperative/consultative body has been dubbed "an incubator of innovative ideas." Flexible approaches and creative suggestions have been a hallmark of the APEC since its creation in 1989. These approaches and suggestions have then been transferred to a more rigid forum of multilateral negotiations, shifting the pendulum of global trade landscape one way or another.

After all, this is an entity whose collective economies account for 57 percent of the global GDP and 48 percent of the global trade.

It is Bali, Indonesia, that hosts this year's 21st APEC Summit Meeting from Oct. 6–8 amid mounting global attention, under the theme of "Resilient Asia-Pacific: Engine of Global Growth." The term "resilient" is said to have been chosen to signify the relatively stable performance of the APEC economies in the tailwinds of the global economic crisis.

In terms of trade, this year's APEC meeting is taking place at the most crucial juncture in the APEC's history since its adoption of Bogor Goals of 1994. It will be a precursor of what is coming up in the same place just two months later: the Ninth Ministerial Conference (MC9) of the WTO from Dec. 3 to 6. The MC9 in December will take up three core issues left on the table: trade facilitation, agriculture, and least-developed countries packages. The outcome of the MC9 will then be used as a crucial barometer to assess the current state of play of the multilateral trading system embodied in the WTO and the possibility to regalvanize it.

As all APEC economies are also members of the WTO taking up a significant portion of global trade, a message from the leaders next week in Bali may well affect, either positively or negatively, how the other 138 members will react in the run-up to the December meeting. Next week's meeting is a critical way station to revive the momentum to reach a deal on the multilateral front at long last. If, on the other hand, the APEC ends up paying only lip service to a multilateral trading regime and establishing mega-regional trade agreements of its own, the breakthrough in December would become that much difficult to attain.

In a sense, the December MC9 in Bali is a "road show" for a multilateral trading regime. Potential investors—countries and governments—will be all ears to check the long-term viability of the company while they check the prospects of another competing company of regional trade agreements. What the APEC members may say and choose at this juncture as opinion leaders in the market stand to affect other potential investors substantially.

The APEC should certainly take pride in its members' "resilience" for stable economic performance despite the continuing economic downturn. The more critical and important "resilience" that the APEC can show is the "resilience" for the support and success of the multilateralism that has framed the world we live in since 1947. The Bogor Goals of 1994 have set the tone for global trade and investment landscapes. Hopefully, 2013 will add another milestone to APEC's achievements.

[The Korea Herald, October 3, 2013]

15. Knowledge Sharing Program

It is remarkable to see the Knowledge Sharing Program (KSP) grow and expand.

This ODA program, jointly administered by the Ministry of Strategy and Finance and the Korea Development Institute, has suddenly become popular among developing countries, and requests to participate are piling up.

This is a program in which Korea "shares" its experience of economic development with developing countries: What is provided here is Korea's own experience since 1960s instead of products or grants. The program has produced as many as 450 projects covering 39 countries since its inception in 2004 for the projects concerning Vietnam and Uzbekistan.

Once a participating country is chosen, the MOSF and KDI organize a group of experts who can provide tailor-made advice and consultation for the country. Korea has earmarked $26 million for this year's projects.

It turns out that many developing countries wish to talk to Korea and learn from her economic development in a short period of time.

They are interested in learning from Korea's failures as well as successes, and setbacks as well as achievements. So, they tend to ask such questions as what Korea would have done differently, having gone through its economic development drive for the past five decades.

Some other countries also run similar programs for developing countries, but the KSP is unique in that it is from a country that has managed to achieve high-level of economic development from a position of poverty in the 1950s. Perhaps nothing would be more valuable to these developing countries than information straight from the horse's mouth, as opposed to grandiose economic theories.

Recent KSP programs have expanded to new areas. Demand is increasing for knowledge about Korea's legal structure and system, in an effort to see how Korea has changed and fine-tuned its laws and regulations during the period of fast economic development. Utilization of IT in the governmental administration and national development is yet another item of high demand.

My personal experience also vouches for the unique contribution of the KSP. I myself have participated in two KSP programs—one for Vietnam in 2005 and the other for Azerbaijan in 2008. The KSP projects' responsibility was to assist these two countries in preparing their integration into the global trading regime.

Multiple meetings of experts from the two sides were held in Seoul and the capitals of the participating countries. Questions were exchanged and answers provided in a candid two-way discussion. It merits attention that there have been 448 other projects for the past ten years.

This program is establishing another kind of solid bridge between Korea and other parts of the world. Recognizing that the program sets a good model for future ODAs, in a recent meeting held in Paris the OECD has adopted the Korean program as a new ODA initiative, describing knowledge sharing as "the third leg to financial and technical cooperation in the changing global development landscape."

Setting the successful launch of the KSP aside, the internal coordination among the government agencies has not been so optimal. Different views still exist between the MOSF and the Ministry of Foreign Affairs on which agency should be in charge of the ODA in general and the KSP in particular. Clearer division of responsibilities together with closer cooperation between the two agencies is just critical to get the momentum going. Based on the program's track record, a successful KSP project arguably requires active participation of both agencies, because what the participating countries expect from Korea spans over a wide spectrum of areas, now going beyond mere economic development planning.

Considering the humble start ten years ago, it is indeed nice to watch the program being expanded to meet the growing demand and recognized as a new route for ODA. To those countries standing on the start line of economic development, having access to someone else's prior experience is sometimes more helpful than simple grants. At the same time, this is also Korea's opportunity to learn from the partner countries.

[The Korea Herald, June 26, 2013]

16. A Red Card from Brussels?

As the Europeans fumble for a red card, Korea is mounting all-out efforts to avoid it. All government agencies are being mobilized to talk the EU out of issuing a red card. The issue at hand is IUU (Illegal, Unreported, or Unregulated) fishing, and the EU still seems skeptical of Korea's plan to eradicate it.

A yellow card was already handed to Korea in November last year when Brussels included Seoul on its preliminary list of IUU fishing countries along with Ghana and Curacao, a Dutch island in the West Indies. Brussels has been of the view that Korean fishing vessels have been engaged in IUU fishing activities while the Korean government has looked the other way. IUU fishing is an illegal fishing activity which is by far the worst type of human maritime behavior universally condemned by the global community. In FAO jargon, IUU is public enemy number one.

The EU delegation's visit to Korea in mid-June was to confirm if a red card should be issued to Korea for failure to respond to IUU fishing activities. A red card here would mean an import ban for Korean fisheries products and a port entry ban for Korean vessels, a significant blow to the Korean fisheries industry. Furthermore, the negative publicity would be immense: the country will be branded as a hub for destructive fishing. A final decision by the EU will be issued by September this year.

Although largely unknown to the general public, 2013 was the year that set off an alarm for Korean distant water fisheries activities. In January 2013, the United States issued a list of ten IUU fishing countries including Korea. The EU then followed in November by designating Korea, through preliminarily, as an IUU fishing country along with Ghana and Curacao. Among a dozen or so countries listed on the US and EU lists, Korea is the only major fishing country. By all accounts, Korea's name just stands out from the pack and cries for attention.

As has been observed by domestic media on the occasion of the EU delegation's visit ten days ago, the issue is not merely about the possibility of a reduction of exports as a result of an EU import ban. The real and long-lasting damage is the negative image to be imprinted from this final designation of IUU fishing. Few realize how damaging it is to carry the tag of an IUU fishing country. Some NGOs almost treat this activity on par with modern-day piracy in that it extorts crucial maritime resources from developing countries.

There is no question that IUU fishing is one of the major culprits of the global depletion of fish stocks. It is also absolutely unquestionable that global efforts to combat IUU fishing cannot be delayed any longer. Also, it is a pity that Korea has not done its homework since 2011 when this issue first surfaced. No one would dispute the fact that Seoul needs to take this issue seriously and find a way to enforce its laws effectively.

That said, however, it begs a question why Korea is the only major fishing power that has been included in the IUU lists, while other major fishing countries are left out. This is difficult to reconcile with recently released reports that discuss IUU fishing activities of other major fishing countries as well. Merely canvassing anecdotal evidence of IUU fishing of a country followed by some unilateral sanction may not be sufficient to offer an accurate picture of the problem. Rather, a global scheme to detect and eradicate IUU fishing should be explored.

In the meantime, watchers are holding their breath waiting for a final decision from the EU after the recent verification visit. Whatever decision the EU makes will also significantly affect that of the United States.

[The Korea Herald, June 25, 2014]

17. What Happened in 1362 and 2012?

Two ancient Buddhist statues were stolen by a group of Korean smugglers from two Japanese temples on Tsushima Island in October 2012. The statues were later found in Korea and confiscated by the law enforcement agencies. Japan has been asking for the return of the statues. This issue has remained an outstanding item in the bilateral relations.

There is an international treaty to which both countries are parties, the 1972 UNESCO Convention, which obligates return of stolen cultural artifacts. Japan has been claiming the return based on this convention.

One of the two statues was returned to Japan in July 2015 after the local law enforcement agency determined that no evidence existed to prove the bronze statue had been illegally brought to Japan.

The other is now being housed at a museum storage facility in Korea pending a court proceeding regarding the return of the religious artifact to Japan. This court proceeding was brought by those who claim the Buddhist statue should now remain in Korea as it was plundered by Japan in the first place.

Confirming what happened in 1362 (the presumed year of the statue's relocation) is practically impossible. This is the year when England was under the reign of King Edward III and the English parliament and court started to use English instead of French. The Black Plague has just killed up to 50 million people in Europe.

Goryeo Dynasty ruled Korea at that time. Not surprisingly, the Korean Cultural Heritage Administration opined the other day that it was impossible to confirm what caused the relocation of the statue from the originating home of Buseoksa Temple in Seosan, Korea.

There is a possibility that the statue was transferred as a result of legitimate bilateral trade in the 14th century.

Furthermore, even if the original relocation is the outcome of plunder by another country, that alone does not mean that it provides legal permission for someone to pry open the treasure storage of that other country. Countries engage in lengthy negotiations and cooperation even in such situation.

In any event, in the absence of any concrete evidence, a reasonable conclusion should be to return this second statue to the temple in Japan as with the first one that was returned last year. While it is not clear what happened in 1362, it is clear, at least, what happened in 2012.

The law enforcement agencies concluded that this cultural artifact was stolen from the Japanese temple. A specific legal obligation is imposed on the parties to the UNESCO Convention to return all stolen artifacts. Korea is a party to this convention since 1983.

It is an unfortunate mistake to confuse this stolen artifact case with the larger endeavor for repatriation of cultural artifacts in foreign countries. Cultural property repatriation is indeed an issue the nation pays keen attention to, sometimes arousing heated emotional response from the people. It is true that cultural artifacts are considered to represent the formation of national identity.

It is also true that sometimes people are frustrated by the time or difficulty involved in bringing the lost Korean cultural artifacts back to Korea.

That said, forceful transfers and illegal smuggling should not be condoned. Defending an obvious crime with an unsubstantiated claim from 650 years ago would only put Korea in an awkward situation in its otherwise legitimate attempt to bring back Korean cultural artifacts from overseas.

It is feared that foreign observers might view Korea as failing to abide by a specific obligation mandated by a treaty.

[The Korea Herald, April 20, 2016]

18. Climate Change Convention with Binding Teeth

As noted law expert Michael Akehurst once opined, treaties are the "maids-of-all-work" for international law. Many countries conclude numerous treaties regularly, with Korea alone signing roughly 100 bilateral or multilateral treaties each year.

All treaties have a legally binding force and contracting states are obligated to abide by them. The nature of the binding force, however, varies from treaty to treaty. Some are enforced with rigorous force through a binding dispute settlement mechanism, while others are enforced merely through a reporting and finger-pointing mechanism.

The truth is the finger-pointing version is not necessarily ineffective compared to the rigorous one. That is because states do care about how they are perceived by other countries and the price they would have to pay if they broke out of the pack. In this respect, soft enforcement version still works, but with one caveat: it works only if the consensus is tight and strong. That is how the national prestige part comes into play.

With extended deadlines, the 21st UN Climate Change Conference (COP 21) held in Paris has finally produced a new treaty on carbon dioxide emission reduction. It now imposes a legally binding obligation on all states—both developed and developing—to limit global warming to no more than 2 degrees Celsius.

The Kyoto Protocol of 1997, the first legal vehicle to tackle global warming, failed to deliver on its promises with major emitters deciding not to participate. The 2009 Copenhagen Accord also failed to produce a legally binding document. So, the Paris pact last weekend is the first global agreement with some teeth—even though the teeth may not be hard enough.

One would hope to see a legal instrument that imposes specific emission reduction levels for individual states. But that is not what is intended by the Paris Agreement. Rather, the agreement is a mixture of voluntary emissions reduction standard setting and global monitoring. So, states are required to set their reduction commitments, and to reconvene every five years from 2023 to monitor how their individual promises are being implemented.

When a state fails to meet its commitments, "naming and shaming" comes into play. So, to say the agreement possesses a legally binding nature is true, but at the same time somewhat overblown. The legal obligation is only for the establishment of self-declared emissions reduction commitments and reporting on the status of implementation.

That said, the unprecedentedly strong consensus shown at the conference in Paris indicates that the name-and-shame part will be particularly effective with respect to this particular agreement. The key is how major countries will implement this agreement domestically.

If some of the key emitting states backtrack on their promises, then the watertight consensus will start to fizzle, at which point the "voluntary" feature of the agreement will be underscored. The Earth will get warmer and warmer, and many coastal cities will be submerged by 2100, as scientists predict.

If, on the other hand, the strong global consensus remains firm, then this agreement with soft teeth will still be a turning point to turn in the fight against global warming. The next generation might remember Dec. 12, 2015, as a historic day.

Judging from the magnitude of the disastrous impact, global warming is by far the most urgent issue for mankind. Nonetheless, the international community has so far failed to find its way around this critical issue. When effective, the Paris Agreement will be the first legally binding document regarding global warming. Now it depends on how individual states implement their obligations faithfully.

This is a very good start, and a good start is half the battle. But the fate of the agreement will depend on how the name-and-shame formula actually works. For it to work, the tight and strong global consensus and a sense of urgency are absolutely critical.

[The Korea Herald, December 16, 2015]

19. Subsidies for Civil Aircraft Development

Ever since Airbus' A380 double-deck superjet made a sensational debut with its luxurious passenger convenience facilities, the aircraft has been advertised as the one that may redefine the term "air travel." Well, the remarkable size and features notwithstanding, the road to the birth of the aircraft may have been paved with illegal subsidies from the European Union member countries.

On June 30, the WTO finally rendered a decision in a high-profile dispute between the United States and the EU concerning the latter's alleged subsidization of Airbus. If found that billions of dollars given for the purpose of facilitating the development and manufacturing of A380 constituted unfair aid. The decision details a long list of support measures, both monetary and non-monetary, that governments of EU members employed to support Airbus in its global competition with America's Boeing.

This may not count as a defeat for the EU just yet. The EU also sued the United States, alleging that Boeing has received its own astronomical subsidies from the US government. A decision on this dispute is expected sometime soon, and given the rationale of last week's finding at the WTO, it is also quite likely that the world trade court will find similar illegal subsidization of Boeing.

These trans-Atlantic aircraft subsidization disputes merit our careful attention because, reportedly, Korea has recently been floating the idea of developing and manufacturing its own civil aircrafts and registering its name in the global civil aircraft market. Although Korea's target is said to be the medium-sized aircraft market, which is dominated by Canada's Bombardier and Brazil's Embraer, rather than the large civil aircraft market dominated by Boeing and Airbus, the June 30 decision still offers us much food for thought. The decision provides a rough guideline as to what a country can do and cannot do with respect to its aircraft industry.

As with any other major Korean products, the idea of manufacturing civil aircrafts would only succeed if those aircraft could be successfully exported to other countries: the small domestic demand in Korea probably will not be able to commercially justify the development and production.

The aircrafts would have to find their export destinations, as Korean automobiles and vessels have done. Then one of the prerequisites to maintain a steady flow of exports in the future is to make sure that no trade norms are adversely implicated or violated in the process.

As the Airbus dispute of last week evidences, however, illegal subsidy claims appear to be the easiest way to disrupt a country's export flow and competition in the global civil aircraft market. The moment Korea manages to produce sellable aircraft and hit the export market, other competitors will be quick in bringing subsidy claims against Korea before their administrative agencies and international tribunals such as the WTO.

This is what is happening between the United States and the EU these days, and what happened between Canada and Brazil at the height of their own aircraft subsidy disputes in late 1990s and early 2000s. All of these disputes were and are being presented as illegal-subsidy disputes. Given the fact that the four economies take up the bulk of the aircraft supply worldwide, it would be fair to say that the aircraft industry is particularly vulnerable to subsidy claims.

Any subsidy program, once initiated and set in motion, is hard to stop or undo. So, the best way of dealing with the problem is to realize the issue early on and adopt a measure to preempt prospective subsidy claims of other competitors. The decision in the Airbus dispute gives us a couple of precious hints in this regard.

For instance, it counsels us that the main entity that initiates and operates a national aircraft development project should be a private entity, if at all possible, as opposed to governmental affiliates. It also indicates that even if the government is involved for various reasons, its role should be confined to providing a general direction of the project from the perspective of managing the national economic policy. If Korea's reported plan for the civil aircraft development and manufacturing is still up and running, one of the indispensable items in the initial checklist will be to study carefully the mistakes other forerunners have made, and think hard how Korea can avoid same pitfalls.

[The Korea Herald, July 14, 2010]

20. WTO Accession: Here Comes Russia

One of the major missing pieces has been finally inserted into the big puzzle picture of the WTO. At the Eighth Ministerial Conference in Geneva from Dec. 15–17, Russia was accepted by the WTO as a new member of the global trade body, ending Moscow's 18-year bid since 1993 involving changes and amendment of more than 300 laws and regulations. Russia has been the only major country that has been left outside the global trade body.

Approval of Russia's accession was hailed as one of the two tangible results of the Ministerial Conference, the other being members' agreement on the amendment of the Government Procurement Agreement. And to those who are weary of the never-ending impasse at the DDA, hopefully these achievements were the two dim lights for the future path of the multilateralism.

Russia's entry is the most important accession since China's in November 2001. As Russia is not as much of a manufacturing powerhouse as China is, the accession would cause less turbulence in the global trade, but the addition of the last big market to the global trade regime would not come without its own share of impact.

Quite a few countries have been gearing up for the competition in the Russian market, expecting Russia's integration into the global trade regime. The sheer size of the country has made it attractive to all manufacturing industries.

Areas in which fierce competition is particularly expected are civil aircraft and automobile industries. Foreign corporations have had keen interest in these industries for a long time and a new horizon of opportunities is now looming. Competition among foreign corporations will become much fiercer. Since these are also areas where Russian domestic industries have had strong bases, competition between domestic industries and foreign corporations will become equally intense.

In the automobile sector, the Korean manufacturers look forward to increased sales in Russia once the tariff rate for automobiles is slashed to 15 percent from the current 30 percent as a result of Russia's WTO accession. The actual outcome, however, will pretty much depend on how Korea fares in the new competitive environment.

The European Union and China are also known to be anxious to expand their presence in the Russian market taking advantage of their geographical proximity.

Accession to the WTO means that exports and imports of all items are now subject to the WTO rules, which further means a member country should administer its export and import policies within the confinement of the terms and conditions of the agreement.

One of the important implications flowing from the requirement is that other countries' access to the vast pockets of Russia's natural resources will become more predictable and stable because exports of natural resources should also follow the rules of the agreement. The recent dispute between the United States and China over Beijing's alleged restriction on the export of natural resources proves how sensitive this issue could be. Although many things are still uncertain, Russia's WTO accession will at least ensure increased access to the Russian raw materials, which is a critical benefit to other countries.

Among the former Soviet Union republics, Kyrgyzstan, Moldova, Georgia, and Ukraine have already joined the world trade body since late 1990s. Other republics have been working hard to accede to the world trade body, most notably Belarus, Kazakhstan, and Azerbaijan.

Now that Russia has registered its name on the members' roster, in all likelihood entry negotiations for other CIS republics will also be accelerated. Most of these republics are inherited with sizable amounts of all sorts of natural resources, and have been approached by many countries seeking a stable line of energy supply.

Russia, Belarus, and Kazakhstan already established a trilateral free trade agreement among themselves in 2010, and expect this FTA to become a magnet for the remaining CIS bloc countries in the future. Thus, regardless of individual accession to the WTO, these former CIS republics are also planning to pursue integration of their own economies. It would be indeed interesting to see how Russia's accession (and accession of these republics) would change the topography of the WTO and how economic integration among the former CIS republics would affect the already complex equation of global trade.

[The Korea Herald, December 28, 2011]

21. WTO's New Director General at a Critical Juncture

A tight race to select a new director general of the WTO has just been completed. Roberto Azevedo, current Brazilian ambassador to the WTO, has been tapped to succeed Pascal Lamy to lead the global trade organization from Sept. 1. Once final confirmation is given at the special meeting on May 14, which is almost certain, he will become the first WTO director general from Latin America.

Ambassador Azevedo is taking the helm of the WTO at the most critical moment for the trade organization. In Azevedo's own words during the campaign: "We are, in my view, on the verge of losing a very valuable system." The eyes of the governments of the 159 WTO members are all upon him now.

The root cause of the current risk the WTO faces runs deeper than it seems. It goes beyond mere discrepancies among members concerning market opening. These discrepancies may be ironed out ultimately with patent negotiators and with timely outside pressure.

But the present impasse stems from something more fundamental than that—lack of trust among members. Without strong trust in other members and their negotiators, the last thing one would expect in such a complex and volatile negotiation as a multilateral trade negotiation is the grand settlement of all outstanding issues, last achieved in December 1993.

In particular, the confrontation between the developed members and developing members has virtually derailed many key negotiations at the Doha Round. It comes as no surprise that Azevedo's and other candidates' platforms all underscored the importance of narrowing the gap between the views of the two competing groups of countries.

As the selection process is confidential, there is no way of confirming which country has supported whom, but the speculation has it that Azevedo's selection has been largely supported by developing members while the United States and the EU, the two most influential members of the organization, favored his opponent, Mexico's Herminio Blanco.

If the speculation holds true, even the director general selection process has largely followed the dividing line. It is against this backdrop that many people are anxious to see how he will deliver his promise of bridging the gap between the developing and developed countries. Each group will be required to make concessions so as to reach a compromise, but again concessions are only feasible when there is trust.

During his campaign, Azevedo indicated that he would make efforts to address the structural problems facing the developing members of the WTO. One of the examples he suggested, as a long-time dispute settlement proceeding participant himself, is to make the WTO dispute settlement system more affordable and accessible to developing countries.

Suggestions like this have obviously helped him garner support from developing countries. The question now is how he will reflect the views of the developed members in addressing these structural issues and manages to find a common ground for touchy and divisive topics.

A first test for his leadership comes just three months after his inauguration. The upcoming ministerial conference in Bali from Dec. 3–6 will be a difficult test for his leadership and his pledges. The outcome of the Bali ministerial meeting will significantly affect how WTO members and other watchers view the future of the WTO and the multilateral trading regime.

Solutions to detailed issues and negotiation topics can come later in time with more discussions and negotiations in 2014 and beyond, but what is critically urgent at the Bali Ministerial is to restore the trust of WTO members among each other.

So, this is the key task waiting for the new director general. At the moment, the expectation seems to be high that this well-known trade diplomat can breathe new life into the WTO.

[The Korea Herald, May 15, 2013]

22. The Perfect Not the Enemy of the Good

Ironically, it was Pascal Lamy, director general of the WTO in Geneva, who made a case for the importance of prompt ratification and implementation of the Korea's free trade agreement with the European Union and the United States. At the Trade Negotiation Committee meeting last Friday, the WTO chief officially acknowledged that the Doha negotiation is now "on the brink of failure" unless a big breakthrough is found to bridge the wide gaps among the countries. He warned that the failure of the round would risk a "slow, silent weakening of the multilateral trading system in the longer term."

The gloomy confession of the WTO chief will further stoke the skepticism for the multilateralism enshrined in the WTO and force the countries to find an alternative in a bilateral setting: i.e., free trade agreements. In fact, FTAs have already become the focal point of the trade policy of many trading powers as a Plan B to safeguard their respective trade interests by ensuring access to the markets of major trading partners regardless of the unpredictable outcome of the Doha Round. China and Japan have recently made significant strides by concluding FTAs with Taiwan and India, respectively. The United States seems ever more enthusiastic about the idea of a trans-Pacific FTA, called TPP (Trans-Pacific Partnership). The EU, on its part, signed a trilateral FTA with Peru and Colombia just two weeks ago. In all likelihood, Lamy's statement last Friday signals that the global FTA drive will further intensify. In that regard, the recent development in Geneva is tantamount to blaring alarms and flashing lights for Korea as well, a country 44 percent of whose gross domestic product depends upon the export. Securing stable access to major markets through bilateral agreements is way more critical to Korea than to any other country.

Coincidentally, last Friday was also the day when the Korean National Assembly was supposed to table the much-debated Korea-EU FTA at the plenary session for the deliberation and voting for the agreement's ratification, following the agreement's passage of the Foreign Relations Committee the previous day. The plenary session deliberation and voting were postponed until May due to the difference of views between the ruling and opposition camps.

Korea and the EU have set the date of the (provisional) entry into force of the bilateral FTA as July 1, 2011. The 27-member EU moved quickly and completed its internal procedure back in February and is now waiting for Korea to do its part. As is well known, the translation issue has turned out to be an embarrassing stumbling block for Korea. Since the issue was raised in early March, corrections have been made and multiple reviews conducted. Obviously, there is no reason to spend another couple of months to go through the agreement article by article and word by word to exhaust all theoretical possibilities. Treaty conclusion is an important national business. That is more so when it comes to treaties like the FTAs now at hand. However, the perfect should not be the enemy of the good.

There are many things to be done to bring a treaty into effect. The Korea-EU FTA is no different. It is not simply as if the president appears on national TV and announces that the FTA is now in effect. To meet the July 1 as the effective date, multiple implementing legislations should be adopted, and various logistical issues should be arranged beforehand. Put differently, ratification is not the end but actually the start of the complex preparation. The longer Korea delays this post-ratification domestic process, the more likely it is for clerical mistakes to pry themselves in at the last minute. As an old proverb goes, the devil lies in the details. Then, an assertion that ratification in June (i.e., after spending one more month) is still sufficient to meet the July 1 deadline is so out of touch with reality. July 1 is just 60 days away.

Partly due to the lame development in Doha Round and partly due to the concern over the EU's early securing of a beachhead in the Korean market, Washington is also moving quickly now to bring the 47-month-old Korea-US FTA to fruition. In his speech in Seoul last week, US Secretary of Commerce Gary Locke even mentioned that the United States is ready to complete the ratification earlier than Korea does.

The recent development in Geneva and the global FTA-frenzy atmosphere further underscores the lucky position that Korea is in at the moment by having signed FTAs with the two major export markets in the world, the EU and the US. The problem is that still one final step is left for Korea to materialize the strategic benefit.

There are many lessons elicited from the recent experiences regarding the Korea-EU FTA and the Korea-US FTA. However, these lessons, as they have been identified so far, are mainly for guidance for future negotiations. These lessons are far from being able to justify further delays of the domestic procedure. Letting this opportunity drift away would be a serious mistake. A mistake Korea's competitors will probably love to capitalize on.

[The Korea Herald, May 5, 2011]

23. Seeking Scientific Rationale

Can a government address consumers' concern over imported products because of a health reason? Of course it can. Governments have always done so and will do so in the future. That is exactly what ordinary people will expect of any responsible government. The real question, however, is how to exercise this authority.

As noted before, the regulatory guideline for this very issue is found in the Sanitary and Phytosanitary Agreement of the WTO. To make a long story short, the agreement basically stipulates that any country can exercise this authority, but a decision to impose an import restriction should be supported by "scientific evidence."

The agreement is carefully drafted to exclude import restrictions stemming from an emotional or unsubstantiated response. Ever since Korea's imposition of import ban on fisheries products from eight prefectures of Japan since early September, the application of this agreement has been another source of tension between the two countries, including the possibility of Japan's lodging of a formal protest at the WTO litigation proceeding.

Viewed from this angle, the IAEA assessment team's recent announcement that it is effectively vouching for the safety of the fisheries products from Japan may offer an important piece of puzzle as to how the international scientific community would perceive the risk from the fisheries products. Obviously, an assessment of an international organization in the area of nuclear science should be a meaningful barometer in the scientific discourse. Many countries dealing with the fisheries imports from Japan will accord significant weight to the findings of the IAEA.

The IAEA's position will raise Japan's challenges by another notch. After all, one of the international organizations tasked with scientific issues has spoken officially. It is now gradually becoming Korea's turn to come up with its own scientific rationale, whether confirmed or temporary, to sustain the import ban. To remain in compliance with the obligations under the said agreement requires an affirmative action as opposed to repetition of consumers' concerns or civic groups' demands. For better or worse, the provisions at issue here are highly technical and not so receptive to the concerns per se, unless accompanied by scientific justification.

One thing to note here is that the findings of the IAEA may not be conclusive in the SPS jargon, given that what was reviewed this time was the "management of the contaminated water." It seems that how the previous discharge may have impacted the fisheries products being imported today has not been evaluated. In any event, the IAEA's announcement has certainly raised the threshold for Korea to meet.

Again, the threshold is not whether the measure is emotionally or politically correct; rather, it is whether scientific evidence is out there to support a country's import ban. Addressing consumers' concerns is necessary but how to address them should dovetail with the science in that area. Korea has focused on the first part of the question, and now it is time for the second part.

Recent trade disputes are replete with the examples in which ostensibly necessary import restrictions to respond to demands from consumers have been found to be in deviation of the treaty obligations. Sometimes legitimate governmental objectives have been criticized in the mires of technical requirements embedded in the agreements. The valuable lesson to be elicited from other countries' experiences is that the legitimacy of an import ban hinges upon satisfying the stipulated requirements. This is the only way to reflect otherwise important consumer concerns within the confinement of treaty obligations.

The IAEA announcement is now turning the attention to Korea: how does it respond and what is in its dossier?

[The Korea Herald, December 11, 2013]

24. A Whale of a Science Project

It was quite demoralizing, to say the least. Last Friday's edition of the South China Morning Post, the leading newspaper in Hong Kong, ran a big cartoon deriding the so-called scientific whaling, and it was obvious which country it was referring to.

Korea's about-face on whaling has become headline news in many parts of the world and invited renewed debates on this issue. The dreaded prospect of Student at Hong Kong University asking me questions about it during my class on international law has already been making me sweat. Many countries interpret Korea's declaration of resumption of "scientific whaling" at the International Whaling Commission's annual meeting in Panama City last week as a virtual denunciation of the country's 26-year-old moratorium on whaling.

The International Convention for the Regulation of Whaling of 1946 imposes international obligations for the protection of endangered whale species. This convention ultimately evolved to impose a global moratorium on whaling in 1986. As a party to the convention, Korea has also implemented its obligation.

Article VIII of the ICRW, however, includes an exception that permits killing and taking whales for scientific research purposes. This exception is for the collection of marine biological data for whales so as to enhance conservation of the species.

What Korea basically declared in Panama City was that it would start this whaling for scientific purposes. While having a burning desire for science is generally praised by peer countries in other sectors, this particular type of scientific activity has been widely criticized for a long time.

The widely held perception in the international community has been that scientific whaling is a pretext for commercial whaling using Article VIII of the ICRW as a loophole. Critics assert that scientific whaling is turning the convention upside down, asking why someone would need such a lethal method of scientific activity to collect biological data. They point out that after producing negligible scientific value the whales killed in the course of "scientific research" are then sold for meat.

The IWC reports that Iceland and Japan are the only two countries currently engaged in the "scientific whaling." Korea's addition will thus expand the list to three.

Korea's unfathomable decision to join this conspicuous list explains the almost universal criticism of its decision of last week. Australia and New Zealand, who have been spearheading international efforts to enforce the ICRW, immediately issued very harsh criticism, deploring Seoul's sudden joining of this "kill-for-science" scheme. Concern was also expressed by Washington.

The wisdom of joining this two-country list would be further questioned if one realizes that this very issue has become a controversial legal question among countries concerned at various international courts for the past couple of years. So, it is hard to fathom why Korea has suddenly volunteers to step into this known minefield.

This turnaround is also puzzling because it contradicts what the country has done and said recently in this particular area. Although still one of the major fishing powers, Seoul has made strenuous efforts at FAO and WTO conferences to help reduce the depletion of fish stocks. Having heard the declaration from Panama City, one would question the good faith of all these statements and papers.

Back-pedaling of this sort easily erases all the hard-earned plus points for the image of a country. Judging from the deep stigma associated with the term of "scientific whaling," and the almost universal outcry against the declaration of Korea to initiate this whaling practice, a dent seems to have been made in the effort to enhance the "national brand image" through all these summit meetings and projects for the past several years.

Unless compelling reasons are given, it seems difficult to refute a widespread perception that this plan for lethal research activities is more about the meat than about scientific data. It is quite disappointing that Korea has suddenly volunteered to carry the torch of this dubious cause.

[The Korea Herald, July 11, 2012]

25. The High Cost of Financial Distrust

Since the financial crisis in September 2008, everybody seems to be talking about banks and financial sector regulation. Can you guess how many banks are operating in Korea? Can you name, say, the five largest commercial banks in Korea? Most of us probably do not have the answers to these questions. Of course, everybody could recite names of some major banks including the one where he or she holds an account, but most of us do not have a general overview of the Korean banking sector.

Believe it or not, however, there are quite a few foreigners who can recite the names of the Korean banks and who are relatively well apprised of the financial system of Korea. Quite surprising, isn't it? This is all because of the seven-year disputes at the WTO between Korea and the United States, Korea and the European

Union, and Korea and Japan concerning the very issue of the relationship between the Korean financial regulatory authorities and the Korean banks. These disputes were finally terminated only recently—April of 2009. These high-profile disputes produced lengthy decisions in which all Korean banks were evaluated and the relationship between the financial authorities and the banks examined. These decisions are all public documents, and anybody can have access to them through the WTO website. In fact, not a few scholars discuss these decisions in their articles and analyze relevant issues in international conferences.

Although Korea made its best effort in these disputes and succeeded in defending itself regarding major issues, it had to spend and mobilize a significant number of resources in the seven-year ordeal. Essentially, these three countries on the opposing side mounted a relentless assertion that the banks in Korea were under the influence of the financial authorities, an example of which was the authorities' intervention in the selection of chief executive officers of the banks. To support these claims, the three countries trawled all Korean newspapers and websites to collect articles that may have indicated such intervention. Fortunately, most of the reports and materials submitted by them turned out to be either inaccurate or exaggerated, but again Korea had to spend a significant amount of time and energy in this process.

Swirling controversies surrounding the election of the chairman of the KB Financial Holdings since last November provide a classic example of déjà vu. The details mentioned (correctly or incorrectly) in the press coverage are embarrassingly similar to those we saw in the just completed disputes. According to the press reports, the elected chairman of the company voluntarily withdrew because of the alleged pressure from the financial regulatory authorities that may have preferred somebody else. I tend to believe this report is either inaccurate or exaggerated. I do so because it is almost unthinkable that a reasonable person or agency with a reasonable sense of a "learning curve" would go down the same path that was a source of seven-year dispute that was resolved only seven months before.

No matter what we say or believe, however, I would bet that many foreign governments and "interest groups" are closely monitoring these developments with a lot of interest. They will probably look into these incidents to find some missing pieces of evidence to build their case next time. Korea cannot afford to remain complacent simply because other countries do not raise similar issues right away, since it takes time to build a case and find the right timing. And again, even if a similar dispute is initiated from the recent fiasco, I am confident that Korea can explain this away as it successfully did the last time around, but only after paying a high price, which prompts us to think about the real problem.

The real problem here is that it is not the financial regulatory authorities or the implicated banks that pay the price in this regard. It is the government agency in charge of defending Korea in future litigations and, more importantly, Korean exporting companies; the former having to bear all the logistical and financial burdens of international litigations spanning over a couple of years and the latter having to pay an enormous amount of extra duties before all these issues are resolved through lengthy litigation. Korea has learned about this mismatch hard way. The recent controversy is particularly alarming because the specter of protectionism is ubiquitous and ready to rear its head at the slightest opportunity. If the reports are not accurate, as the financial authorities claim, that is good. But the authorities should ensure, at all costs, that similar "misunderstandings" do not occur in the future.

By the way, there are 18 banks operating in Korea as of today. For more information, please check the materials posted in the WTO website.

[The Korea Herald, January 26, 2010]

V

INTERNATIONAL LAW IN THE FIELD—DISPUTES, TREATIES, AND INTERNATIONAL COURTS

Korea has demonstrated active engagement in the creation of international law and participation in the dispute settlement proceedings. The act of creation is primarily accomplished through the process of concluding treaties. Korea concludes roughly 50 to 100 treaties annually. Due to a prevailing sense of caution within its national psyche, Korea seldom assumes a leading role in initiating international discussions on emerging issues in uncharted domains. It is a faithful follower once a rule is adopted, but not enthusiastic about becoming a rule-setter for the first time. However, on certain occasions, it spearheads the adoption of treaties ahead of other states. Free Trade Agreements (FTAs) serve as a notable illustration in this regard. Between 2005 and 2015, Korea's FTAs were trailblazers in addressing some of the novel issues that subsequently influenced the FTAs of other countries. Tariff elimination at the border is merely one aspect of the commitment to opening up the market. How the imported products are treated within the market, specifically behind the borders, is increasingly crucial in terms of commitment. The focus of international trade has transitioned from at-the-border issues to behind-the-border issues. There is also an irony related to an FTA. The conclusion of an FTA leads to the removal of tariffs, but it also tends to induce robust trade remedy investigations—the trilogy of trade remedy investigations, namely antidumping, countervailing duty, and safeguards measures, has become a widely used instrument as a means for domestic industries to address the increased penetration of products from FTA partners.

Korea also participates in dispute settlements when deemed necessary. To date, it has not been involved in any proceedings before the ICJ. Nevertheless, it is one of the active participants at the WTO dispute settlement proceedings with 41 cases as of February 2021. Its participation in international investment disputes has also been steadily increasing, with a total of ten cases filed against Korea, while Korean

DOI: 10.4324/9781003501749-5

companies have initiated seven cases against foreign countries. The inclusion of a dispute settlement mechanism between an individual and a foreign government through an international tribunal may result in complex legal consequences, which can be either advantageous or disadvantageous. In situations where both negative and positive aspects co-exist, a proper way of evaluating the overall consequence would be to consider both aspects in their entirety and give them equal weight. Limiting one's attention to sporadic glimpses of either positive or negative aspects results in an incomplete and inaccurate picture of the matter. Instead, one would need to take one step backward and pause in order to gather a more comprehensive view of the entire silhouette of this dispute settlement mechanism.

As a matter of fact, international law has a comparatively weak enforcement mechanism. While certain contemporary norms are equipped with more robust enforcement mechanisms, such as those related to trade or investment, there are other norms that lack or do not have such mechanisms. One commonly overlooked fact is that states comply with judgments of international courts at a remarkably high rate. This high compliance rate of international court decisions can be attributed to various factors. One major reason is that states are highly sensitive to international peer perceptions. States assert their entitlement to choose policies based on their own judgment, yet they exercise great caution in considering how their policy choices would be perceived by other states. Upon the issuance of a judgment by an international court, states are inclined to abide by it, regardless of the presence or strength of an enforcement mechanism.

To scholars of trade law researching WTO disputes, the English names of major Korean banks like KB are no longer unfamiliar. From 2002 to 2009, three disputes regarding the relationship between the Korean government and financial institutions involving the US, the European Union, and Japan unfolded consecutively, bringing these names repeatedly into the spotlight. In all three disputes, the relationship between Korea's financial supervisory institutions and major banks was a central issue. The US, EU, and Japan presented extensive evidence to demonstrate that Korea's financial regulatory agencies had direct and indirect involvement in the appointment and operations of key executives at these institutions. The Korean government also submitted considerable evidence to refute these claims. Despite persistent rebuttals, some arguments from these countries were upheld, and the disputes, which culminated with Japan, were only narrowly resolved in April 2009 after significant effort by the Korean government. However, the controversy surrounding the recent appointment of the KB Financial Group chairman since last November suggests that the hard-earned lessons and experiences from the past seven years of disputes have faded into institutional amnesia. Reports on the selection process continued to stir discomfort, culminating in the resignation of the newly appointed chairman. Many point to implicit or explicit pressure from related authorities as the reason behind the resignation. While one can only hope these reports are unfounded, it is difficult to imagine repeating the same issue under international scrutiny within just seven months, given the sensibility of the situation.

Unfortunately, in some of the past disputes, the WTO Dispute Settlement Body accepted the claims of countries like the US, asserting that Korean financial regulatory agencies exercised control over the financial sector. Key evidence in this process included materials showing governmental influence over the appointment of bank executives. Unlike the past, where such information might have been less accessible, nowadays, due to increased disclosure of regulatory data on websites, media, and academic publications, it is not challenging to gather evidence depicting the relationship between specific governments and financial institutions. In the case of KB, for instance, information disclosed to the US Securities and Exchange Commission (SEC) was thoroughly examined and used as crucial evidence in WTO litigation. As foreign investments in Korean banks increase, so does international interest and accessibility to the circumstances surrounding these banks. In fact, numerous foreign media outlets have begun reporting on the matter, drawing international scrutiny. The issue is that the damage from such disputes does not fall on regulatory authorities or financial institutions but ultimately affects Korean exporters. Efforts by the US, EU, and Japan to link Korea's financial regulatory authorities with financial institutions were aimed at confirming industrial support policies through financial sector control, ultimately justifying the imposition of countervailing duties on Korean exports. The indirect and direct costs borne by Korean companies, the ultimate target of these disputes, in legal fees and additional tariffs, have been astronomical over the past seven years. While one hopes otherwise, if a similar dispute arises targeting specific companies, the current developments might unwittingly serve as critical evidence, creating challenges for the Korean government and businesses.

This is especially concerning as protectionism resurfaces in various regions in the aftermath of the financial crisis. As the urgency caused by the financial crisis subsides, countries are increasingly imposing anti-dumping and countervailing duties on key products of competing trade nations to weaken their competitiveness in domestic markets. Moreover, many nations are viewing Korea's surging exports, which have thrived even amid the financial crisis, with wary eyes. Amid this environment, the controversy surrounding the appointment of a CEO at a major bank, where foreign shareholders hold a 58 percent stake, resembles an act that invites suspicion regardless of intent—regardless of how justified it may be, the circumstances alone are enough to trigger concerns among observers. As the host country of the G20 Summit this November and a core player in international trade, Korea's every move is closely monitored by all its trading partners. Any lapse could quickly escalate into an international trade dispute, causing massive losses for Korean companies. This reality needs to be reaffirmed.

Sometimes, Korean courts render judgments on issues of an international nature. These issues are covered by the foreign press. At times, these issues themselves give rise to fervently contested diplomatic and legal debates. For example, the 2012 decision of the Korean Supreme Court concerning the 1965 Korea-Japan Claims Settlement Agreement is exactly the opposite of the 2007 decision of the Japanese Supreme Court. The highest courts of the two countries have two contradictory interpretations of the same treaty provision. Obviously, the most appropriate approach to resolve the deadlock would be to pursue a diplomatic solution to this issue. If, however, the comparable stances of the two countries do not exhibit any indication of flexibility, then the only remaining recourse appears to be the arbitration process as stipulated in the agreement.

These issues of the creation of international law and dispute settlement are inevitably intricate. And yet, they attract keen interest from the general public and garner broad press coverage. Mindful of this, these issues were regularly discussed in the columns. The demonstration of international law can be observed in both its legislative and dispute settlement aspects. Globally, many countries are in support of their key domestic industries to help them compete in the world market. If anything, this is one of the most important tasks for any government at a time of national crisis, be it an economic or geopolitical one. The United States and China are mobilizing their national resources to support their key industries. Semiconductors and core technology sectors provide good examples. The Europeans are trying to support their domestic electric vehicle manufacturers as well. National support for key industries is not unprecedented. In fact, such support has been adopted by many countries, including both developed and developing states, in many sectors. The American and European support for civil aircraft manufacturers has been well known for many years culminating in high profile disputes at the WTO.

But few people are aware of the fact that there have been similar disputes between Canada and Brazil concerning national support for the civil aircraft manufacturing sector. These disputes have also proceeded to the WTO dispute settlement proceedings. Both Canada and Brazil have invested a great deal of their respective national budgets in the development of their respective domestic aviation industries. Both as countries of continental proportions, the only means of transportation would have been airplanes. To move from one city or region to another, airplanes would have been the most efficient and practical means of transport, which may have boosted the aeronautical industry in Brazil and Canada. As a result, the Bombardier of Canada and Embraer of Brazil have played an important role in their respective domestic economies. It would be natural for the two countries' governments to introduce supportive measures for these aeronautical companies. In the case of Embraer, it started as a public company, maintained by the Brazilian government. Although the company was privatized in 1994, the Brazilian government's effort to support the company did not cease. For instance, the Brazilian government established a program called PROEX (Export Financing Program), which allowed Embraer aircraft to be exported more easily, since the Brazilian government would equalize or neutralize the interest charged on the sale of airplanes. The Brazilian government argued that PROEX was necessary to neutralize the effect of the "Brazil risk" on the international market.

The same national desire to establish and support key national industries equally applies to Korea. Like its counterparts, the Korean government has been keen to provide its policy guidelines and support for core sectors of the national economy—some of which have prospered in the global market. However, although such national support is widespread and common, its legal status under relevant international law—such as trade agreements and investment agreements—has not always been solid or watertight. Accordingly, such support measures have led to disputes in which both parties claim violation of relevant international law. The WTO disputes on civil aircraft involving the United States, the European Union, Brazil, and Canada offer the most prominent example in this respect. This gap between norms and reality places a constant burden on the many governments, as they are caught between domestic demands and international legal obligations. Korea has also been struggling with this dilemma for a long time. Interestingly, the dilemma is getting less acute these days because of the weakening of multilateralism and the rule of law.

Resolving disputes through legal means is essential—and at times, the only viable option. However, pursuing a legal path can sometimes escalate the dispute and ultimately damage the relationship. This aspect of the legal approach has been well recognized in Korean society. One often-heard compliment in Korea is that "he is the person who can live without law." Traditionally speaking, Korean society is particularly receptive to non-legal avenues as a means to resolve disputes among societal members. Although this traditional attitude is changing fast with the rapid permeation of a Western-style business-as-usual attitude, it still remains deep-rooted in the mind of Korean society. More often than not, people tend to look at societal reactions beyond legal compatibility when socially sensitive issues arise for high-ranking officials or socially influential figures. These non-legal reactions display both the strength and weakness of Korean society.

In any event, this focus on the non-legal approach to settling disputes is now receiving renewed attention globally as businesses and governments encounter difficulties in resolving their disputes through purely legal avenues. For instance, the entry into force of the Singapore Convention in September 2020 reflects this global trend. The convention demands enforcement, in third countries, of a settlement agreement resulting from mediation, which will help facilitate the spread and utilization of mediation among the global businesses and industries. Mediation is a non-legal dispute settlement process wherein disputing parties consider resolving disputes amicably with the help of a third party—a mediator. Similarly, some recent treaties and agreements undertake new experiments to adopt and apply mediation to settle disputes between states. The most representative example is the dispute resolution procedure stipulated in Chapter 13 (Trade and Sustainable Development) of the Free Trade Agreement between Korea and the European Union. This procedure has, in fact, been invoked recently. The EU initiated the process in July 2019 in connection with the violation of the principles of Korea's International Labor Organization (ILO) Charter and the delay in ratifying key conventions. Accordingly, the mediation process between Korea and the EU was not carried out until January 2021. The Korea-China FTA between Korea and China also introduces adjustment procedures to deal with non-tariff trade barriers.[1] Furthermore, ISDS, which is currently drawing keen attention from the international community, is also considering the mediation process as a complement to the existing ISDS procedure.

These recent moves on mediation as a means of resolving state-to-state disputes also begin with a reflection on existing dispute resolution procedures. This is because, even when a dispute is officially resolved through established procedures, relations between the parties often deteriorate. If there is a way to resolve the dispute with the help of a third party but maintain the relationship as harmoniously as possible, the countries will inevitably pay attention to it. This is the background of recent interest in coordination. If institutional development and experience in mediation is achieved in the future, the introduction of such a "relationship-keeping" dispute resolution system may be more actively sought throughout international law. This new approach is particularly timely at this juncture. The current global environment wherein cherished multilateralism has been steadily weakening may find mediation or other Alternative Dispute Resolution (ADR) options more useful and appropriate considering (i) a growing gap between treaty texts and reality because of the fast development of technology and human activities, (ii) ever deepening fragmentation of respective branches of international law, and (iii) the glaring inherent limitation of existing binding dispute settlement mechanisms to ensure effective resolution of disputes satisfying the disputing parties. Mediation and other ADRs are believed to contribute to alleviating these structural problems of international law and dispute settlement proceedings.

Consider the following example. A diplomatic tension between Qatar on the one hand and Saudi Arabia, the United Arab Emirates, Oman, and Bahrain on the other hand evolved into a series of legal disputes on multiple fronts at various global forums and courts starting in 2017. These issues spanned a wide range of areas, including trade, investment, human rights, and airspace restrictions. As the disputes concerned both diplomatic, political, and legal issues, it was not necessarily easy to resolve them through conventional avenues of "legal" proceedings. Mediation initiated by the Gulf Cooperation Council (GCC) and Kuwait helped ease tension, which then led to reconciliation in 2021. Mediation and ADRs are particularly useful when legal norms are in conflict, which is increasingly the case at the moment in the global community. Climate change offers a good example. As climate change becomes one of the imminent problems facing global society, many governments are adopting a variety of governmental measures to achieve a reduction of greenhouse gases. Other governmental measures are also being introduced to support environmentally friendly activities and products. All these measures are

1 See Articles 20.5(4), (5), and (6) of the Korea–China FTA. For reference, the Korea–China FTA marks this procedure as "conciliation." This term is also translated as mediation in Korean, but it is assumed that it corresponds to "mediation" and "adjustment" in this article, reflecting the need for the unified use of the term described earlier.

important and critical to attain the basic objective of the global community. These measures are also encouraged and even required by international agreements such as the Paris Agreement of October 6, 2016.

At the same time, however, trade agreements restrict governmental support measures if they lead to the facilitation of manufacturing and exportation of products. The WTO's SCM Agreement is directly implicated in this regard. In principle, the SCM Agreement does not provide exceptions for government measures supporting environmental objectives. As a consequence, governmental measures to support environment enhancement or protection are subject to the regulation of the SCM Agreement and possibly constitute a violation of the agreement. As a matter of fact, some of the environmentally friendly measures have become issues of international disputes, either in the domestic countervailing duty investigations or at the WTO dispute settlement proceedings. This reality underscores the gap between the trade norms and the climate change norms. This gap seems to invite further controversies and disputes as time passes. Mediation and ADRs can be useful in resolving disputes as they can explore legal texts and compromise deals in a more flexible way, breaking away from the straitjackets of the binding legal norms. A similar logic may apply to other politically sensitive and legally complex disputes that the global community faces at the moment.

Many people in Korea mention the International Court of Justice (ICJ) when there is an issue of international law. The ICJ is sometimes misunderstood as the supreme court for all matters of international law. In fact, its jurisdiction is narrowly defined and requires the satisfaction of certain pre-conditions. Despite the continuing attention on the ICJ, Korea has not paid adequate attention to cultivating experience and accumulating expertise for the ICJ practice. It is juxtaposed with the effort of Japan, a country most frequently mentioned in the discussion of ICJ in Korean society. Japan experienced its first ICJ contentious proceeding as a disputing party in the Antarctic Whaling dispute with Australia between 2011 and 2014. While Japan lost the dispute, it has apparently accumulated experience with regard to contentious ICJ proceedings. Although Korea does not have to entertain a contentious dispute proceeding at the ICJ at the moment, it at least needs to initiate its preparation for future proceedings at the ICJ in order to keep up with neighboring countries' accumulation of ICJ experience.

National security exception provisions have recently come under a new light. This is because these provisions included in trade agreements and investment agreements are being actively utilized. It all started with the US import restrictions. The US government implemented import restrictions on foreign steel products in June 2018, citing the national security exception in Article XXI of the GATT. This unusual move led directly to a WTO dispute. The US government is considering similar import restrictions on imported automobiles. The Korea–Japan dispute over Japan's export restrictions, which began in July 2019, serves as a key backdrop to the invocation of security exceptions under Article XXI. Japan explains this as a legitimate export control measure based on national security concerns, and argues that even if there are problems, they are justified under Article XXI of

GATT. Regarding this measure, our country filed a complaint against Japan with the WTO in September 2019, and two rounds of bilateral consultations between the two countries have now been concluded.[2] As part of efforts to reach a diplomatic settlement between the two countries, WTO proceedings have been suspended as of March 2020.

Meanwhile, GATT Article XXI also figures in other major disputes within the WTO. An example is the conflict between Qatar and the United Arab Emirates (UAE),[3] which was triggered by collective sanctions from neighboring countries over Qatar's pro-Iran policy. In the ensuing WTO dispute, the UAE invoked GATT Article XXI(b)(iii), claiming that its trade restrictions against Qatar were necessary to protect its essential security interests in the context of a regional diplomatic crisis. This case marked the first time the WTO panel explicitly analyzed the scope and limits of the security exception under Article XXI, emphasizing that such invocation is subject to objective review and cannot be entirely self-judging. The growing invocation of national security exceptions is also evident in other treaties. The Ukrainian-Russian conflict[4] over Russian military support for pro-Russian militias in eastern Ukraine began in January 2017 and is currently before the ICJ.[5] In this dispute, Russia also cited its national security interests.[6] Two cases are currently pending before the ICJ,[7] which were sparked by the US withdrawal from the nuclear freeze deal with Iran in May 2018. The national security exceptions stipulated in the consular treaty between the two countries are also a key point of contention here.[8] Meanwhile, Qatar and the UAE[9] are currently engaged in mutual

2 *See Japan—Measures Related to the Exportation of Products and Technology to Korea*, Request for Consultations by the Republic of Korea (G/L/1325; G/TFA/D3/1; G/TRIMS/D/45; IP/D/42 (Sept. 16, 2019).

3 *See Qatar—Certain measures concerning goods from the United Arab Emirates* (DS576), available at www.wto.org/english/tratop_e/dispu_e/cases_e/ds576_e.htm.

4 *Russia—Measures Concerning Traffic in Transit*, Report of the Panel, WT/DS512/R (Apr. 5, 2019) [hereinafter *Russia-Traffic in Transit*].

5 *See Application of the International Convention for the Suppression of the Financing of Terrorism and of the International Convention on the Elimination of All Forms of Racial Discrimination (Ukraine v. Russian Federation)* (2017).

6 *See ibid., Provisional Measures, Order of 19 April 2017, I.C.J. Reports 2017*; *ibid., Preliminary Objections* (Nov. 8, 2019), paras. 36, 93.

7 *See Certain Iranian Assets (Islamic Republic of Iran v. United States of America)*, Application instituting Proceedings (Jun. 14, 2016); *Alleged Violations of the 1955 Treaty of Amity, Economic Relations, and Consular Rights (Islamic Republic of Iran v. United States of America)*, Application Instituting Proceedings (Jul. 16, 2018).

8 *See ibid., Preliminary Objections, Judgment, I.C.J. Reports 2019*, Judgment of 13 February 2019, p. 7; *ibid.*, paras. 39–44, paras 46–47; *Alleged Violations of the 1955 Treaty of Amity, Economic Relations, and Consular Rights (Islamic Republic of Iran v. United States of America), Provisional Measures, Order of 3 October 2018, I.C.J. Reports 2018 (II)*, p. 635, para. 41.

9 *See Application of the International Convention on the Elimination of All Forms of Racial Discrimination (Qatar v. United Arab Emirates), Provisional Measures, Order of 23 July 2018, I.C.J. Reports 2018*, p. 406; *Application of the International Convention on the Elimination of All Forms of Racial*

expulsion and denial of entry of nationals of the other country, triggered by the heightened diplomatic conflict over hegemony in the Middle East. The ICJ dispute between[10] Saudi Arabia, Bahrain, Egypt, and Qatar also raise issues related to national security exceptions under the relevant treaties.[11]

In this way, national security issues have recently become a subject of fresh attention. In this extension, an active review of national security exception provisions is underway. However, the review of this provision has so far mainly focused on the part where the governments of the contracting parties can "take necessary measures that conflict with their obligations under the agreement" for reasons of national security. Or, sometimes, it has been developed around the part that says, "[i]f necessary to fulfill obligations under the UN Charter, measures otherwise inconsistent with the agreement may be taken." However, another provision included in the national security exception clause is the "refusal to provide information" provision. This provision states that a Contracting Party may not provide any information for reasons of national security. However, the content examining this regulation has been minimal, both domestically and internationally. There have been some occasional reviews, but they are limited to brief mentions. Moreover, even when national security exceptions are addressed in their entirety, there is little focus on refusals to provide information. As already noted, the emphasis was primarily on the power to take measures that violate the agreement.

1. Disputes in the East China Sea

As if the current load of disputes was not sufficient, a big sleeping giant is about to wake up—competing claims by Korea, Japan, and China over the continental shelves in the East China Sea.

Rather unnoticed in the waning moments of 2012, an 800-page report was submitted by Korea to the UN Commission on the Limits of the Continental Shelf. Included in the submission was scientific and technical information on how far Korea's landmass extends under the sea toward the Pacific.

In more technical terms, Korea basically claims that the "natural prolongation" of her land territory extends beyond the 200 nautical miles from the baseline, all the way to the Okinawa Trough, deep inside the exclusive economic zone claimed by Japan.

Discrimination (Qatar v. United Arab Emirates), Provisional Measures, Order of 14 June 2001, paras. 25–30, para. 23.

10 *See Appeal Relating to the Jurisdiction of the ICAO Council under Article 84 of the Convention of the International Civil Aviation*, Joint Application Instituting Proceedings (Bahrain, Egypt, Saudi Arabia, and the United Arab Emirates v. Qatar).

11 *See ibid.*, Annex 2, pp. 8, 26–30; Annex 3, pp. 34–39.

Korea's submission followed China's submission of its own information on Dec. 14 to the same commission. In the report, China also claimed its continental shelf should reach the same Okinawa Trough.

The 1982 UN Convention on the Law of the Sea stipulates (in Article 76, paragraph 8) that any country claiming a continental shelf beyond the 200 nautical miles should submit such information to the commission. The same convention also acknowledges a continental shelf of a coastal state in terms of the natural prolongation of the land territory. Korea and China thus purported to submit marine scientific information to substantiate their claims. It turns out that the natural prolongation of the landmass of the two countries nearly touches Japan's territorial waters in the region.

Not surprisingly, Japan has made clear that these claims are not acceptable and asserted instead that delimitation on the basis of an equidistant median line (i.e., dividing in half) is the most equitable solution to the problem.

The December moves of Korea and China, although expected for some time now, must have displeased Japan, to say the least. Japan dismisses the two neighbors' positions by referring to international court decisions which seem to have endorsed median line delimitations in similar situations.

In a nutshell, the areas claimed by Korea and China mainly overlap in the region and Japan does not recognize at all the claims made by Korea and China to the extent they exceed the median line. Once the scientific and technical information is confirmed as accurate by the 21-member commission, the next step is for the three adjacent countries to sit down together for negotiations to delimitate the overlapping regions.

Korea's Dec. 26 submission also makes clear that future negotiations are necessary by putting a disclaimer that its submission is "without prejudice to the questions of delimitation of the continental shelf."

In other words, these two submissions were meant to mark the beginning of trilateral negotiations, perhaps long negotiations. Some experts are even talking about a couple of decades. Between Korea and Japan, this is to take an old issue from the shelf and dust it off. The two countries concluded a Joint Development Agreement in 1974 that is set to run through 2028, only 15 years away.

The maritime territorial flare-ups among the three countries are showing no signs of letting up. A likely scenario of how they will jockey for the enormous pockets of natural resources buried under the seabed could make the recent confrontations look tame.

Once the current spell of bad weather passes by, a breakthrough needs to be found in order to unlock the impasse. A breakthrough would only come with confidence building and mutual trust—the same spirit shared when the three countries set up a Trilateral Cooperation Secretariat in 2011. Given what has transpired since 2012, almost anything would look easier than reviving that spirit.

As long as it is continued, genuine efforts are made, it may be slow in coming but come it will. Failing this, the East China Sea will be known for all sorts of bickering.

The sea of confrontation should turn into a sea of cooperation (why not joint trilateral development projects?). Otherwise, it may become a sea of heartbreak for all three.

[The Korea Herald, January 9, 2013]

2. Racing against the Clock

It is everybody's nightmare when a deadline for a project is approaching but progress is slow. A deadline, if well managed, works as a catalyst for a positive outcome—we all experience last-minute creativity and efficiency sparks under extreme time pressure.

When, however, a deadline is imposed but the task is unrealistic, this positive last-minute drive does not work. People just have to let the chips fall where they may.

Ever since a deadline was set as the end of this year at the July summit meeting in Seoul, the Korea-China FTA negotiations have intensified on all fronts to meet it. It is now being mentioned that a summit meeting on the sidelines the November APEC meeting in Beijing may declare the completion of the negotiations.

For this to happen, some miraculous strides need to be made to narrow the gaps between the two countries' positions in the next two months in key sectors such as industrial goods and agricultural products. It is theoretically feasible, but stars must align first.

The pressure of meeting the deadline is already pushing Korea to reduce its ambitions and kick the can down the road. In the 12th round of negotiations held in Daegu in July, the two countries reached a compromise on services. One of the critical differences between the two sides was whether to adopt a "negative" listing system in services trade as suggested by Korea or a "positive" system championed by China. In the negotiation held right after the summit, Korea agreed to accept a "positive" listing approach in exchange for a promise that the two sides will seek to amend the agreement in the future to adopt a negative scheme after the agreement enters into force.

Once concluded, any treaty is difficult to amend. Particularly so, in the early stage of implementation, and more so if the issue has been one of the key pillars of the negotiation. Today's complacency can be tomorrow's headache.

What has been put on the backburner in the heat of the Korea-China FTA is the mega-FTA that stands to affect Korea's interest significantly in the long run—the Trans-Pacific Partnership. In an effort to find a breakthrough, 12 TPP negotiating countries are having meetings in Hanoi this week. Interestingly, they also have the same deadline in mind—the November APEC meeting. Wide gaps in views between the United States and Japan, and the upcoming US mid-term election in November still make it quite challenging to meet the deadline.

If TPP participants miss the November deadline, it might prolong the entire negotiation and this may open up a small but new window of opportunity for Korea to join the TPP as an original member. If Korea's ultimate plan is to join the TPP at some point, doing so as an original member would make more sense. Once a trade agreement is concluded, membership fees for newcomers are usually high.

Noting the importance of a mega-FTA as a venue of new rulemaking in many areas of trade, a country's accession to the agreement after all deals are completed would mean losing an opportunity to have its voice heard in the rule formulation stage. If Korea has strong interest in TPP, this fall and winter may provide the last chance to get on the bandwagon. The benefits to be flowing from a prospective FTA between Korea and China are obvious and undeniable, but meeting the deadline for deadline's sake should not blind Seoul to other important developments in the trade front.

As much as a prospective Korea-China FTA is important, every step and decision should be carefully made. If the bilateral FTA, in practical sense, cannot be reached by the desired deadline or can only meet the deadline in a hollowed-out form, the approach should be shifted to account for other pending issues such as the TPP. There is no need to put all eggs in one basket.

[The Korea Herald, September 3, 2014]

3. Issues in FTA with China

The year 2014 has been quite productive for Korea in terms of Free Trade Agreements. Australia, then Canada, and now New Zealand have agreed to free trade deals with Korea. While all these FTAs are important for Korea, the one with China, Seoul's largest trading partner, marks a watershed moment for Korea' s FTA policy started in the early 2000s. Many things are still on the drawing board and both countries will now conduct "legal scrubbing" to polish the text to reflect what has been agreed upon.

The balance sheet for the Korea-China FTA has been analyzed by different entities from many different angles. This exercise will continue and perhaps intensify once the whole ratification procedure starts at the National Assembly early next year.

The usual assessment—whether for the agreement or against it—is based on the direct economic impact as a result of tariff elimination "at the border." This is of course important, but the real impact of an FTA can only be assessed—and felt—by evaluating how the consumers access to goods in the partner country is guaranteed. This assessment is called calibrating "behind-the-border" issues and is getting more attention in the global trade regime.

The elimination of tariffs at the border is just one aspect of the market opening commitment. How the imported products are treated inside the market—behind the borders—is becoming more important in the commitment. The pendulum of international trade has shifted from the at-the-border issues to behind-the-border issues. The balance sheet for the Korea-China FTA also hinges upon how these behind-the-border issues will be dealt with. With respect to this particular FTA, here are some of the important issues to look for.

First and foremost is the local government. China is known for the broad autonomy and wide discretion accorded to its local governments of all levels across the vast territory. In many instances, trade frictions with China concern what has taken place at the local government level. So, it is critical to ensure that the FTA is implemented at the level of local governments as promptly as possible. It usually takes time for many countries, and it may take longer, even with good faith, for a country with a population of 1.4 billion. Just look around us—after all, it is the local governments (City Governments and District Offices) that stand to affect our daily business operations and sales of goods.

Let's then consider the Non-Tariff Barrier issue. Navigating the web of laws and regulations, both written and unwritten, in some countries is like walking down the labyrinthine streets of an old city. Unpredictable exercise of discretion and invisible regulatory restriction couched in vague terms may well neutralize the benefits from tariff elimination. NTB detection and elimination is therefore critical. As with any other FTA, a mechanism to detect, monitor, and address NTBs is all the more necessary in this FTA as well.

Finally, the irony of an FTA. The conclusion of an FTA eliminates the tariffs but tends to induce robust trade remedy investigations. The trilogy of trade remedy investigations—antidumping, countervailing duty, and safeguards investigations—have become a more popular tool for domestic industries to cope with the increased penetration of products from FTA partners. Over the past several years, China has become one of the active users of these trade remedies, and it may be forced to target Korean products when the increased market shares threaten its domestic competitors.

The final balance sheet of the Korea-China FTA will be drawn up only when it is clear how these behind-the-border issues are shaping up through the implementation of the FTA. Of course, China will have its own checklist for Korea. The conclusion of an FTA is just the beginning of a long process, and it is its (faithful) implementation that matters.

[The Korea Herald, November 19, 2014]

4. Elephant in the Room

One common mistake in understanding the Trans-Pacific Partnership deal is to view it as just another free trade agreement. This one is quite different.

People tend to forget the unique feature of this particular agreement: it introduces many new rules of trade, rules that will form new codes of conduct for governments and serve as a platform for future discussions in other settings.

When new rules are being discussed, waiting out has its own benefits and risks. As few can gauge the exact impact and consequences of a new rule, we can wait and see how other early adopters fumble and struggle. We learn from others' mistakes and adjust our footsteps in following them before we adopt the rules. A temptingly safe choice.

The downside of the waiting strategy is also obvious. Once the trailblazers establish the basic structure of rules as they see fit, you lose the opportunity to give your inputs for the general architecture of the rules. You just follow the footsteps of the pathfinders, but you can hardly change the general direction they are heading. The followers have less control over where to and how to get there. So, sitting on the fence has both benefits and risks. You weigh benefits and risks and make a choice. Once a choice is made—either to wait or plunge—then you will have to see how the chips may fall.

That is exactly what has happened with respect to Korea's position toward the TPP. It decided to wait. The appropriateness of the decision can be challenged, but a decision has been made and the consequence is ours. Kicking ourselves for the past decisions made will not help. Now that the mega-FTA has been agreed upon among the 12 participating states, what is left is how to proceed from this point onward—to maximize the benefits and minimize the risks.

Once the full text of the agreement is disclosed in early November, we can fathom the real impact of the new rules included. And, more critically, then we can watch how other countries adjust themselves to implement the new rules. This is the advantage of the waiting strategy.

On the other hand, once Korea is ready and sends in its request to join, the accession fee can be quite high. Just like any group, once it is formed by core members, any new member desiring to join it afterward is expected (and requested) to pay an admission fee. This has been the case for trade agreements as well and quite a few accession negotiations have been brutal and difficult. As Korea is one of the most active trading partners with these 12 nations, it would not be surprising to see long lists of preconditions. Under this scenario, it is theoretically possible that despite Korea's desire to join the mega-FTA, the accession fee may turn out to be prohibitively high because all these 12 countries are trying to settle all the outstanding bilateral issues at this juncture, in which case accession may become infeasible.

Since the announcement of the TPP breakthrough in early October, statements have been made indicating Korea's interest in joining the agreement "at whatever costs." Expressing the desire to accede by paying whatever it takes would not serve Korea's interest. Nor would it solve the problems. It would only weaken Seoul's position in future negotiations.

Given Korea's economic status in the Pacific Rim, it does look odd if it does not participate in this mega-FTA with important new rules. So, all things being equal, it is reasonable to expect Korea's participation in the agreement. But it is the terms and conditions of the accession that determine Korea's ultimate accession. And it is still too early to tell.

With the announcement of the final agreement on TPP, all sorts of "what if" talks have been engulfing Korea. Monday morning quarterbacking really does not help anyone and the remaining, and meaningful, question is what to do next.

[The Korea Herald, October 21, 2015]

5. Pirates, Private Security Firms, Consuls

No. 1: one way to sail through the pirate-infested Gulf of Aden with peace of mind is purchasing security service. Protection Vessels International, Ltd. is one of such security corporations founded by former British special forces personnel. It provides escort and protection services to merchant ships. PVI is a maritime version of Blackwater Inc., which provides security service to officials and military personnel in Iraq and Afghanistan.

When a security vessel of the PVI visited the port of Masswa, Eritrea, on Dec. 24 for refueling, the company's employees were arrested by the Eritrean police on charges of possession of illegal firearms.

Then came exchanges of barbed words between Britain and Eritrea. Britain has been criticizing the Eritrean government for denying the right of consular access to the detained Britons. This is the right of the consul to visit its own nationals who have been arrested by the state where the consul is posted. Under the 1963 Vienna Convention on Consular Relations, to which almost all countries have acceded, a country putting a foreign national to a criminal proceeding has an affirmative obligation to notify the consul dispatched from the foreigner's country. The foreign arrestee should also be informed of the right to communicate with the consul from his or her home country. The consul should then be permitted to have access to the person in custody.

This convention constituted the basis on which the US demanded consular access when its citizen was arrested by the Syrian government earlier this month. When four Japanese nationals were arrested for allegedly filming a military installation in China last fall, Tokyo also demanded full consular access. China also raised the same issue upon the arrest of its nationals by the Indian authorities at the Indo-Nepalese border in January this year.

From time to time, this obligation evolves into an international dispute. Mexico and Germany raised this issue at the International Court of Justice in The Hague against the United States (in Avena case and LaGrand case, respectively) when their consuls have not been notified of their nationals' arrest and trial in the United States. Mexico and Germany ultimately prevailed in these litigations. In a 2010 dispute, the world court also found similar violation when the Democratic Republic of the Congo failed to notify the Guinean consul when a Guinean national was arrested in Kinshasa.

In these disputes, regarding the notification obligation, an argument was made that the arrest and nationalities of the detained were already made public through press reports, rendering consular notification unnecessary. The court disagreed with this line of argument by effectively holding that irrespective of the public knowledge, what is necessary under the 1963 Vienna Convention is the official notification.

No. 2: the first foreign piracy trial by Korea was completed last Friday. With journalists from roughly 50 international news outlets covering the trial, the Busan District Court sentenced four Somali pirates arrested on Jan. 22 to harsh punishment, spanning from 13-year imprisonment to life imprisonment.

As this was the first attempt of this kind, quite a few logistical and procedural issues have surfaced since the pirates' arrival in Korea in late January, including attorney appointment, arranging interpretation, and adjustment to detention facilities. The recent confession of some pirates that they would like to settle down in Korea may allude to the effort of the law enforcement agency to preserve their procedural due process rights.

As noted earlier, to the extent the pirates are foreigners subject to a criminal proceeding in Korea, the checklist should also take note of the procedural requirements applicable in the international plane including the consular notification and access.

Since the Somali pirates' arrival in Korea, the press coverage of their investigation and detention has presented a detailed account of the proceeding in Korea. None of the press reports, however, refer to notification to or communication with the Somali representatives or their delegates as the proceedings were pending. The only contact, according to the media, seems to be the discussion with the Somali official in Oman relating to the repatriation of the bodies of the pirates killed in the rescue operation.

If the necessary communication has been done already or Somalia has somehow waived its right to it, that is good. But if that is not the case as it appears to be, the relevance of the obligation in this particular context should be explored without any further delay. In case one wonders, both Korea and Somalia are parties to the 1963 Vienna Convention along with 171 other countries.

Not surprisingly, Somalia does not maintain a diplomatic mission in Korea. The nearest one is in Beijing. It is not clear whether under the circumstances the consular notification and access should be given to the country's Beijing mission or to the Foreign Ministry in Mogadishu, or whether such notification and access can be excused entirely.

Alternatively, maybe there is an honorary consul in Korea for the country, which is often the case for countries without permanent embassies or consulates. In addition, sometimes countries delegate their consular access rights to a third country when its mission does not exist in a given country as seen in the 1995 US-Sweden agreement under which the Swedish embassy in Pyongyang provides basic consular protective services to US citizens traveling in North Korea. These alternative scenarios might be relevant in the present case.

Although the factual situation is not clear, this aspect of the procedural requirements is something that should be carefully examined lest Korea faces unintended embarrassment in the future.

[The Korea Herald, June 1, 2011]

6. Sharing Benefits of FTA—But How?

From the angle of domestic politics, the fundamental problem with free trade agreements is that certain segments of the national economy end up with the short straw even if the country as a whole benefits.

When someone asks, "Why should I sacrifice for the benefit of others?," there's got to be an answer from the government: "Do not worry, we've got your back." In many countries, that is the only way any trade deal can survive domestic politics. How to formulate an assistance package for those who may get shortchanged from a trade deal has now become the most difficult homework for a government negotiating an FTA.

Many trade agreements commonly restrict targeted governmental support for certain industries or allow support only in prescribed ways. So, a government is left in a catch-22 situation: it should help and is willing to help, but is largely not permitted to do so under applicable trade pacts.

Forget about trade pacts. From the political perspective, promising to offer a package of compensation and emergency rescue is virtually the only way to secure the necessary domestic support for trade deals.

This debate over "how to" and "who to" save had delayed the ratification of the Korea-China FTA since June. On the last day of November, the National Assembly finally ratified the deal along with New Zealand and Vietnam FTAs. This is relieving news, as the absolute deadline for the legislative process to bring the treaties into effect within the year was Nov. 30—the latest point to complete all the remaining proceedings in time after the legislative voting: a treaty conclusion entails a complex domestic process under the law. Now it seems that the entry into effect within the year is within reach.

This agreement with China adopts a tariff reduction schedule purely based on the calendar year of the final consummation of the deal. The first-year reduction schedule applies even if the effective date becomes Dec. 31, in which case the second-year reduction schedule kicks in the next day, Jan. 1, 2016.

If, on the other hand, the final completion comes on Jan. 1, the whole year next year will have to stick to the first-year schedule.

Think tanks calculate the monetary loss from missing the Dec. 31 deadline as 1.5 trillion won ($1.5 billion): to put it visually, this is roughly 70,000 compact sedans. As the reduction schedule applies for 20 years, the one-year delay in the front end also means that the total schedule is pushed back by a year. So, the potential cumulative effect could be larger than 1.5 trillion won annually. Making efforts to meet last Monday's deadline was thus critical, at least for Korea.

As a condition for the clearance of the legislative process, a new fund is going to be established using contributions from manufacturing companies and trading entities that stand to benefit from freer trade with China. Monetary assistance will then be provided to "affected" industries, mainly the agricultural sector.

There is no information available yet as to who will contribute and how much. If the contribution is somehow allocated to paying companies based on export performance, it may raise a consistency issue with existing trade agreements. Doling out monetary support to designated industries would also raise another legal issue under the agreements. It all depends on specific components of the proposed assistance fund. As far as we can tell, no country has adopted this type of scheme before—arranging to transfer money from the beneficiaries of a trade deal to affected sectors.

Unquestionably, we have to make sure that the benefit of a trade agreement is fairly distributed among domestic constituents. But having exporters and manufactures pay as they profit is a new formula that has not been tried before. Will it set a new precedent?

[The Korea Herald, December 2, 2015]

7. Hot Pursuit, Cold Relations

Liquor smuggling was a lucrative business in the American Prohibition era of 1920–1933. A Canadian ship named "I'm Alone" was one of the vessels engaged in smuggling. In March 1929 the ship was approached by US Coast Guard cutters for inspection within the jurisdictional waters of the United States. Not surprisingly, it sped away. The Coast Guard cutters continued their chase for the next two days, and finally caught the ship on the high seas.

A dispute arose between Canada and the US since the ultimate arrest was made on the high seas. As the initial chase began from within jurisdictional waters, the apprehension on the high seas was found by an international arbitration court to be consistent with international maritime law.

Look at another more recent example. In 1997 an oil tanker of Saint Vincent and the Grenadines, named Saiga, was seized by a Guinean customs patrol boat on the high seas for allegedly violating customs regulation within the Guinean Exclusive Economic Zone. In this incident, the patrol boat originally initiated the chase but gave up and returned to the port. The next day the boat resumed its search and found Saiga in high seas and detained her.

Here, the International Tribunal for the Law of the Sea deemed the clear interruption of the pursuit to nullify the right to pursue and apprehend in high seas. So, Guinea was found to have violated the UN Convention on the Law of the Sea.

As long as a chase proceeds without interruption, it can continue for many more days. In August 2003, the Australian navy conducted the longest pursuit on record: it pursued a Uruguayan vessel Viarsa, which was engaged in illegal fishing, for 21 days over 7,000 kilometers. The vessel was near Cape Town, South Africa, when captured and escorted back to Australia for a legal proceeding.

This concept of maritime law is called the right of "hot pursuit." It is included in the UNCLOS as well. There are several conditions. A pursuit should be "hot," meaning it should be continuous and uninterrupted. It should also be initiated from the jurisdictional waters such as an EEZ or territorial waters where a coastal state has jurisdiction. In addition, a visible and audible signal to stop must be provided first.

In many respects, the Oct. 7 incident in the Yellow Sea is a typical example of the right of "hot pursuit." It was on the high seas that Chinese fishing boats rammed into a Korean Coast Guard patrol boat and sank it. The ensuing arrest of Chinese fishermen was made on the high seas.

The Chinese Foreign Ministry claimed that the arrest was illegitimate because it was made on the high seas and outside the Korean jurisdictional waters. As noted in the preceding examples, what matters is not the location of the ultimate arrest but whether laws and regulations were violated within the Korean jurisdictional waters before fishing boats started to flee and whether the pursuit was "hot" throughout the chase. The accounts of both countries apparently indicate that these requirements were satisfied here.

The ramming and sinking of the law enforcement boat marks a new high in the level of violence in the Yellow Sea. Seoul vowed to dial up the level of force in future altercations. It was not prudent, however, to mention specific types of weapons on board, such as cannons, to be employed in future confrontations. Such a statement may cater to the short-term feelings of the national audience, but it can easily backfire, as the words can be interpreted as Korea's unwillingness to pay due regard to the need to use reasonable force proportionate to specific situations at hand. A short, but stern statement would have been more effective.

Given the intensity of illegal fishing in the Yellow Sea, pursuits, clashes, and arrests will continue. The two countries are now negotiating EEZ delimitation in the Yellow Sea. Any delimitation would be effectively vitiated if the likes of Oct. 7 stand to describe an archetypical environment in the Yellow Sea.

[The Korea Herald, October 18, 2016]

8. Nonbinding, Amicable Procedure Does Not Just Bark, It Bites, Too

A dispute settlement proceeding between two states usually conjures up the image of stern-faced judges in robes under tightly controlled timeframes, and most importantly, a legally binding judgment with a serious penalty. This is very important, and many disputes go down this path.

In the meantime, a notable new trend is forming. Nonbinding dispute settlement procedures that seek an amicable solution are making inroads into new treaties and agreements. This is, so to speak, a state-to-state version of alternative dispute resolution.

Yes, the decision from such proceedings is nonbinding and unenforceable, so one might shrug it off, saying, "It is not legally binding, so why bother?" That is true but not quite. The outcome from the proceedings still carries significant weight for disputing parties. An objective assessment by a third party is rendered from the proceedings, stating the violation or non-violation of a treaty. Any responsible government would view its national policy being branded as the violation of a treaty as a serious matter. At that point, whether it is legally binding or nonbinding doesn't matter that much. In addition, nonbinding proceedings cost less and conclude fast. Knowing this, treaty parties are introducing and experimenting with these proceedings in many varieties and kinds.

The best testing grounds are, not surprisingly, free trade agreements. Recent FTAs offer a variety of nonbinding dispute settlement proceedings for various purposes.

The first instance of the invocation of this new type of dispute settlement proceeding came on Dec. 17, when the EU initiated an official proceeding regarding the implementation of "sustainable development commitments" under the Korea-EU FTA. As far as Korea is concerned, this is the first instance of an official dispute settlement proceeding of an FTA—whether binding or nonbinding—being initiated, after 15 FTAs in 14 years since 2004.

In a two-page letter uploaded on a website, Brussels complained about Korea's slow progress in the ratification of the four "fundamental" conventions of the International Labor Organization. Among the eight fundamental conventions of the ILO, Korea has so far ratified only four. The remaining four concern freedom of association and prohibition of forced labor (Convention Nos. 29, 87, 98, & 105). The EU claims Korea's continued delay of the ratification of these four remaining conventions constitutes violation of the FTA. In the bilateral FTA (Article 13.4), the two countries committed themselves to making "continued and sustained efforts" toward ratifying these core ILO conventions. From the EU's point of view, Korea has not made continued and sustained efforts for this ratification to happen, therefore it argues that the FTA has been violated.

The official proceeding will start with government-to-government consultations. If the matter remains unresolved after 90 days, an expert panel will be formed to hear the two governments out and issue a decision. Again, this decision of the panel would be nonbinding. But whatever comes out of the panel would have significant impact, in a practical sense.

Let's set aside whether Korea has made continued and sustained efforts and whether there is a violation of the FTA. Future proceedings will determine it in due course.

What is symbolic of this development is that various mechanisms and proceedings contained in FTAs are now waking up from hibernation. FTA proceedings have not been active so far, but the EU's request heralds that the tide is changing, and nonbinding proceedings in particular are moving briskly.

For trade disputes, only WTO proceedings have been on our minds. Now diverse FTA proceedings are springing up. The question is: how do we handle the logistical burden? Each FTA contains several new proceedings. If we have 15 FTAs so far, that means we would have to deal with at least dozens of new proceedings soon. Obviously, administration of and participation in these proceedings need tremendous resources. Nonbinding, amicable proceedings are particularly important: they are not just hortatory; they do bite sometimes. Therefore, thorough preparation is necessary, and it requires resources.

Up until now, this possibility has been largely theoretical. The EU's latest request shows that the theoretical concern has now started to become a real one.

[The Korea Herald, December 25, 2018]

9. Cheonan and UN Security Council

As the Icelandic volcano covered the European sky over the weekend, the ashes from corvette 772 (aka The Cheonan) explosion in the West Sea four weeks ago have covered the entire Korean peninsula. The ashes were so thick that all is dark and rumors of all sorts are jockeying for the attention of the media. Shaking off its initial clumsy handling of the matter, the government is currently mounting an all-out investigation to confirm the cause and source of the explosion, and who is responsible for the tragedy. It may never be easy, but sooner or later the government investigation will find answers to all these questions as in the following cases.

Case No. 1 (Dec. 24, 1988, Lockerbie, Scotland). The 1988 bombing of Pan Am 103 over Lockerbie, Scotland, also seemed at first to be an insoluble incident. The evidence was untraceable: the entire airplane was destroyed in midair, reduced to small pieces, all of which were then scattered all over the ground. The US and UK joint investigation team, however, spent almost two years collecting debris from the ground to basically reconstruct the airplane and what was inside. The investigators in this process managed to collect some foreign plastic debris. What emerged from the assembly of the debris over time was a small Toshiba radio with a faint serial number on the back. With the number, the investigators could confirm that the radio had been sold from a Swiss merchant to an agent of the Libyan intelligence agency. This evidence played a key role in the UN Security Council's imposition of harsh economic sanctions against Libya for the next 15 years, to which Libya finally succumbed by surrendering those responsible to an international trial.

Case No. 2 (Oct. 22, 1946, in the Corfu Channel between the Greek island of Corfu and Albania). In this incident of 1946, British warships were damaged and sailors killed by sea mines as the warships were cruising through the Corfu Channel off the coast of Albania. The United Kingdom brought a case against Albania at the International Court of Justice, a UN organ, asking for damages. Albania refused to acknowledge its responsibility, arguing that the sea mines were in fact deployed by some other countries, including Yugoslavia. In 1949, the court went on to rule for the United Kingdom. This case also involved a lengthy investigation and evidence-gathering process in order to determine who had rigged the channel with the sea mines and whether or not the government of Albania had been involved in the whole process.

These precedents may teach us three things at this painful juncture: first, it may take a long time to put all pieces of the puzzle together, but a culprit will emerge; second, what is critical now is an extensive and thorough investigation to turn up clear evidence, rather than an emotional or hasty response; and third, once those responsible are confirmed we will probably have to resort to the United Nations, unless another military attack occurs. With respect to the third point, as much as military retaliation may be tempting, the legal principle in this situation dictates that use of force for retaliation is prohibited, unless another military attack is imminent or underway. At this point it may be difficult for South Korea to justify military retaliation based on the concept of self-defense.

The only option available then would be to take the issue to the UN Security Council and request a sanction measure under Chapter VII of the UN Charter. Bringing a case to the ICJ would also be an option, but it is doubtful whether the court will have jurisdiction for the incident as the establishment of the court's jurisdiction requires prior consent from the defendant state. A sanction under Chapter VII may include an economic or diplomatic sanction and in fact could be as lethal as a military sanction depending on how the sanction is formulated with how much international support. The preceding Lockerbie example proves this. It should also be noted that this sanction by the Security Council would be possible only with concrete and specific evidence. Circumstantial evidence and vague linkage will not be able to gather the yes votes from the five permanent members possessing the veto right.

International law confers a special status on a warship. Indeed, the 1982 UN Convention on the Law of the Sea, which is a constitution of an international maritime law, treats a state's warship as if it were a "floating island" of the nation and exempts it from jurisdiction of another state. So, South Korean naval vessels operating off the coast of Somalia and visiting the port of Hawaii are all regarded as part of Korean territory, not as a mere vessel. That is why the recent attack and sinking of the Cheonan shakes us all to the core: the ship represents Republic of Korea and thus all of us. And probably that is why some people say that the tragedy is the Korean version of Sept. 11.

[The Korea Herald, April 21, 2010]

10. A Whaling War in the Hague

As the prime ministers of the two countries publicly acknowledge, fish conservation is the only area where Japan and Australia have differing views. Japan is one of the major fishing countries in the world and Australia has long been the spiritual leader of the global fish conservation group. The diplomatic wrangling between the two countries has been particularly tumultuous over Japan's Southern Ocean whaling program.

The "whaling" tension has continued to intensify in recent years as the Japanese whaling vessels have become frequent targets of anti-whaling activists from Australia and other countries. The anti-whaling protesters have boarded Japanese whaling vessels in high seas off the coast of Western Australia, and sometimes thrown paint or rancid butter in bags at the whaling ships.

Two years ago, a New Zealander who had boarded a Japanese whaling vessel in protest was later convicted by a Japanese court on charges of assault and trespass before his deportation to his home country. An Australian Federal Court even issued a judgment in 2008 declaring that Japanese whaling in the Australian Whale Sanctuary in Antarctica is a breach of Australian law.

Having seen all this, Australia and Japan are now attempting to resolve their differences, once and for all, at a forum of last resort: the UN's International Court of Justice in The Hague.

The ICJ is the highest adjudicating body for international disputes to which countries refer their most sensitive legal problems with other countries—including territorial disputes, treaty interpretations, and military conflicts.

All 192 members of the UN are automatically parties to this court. Among them, 67 states have voluntarily accepted the "compulsory jurisdiction" of the court, meaning that they allow other countries to bring a legal action against them in the court, as is commonly observed in a domestic legal system. As for the other 125 countries, a case-by-case consent is a prerequisite. Japan has been one of the most significant recent additions to the list of 67 "compulsory jurisdiction" countries when accepted it in July 2007.

The acceptance of the jurisdiction may have been most welcomed by Australia. In May 2010, Australia filed its complaint with the ICJ, alleging that Japan's whaling program had violated the 1946 International Convention on the Regulation of Whaling. The US diplomatic cables sent from Canberra released by WikiLeaks detail the internal discussions on pros and cons inside the Australian government concerning the appropriateness of initiating an ICJ proceeding against a close economic ally and the strength of its case. So started Japan's first (and Australia's fourth) ICJ proceeding and intermediate court deadlines have been set and met. Under the current pace, the judgment is expected to be released by sometime next year.

Perhaps the outcome of this dispute is a matter of concern for the two countries only. But watching how two friendly countries negotiate, get frustrated and end up in court is both suggestive and informative. As for those countries in this part of the world, who have possibilities of encountering each other at adjudicative proceedings in the back of their mind, Japan's decision to be more actively involved in the ICJ proceeding is an interesting development to keep an eye on.

As with domestic trials, international litigation requires experience and expertise. There is a huge difference between those who have "been there, done that" and those who haven't. Most countries scramble to cram when a proceeding is imminent, but it is usually too late.

This proceeding and future proceedings with other countries at the ICJ may enable Japan to solidify its status as the leading country in Asia in the field of international law. What prompted Japan to accept the compulsory jurisdiction in 2007 and how it has prepared to participate in the present and future proceedings would offer an interesting case study material for countries in the region.

Contrary to common notion, all this state-to-state litigation at the ICJ is open to the public, so anybody can watch it after prior registration. And the schedule for the "oral hearing" of the Australia-Japan dispute, in which the top professionals of the two countries appear and make argument for their countries, will be released sometime soon, so stay tuned.

[The Korea Herald, April 18, 2012]

11. One Treaty, Two Interpretations

When a government negotiates and signs a treaty, lay people have one simple question: how would it affect me? With a little bit of elaboration, the question then can be further divided into two different categories of retrospective queries and prospective ones.

A good example of a prospective query is whether I, as an individual, can refer to the treaty as a basis to bring a claim in domestic court on my own accord. This has been one of the key issues in the context of free trade agreement negotiations these days.

A good example of a question falling under the retrospective category, on the other hand, is whether the treaty at issue has settled the existing claims that I may have. This very issue lies at the core of the May 24 decision of the Korean Supreme Court, in which it examined the meaning and scope of the 1965 Korea-Japan Claims Settlement Agreement attached to the simultaneous Basic Relations Treaty.

In the 20-page decision, the nation's highest court opined that the 1965 Claims Agreement cannot be interpreted as having settled all individual claims held by individual victims. It thus reversed the previous judgment of the Busan High Court and remanded the case back to the lower court for further deliberation in accordance with its May 24 decision.

Though a final disposition in the lower court is still to come, the official pronouncement of the highest court concerning the 1965 treaty is expected to have far-reaching implications particularly because this decision does not entirely dovetail with the existing position of the government. The highest court's decision may incentivize other claimants to consider similar proceedings. Expectedly, the government offered a cautious response and commented that it would continue to carefully watch future proceedings at the lower court.

This decision of the Korean Supreme Court is exactly opposite of the 2007 decision of the Japanese Supreme Court over the same claim and the same issue. In the decision, the highest court of Japan concluded that all individual claims of Koreans were espoused by the Korean government and were settled, once and for all, by the 1965 agreement. In last week's decision, the Korean Supreme Court offers a lengthy discussion on the 2007 decision of Japan and stated in no less unequivocal terms that it does not agree with the decision. Put another way, the highest courts of the two countries have now two contradictory interpretations of the same treaty provision.

The effect of the conflict will become more palpable when the plaintiffs try to enforce the judgment once they finally prevail in the lower court. In theory, the defendant Japanese corporation's assets in Korea may be subject to the attachment application by the prevailing plaintiffs. Once (or before) the dispute reaches this stage, the two governments will have to find a resolution.

The Korea-Japan Claims Agreement sets forth a two-step process to deal with this kind of situation. Under Article 3 of the agreement, the two countries are obligated to settle the dispute through the diplomatic channels, and if this attempt fails one of the parties can initiate an arbitration proceeding. A three-member arbitration tribunal will be composed within 60 days of initiation. After deliberation, this tribunal then issues a binding decision.

Obviously, the most appropriate way to break the stalemate would be to explore a diplomatic solution to this issue. If, however, the parallel positions of the two sides do not show any sign of flexibility, then the only remaining solution seems to be the arbitration process as stipulated in the treaty provision.

Of course, this route would not be stress-free or cost-free. By having a third party issue a binding decision on this politically and diplomatically sensitive issue, both sides would encounter immense domestic pressure throughout the proceeding. The burden for Korea would be no less onerous since Korea has not participated in any state-to-state arbitration of this sort.

Sadly, unless some area of convergence is found one way or another, this path appears to be the only remaining way to put a punctuation mark on this issue. Hopefully, the two countries will be able to come up with a wise solution to break the deadlock before the problem is further complicated.

[The Korea Herald, May 31, 2012]

12. Chasing Two Targets in Oil Imports

The European Union's imposition of tough sanctions against Iran starting from July 1 is really pushing Korea into a corner. One of the core elements of Brussels' sanctions is to prohibit insurance companies in the EU from providing coverage for foreign tankers transporting oil shipments from Iran. As Korean tankers are insured or re-insured by big name insurance companies in Europe, this sanction is virtually halting Korea's oil importation from Iran. No insurance simply means no seafaring.

In 2011 Iran was Korea's sixth-largest oil supplier accounting for 9.4 percent of total petroleum imports. An abrupt suspension of oil imports from one of the major suppliers is adding up another woe to the country's general economic performance.

Even before the EU's sanction, Seoul has already been tightening its energy belt, fearing an energy shortage this summer, by forcing to dial up the thermostats of downtown coffee shops and spreading a "cool casual" dress code. And the recent development may require punching another hole in the belt. What's more, no oil imports from Iran also means no Korean exports to the country since both in-bound and out-bound bilateral transactions are presently cleared through the Iranian Central Bank accounts opened in the Korean banks.

It was just a few weeks ago that Seoul breathed a sigh of relief when the United States decided to exempt Korea from the application of its new Iran sanction statute for the next six months, on the condition that Seoul would significantly reduce the oil imports from Iran. Seoul's effort to secure a similar waiver from the EU was to no avail.

Interestingly, Iran is now offering a new type of service to countries like Korea. Iran is floating the idea that it can use its own tankers to deliver the crude oil to the importing states. This can be seen as an international version akin to a home-delivery service for people whose cars are grounded because their insurance policies were canceled.

Whether this scheme will work is uncertain yet, because the home-delivery service still carries the issues of who pays for the insurance and what kind of an insurance package is purchased. This is the most recent attempt by some countries to find a "magic formula" to pursue two rabbits at the same time: joining the UN-imposed sanction against Iran, while also minimizing the negative impact on their economy. Achieving the goal does defy an easy solution.

The UN Security Council sanctions is legitimate in all respects under the circumstances, and individual countries' authority to enforce its own sanction measures within the framework of the UN resolution seems also unquestionable. In the meantime, the government's relentless efforts to get waivers from Washington and Brussels over the past several months have exposed how vulnerable Korea is in the overall chain of international transactions. Korea manufactures goods and exports them.

That is entirely within its control. But key elements to bring the goods into the stream of international commerce are within the jurisdiction of other countries. International banking and financing, and maritime insurance are two examples of such key elements. The former was the reason for Korea's effort to get a waiver from Washington, whereas the latter explains the recent fire drill concerning the EU sanction. Both countries control the critical check points of the long road of international trade. If any checkpoint is closed or tightened, the effect would be more immediately felt by countries like Korea with a lot of traffic volume and no other alternative routes in sight. So, a similar situation could easily happen in the context of transactions of other ordinary goods as well.

Some countries' decision to introduce their own maritime insurance programs to cover their oil shipments from Iran in the face of the EU sanction is the recognition of this reality. This also suggests that a network of Plan B options be reviewed and prepared by Korea well in advance for future contingents.

Exploring creative ways to get around other countries' sanction is one thing. But a more difficult problem is how to deal with the cold stares from these countries watching an array of circumventive maneuvering, countries that exert significant influence at every corner of international transaction. Finding a balance between preserving commercial interest and falling in line will continue to be a daunting task.

[The Korea Herald, July 25, 2012]

13. Who Are Subject to Treaties?

One of the common misunderstandings about treaties (i.e., international agreements) is to believe that they bind all people and corporations of the contracting states. That is just wrong. Treaties only bind "governments" of the contracting states and do not reach private entities.

So, individuals like you and me or corporations, big or small, are not bound by treaties that our governments sign. What bind us are the domestic laws that our governments adopt as a result of their obligations under the treaties.

Now, this simple cardinal rule is not simple anymore. Increasingly, it is becoming more difficult to say which is which. In quite a few countries, the governmental sector and the private sector are sometimes closely intertwined to undertake joint tasks or achieve common policy objectives.

This phenomenon is more observable in the economic sector where governmental entities and private players are more closely working together to ride out financial storms.

This explains why states frequently collide, in the course of treaty interpretation or implementation, on the "scope" of a government.

Treating an entity as a governmental organ or as a nongovernmental player makes a night-and-day difference in terms of treaty application because if it is deemed to be a nongovernmental one the whole set of treaty obligations simply becomes moot: again, treaties are supposed to create binding force only for the governmental agencies. This has become an acutely touchy issue in trade agreements and investment agreements. This has been a headache for many governments, and Korea has had its own share of agony for this issue in a series of disputes during the past decade.

This topic has recently flared up in the context of China. China has traditionally maintained a hoard of state-owned enterprises in key economic sectors, which account for almost half of the gross domestic product according to some recent statistics. The question then is how these unique enterprises should be treated in terms of treaty application and implementation. Stated differently, are they some sort of governmental apparatus or not?

Particularly vigilant here is the United States who puts this issue as one of the priorities in its negotiations of various agreements including Trans-Pacific Partnership that may have relevance to China. During the WTO's Trade Policy Review of China conducted this past August, questions concerning the SOEs took the center stage.

This sensitive "hot potato" is now about to be dumped on the lap of Korea as its negotiation with China to conclude a free trade agreement intensifies.

Depending on whether and how the SOEs are covered by the prospective FTA, we are virtually talking about two different agreements—this is a threshold question which determines the whole universe of treaty obligations. If a big chunk of government-related players is left out for whatever reason, the landscape of treaty implementation might be quite different.

This doesn't mean that the Korea-China FTA will have to find a definitive answer to this sensitive question. Perhaps there isn't any magic formula here. As the entirety of the problem is so massive and complex, an easy answer is not just probable.

What the agreement can do, however, is to spell out what the criteria of the SOEs are for purposes of the FTA and how they are (or not) subject to the norms of the agreement. This value-neutral clarification would help crystallize otherwise opaque parameters of the scope of the agreement and avoid unnecessary bickering in the future. An agreement whose clear contours are not known to the parties at the time of signing would only invite unexpected surprises at best and deep frustration at worst.

The success of this particular FTA would hinge upon finding a workable middle ground, reflecting the interest of the two countries, to address the issue of SOEs.

[The Korea Herald, December 12, 2012]

14. A Rare Rush to Apple's Rescue

An unexpected turn of events occurred las Saturday in the three-year legal battle saga between Samsung and Apple. Since 2011, the two digital giants have been engaged in more than 30 legal proceedings in more than a dozen jurisdictions worldwide claiming patent infringement. And now the plot thickens as the US government enters the fray between the two private corporations.

So came the veto by the Obama administration of the United States International Trade Commission's June ruling in favor of Samsung in which the US federal agency banned imports of selected Apple products into the US market. In its June decision, the USITC basically ruled that the Chinese-made Apple products infringed a Samsung patent. The highest echelon of the administration has now overturned this agency decision citing "effect on competitive conditions in the U.S. economy and the effect on U.S. consumers." This intervention by the administration is the first time in 26 years, since 1987 during the Reagan administration.

The unexpected and unprecedented move by the US government has started the talk of "creeping protectionism" on the way back. This immediate response is largely an emotional one with hardly any evidence, but the administration's first-in-three-decades overturning of a USITC decision certainly gives a perception to outside watchers that the government is stepping in to preserve the interest of a key corporation. The political motivation is inescapably suspected. It is true that an overturn like this is entirely consistent with US statutes. But what matters in this kind of situation is not the statutory consistency but rather the perception being created.

Perhaps with danger of overstatement, this direct intervention by the government in otherwise purely legal disputes between the two private corporations could bring a small but ripple effect to the trade landscape. The Samsung-Apple litigation has drawn enough global attention for the past several years for many reasons, but it has been merely a company-to-company issue concerning contracts and intellectual property rights. The sudden intervention by the US government and Korea's quick registration of its concern the following day are now seemingly putting a new face on the dispute: there is an untoward potential of governments being drawn to the hitherto private dispute. For the two governments still occupied with all the complex homework, both domestically and toward each other, for the implementation of the 15-month-old bilateral FTA, this development will be far from being helpful.

Now consider how this latest decision would be viewed by other countries. Even if the decision is entirely legitimate and necessary for the United States, it might send the wrong signal to other countries that even America leans toward the protectionist tendency when a key domestic industry is concerned. Which would arguably embolden hesitating countries to explore ways to protect their domestic industries, and also prod domestic industries to look to their own governments for rescue measures of their choice. A downward spiral of race to the bottom to be stemming from such a phenomenon will deal a significant blow to the global effort to deter protectionism since 2008.

In the debate of protectionism, an argument that a domestic statutory basis exists for a measure or a decision hardly solves a problem. It would only induce other countries to invoke a similar provision if it already has one, and to enact a new one if it doesn't. Then come, quite possibly, the escalation and tit-for-tat.

It is just ironic that a blunt and un-innovative method is being chosen to the rescue of the most innovative company in the world. As a Tale of Two Digital Giants turns a new twist, everyone is holding their breath. Stay tuned for the next episode.

[The Korea Herald, August 7, 2013]

15. To Err Is Human, but Not Granted

What would it be like to watch a live broadcast of a court decision on a highly political territorial dispute with another country? Just ask those who are in Bangkok and Phnom Penh. As the critical decision on the 100-year-old Thai-Cambodian territorial dispute was being rendered two weeks ago by the UN's International Court of Justice in The Hague, the two nations were holding their breath.

This proceeding, a sequel to the 1962 dispute between the two at the same court, concerns an 11th-century Hindu temple called Preah Vihear located at the border between the two countries. Again, in the Nov. 11 judgment, the judges sided with Cambodia in material respects, although some of its claims were rejected.

Interestingly, for a long time this dispute has been associated with the term "error": the consequence of inadvertent errors committed in the course of negotiation and implementation of a treaty. The whole thing dates back to 1904 when Siam (as it was then called) and France (on behalf of Cambodia) negotiated and concluded a boundary delimitation agreement.

According to the agreement, the Preah Vihear temple was supposed to belong to Thailand. In fact, this temple sits atop a cliff which is only accessible from the Thai side of the border.

Then came a twist. One of the four French officials working to draw the border demarcation line made an apparent mistake and put the temple on the Cambodian side. Oddly, Thailand did not take issue with the situation, at least not officially, even after the mistake was known to the country.

In their 1962 judgment, the judges put more emphasis on this 50-year absence of protest by Thailand than on the original agreement and the inadvertent errors, and ruled for Cambodia. Jurisprudence basically teaches that a country is stopped from citing an error in dealing with other countries if a remedial action is not taken promptly once it is known.

In yet another ICJ dispute, between Singapore and Malaysia in 2008 over the island called Pedra Branca in the Singapore Strait, it was a short letter from 1953 that determined the ultimate fate of case. The court confirmed Malaysia's original title to the islet, but pointed out that the title was given up in a letter of 1953 from the then ruling government of Malaysia to the British colonial government in Singapore.

In fact, the letter was composed of only seven lines and acknowledged the ownership of the islet by Singapore. Noting the original, historic title of Malaysia to the islet, this short letter was apparently drafted by mistake, whatever had caused it.

These examples tell us that sometimes errors do take place even in the most important business of nations—treaty negotiations and interactions with other governments. These errors are not to be taken back easily and create their own legal consequences for the future.

After all, to err is so human and sometimes making an error is just inevitable. But the distance and separation between countries on the international plane will not necessarily allow one party to shrug off a mistake. We can see that international adjudicators have not always been kind about mistakes and errors. These examples also show that once a mistake is found all efforts should be mobilized, despite some embarrassment, to correct it as promptly as possible.

For all countries, a myriad of international negotiations is taking place all over the world as we speak. Promises are given and documents exchanged in various contexts. It may be a small mistake or error of today that will determine the fate of a critical issue of a country in the future.

[The Korea Herald, November 27, 2013]

16. From Coral Reefs to a Power Hub

Perhaps we don't have to worry about the rising sea levels as a result of climate change. We can "outland" it by pouring sand on tiny islands and coastal cities. The recent experiment in the South China Sea is proving it works.

The South China Sea has been a flashpoint of international tension for some time now, but the most recent dispute this year involves something entirely new—an "island building" project. China is virtually building a new island there (Spratly Archipelago) by digging sand from the nearby seabed and piling it on coral reefs. The once submerged reefs are now morphing into parcels of land on which an airfield is constructed and presumably military equipment is deployed.

These reefs have been also claimed by the Philippines, Vietnam, Taiwan, Malaysia, and Brunei, and some of them have also sporadically engaged in the land reclamation in the archipelago, but the speed and scale of the Chinese construction this time gives the term a new definition.

Criticism has been increasing. In a recent meeting, G7 countries warned that the island building was a violation of international law. Tensions were also running high at the recently concluded 14th Asia Security Summit in Singapore. China's response was simple: the reefs are Chinese territory, and China is simply exercising its lawful sovereignty over them.

The creation of a new island, if we may call it that, is an attempt to take advantage of the special status given to an island and nearby maritime zones under international law. International law—the 1982 UN Convention on the Law of the Sea—indeed accords a significantly different treatment to a submerged reef (officially called low-tide elevation) and an island. Submerged reefs do not allow for any maritime zones of their own, while an island commands a territorial sea, an exclusive economic zone and a continental shelf—a vast area of water indeed.

Moreover, in the territorial sea, freedom of navigation and freedom of overflight can be controlled or restricted. Construction of airfields and military-related facilities on the new island would enable the assertion of such controls. On top of that, an additional layer of Air Defense Identification Zone may be contemplated as seen in a recent video clip on YouTube featuring communication between a US reconnaissance plane and a Chinese ground controller. No wonder other countries in the neighborhood respond sensitively.

Placing an island in the middle of an ocean, if you can, therefore comes with a package of sizable benefits. If anything, this seems to be the most lucrative infrastructure investment program that a country can consider.

The problem of the island-building scheme, however, is that the definition of an "island" under the UNCLOS is confined to "a naturally formed" one. As such, a man-made island, however large it is, does not fall under the category, and so is unable to enjoy the rights accorded by the convention.

When the G7 countries mentioned a violation of international law, they must have been referring to this aspect of the situation. While the technological development in the dredging and construction sectors has made it feasible to turn a submerged maritime area into a man-made island, the UN convention is clear that an island, to be legally recognized, should be a naturally formed one.

Irrespective of the legal status of the new islands, once created they can become "power hub" from which regulatory authority or sometimes military influence can be projected. As other countries pledge not to recognize the status of new island by exercising complete freedom of overflight and navigation as before, a new level of tension is feared to be introduced to the already volatile maritime area. As the South China Sea is a key sea line of communication for Northeast Asia, escalation of tension there is not a good sign for us at all.

[The Korea Herald, June 17, 2015]

17. International Law and Sea Dispute

When I mention my profession, the first question people usually ask is how international law is enforced.

As a matter of fact, international law has a relatively weak enforcement mechanism. While some of the newer norms are equipped with stronger mechanisms of enforcement, such as trade or investment, there are other norms that are characterized by the lack or absence of enforcement mechanism.

One thing people usually miss here, however, is that states abide by judgments of international courts at an extremely high rate. The compliance rate here is higher than that from municipal jurisdictions.

Of course, we remember instances of noncompliance, but they are indeed exceptions of rare outliers. Perhaps compliance does not have newsworthiness, but noncompliance does, so what is etched in our memories is usually instances of noncompliance.

There are many reasons behind the high compliance rate of international court decisions. One major reason is that states are considerably "peer sensitive." States behave as if they are entitled to choose whatever policies they deem appropriate, but in fact they exercise the utmost care as to how other states would view their policy choices. When a judgment is rendered by an international court, states feel compelled to abide by it even if enforcement mechanism is weak or even absent. A state might muster the courage to tell other peers that it will ignore an adverse ruling—sometimes it happens, but it is extremely rare.

Attention is currently on the Permanent Court of Arbitration in The Hague, Netherlands, as the international court is scheduled to issue its final decision on July 12 on a highly sensitive and complex dispute between the Philippines and China. The legal proceeding was initiated in 2013 by Manila concerning various maritime and territorial issues in the South China Sea. China's objection to the jurisdiction of the court was dismissed and it has subsequently boycotted the proceeding. The PCA proceeded and completed its deliberation nonetheless.

Given the volatility and complexity surrounding the South China Sea, the upcoming award from the PCA, regardless of which side prevails, will mark a turning point for the maritime and territorial disputes in the region. The award will rule on the legal status of the geographical features and maritime zones in the region, including the legality of China's "nine-dashed line."

So, while this case just handles the disputes between Manila and Beijing, assessments of legal and factual issues will directly affect the interest of other states vying for maritime and territorial jurisdiction in the South China Sea.

As the award issuance day approaches, the lack of enforcement mechanism of the PCA proceeding is being highlighted. Speculation is that the losing party may declare the decision legally erroneous and refuse to comply. Quite frankly, as long as an enforcement mechanism is lacking in the PCA proceeding, twisting the arms of a noncomplying party is neither feasible nor realistic.

Thus, noncompliance or partial compliance is certainly a possibility. Nonetheless, considering the historical record of faithful implementation of international court judgments, it is still much more likely than not that a losing party is going to comply with the award.

A losing party or two parties in the case of a partial or split judgment may declare noncompliance initially, but such declaration may be employed for political or strategic purposes, and compliance will come slowly and gradually. Almost all of the time countries end up abiding by the decisions of the courts at the end of the day, because they know that doing so serves to protect their long-term interest.

That conventional logic, however, would work only if the parties perceive this dispute as one of many outstanding disputes and address it as business as usual. If parties attach historic significance and treat it as a strategic turning point as they seem to now, it may take longer, with fierce confrontation, before the final resolution of the disputes in the South China Sea.

[The Korea Herald, July 13, 2016]

18. Tricky Path Ahead: Triangular Talks

As the United Kingdom officially notified the European Union on March 29 of its intention to leave the common market, South Korea is quick in preparing to start negotiations with the UK to conclude a bilateral FTA. The UK also chimed in by underscoring the importance of a bilateral FTA to sustain and expand bilateral trade. Article 50 of the Lisbon Treaty will validate the UK departure as of March 29, 2019, when two-year negotiations between the UK and the EU end.

Surely, given the magnitude of the bilateral trade (the UK is Korea's 15th-largest export market and fifth largest source of investment), the two countries cannot afford to have any interruption in the flow of goods and services on March 29, 2019. Hence, both Seoul and London are echoing a strong willingness to conclude an FTA without delay. But there are tricky curves and treacherous paths in the road to the Korea-UK FTA. This particular FTA is bilateral in form but "triangular" in substance.

Here are some things to consider. Many provisions to be included in a prospective Seoul-London FTA will have mirror or corresponding provisions in the present Korea-EU FTA. Terms in the Korea-EU FTA will similarly appear in the bilateral FTA mutatis mutandis. After all, the Europeans seem to share similar perceptions and concerns when it comes to regulating trade with Korea. Now, the Korea-EU FTA is waiting for its own amendment negotiation: it was last July when Korea and the EU reached consensus to explore amendment of the now six-year-old trade pact.

In other words, the next two years will probably see parallel negotiations of a Korea-UK pact and a Korea-EU amendment. This further means the UK will look at Korea-EU development with great interest and Brussels will follow every step of Korea-UK talks. In effect, the two sets of negotiations for the next two years are interlocked.

Between London and Brussels, everything indicates that their own separation negotiations will be anything but easy. Since the March 29 official notification, both sides have been digging their heels in deeper and harder. As of now, no one knows for sure what kind of relationship the UK and the EU will agree to form when the two-year negotiation period runs out. All we know now is that this divorce negotiation will probably dwarf any previous negotiations in complexity and bitterness. In any event, what comes out of the UK-EU separation package will then affect Korea-UK and Korea-EU (minus UK) FTAs in two years.

So, what awaits us is a triangular negotiation in a short timeframe. Multiple negotiations with several countries are common. But a simultaneous, triangular bargaining is a novel concept. Certainly it has not been in Korea's playbook.

Since the FTA in 2011, Korea and the EU have had some important outstanding issues in the trade front: Korea's domestic service market regulation and non-tariff barriers have been the EU's major concerns, whereas the EU's own import regulations in 28 different member countries have posed challenges to Korean exporters. As the EU finalizes its investment policy, agreeing to an investment chapter to be added to the present FTA to replace existing bilateral investment agreements between Korea and individual member states has become new homework for the two sides. None of them are easy to deal with. In all these outstanding issues, the UK will now have its own voice and agenda. So will Korea vis-a-vis the UK. The upcoming triangular negotiations will be quite challenging, to say the least, for the three sides involved.

The strong willingness for a bilateral FTA expressed by Korea and the UK in the past week is a good sign. While there is certainly a long way to go with unexpected twists, with such strong determination the two countries will be able to find a way to overcome the challenges and difficulties from the first ever triangular interaction. Hopefully, a new agreement may breathe fresh air into the already vibrant bilateral trade between the two countries.

[The Korea Herald, April 4, 2017]

19. Better Late than Never

We were hoping that 2018 was an aberration. That countries were just reacting emotionally. That things would return to normal come next year. Sadly, those hopes were just hopes and recent reports confirm what many of us suspected and still dread: global trade will not exit the "protectionist" orbit anytime soon, and China-US trade relations will continue on a collision course. To a country struggling to overcome an economic slowdown, with red lights flashing on major indicators, nothing could be more disappointing than this gloomy forecast. That is especially true considering that 70 percent of the country's GDP depends on exports. This year alone, we are already seeing thinning patches in the "trade forest."

Can we ride out this storm? What should we do? We can explore many "outside-the-box" ideas, but the most proven and reliable path is to mend and solidify our base of friends and liaise with them to cope with new challenges.

Traditional 1-to-1 bilateral FTAs are important. But what we saw in 2018 underscores their inherent limitations. These pacts compartmentalized and segmented piece by piece, apparently do not form a critical mass. Nor do they build on each other to establish a breakwater when it is most needed.

Which then draws our attention to a long-titled trade agreement, the Comprehensive and Progressive Agreement for Trans-Pacific Partnership or CPTPP. This is an 11-state mega-FTA to preserve the Trans-Pacific Partnership despite the US withdrawal. Against all odds, its entry into force may soon be imminent.

Under normal circumstances, it would be just one of those agreements. Nothing peculiar. In the barren landscape of global trade in 2018, however, this is a nice breeze—a modest but still meaningful breakthrough for free trade. It will definitely serve as a morale booster for many "undecided" countries.

The survival of the CPTPP is forcing Korea once again to confront the hard question of whether to join. I say "again" because Korea faced the same question several years back when the TPP was in its prime. The accession plan didn't go through for many reasons. Looking back on what has happened since then, Korea would have more maneuvering room by now if it had chosen to take part. Cooperation with like-minded countries is sorely missed when the environment is harsher.

The question, again, is "What should we do?" The government has expressed its strong interest in joining the mega-FTA. A difficult but wise decision, indeed. True, there are industries that will be thrown into a different type of competition, but the circumstances require us to find a platform to anchor ourselves on. Regrettably, prior opportunities were missed, and we stand here again. Well, as they say, it is better late than never. Depending on how we coordinate and align with the other parties, we could earn friends on rainy days or miss out again.

There is a practical obstacle, though. A high admission fee. These 11 countries have outstanding bilateral issues with Seoul. Not surprisingly, they will purport to settle them during accession negotiations. Exorbitant admission fees might well derail Korea's effort to join, because eagle-eyed domestic industries will be watching the government's every move.

At the same time, the 11 countries need Korea too. After all, Korea is the seventh-largest trading nation, and our membership will reinforce the stature of the agreement—all the more so if the desired US return does not materialize in the near future. A changed trade landscape with hawkish and hostile environments is what we will see next year, the year after, and probably beyond. Having like-minded countries on our side is always a good idea in times of need. Of course, to make friends, Korea should be prepared to be a good friend to them as well.

[The Korea Herald, October 16, 2018]

20. Tackling Non-Tariff Barriers

It is no secret that one of the final sticking points in the Korea-US FTA is the alleged Korean non-tariff barriers (NTBs) in the automobile sector. The United

States takes the position that the enormously low penetration of the US automobiles into the Korean market can only be explained by NTBs.

The Korea section of the USTR's 2010 National Trade Estimate for Foreign Trade Barriers lists "a range of NTBs" in Korea that Washington takes issue with. They include standard compliance issues, environmental regulations and even "inability to provide input in early stages of developing regulations and standards." At this juncture, US automakers are vowing to oppose any free trade agreement with Korea unless Korea commits itself to fully dismantling all these NTBs.

NTBs refer to invisible, disguised import restrictions other than tariffs. They cover various maneuvers to circumvent otherwise applicable international trade norms so as to keep out foreign products from one country's domestic market. They distort international trade and possibly constitute violations of various trade norms.

The problem is, it is difficult to tell NTBs from incidental negative business consequences flowing from legitimate government regulations that people and companies usually encounter in their daily operation. It indeed requires an extensive inquiry to see which is which. So, broad complaints about NTBs in general would not do much good in addressing the problem. Instead, what is helpful would be to identify the measure, pinpoint the problem, and present explanations. Put differently, a fine line would have to be found between negative consequences from NTBs and mere unsatisfactory business performance caused by other factors than NTBs.

Now, again the Korean automobile NTBs. If there are NTBs that are designed to restrict US automobile imports as the US automobile industry argues, they should be abolished or dismantled, pure and simple. An NTB would not only violate a laundry list of provisions of trade agreements; it would also foment distrust between the two countries. This seeds of distrust will then bloom into more NTB claims in more sectors in the years ahead. They will certainly hurt Korea's long-term interest.

However, as noted earlier, an NTB inquiry requires more than simply throwing a general NTB accusation. In order for there to be meaningful discussions to find solutions, the alleged NTBs must be substantiated with specific information and materials beyond US automobiles' less than optimal business performance in the Korean market. It is then Korea's turn either to explain why the US perception is wrong or inaccurate, or to accommodate US concerns and take necessary follow-up measures without delay.

This has yet to take place in the automobile NTB showdown in the context of the Korea-US FTA. Most of the statements on Korean NTBs apparently only point out the imbalance in the automobile trade. The dramatic imbalance that we see between the two countries is indeed embarrassing (it was 6,140 vs. 735,000 in 2009). It does show that there is an issue that requires immediate attention from and cooperation between the two governments. The imbalance alone, however, would not directly translate into the existence of NTBs in a way that violates relevant trade rules. The trade imbalance becomes meaningful only if it has been caused by a disguised trade measure, an NTB. As there are numerous factors that contribute to the specific performance in the domestic market of another country, one could not simply attribute any imbalance to the existence of NTBs.

In fact, sincere discussions on the NTBs in the automobile sector at this juncture may also be important to Korea. Regardless of whether there are NTBs in the automobile sector in Korea, the current situation at least shows that there are areas that require more explanation and clarification from Korea. If so, it would be better if these issues were raised and resolved as early as possible, preferably before the agreement goes into effect. Korea may be able to explain away the misperception of US automobile manufactures, or Washington may end up clarifying its source of concern which may turn out to be NTBs. Either way, chances are the two governments will be able to find a solution to this old issue. In fact, the automobile sector has been the source of attention throughout the negotiations of the FTA, so facing the problem head on early on may not be such a bad option for Korea as opposed to kicking the can down the road for someone else's future agony.

[The Korea Herald, August 25, 2010]

21. Here Comes the Korea-EU FTA

"Will you really love me?" Just one week before the marriage the concerned bride asks the groom (or the groom asks the bride). Not in private, but in public. The bride (or groom) appears before the friends and relatives and pronounces her (or his) expectation of the upcoming marriage with a list of dos and don'ts and past sins. Friends would then wonder what they have said to each other during the courtship.

Probably, people would have felt the same untimely awkwardness on June 24 when the European Chamber of Commerce in Korea in Seoul held a press conference to raise the contentious issue of Korean non-tariff barriers asking for prompt changes and their abolishment in as many as 20 industries. This was exactly one week before the Korea-EU FTA goes into effect on July 1. In the press conference, the EUCCK made it clear that the NTBs would continue to be their major concern and priority in penetrating the Korean market even in the post-FTA era. In fact, the NTB issue was one of the top priorities of the EU during the Korea-EU FTA negotiations.

Let me be clear. All NTBs, if found, are potential violations of the Korea-EU FTA and any trade agreements for that matter, and should be abolished promptly. NTBs are one of the common ways of circumventing the promises and covenants made in trade agreements. And it cannot be denied that foreign trade partners have long complained about the visible and sometimes invisible NTBs in the Korean market.

The EU's concern over the NTBs led to the inclusion of provisions in the Korea-EU FTA to eliminate or shrink potential NTBs in key industrial sectors where the EU possesses interest, such as automobiles, electronics, pharmaceuticals, and medical equipment sectors. At the same time, at the EU's insistence, a new annex was included in the Korea-EU FTA wherein a special dispute settlement mechanism is introduced to deal with the NTBs exclusively. Although many countries have talked about this NTB-specific procedure for a couple of years at the WTO level, the Korea-EU FTA is the first trade agreement that actually incorporates the idea for implementation.

This mechanism is different from the regular dispute settlement procedure under the agreement in that it is a nonbinding mediation procedure conducted before a mediator. Nonetheless, this is still a procedure to settle trade disputes over the NTBs: a party against which a complaint is lodged by the other party should provide materials and explanations to the mediator in a short timeframe, followed by conferences. Given the number of alleged NTBs and the number of industrial sectors implicated in the EUCCK's report, there is certainly a possibility that the mediation procedure in the agreement will become quite active. As Korea has also been concerned about the NTBs of various sorts in the 27 member countries of the EU, mainly regarding the trade remedy regulation regime, Korea may find this procedure tempting as well.

The inherent problem concerning the NTBs, however, is that it is sometimes difficult to discern illegitimate NTBs from legitimate governmental regulation. In fact, most of the NTBs raised in the EUCCK's June 24 report are related to Seoul's regulation and requirements one way or another. If regulation is designed in a way to discriminate foreign goods and investors in the domestic market in a subtle manner, that would be a classic example of NTBs. On the other hand, if a complaint concerns a logistical burden as a result of the governmental regulation and the regulation equally applies to domestic goods and investors, then it is questionable whether such a measure constitutes an NTB. All these complex issues will be handled by the NTB mediator under the Korea-EU FTA regime. If the mediator fails to resolve a particular dispute, Seoul and Brussels will then have to move to the full dispute settlement procedure. But resolution of the disputes over the NTBs would be far from being easy and simple.

The scope and intensity of the EUCCK's concern over the NTBs last week offer a glimpse of the new challenges in the FTA era. As much as the negotiations and conclusion of the agreement have been extraordinarily difficult and complex, so will be its implementation and management. With the same friendship and flexibility shown so far, the two countries will certainly be able to manage and overcome these challenges.

As of today, the Korea-EU FTA finally goes into effect. This agreement will certainly open a new chapter for Korea's trade and economy. My last question is, is it on Seoul time or Brussels time? As people say, the devil always lies in the details.

[The Korea Herald, July 1, 2011]

22. FTAs and Trade Remedy Measures

Import restrictions are detested by trade agreements. The purpose of such agreements, most notably FTAs, is to dismantle trade restrictions between the signatories.

There is one important exception to this general rule: raising an import barrier against unfairly traded goods is permitted.

Unfair trade, as the term is used in trade agreements, refers to two situations. One is "dumping" where a foreign exporter sells a product at an illegitimately low price. The other is "subsidization" where a foreign exporter's competitiveness is artificially enhanced by the provision of monetary support from its home government.

In both situations, the domestic industries of the importing country are harmed and the importing country is permitted to impose extra tariff rates to the amount commensurate with the level of such dumping or subsidization.

Every country has one agency designated for anti-dumping and anti-subsidy measures (collectively called "trade remedy measures"). In Korea, the Korea Trade Commission was established in 1987 as an agency in charge.

All FTAs stand on the proposition that trade partners will resort to these measures against unfairly traded goods. As long as substantive and procedural requirements are satisfied as stipulated, these are legitimate measures against unfair imports.

In fact, these trade remedy measures are not only permitted, but stand to play an important role when tariff rates are eliminated as a result of FTAs. A surge of foreign imports would arguably increase the likelihood of products being unfairly traded.

So, in a sense, the FTAs necessitate vigorous pursuit of such regulation. As much as the tariff barriers are gone, the policing of dumped or subsidized products will become that more important. It is no wonder the NAFTA countries have been actively applying anti-dumping and anti-subsidy measures against each other.

When 30-plus FTAs are in operation in the next ten years as Korea envisions, surges of foreign imports will be observed in all sectors. This is a perfectly natural result of FTAs and foreign imports should never be subject to illegitimate trade barriers in Korea. But, at the same time, if there are dumped or subsidized imports, arriving in the domestic market, they should be addressed so as to preserve the basic premise of trade agreements.

The problem is the application of anti-dumping or anti-subsidy measures requires extensive prior preparation. Challenges are mainly presented in three different fronts: they involve logistical, procedural, and substantive aspects.

From the logistical aspect, the administration of anti-dumping or anti-subsidy proceedings requires significant manpower and resources. The United States and the European Union have been able to stay active in this area due largely to the abundant logistical infrastructure they enjoy. Recently, China has been expanding its trade remedy investigation agency fast to cope with the increase of foreign products in China.

The fact that the KTC has yet to make its first anti-subsidy action may probably offer a telling glimpse of the current situation. This is in contrast with neighboring Japan or China, let alone other major trading partners such as the United States and the European Union. Thus, if the FTA drive requires the KTC to be a more active player as in other FTA partners, the infrastructure of the agency will have to be enhanced accordingly.

A challenge in the substantive front is the complexity arising from multiple FTAs. Although FTAs do share things in common in terms of anti-dumping or anti-subsidy measures, different FTAs have different requirements for the application of specific measures. So, in the future officials at the KTC would have to look at a particular FTA with the country in question on a case-by-case basis. If 30-plus FTAs are ultimately in place, this would mean having thirty different sets of rules. This would also mean that different rules apply in the same process depending upon the nationality of the products.

Thirdly, a challenge in the procedural aspect. These proceedings are composed of a long list of procedural hurdles which should be cleared by the government imposing anti-dumping or anti-subsidy measures. Other countries have been quick (and Korea has been quick) in taking issue with any minor procedural shortcomings in the course of lengthy proceedings. Procedural integrity and transparency would be further underscored in the new environment.

Anti-dumping and anti-subsidy measures should never be abused to restrict foreign imports. That said, they are the only measures available to address the surge of unfairly traded goods and the FTAs envision that these measures will be vigorously applied. As the FTA drive is in full swing, Trade Adjustment Assistance is being considered by government agencies in Seoul. But one of the most effective ways of ensuring adjustment may lie in setting an effective trade remedy mechanism in motion.

[The Korea Herald, August 24, 2011]

23. Perils of Investment Disputes

The US ratification of the Korea-US FTA on Oct. 13 lobbed the ball into Korea's court one final time. It is being reported that Korea's ratification procedure will begin soon. One of the key points that the opponents of the agreement raised (again) after the last week's US ratification was the investment dispute settlement procedure contained in the agreement. This dispute settlement mechanism has been criticized as a loss of Korean sovereignty for the benefit of foreign business interests. The critics portray this procedure as a genie coming out of the bottle that gobbles up a country's sovereignty. This is a dispute settlement mechanism under the FTA framework exclusively applicable to bilateral investment disputes between an investor from one party and the government of the other party.

To the extent it introduces a dispute settlement mechanism between an individual and a foreign government through an international tribunal, this procedure stands to present peculiar consequences, both positive and negative. Where, as here, both negative aspects and positive ones co-exist, a proper way of evaluating the overall consequence would be to look into both aspects in their entirety, by according equal weight. Only focusing on sporadic snapshots of negative aspects or positive aspects fails to give an accurate picture of the matter. Instead, one would need to take one step backward and pause to catch a better glimpse of the entire silhouette of this dispute settlement mechanism as applied to the Korea-US bilateral context. The way I see it, positive elements far outweigh negative ones, and the assertions of the critics are mostly exaggerated. Following are the realities that have been mostly forgotten in the controversy over this issue.

More than anything else, this system is not new. Among the 85 investment treaties that Korea has signed so far since it first signed one with Germany back in 1967, 80 treaties already contain this very system. So, describing the Korea-US FTA as if it were the first instance of introducing this "unheard of" mechanism is simply misplaced. So, such an argument is at least 40 years late.

Second, and more importantly, what has been missing in this controversy is the contemplation of the fact that Korean investment in foreign countries is on the rise. With respect to the United States alone, since 2006, the Korean investment in the United States has surpassed the US investment in Korea by a ratio of 3 to 1. So, if anything, this dispute settlement procedure may provide further (or equal) protection for the Korean investment and investors in the United States. Chances are, the US government is equally concerned about this dispute scheme, given its experience in the investment disputes with Canadian and Mexican investors under the NAFTA.

Third, under these circumstances, a more appropriate question at this juncture should be how Korea prepares and manages this mechanism down the road instead of raising all sorts of hypotheticals that may or may not happen in the future. Should problems be identified as we go along, we can come up with a plan to minimize or address them. Of course, the investment dispute settlement procedure has given a list of homework for Korea that requires continued attention. Once all homework is done properly, this will ultimately become business as usual that comes and goes, as opposed to a genie out of the bottle. Korea's experience at the WTO dispute settlement procedure provides a good precedent: Korea had similar concerns and uneasiness in 1995 when a new dispute settlement procedure was introduced. But Korea turned out to prevail in 70 percent of its 29 disputes so far, much higher than the average. So, it raises the question: where have all these people have been during the 29 disputes at the WTO where Korea has sued or been sued since 1995. Nothing serious happened. The Korean economy has fared relatively well during this period.

The over-exaggeration of the problems of the investment dispute settlement mechanism is neither accurate nor appropriate. This does not provide a rational basis to oppose the free trade agreement with the United States, or with any other country for that matter.

[The Korea Herald, October 19, 2011]

24. Trade Disputes and Domestic Policies

Antigua and Barbuda is the seventh-smallest country in the world with the population of 70,000. This country, as its name connotes, is composed of two main islands and located in the middle of the Caribbean. It is a former British colony where a

British naval fortress was located in the 1700s (this fortress was featured in the movie "Pirates of the Caribbean").

In 2003, this small country waged a David and Goliath battle against the United States by bringing a claim against Washington at the WTO dispute settlement panel. The country took issue with US domestic policies relating to online gambling regulation, and it prevailed. With the authorization of the WTO, the island country further cornered the United States by imposing a trade sanction against US intellectual property rights. This case is frequently referred to as an example showing that a norms-based system also benefits smaller countries.

Similarly, in 1997 Costa Rica prevailed over the US in a dispute over a US import restriction against its textile products. In 2001, Pakistan successfully challenged a US measure against its cotton yarn products.

The European Union has not fared any better. Thailand prevailed over the EU at the WTO in 2005 when it challenged the Brussels' classification of its frozen chicken cuts. In 1999, Ecuador successfully brought a challenge against the EU's preferential trade relationship with the so-called ACP countries.

The list of trade disputes at the WTO over the past 16 years (427 in total) is replete with cases where developing countries prevailed over developed ones and where small states have cornered big ones. The United States and the EU are the two strongest and most influential members of the world trade body.

This reality brings us back to the never-ending controversy over the investor-state dispute settlement clause contained in the Korea-US FTA, because the formation of the dispute settlement panels and application of treaty provisions are quite similar between the WTO and the ISD.

Criticism has been raised that the ISD clause is problematic because its decision-making process will be somehow controlled by stronger countries. Not only does this assertion turn a blind eye to the detailed procedural checks contained in these agreements, but also it fails, to explain the reality of similar international litigations at the WTO where claims of small countries have been arguably equally vindicated, and where big countries' domestic policies are also extensively reviewed by the international tribunal.

As noted in a previous article of Oct. 18, Korea has been quite active in the trade dispute settlement process at the WTO, ranking in the fifth in terms of the number of disputes, with 29. Of these, 12 concern instances where Korea's national policies were extensively examined—including tax policies, financial policies, and exercises of governmental regulatory authority. Korea sometimes won and sometimes lost.

Nonetheless, few people call this an infringement of Korea's national sovereignty. This is not unique to Korea and all WTO members are subject to the same norms and regulation. In fact, recent high-profile disputes between the US and EU, and the US and China have been all about their respective domestic policies.

If the main cause of concern for the ISD clause contained in the FTAs (including the Korea-US FTA) lies in the fact that Korea's national policies can be subject to review by an international tribunal, it is forgetting the reality that Korea has already been living in such an environment, at least for the past 16 years. Portraying the ISD as a mechanism that puts the Korean national policy under the review of an international tribunal for the first time, therefore, seems disingenuous.

Since the ISD procedure was first introduced in 1966, almost 70 countries have participated in this process. Moreover, 81 investment agreements and many FTAs that Korea has signed have this proceeding already in place. Under these circumstances, setting the Korea-US FTA aside, it would be a matter of time for Korea to encounter its first investment dispute. It would require tremendous luck for Korea to avoid this hassle forever.

Vanuatu is on the verge of joining the WTO as its 154th member. Japan also declared its participation in the Trans-Pacific Partnership. Following the logic of the ISD criticism, one would wonder why these countries, both big and small, and developed and developing, are so desperate to join the network of evil that encroaches upon their national sovereignty.

[The Korea Herald, November 17, 2011]

25. The FTA Journey Has Just Begun

The long odyssey has finally come to an end. Fifty-seven months after the jubilant signing ceremony and ensuing heated debates in the legislatures of both countries, the Korea-US Free Trade Agreement went into effect on March 15. Despite all the controversies, the majority view is that this agreement reflects long-term trade interests of the two countries in a balanced manner and opens up a new horizon for the bilateral trade.

Not surprisingly, a huge sigh of relief is being heard in both capitals. The efforts of the two governments for the past seven years (since the idea was first floated) to bring this agreement into existence should be fully commended. At the same time, however, it should not be forgotten that this is just the beginning and the hard part has yet to come. The ultimate success of the KORUS FTA hinges upon how effectively the two countries handle this hard part down the road.

The hard part started after March 14, because full implementation of all the provisions in the agreement will be tough and time-consuming for both countries and thus require continued attention from the two governments. Yet still, quite a few people in the two countries tend to look at the agreement as if it were a static document, focusing on who gets what and who benefits from which sector. That is always important. This agreement, however, is not about a snapshot picture on March 14, but about a continuing process whose final score sheet can only be confirmed once the agreement is fully implemented over time.

As with any other FTA concluded these days, the KORUS FTA is notable for its comprehensive coverage: the almost 1,000-page treaty text covers virtually the entire spectrum of economic activities. The voluminous nature of the treaty text sometimes belies the fact that many provisions in the treaty only set forth basic principles and general guidelines whose specific implementation is reserved to the two contracting parties' agencies. Implementation of the agreement does not merely stop at amendment or enactment of laws and regulations, but goes even deeper than that.

Bringing tariff rates for goods to zero is easy to implement and, more importantly, easy to verify. What is difficult, however, is when the treaty commitments concern abstract obligations susceptible to relational concepts such as transparency, fairness, promptness, due process, market principles or the proper role of governmental agencies, and the like. The more grandiose the covenants are, the more difficult they are for a party to implement.

The difficulty actually is twofold. First, with respect to a relational concept, your best effort does not always guarantee the satisfaction of the other party. The two contracting parties look at the same words and terms in the treaty, but their expectations concerning the words and terms may significantly differ. Secondly, these types of commitments are not susceptible to easy verification. You basically rely on good faith of the other party until a serious problem arises. In fact, difficulties of various kinds have been presented during the negotiations and ensuing discussions, but most likely we have only seen the tip of the iceberg.

Another twist in this regard is the fact that the agreement introduces new dispute settlement mechanisms that have not been tried before in the Washington-Seoul bilateral relationship. Although it is difficult to quantify, the experiences tell us that increased interaction usually leads to increased occurrences of disputes of all sorts. The agreement is premised upon this assumption and introduces various mechanisms to handle these situations. How these dispute settlement mechanisms are administered so as to address these disputes will significantly affect how the two countries evaluate this FTA in the long run. The gaps will be filled, and the contours will be clarified by these treaty-based adjudicating bodies. Not now, but over time.

In a nutshell, with respect to the KORUS FTA the basic plot is there, but you never know whether the final story will be a happy ending of common economic prosperity in an ever-volatile global economy, or a saga of dashed hopes and broken promises. It can go either way depending upon how the two countries proceed from March 15 onward. After all the rehearsals, the curtain is now going up, and the hard part has just started.

[The Korea Herald, March 21, 2012]

26. Rare Earths Require Rare Solution

There is an old Chinese saying that goes "without rice, even the cleverest housewife cannot cook." A modern version of that proverb would go like "without rare earths, even Apple cannot make its iPads." "Rare earths" refers to 17 minerals, such as tungsten and molybdenum, indispensable for the production of key industrial products such as smartphones, LED flat screens, hybrid cars, and even a variety of defense equipment.

Now, it is China that singlehandedly covers the global demand of rare earths: the country accounts for 97 percent of the world's rare-earth minerals being consumed at the moment. So, when China started restricting exports of these minerals to other countries through various measures citing several reasons, other countries reacted in shock.

The concern and criticism voiced by other countries over the tightening export restrictions of China have now evolved into yet another round of international litigation. Just two weeks ago, the United States, the European Union and Japan joined forces to file a complaint against China over this export restriction. The way the initiation of the litigation was announced is a testament to the sensitivity and urgency these countries are presently feeling.

On March 13, US President Barack Obama announced his government's decision to seek a legal recourse in person before the press corps. The unusual appearance by a head of state to publicly announce an initiation of a legal dispute with another country reflects the degree of importance the United States is attaching to the situation.

These three countries claim that the Chinese measure is in violation of Beijing's obligation under the GATT, which prohibits member countries from adopting export restriction unless carefully carved-out exceptions apply. The three complainants further allege that the Chinese measure is to meet the domestic demand first and control the prices of those minerals in the international market.

The fundamental question China has raised since this issue first came up a couple of years ago is emotional rather than legal. It basically asks why the other countries are not so eager to mine their own pockets of rare earths, if it is so important to them. In fact, while China possesses only 36 percent of the confirmed global rare-earth minerals, its global production reaches as high as 97 percent. According to statistics, countries such as Russia, the United States and Australia are countries with significant possession of these minerals.

The environmental degradation involved in the excavation of these minerals is commonly referred to as one of the main reasons of other countries' lack of enthusiasm for domestic production.

Beijing is thus sending a message that it cannot let other countries take advantage of Chinese production while they are attempting to avoid environmental impact on their own territories. On top of that, the growing demand for these minerals inside China has given Beijing another reason to limit their exportation. China apparently sees this confrontation as another form of "China bashing."

Judging by the jurisprudence of the GATT and the WTO, it is likely that the complainants will prevail at the end of the day, as the violation of the treaty provision seems to be apparent. Irrespective of the legal jargon and evaluation of the merits to be rendered in a prospective judgment, however, as long as China continues to harbor suspicion about "China-bashing," an ultimate solution to the standoff does not seem to be in sight.

The reason this issue has ended up in the docket of the WTO is because it has been formulated as "export restriction" and "export quota." Should China adopt a different mechanism to achieve the same objective, such as reduction or cancelation of excavation permits for domestic producers of these minerals, it could probably avoid implication for its obligations under the trade agreements, but still maintain its virtual dominance in the global market. An easy victory or clear-cut determination for a sensitive dispute like this hardly guarantees an ultimate resolution of the core problems.

If the international community has to be heavily dependent upon the production of these materials by China, it should find a reasonable way to incentivize such continued production, so that both China and other countries can benefit in the long run. Simply forcing one country to take the role of global provider of rare earths against its will may further complicate the problem. More so, if that one country turns out to be not so shy about flexing its muscles. That is why, in parallel with the international litigation, countries concerned should talk to build long-term consensus.

In the meantime, Korea's reliance on Chinese export of rare-earth is also significant. In the month of February, 65 percent of the rare-earth imports were Chinese origin. Well, the upcoming negotiations for Korea-China free trade agreement could be a useful forum to discuss a stable access to these key minerals from China.

[The Korea Herald, April 4, 2012 "Rare Earths Require Rare Solution"]

27. Korea's First International Investment Dispute

With the expiry of the six-month cooling-off period, Lone Star officially started an international investment dispute against the Korean government last week by filing its notice of arbitration with the ICSID in Washington, DC. This is the first international investment dispute for Korea under a bilateral investment treaty since Korea's subscription to the investor-state dispute settlement (commonly called as ISDS) mechanism in 1975. Korea is now joining 85 other countries in the world that have previously participated in the international investment litigations. The government vows an "aggressive defense" during the upcoming proceeding.

The first reaction in Seoul seems to be calm and sober: no panic buttons or emotional response. Understanding this development as "business as usual" is itself a big stride forward. It was just this time last year when the whole country was engulfed by the controversies over the investment chapter of the Korea-US Free Trade Agreement in the course of the agreement's ratification.

The debates last year must have vaccinated the country against the overblown concern and exaggerated outcome. The Lone Star dispute, which has nothing to do with the FTA but is unfolding within the framework of the 2006 Korea-Belgium BIT, sets a good example of divulging the true nature of investment disputes. Portraying this mechanism as a unique issue in a particular FTA or with respect to a particular trading partner misses the mark by a wide margin. If 85 countries have done this before, it was only a matter of time for Korea.

Hopefully, the business as usual response in the country will continue throughout the proceeding. Critical views are being expressed in Korean national newspapers concerning the Lone Star's decision, but such a patriotic rhetoric would be neither appropriate nor helpful. The Korea-Belgium BIT acknowledges a foreign investor's right to pursue its claims through an international tribunal.

Lone Star's decision to exercise its right under the BIT should not be criticized to the extent it is compatible with the agreement. We should stay mindful that it won't be long before Korean investors turn to this scheme in other parts of the world. There's no need for an emotional response. Simply, the remaining task is for an international tribunal to interpret and apply the BIT as it is written.

One could safely assume that Lone Star will vigorously pursue their claims in the upcoming litigation given the enormity of what is at stake. In response, Seoul is expected to rebut the allegations and defend its positions aggressively, as it vowed the other day. Through this first international litigation in this field precious opportunities will be presented to accumulate hands-on experiences and future guidelines.

As shown in the Lone Star example, an investment dispute usually arises when a foreign investor departs the host state and burns the bridge. What has transpired in this case for the past nine years—from the Dallas-based fund's arrival in Korea in August 2003 to its initiation of the investment dispute in November 2012—would serve as a robust case study material for future interactions with foreign investors.

Once three arbitrators are selected soon, the litigation will begin its life cycle for the next two or three years. As there is no appeal available in this proceeding, the three-member arbitration panel's decision is final. Korea's first international investment dispute will be closely watched by many governments and interested entities. Handling this first dispute appropriately will be a crucial first step for Korea in this area. To that end, again, it is imperative to approach and view this dispute with a steady business-as-usual mode.

[The Korea Herald, November 28, 2012 "Korea's First International Investment Dispute"]

28. An SPS Dispute on the Horizon?

The lingering consequences of the Fukushima disaster are now taking a new form—trade agreements and international dispute settlement proceedings. Japan is now formally contesting the import ban imposed by the Korean government against fisheries products from eight prefectures due to the consumer concern over the contaminated water along the Fukushima coastline. The possibility of Japan filing a suit with the WTO is also being mentioned. If this plan materializes, this will be the third bilateral trade dispute brought to the WTO, after the laver quota dispute (2005) and the DRAM countervailing duty dispute (2006). As Korea was the complainant in these two previous disputes, this would be the first case brought by Japan against Korea.

Last week's visit of the Japanese government's delegation indicated that Japan's contention is apparently based on the WTO's Agreement on the Application of Sanitary and Phytosanitary Measures (SPS Agreement). This agreement allows a country to adopt an import restriction measure to guard against health risks and concerns, but only subject to fulfillment of specific homework—(i) gathering relevant scientific evidence and (ii) conducting a scientific risk assessment before a measure is taken. Japan thus challenges whether Korea has completed these requirements.

The agreement carves out one exception, though. Article 5.7 permits a country to take an emergency import restriction (called a "provisional measure") even if scientific evidence is insufficient, on the condition that the country continues to seek to obtain additional scientific information. Given the paucity of information and the urgency of the situation, Korea's measure appears to have relied upon this provision at the moment. The provision, however, also imposes an affirmative obligation on the importing country, after a provisional measure is taken, to continue to gather scientific evidence and conduct a risk assessment in accordance with the SPS Agreement. So, even if Korea's measure falls under the category of a provisional measure, the agreement still imposes specific homework to be completed.

In short, either before or after an import ban is put in place, an importing WTO member is obligated to carry out its conventional requirements of collecting scientific evidence and assessing the risk. Since 1995, there have been 11 WTO disputes involving the SPS Agreement, and the core issue posed consistently, in a nutshell, has been whether these requirements have been indeed fulfilled. Detailed guidelines have been developed from these precedents. So any prospective SPS dispute between the two countries will examine whether Korea, as an import ban imposing country, has checked off all the boxes.

What is meant by the scientific evidence principle of the SPS Agreement is that mere fear and public emotion, without the support of scientific justification, do not offer, at least among WTO member, legitimate bases for an import restriction. Invocation of such grounds has been consistently found insufficient in previous SPS disputes.

Responding to the consumers' food safety concerns is of utmost importance to any government. But the relevant trade agreement stipulates detailed substantive and procedural requirements that each government should follow in the course of imposing an import prohibition in a WTO-consistent manner. Following the Sept. 6 import ban, some research institutes and consumer groups advocate the expansion of the ban: for instance, the National Assembly Research Institute proposes a total ban on fishery products from Japan mentioning cost-efficiency. Hopefully, these suggestions and proposals are based on the clear understanding of the web of rules imposed by the trade agreements.

Setting aside whether Japan's measure have been sufficient to allay concerns of the consumers in the neighboring countries, once an import restriction measure is imposed it is Korea's obligation to touch all the bases enumerated in the trade agreements. It is not about whether a concern is legitimate. It is just a starting point.

Once an import ban is applied, it is now about whether the enumerated homework under the treaty has been adequately checked off.

[The Korea Herald, September 25, 2013 "An SPS Dispute on the Horizon?"]

29. Time for Rice Tariffication

The 10th anniversary has come—again. Among the many issues on the national agenda in the new year is how to address the perennial problem of rice market opening. This issue was on the radar throughout last year, but apparently put under the rug with a policy of hush because of the political explosiveness. Now the moment of truth is coming up soon.

Last time this issue erupted was in fall of 2004, when Korea's ten-year obligation to suspend the rice market (called tariffication) was coming to an end. Amid much debate and difficult negotiation, Korea was able to secure one more extension for ten years to fulfill its tariffication obligation. This extension is now going to expire as of Jan. 1, 2015.

This, then, means that negotiations with other interested countries and, more important, eliciting consensus among domestic constituents should be done for the next 11 months or so—a doable but a very challenging task. Remembering how much effort was put into this volatile issue last time around, tackling this homework is already long overdue.

At the moment, Korea and the Philippines are the two countries that have extended their rice market tariffication obligations. Japan and Taiwan converted to tariffication in 1999 and 2003, respectively.

The problem is a second extension is not permitted under the WTO's Agricultural Agreement. So, talking about securing another extension misses the point. The only available alternative to avoid the market opening obligation is to receive a "waiver," wherein a country receives an exception for a measure that is otherwise in violation of applicable trade agreements with an approval from the supermajority (three-quarters) of all members.

The "no free lunch" canon equally applies here, and a country applying for a waiver is usually forced to offer something equally valuable in return. Just imagine how many countries would voluntarily sympathize with the difficult situation of another country and agree to provide an exception for free while they struggle to abide by the obligations despite their own domestic headaches. A waiver is theoretically feasible, but will most likely come with a high price tag.

By looking at what the Philippines has gone through since last March in this regard, we can do a dry run. In an effort to continue to postpone its rice market liberalization obligation, Manila has chosen to pursue a waiver option. In response to the waiver request, other countries were quick to put their wish lists on the table covering many outstanding issues in bilateral trade. Considering the volume of Korean trade, we should expect much longer wish lists from other countries in any waiver proceeding.

The real cost of a waiver, however, is beyond the visible compensation packages. During the 19 years of the WTO's lifespan, there have been only 31 instances of waivers, mostly developing countries. Korea's pursuit of a waiver to get away with an explicit legal obligation, even if approved, would put a stigma on its trade liberalization effort and probably haunt the country in other areas.

One of the pitfalls many debates fall in the course of discussing issues like this is an illusion built on a theoretical possibility, which in fact is far from being practically available. If the cost to be paid is extremely high, the deal is not practically feasible, even if it is permitted in the rule book.

That is why a careful and candid comparison between the waiver option and the tariffication alternative is now necessary. The time is running out fast. With much more at stake, we are moving at a slower pace than the Philippines. Obviously, this issue just can't wait until after the local election in June. From June, only five months remain—a very short window to untangle this complex 20-year-old problem.

[The Korea Herald, January 8, 2014 "Time for Rice Tariffication"]

30. It Is All about NTBs

Frozen orange juice concentrate has been a thorny issue for almost a year. Washington has complained that the Korean Customs Service has been imposing unreasonable "country-of-origin" verification requirements on citrus growers from Florida. These are based on unsubstantiated suspicion that some orange juice concentrates from Florida may in fact originate from Brazil.

Ginseng chicken soup (samgyetang) exports have been on Korea's to-do list since 2004. The necessary sanitary certification has not been provided by the US Department of Agriculture and export of the broiled poultry product to the US market has not been stalled.

It is indeed great to hear that the just-completed summit meeting between Presidents Park Geun-hye and Barack Obama was able to resolve these outstanding issues. The trade volumes of these two items are not that big, but their symbolic nature as persisting nontariff barriers (NTBs) in the post-KORUS era is making the last week's resolution all the more encouraging and laudable.

Perhaps a single term that characterizes President Obama's two-day visit to Seoul in the economic sector is "full implementation" of the KORUS FTA. He used the term on different occasions in a subtle and nuanced manner given the somber mood in Korea after the recent ferry tragedy, but the message was loud and clear. His statement connotes that Korea's implementation of the trade pact has proved less than satisfactory with the introduction of a series of stringent measures bordering on NTBs. Country-of-origin issues, as with orange juice, are one of such examples. So, the request for full implementation is another way of saying that NTBs should be eliminated at all costs.

The fact that such mundane items as orange juice and chicken soup were mentioned at a presidential summit meeting is quite telling. Obviously, these issues should have been resolved at the working level. In fact, there are numerous mechanisms in the FTA to address all the garden-variety issues. If all these issues are somehow forced into the agenda of presidential meetings, this means either that such mechanisms do not operate as they should or that these issues are too sensitive to be resolved at the working level. Either way, arguably situations like this bodes ill for a scheme of full and prompt implementation of the obligation under the agreement.

The problem is this may well be just the beginning of the whole laundry list of outstanding issues on the road to full implementation. Many issues are lined up waiting to receive (presidential) attention. Automobile sunroofs, carbon tax, chemicals, agricultural products, customs classification, and sanitary regulation, to name a few. In the interim, the level of frustration will go up.

The cardinal rule is simple. All sorts of NTBs should be abolished no matter what. The difficult question, however, is where to draw a line between an NTB and aggressive enforcement of the provisions of the trade pact. Unless a workable guideline is somehow adopted, FTA meetings will be filled with mutual outcries about NTBs and broken promises. This would be the last thing any government would want from an FTA.

Which then leads to another aspect of the KORUS implementation—a membership fee for the Trans-Pacific Partnership. President Obama described the full implementation of the KORUS FTA as a "precondition" for Korea's prospective participation in the TPP. So, the TPP accession has now become Washington's leverage to address outstanding issues in the bilateral FTA front. Assuming Korea desires to join the Pacific Rim deal, Washington may attempt to use the TPP pathway as a one-stop customer service center for a plethora of outstanding issues.

So, in a word, FTA negotiation is all about market opening. FTA implementation, on the other hand, is all about NTBs. How to manage them almost determines the success and failure of any free trade agreement.

Lastly, on a personal note, my heart goes out to the innocent victims and their families of the April 16 Sewol tragedy. They will be in our thoughts and prayers in this most trying moment.

[The Korea Herald, April 30, 2014 "It Is All about NTBs"]

31. Writing the Rules on Trade

In President Barack Obama's State of the Union address last Tuesday he expressed confidence that the economy was showing strong signs of recovery, as best summarized by his "shadow of crisis has passed" statement. In the hour-long speech, he touched upon many US domestic issues such as childcare, immigration, minimum wages, and middle-class economics. He also talked about issues of global concern including climate change, cyberterror, and the fight against the Islamic State. Interestingly, there were also two paragraphs in his address that showcased a difficult equation that Korea is trying to solve. These paragraphs were on China and on trade negotiation.

Obama's reference to China in the context of trade was both direct and pointed. Roughly in the middle of his speech, he said that "China wants to write the rules for the world's fastest-growing region" in a way "that would put (US) workers and (US) businesses at a disadvantage." He then stated, the US "would (not) let that happen" and that the United States "should write those rules," to "level the playing field" in the area of global trade.

He then moved on to ask for the Trade Promotion Authority—namely, fast-track authority to negotiate trade deals under which US Congress can vote only up or down for completed deals. According to Obama, with this authority he would negotiate "new trade deals from Asia to Europe that aren't just free, but are also fair."

So, when the two paragraphs are combined, Obama basically says that he needs fast-track authority to negotiate trade deals which would keep China at bay in terms of writing new rules on trade. As the 12-nation TPP is the most important US trade agenda at the moment, the fast track authority being requested is to complete the deal on the TPP, which is now entering a wrap-up mode. This authority is critical for getting the participating nations to put the final offer on the table.

Now, some important implications can be gleaned from these statements. First, they signal that the Sino-US rivalry on the trade front will show no signs of letting up in the new year. If anything, Obama's statement on Tuesday almost admits that one of the major goals of the TPP is to counter the expansion of Chinese influence in this part of the world. And second, the Obama administration will pursue trade deals so as not to let China "rewrite" trade rules.

With the new year's game plan shaping up this way, Seoul will be walking a tightrope in 2015. The new FTA with China will be initialed, signed and put into effect this year. It is not clear whether and how the rules in the trade deal with China are different from the one with the United States, as the China text has not been disclosed yet. Accepting Obama's statement at face value and assuming that different rules are inserted here and there in the voluminous agreement with China, this situation would then mean for Seoul two different playbooks with the two most important trading partners. Navigating through the myriad of different rules will be a serious challenge, if not entirely impossible.

Not only that, consider also the TPP. Korea has proclaimed its desire to join the TPP. If this plan materializes, and if the TPP turns out to be a vehicle to contain China, again as Obama indicates, the rules-friction or the rules-mismatch, whatever one may call it, will become more conspicuous at that point.

It is like they are playing the same tune under the same name of trade deals, but the rhythms are different. If one has to dance to two different rhythms at the same time, and if the partners are all so important, masterful choreography is everything.

[The Korea Herald, January 28, 2015 "Writing the Rules on Trade"]

32. CPTPP Is a Good Club to Join, but Membership Fee Is a Question

In the article, the writer says Seoul should consider the costs of joining the new Comprehensive and Progressive Trans-Pacific Partnership (CPTPP).

Still a bit of a tongue twister even to experts: hard to pronounce and difficult to remember. Many tend to get the sequence of the letters wrong.

The CPTPP stands for the Comprehensive and Progressive Trans-Pacific Partnership. As the name speaks for itself, this is a treaty to save the TPP—an originally 12-nation trade agreement in the Pacific region, spearheaded by the United States.

Upon Washington's withdrawal in January 2017, the remaining 11 states joined forces to rescue the deal. They agreed to go ahead with it anyway (with a new name), waiting for the US to return. And it worked. The CPTPP finally came into force on Dec 30, and is now getting into full swing. This is a laudable effort. Come to think of it, this was (almost) the only positive development in trade in 2018. One could find a small ray of hope through the thick cloud of global protectionism, so to speak. Very well done.

Well, to Korea this means the Hamletian question returns—"to join or not to join." It is the question that South Korea has agonized over for the past eight years. And without an answer. The TPP and its successor CPTPP have been elusive to South Korea for many reasons. When they wanted South Korea to join, Seoul hesitated. When South Korea longed to participate, they turned lukewarm.

But now the time has come. With the CPTPP in full operation, South Korea must confront the question upfront. What should we do?

The painful contemplation this year has to juggle two aspects: theoretical and practical. From the theoretical aspect, the answer seems to be relatively easy. South Korea should join the 11-state trade pact. National consensus seems also strong. Among others, this pact offers the most recent version of trade agreement with new norms and rules. We should stay in tune with these new developments.

Furthermore, the wide spectrum of membership is also enticing; almost all key states in the Pacific region, both developed and developing, are participating. South Korea's absence just stands out.

Quite odd, indeed. After all, South Korea is the sixth largest exporting country and seventh largest trading country, located in the Pacific Rim. So, purely theoretical point of view, joining seems to be a natural course of action. But here is the practical problem—the price tag. Just how much would the membership cost?

The bad news is that it will be substantially high. Just about a month ago (Jan. 19), the 11 states released public documents, detailing accession procedure for prospective aspirants. Not surprisingly, they expect a basically take-or-leave-it negotiation. Imagine you try to join an exclusive membership club. You probably have to accept existing members' demands. So, they envisage a process where all 11 states start bilateral negotiations with a new candidate. All of them should sign off before a new member is accepted.

What would happen to South Korea under this accession scheme? Unfortunately, its future accession appears all but impossible. South Korea will have to accept almost all the demands and requests from the existing members. Quite naturally there are numerous outstanding trade issues between Korea and these 11 countries at the moment.

They will obviously aim to settle these individual issues first before they throw their support for Seoul's accession. Which means it will always be an uphill battle for South Korea. Not just an uphill but a steep uphill indeed. Simply, accepting all demands from as many as 11 key states would be probably unacceptable to South Korea. More so, given the slowdown of the national economy and deteriorating job market and a general election coming up. So, practically, South Korea's accession will be very, very difficult. So, you say, "we should join," but the question is the price of the membership. Without knowing this, and without calculating this, there is no point of agreeing or opposing the accession to the CPTPP.

Let's see the demand list and price tag, and then we can go from there.

A decision here is an important national agenda for 2019.

[The Straits Times, February 20, 2019]

33. Just One Word, but a Sea of Difference

It was about ten years ago when I visited Baku, Azerbaijan, several times, right by the Caspian Sea. A seaward view from the city was like that of any other city at the tip of an ocean. Its vastness matches almost that of the Black Sea, with five countries bordering it. The sea contains a variety of fish. Rich pockets of gas and oil, you bet. Beaches, of course. It even has salty water. In a sense, it contains everything a "sea" would have. Except one thing: an outside route. It is landlocked.

The unique features of the Caspian Sea have made it a flashpoint for two decades among the five neighboring states—Russia, Iran, Kazakhstan, Turkmenistan, and Azerbaijan. Some say it is a sea while others claim it is a lake. It is not because these five countries have a particular interest in marine geology or oceanography. Depending upon which way you go, there is a "sea" of difference, literally and figuratively.

If it is a sea, then there is a particular set of international laws applicable—the well-known 1982 UN Convention on the Law of the Sea (UNCLOS) and comparable customary international law. If it is a lake, on the other hand, it is pretty much down to the agreement among the five littoral states. Between sea and lake, different distribution formulas and delimitation principles apply. It also determines whether the vast majority of the water will be open for navigation for other countries—even those from outside the region. So, a lot is at stake behind the name game.

Interestingly, there is no legal definition of a sea in the UNCLOS. It has 320 articles and 9 annexes to regulate almost everything at sea and about sea. So, the convention has become the sword and shield for countries when they encounter anything maritime. But, critically, it does not define what a sea is. To drafters perhaps, it was obvious. Well, according to the Caspian case, it is actually more complicated than that.

This old question has been answered, at least for now. Five coastal states signed a treaty on Aug. 12 to deal with this issue—the Convention on the Legal Status of the Caspian Sea. The answer provided in the new regional convention, however, is rather tricky: it is neither a sea nor a lake, but something in between.

A short summary of the regional convention: among five states themselves it is treated as if it were a sea. Each state has territorial waters extending 15 miles (22 kilometers) from the coast, together with an additional ten miles of fishing water, leaving the vast majority of the remaining maritime zone as a jointly managed area. This is a scheme very similar to the UNCLOS. To outsiders, however, it is pronounced as a lake, rendering it off limits to other countries. So, the new convention adopts a sort of hybrid system to settle this long dispute.

The fact that the five countries have agreed on the legal regime of the important body of water is a welcome development. In particular, if the legal instrument is fully implemented as agreed upon, more concerted efforts stand to be mobilized to deal with environmental degradation and depletion of fish stocks in the Caspian Sea. An important objective.

But the hybrid approach of the convention still leaves the question open—is it a sea or lake? In a sense the structure and contents of the convention make the maritime area look all the more like a sea. Perhaps, other countries may raise the issue when the "accessibility" dimension somehow changes in the future, either through technological development or through business cooperation arrangements involving some of the littoral states.

When a core definition is missing in a legal instrument with a lot at stake, situations become tense inevitably. Consider how the definition of an "island" has become the focal point of the US-China tension in the South China Sea. Sometimes clear legal definitions are sorely missed when countries disagree even on something thought to be so obvious in the beginning.

[The Korea Herald, August 21, 2018]

34. Korean-Made Civil Aircraft Soars

Korea has gotten one step closer to manufacturing passenger aircrafts for commercial purposes as KC-100, dubbed as "Naraon," soared into the sky last Wednesday in Sacheon, Gyeongsang Province.

According to the Ministry of Land, Transport and Maritime Affairs and Korea Aerospace Industries, this has made Korea the 28th country to manufacture civil aircraft. Obviously, this is another big stride for the Korean aviation industry after the recent achievements in the export of its first indigenous military trainers, the T-50s.

Not surprisingly, the development of the civil aircraft looks beyond the Korean domestic market. The aviation industry has been marked as a new frontier for the future of the Korean manufacturing industry, as indicated by sporadic statements from officials in the governmental agencies repeating Korea's interest in the global market of medium size (50-to-100 seat) passenger aircrafts.

This is the market that is dominated by a handful of major players, including Bombardier of Canada and Embraer of Brazil. Unlike the large-passenger-aircraft market, which is dominated by Boeing and Airbus, the medium-size market has been expected to present a small window of opportunity for new participants.

The successful test flight of Naraon was a meaningful first step for the ambitious plan of KAI. Having watched Korea's penetration into the global markets of automobiles and commercial vessels as latecomers, other countries and aircraft manufacturers may have observed the debut with interest.

The global civil aircraft market has been very competitive. Development and export of civil aircraft have frequently caused all-out trade wars between the competing countries. In the late 1990s and early 2000s, Brazil and Canada were involved in multiple trade disputes at the WTO, accusing each other of illegal support for their respective aircraft manufacturers who were competing in the global market.

Since 2004, the battle front has moved to the large civil aircraft market, where the United States and the European Union have been engaged in a series of high-profile subsidy disputes of their own. The US-EU disputes concern large civil aircraft manufactured by Boeing of the United States and Airbus of the EU.

As the competition between the two aviation giants in the international market intensified with the introduction of new aircraft (Boeing's B777 and Airbus' A380), the two countries started to accuse each other of providing illegal subsidies in many forms to Boeing and Airbus, respectively. Although decisions for some component disputes have been rendered, the US-EU aircraft disputes are still pending.

The aircraft disputes for the past decade tell us many things. First of all, they indicate that development and establishment of the aircraft manufacturing industry are only feasible through long-term planning and thorough coordination of a national government.

At least in the initial stage, that is the case. With the enormity of the initial investment in research and development and the magnitude of mobilization of the national technologies and resources, this is rarely an industry in which an individual company can decide to join and thrive.

At the same time, the WTO Agreement basically stipulates that a government should not intervene in the private sector such as the aviation industry. So, there is a de facto conflict between the reality and the norm. This dilemma explains why we have seen all these disputes involving aircrafts of all sizes during the last decade.

Once the Naraon four-seater evolves to a 50-seat passenger plane, as envisioned by the blueprint and Korea's own commercial aircraft make a splash in the international market, it is quite possible that these aviation trade battles will repeat themselves.

As a matter of fact, Korea has been particularly vulnerable in subsidy disputes. It was not long ago when Korea was involved in subsidy disputes with major trading partners because of commercial vessels and semiconductors, two major Korean exports.

One good thing is that there is always a benefit for latecomers. The recent disputes between the United States and the EU provide ample examples that other countries might want to carefully scrutinize, if they want to avoid future pitfalls in their own endeavors. One can see that all things being equal, a significant difference can be made depending upon how governmental policies and assistance programs are formulated and structured.

Framed differently, a rough map of pitfalls is already available for a new entrant and there is no need to reinvent a wheel. The KC-100's successful virgin flight provides another reason that Korea should remain apprised of the continuing saga of the aircraft disputes.

[The Korea Herald, July 27, 2011]

35. BSE Doesn't Light Candles This Time

It was exactly four years ago when candlelight vigils almost engulfed the Korean society because of the concern over bovine spongiform encephalopathy, widely known as a mad cow disease. The recent occurrence of BSE in California in late April has led to déjà vu, but not a repeat of similar protests.

Upon the return of the on-site verification team from its visit to the United States, confirming that the April outbreak is "atypical" and the risk has been found to be contained, some retailers in Seoul even resumed sales of the US beef. The only difference after the outbreak is the heightened inspection at the border.

Critics of the government's response argue that import prohibition or, at a minimum, suspension of inspection is in order, but the public response has been largely cooler than four Mays ago. The headline of the website of the Ministry for Food, Agriculture, Forestry and Fisheries notes that none of the 177 other American beef importing countries have taken any meaningful new measure since the April outbreak.

Not surprisingly, import restriction arising from food safety concerns is yet another area in which national sovereignty meets a treaty obligation. This issue is now regulated by the WTO's Agreement on the Application of Sanitary and Phytosanitary Measures (or the SPS Agreement).

With the danger of over-simplicity, the complex web of provisions in the agreement can be summarized into one bullet point: a country can do whatever it wants as long as there is scientific evidence to support it. The concept of "sovereignty" is captured in the first part of the sentence, while the second part sets forth the homework to be done. People are obsessed with the first part but tend to forget the second one.

To apply this principle to an actual food safety regulation, any country can declare, on its own accord, which food is safe to consume and which is not. One country could even say that it wants to be more sensitive or even hyper-sensitive when it comes to a particular product. Or one country could even say that it respectfully objects to the mainstream view of the international community. Nobody is telling anyone to change their view.

But this national position should come with scientific evidence and a risk assessment based on it. So, in the realm of the SPS Agreement, only a concern expressed in scientific terms and supported by scientific evidence is taken into account. Perhaps an argument can be made that doing this homework imposes too high a standard, but like it or not, that is the yardstick applicable to the situations at hand until an amendment is somehow made in the future.

Thus, a country wishing to impose an import restriction is required to conduct a scientific analysis as to why this April occurrence represents a systemic failure to regulate BSE on the part of the exporting country and why an import ban is the only way to allay the concern. The relative silence of the 177 countries perhaps stands for the proposition that the situation has not yet risen to the level of clearing the threshold.

As one may have guessed by now, the legal framework is somewhat counterintuitive. It is not like an exporting country proves that its product is safe to consume; rather it is the importing country that should show why an import restriction is required. Criticism has been raised whether this framework adequately reflects reality.

Obviously, public opinion is rarely affected by legal discourse. What forms public opinion, at least in the initial stage of the event, may well be reflexive emotional reaction. Only a solid explanation from a government accompanied by full disclosure of information may help people follow the voice of reason over emotion.

Although an SPS measure requires scientific analysis, talking to people does not always require rocket science. Perhaps the government's candid discussions early on explain the cautious public response in Seoul this time around.

There may be instances in the future in which Seoul would have to consider an import restriction for food safety, whether it is for a BSE occurrence or for any other contagious disease. The validity of such future restrictions always hinges upon the scientific evidence and a risk assessment. Completing the task takes time and longer time if resources and infrastructure are not in place in advance. As much as SPS measures are sensitive and important, commensurate efforts should be put to cover all bases.

[The Korea Herald, May 18, 2012]

36. Final Ending of Lone Star Story

"A good ending makes everything good as well," or so goes an old saying in Hebrew. The raucous relationship between the Korean government and Lone Star, a Texas-based private equity fund, perhaps shows the converse is also true: a bad ending makes everything ugly. With the PEF's delivery of a "notice of intent" to the Korean government under the Korea-Belgium Investment Promotion Treaty on May 22, the relationship is now heading to a point of no return. Perhaps it has already crossed it.

In the notice, Lone Star expressed its intention to initiate an investment arbitration proceeding under the treaty alleging Seoul's violation of the treaty provisions. The two agencies implicated in the notice are the Financial Services Commission, the nation's financial watchdog, and the National Taxation Service, the nation's tax authority.

Lone Star claims that it has suffered financial losses because of the FSC's "unwillingness to approve a string of prospective buyers of the fund's majority stake in the Korea Exchange Bank," and the NTS's arbitrary taxation on the sales of the investment. As the entire universe of claims of Lone Star has not been disclosed yet and as the merit of the claims will only be confirmed by a prospective investment tribunal, it is still too early to tell how the story will unfold.

In a sense, this latest episode makes us aware that the chapter of the 1997 financial crisis has not been closed yet. It was October 2003 that the US fund acquired the controlling share of the KEB from Germany's Commerzbank which had purchased the KEB shares in August 1998 in a fire sale in the wake of the 1997 financial crisis. For its part, Lone Star attempted to sell its shares to other banks in 2006 and 2008, but the deals fell through. A deal was finally sealed this past January with Hana Financial Group with a sale price of $3.45 billion. The US fund now blames the FSC for the two botched sales that may have offered a higher sales price. Again, the situation is murky, and conflicting stories are being presented.

With the delivery of the notice of intent, the clock starts ticking for a six-month cooling off period. It is still possible that the two disputing parties agree to settle during the period, but oftentimes the filing of a notice of intent itself reflects that the efforts to settle have already been exhausted or that a possibility of an amicable solution does not look so promising. In practice, the six-month waiting period is like two race cars revving their engines on the starting line waiting for the green signal. As fate would have it, if the dispute fails to be resolved during this six-month window, the dispute then moves on to the formal dispute settlement proceeding, which means real action will take place in late November this year. It may then continue for the next two to three years. This evolution will force Korea to face its first international investment dispute ever.

In part hardened by the relentless national debates on investment disputes since last fall, the government agencies seem to show no signs of panic, which is in stark contrast to the situation in 1996 when Seoul encountered its first international dispute settlement proceeding on the trade front. The interviews of the FSC officials include mentions of a vigorous defense and business as usual. Considering the future implications of the first dispute, the Seoul government will have no other choice but to participate in the proceeding until the end. If Lone Star's underlying intent was to threaten and wait Seoul to budge, that would be misreading the crystal ball. Seoul's general litigation-averse tendency doesn't apply to an investment dispute at this particular juncture. Anyone who has read the Korean press since last fall would know that the government has only one choice in the area of an investment dispute, at least for the time being: defend its case to the best of its ability and see what happens.

The fact that the Dallas-based fund used the Korea-Belgium investment treaty, originally signed in 1974 and revised in 2006, as a vehicle to drive its claim provides some food for thought. Multinational corporations, existing in multiple jurisdictions at the same time, have multiple treaty vehicles ready to go, and pick one that suits the road best. Focusing on a treaty with a particular country does not always extend a shield against this hassle: an armada of vehicles may still be available to these corporations from other treaties with other countries. Well, a company's pursuit of the best forum available is nothing to blame. It only means a responding government's defense becomes that much more difficult.

Lone Star's eight-year stint in Korea has already brought a plethora of legal issues. An investment dispute will top them all.

[The Korea Herald, June 13, 2012]

VI

OUTER PARAMETERS OF LAW—LIMITATIONS OF LEGAL DISCOURSE

Law is a crucial element in maintaining modern human society, whether domestic or international. Any country's genuine development depends on the level of permeation of the rule of law. Thus, the importance of law and legal discourse cannot be overemphasized. The development of the global community after the Second World War, although still imperfect in many areas, is largely attributable to the strengthening of the rule of law in the UN regime. Despite its acute shortcomings, the UN regime has made undeniable contributions. Compared to previous generations, the past 80 years have been the most stable period in international relations.

Korea's economic rise and political improvement have also been made possible by intensifying the rule of law in its society in general. Certainly, Korea still has many problems and in some areas it has not changed that much. That said, it has made strides in many areas over the past couple of decades. The rule of law has played a crucial role in this regard. At the same time, law has also displayed inherent limitations. It is increasingly lagging behind in a rapidly changing society. Laws from the analogue age continue to govern what is now a digital society. Once enacted and codified, laws must be followed by all, regardless of their growing disconnect from reality. Sometimes statutes are too narrow or too broad. Either way, innocent victims result. Most importantly, law is adopted to reflect the view of those who can influence the legislative process. The voice of the less influential is sidelined or sometimes ignored. The advantage included in the law becomes further institutionalized as time passes. All these inherent limitations can be observed both in a domestic legal setting and the international legal setting.

The columns do not simply underscore the importance and contribution of law. They also point out its inherent limitations. Law is an important tool, but it cannot serve as the sole or decisive factor in addressing complex social issues. Decisions that disregard the law are risky and illogical, whereas decisions based solely on

DOI: 10.4324/9781003501749-6

legal considerations are unstable and unwise. The columns convey this message and underscore the importance of a balanced approach. This is evident in Korea's transformation over the past several decades, where legal frameworks have contributed, but non-legal factors such as culture, economy, and technology have played an equally crucial role. For instance, Korea has seen drastic changes for the past several decades. Seoul has become one of the major global cities in Asia attracting foreign businesses and visitors. Before COVID-19 hit the global community, Seoul had become one of the most popular destinations for young people from other countries. Its economy has continued to thrive: the nation's per capita GDP in 1980 was US$1,700 and it rose to US$30,100 in 2020. Korea is synonymous with ultra-fast, reliable internet networks and advanced digital products. This digital prowess has further fueled its economic and social transformation.

Recent changes have exacerbated existing issues. The country has become increasingly polarized: the gap between the haves and have-nots has been steadily widening, and the political confrontation between conservatives and progressives has been ever deepening. Remarkably, Korea is now a country with the lowest birth rate. Its population is aging at the fastest pace. 2020 was the first year in Korean history when its population shrank. We may see further shrinkage next year and the year after. Despite Korea's world-renowned companies, its political system has long been regarded as an impediment to national development. Its legislative body has been polarized and slow. Corruption scandals embarrass ordinary people. The columns have identified new challenges in Korean society. They have explained the current situation and the emerging problems, and offered possible solutions. Needless to say, none of these problems lend themselves to easy solutions. And yet, I tried to provide some of my own ideas and proposals to address or alleviate the problems. These changes and resulting problems invoke legal issues. These legal issues sometimes pertain to Korea's domestic legal system but often bring international law to the forefront as well. Disputes with foreign entities and governments then ensue. Columns examine these legal issues from various angles.

As the era of polycrisis arrives with the conflicts among states surging, people realize the importance of a rules-based system. Many global leaders and scholars underscore and emphasize the need to resurrect and strengthen a rules-based global order. Needless to say, this should be an urgent objective of the global community. One should not forget the critical pre-condition for this endeavor: there must be a rule or rules in the first place on which the global community is to be based. Without rules, a "rules-based" system cannot begin or survive. In that regard, it is alarming that rules are either insufficient or missing in many areas of global concern at the moment. This is mainly because the global community we live in has changed so fast and so dramatically for the past couple of decades and the pace of change will further accelerate for the next couple of decades. At the same time, these new areas do not have an up-to-date regulatory regime, causing a "legal vacuum." Two primary approaches appear to exist for addressing the legal vacuum. One approach involves promptly and rigorously introducing legal norms under a strong regulatory regime to protect people from sometimes aggressive business entities. The other is to let the market sort out the problem and foster innovation while government is taking a backseat and step in only if big problems are identified.

On the one hand, humanity is advancing into new areas. We are paying new attention to the space industry, which was previously an unknown area, and the Mars exploration plan is being promoted in earnest. Space, once an object of curiosity, has now become a business and a subject of fierce competition between nations. The Arctic Ocean, now accessible due to global warming, has become a new arena for geopolitical competition. These new areas do not have clear legal norms or standards. We are now in the process of forming new norms. The momentum of the new Cold War is reaching these new areas as well. As new areas of human activities are emerging, business entities are actively pursuing new business opportunities in these areas. Korea is caught in the middle. It still moves back and forth between the two lines of policies. This is the place where the government, business entities, and people have different views whenever new issues emerge in Korean society. For instance, outer space has now become a new frontier for many countries and businesses. The legal framework governing outer space is grounded in the 1967 Outer Space Treaty. The treaty is based on the notion of outer space exploration at that time; national agencies (such as NASA) sending rockets to orbits around the Earth allied to scientific research. It does not envisage the current situation where companies are sending their own rockets to orbit and to other celestial bodies for the purpose of making profit. Most notably, the 1967 Treaty adopts a view of the common heritage of mankind in relation to outer space. No country can appropriate outer space on its own. The economic benefit of outer space is for humankind in general. This conceptual framework does not fit with the current business practice where companies are jockeying for position in the universe to make money. Despite robust business activities, the norms therefore negate such phenomenon. Once money starts to flow, tension is bound to increase, probably leading to legal disputes.

The digital domain offers another example: regulatory approaches to digital companies remain unclear. New norms are being introduced but there is still a long way to go. On June 6, 2024, the US Justice Department and Federal Trade Commission came to a mutual understanding as to how future anti-trust investigations against digital companies might proceed. Due to concerns surrounding the dominant position that these firms occupy in the digital market, and potential anti-competitive industrial advantages and practices, the US government is exploring various regulatory avenues. Similar regulatory trends are emerging in many countries, including Korea. People did not think about new business activities in outer space or in cyberspace. The conventional norms are all based on the notion of territoriality. Now that these new business areas have emerged, these existing norms are showing their limits. To some extent, they can still apply, but in many respects they do not reflect current business realities and the market environment. Consider the digitalization of our daily lives. The advent of the digital age has fundamentally transformed our daily lives. New industries are emerging and borderless transactions are expanding. The value of 'information' is increasing. Conflicts between countries over the cross-border transfer and use of information are also growing. At the same time, efforts to protect personal information are also seen.

The advent of the era of AI is fundamentally transforming how society operates. The recently introduced ChatGPT clearly illustrates this potential. The ability to conduct key social activities and make decisions without human intervention marks a previously unimaginable shift. The rapid penetration of digital technology is reshaping our daily lives in multiple dimensions. In particular, the advent of artificial intelligence (AI) signals fundamental changes or possibly structural transformations in the way we live, work, and interact. Mindful of this, key players in the global community are now engaged in fierce competition in areas related to the digital economy and AI. The United States and China are saying that their hegemonic competition will be determined by which side prevails in this digital and AI arms race. Having realized the potential offered and threats posed by AI, countries have started to debate rules on AI. These debates take place both on international and domestic planes. Some countries have begun legislative processes as well. On May 17, 2024, the Committee of Ministers of the Council of Europe adopted *The Framework Convention on Artificial Intelligence and Human Rights, Democracy, and the Rule of Law*. This document, the first legally binding international treaty in the field, if accepted by other countries, identifies human dignity and social, economic, and political democratic inclusion as subjects that must be protected from potential algorithmic discrimination and other unintended negative impacts. It is expected that the EU will begin to offer this treaty text to its counterparts one by one.

On May 21, 2024, The EU AI Act was voted forward by the European Council. Once signed by the presidents of the European Parliament and Council, this act will be published in the EU's Official Journal and enter into force twenty days later. The new regulation will apply two years after its entry into force, with some exceptions for specific provisions. This risk-based framework would categorize AI risk into four tiers of ascending severity, from low risk to medium risk, high risk, and finally unacceptable risk. Examples of prohibited AI functions provided by this summary include aggregated facial recognition databases and "subliminal, manipulative, or deceptive techniques." There are exceptions for AI systems that exhibit "unacceptable risk," however, such as in technologies developed explicitly for military applications. As regards the United States, in May 2024, the Bipartisan Senate AI Working Group released the Roadmap for US Innovation in Artificial Intelligence Policy. In it, the group builds upon previous educational meetings held in the summer of last year and a subsequent confidential all-senators classified briefing. The roadmap seeks to address long-term challenges such as AI societal-level risks like job displacement and national security issues as well as short-term challenges. Some states have already moved forward with AI regulations of their own, such as the Colorado AI Act and the Utah AI Policy Act.

AI is now affecting every aspect of our daily lives and business transactions. Its penetration into our lives will become faster and deeper with each passing day. As a result, there seems to be a wide consensus that AI should be regulated, and the regulation should come as soon as possible. As such, many countries are now contemplating, preparing, and/or adopting laws and regulations to regulate AI. These efforts are important and timely, and should continue with more attention and higher intensity. These laws and regulations, however, are all different, fragmented, splintered, and compartmentalized along state borderlines. Every country is on its own. This is because there is no basic framework or principled template at the global level. A global framework or template is critical so that domestic laws and regulations of many countries are not in conflict with one another or proceed in different directions. Ultimately, people and business entities using AI around us are not confined by any territorial restriction, so if the core elements of one country's law differ from those of another, individuals and companies around the world may face confusion and uncertainty. It becomes unclear what is permissible or prohibited in an AI-enabled world. To preempt this unseemly situation, the basic elements and the general direction of AI regulation should be discussed and agreed upon at the global level first. Domestic laws and regulations could then be elaborated and fine-tuned reflecting each country's different sensitivities and policy objectives. This is not to pursue complete harmony or complete agreement at a global level. This would be difficult and take a long time to achieve. Instead, the aim would be to realize and underscore the importance of having all countries on the same page at least on the fundamental issues. Every country's laws and regulations will be different, and different countries will have different views and policies on AI in their daily operation. And yet, as regards core elements at least, countries will be able to and in fact should find common ground.

While these endeavors are meaningful, they still miss the critical part of the rules discussion. They do not address the issue of regulating AI from the perspective of establishing a legal system where individuals, corporations, and government agencies are aware of their rights and obligations in advance and adjust their behavior and decision making appropriately. The current discussion is mainly focused on moral, ethical, and trust issues. Although morality, ethics, and trustworthiness are important, they, in and of themselves, do not resolve disputes in the field. Nor do they tell stakeholders what to do and what not to do in their daily operations. For AI-regulation to apply to the real world, it must be designed to address the issues taking place in the real world. Pleas for moral, ethical, and trustworthy use of AI do not provide concrete rules applicable to real-world transactions.

As regards a prospective treaty on AI regulation, it may be difficult to form a consensus on these areas. And yet, an earnest effort could lead to the successful conclusion of such a treaty. This is possible because many countries share common concerns about the threats posed by AI and can agree on collective responses. For instance, while the United States and China are competing in many fields, they are also trying to find some common ground in the area of AI. Talks in Geneva led by senior US and Chinese officials held on May 14, 2024, established "a new platform to draw on each other's governance experiences and contribute to global AI regulation," according to China Daily. Both sides labeled the talks "constructive." Liu Wei, director of the human-machine interaction and cognitive engineering laboratory at the Beijing University of Posts and Telecommunications told The Global Times that "while there is competition between the two sides in the field of AI, there is also room for cooperation."[1]

As a country deeply interested in global trade and the digital economy, Korea has been recently trying to lead the global discussion in this regard. On May 21–22, 2024, the UK and Korea hosted the second AI Safety Summit. The first summit, hosted in the UK in 2023, culminated in the Bletchley Declaration, wherein developers pledged to prioritize safety and focused on bringing together national and industry leaders to align on the issue of AI safety. The Bletchley Declaration, intended to drive international cooperation on AI safety, includes assurances by AI frontier model developers to cooperate with governments like the UK in assessing safety prior to releasing their models to the public. These expectations of transparency are part of two key focuses: identifying AI safety risks to create shared global understandings of approaches, and building respective risk-based policies that integrate public and private actors across the globe. Prime Minister Rishi Sunak and Korean President Yoon Suk Yeol co-chaired a virtual leaders' session at the summit. Leaders from other countries were invited as well as leadership from prominent AI companies who were expected to update how they have fulfilled transparency and model safety commitments made at Bletchley Park. Although the declaration adopted in Seoul represents a timely and significant achievement, it remains constrained by a narrow focus on ethics and morality in AI regulation. It is time to approach this from a legal perspective so as to establish rules in this field. The global community should begin to confront this task. Countries like the UK, Korea, and Singapore may play an important role in this area.

Over the years, we have frequently used the term "paradigm shift" to refer to various aspects and occasions. In most cases, the term was closer to a rhetorical expression. However, events in the international community in recent years clearly show that this "paradigm shift" is taking place right before our eyes. The US-China conflict is intensifying across the board. The Russia-Ukraine war continues. The world is on edge over the possibility of armed conflict surrounding the Taiwan Strait. Countries such as the US, the EU, Japan, Russia, China, and both North and South Korea are increasingly confronting one another in global affairs. The era of a new Cold War has arrived. Between developed and developing countries, long-standing conflicts still persist. Even in this crisis situation, the UN Security

1 Liu, W., 2024, While there is competition between the two sides in the field of AI, there is also room for cooperation, *Global Times*, May 14, 2024, available at https://www.globaltimes.cn/page/202405/1312269.shtml (last visited July 31, 2025).

Council, which is supposed to manage and control it, is not visible. It is clear that the UN system, which was launched in 1945, is now being shaken to its very foundations. In this situation, the international economic system is also undergoing major changes. The basic framework and principles that have maintained the existing international economic system are rapidly changing. Free trade and the principles long promoted under the motto of expanding investment are now undergoing significant changes. At the heart of these changes is what is now being called "supply chain (global value chain)" reorganization. This is probably the phrase most frequently mentioned in the media and books these days. If the emergence of new global challenges and the resulting shifts in international relations help explain the current state of affairs, the phenomenon in which these changes are manifested in the workplace where companies and individuals operate can be called the problem of supply chain reorganization.

1. Sweet Dream, Harsh Reality Jumbled Up

The movie *Inception* is about a man who can penetrate into somebody else's dream to reach the target's subconscious and plant an idea in the target's mind, which then leads to a decision the penetrator hopes for. Looking into the most secretive corner of someone's mental universe must be intriguing, but the adventure does not come without baggage. Shuttling between dream and reality, the penetrator reaches the point where he himself is sometimes confused which is dream and which is reality. Let me stop here for those who have not seen the movie yet. But the confusion of dream and reality or mixture of two different worlds is not simply something that we can see only on screen.

The US counterintelligence agency's sting operation to arrest alleged Russian intelligence agents operating in the United States, and the ensuing swap of intelligence agents in custody between the United States and Russia have received wide media coverage. The profile of the alleged Russian agents arrested by the US government simply shattered any common notion of parents who held ordinary occupation, mingled with neighbors, and worried about the children's grades and behavior at school. They were far from James Bond, but rather as ordinary mom and dad as one could imagine. In a sense, they had been completely embedded with the target country's culture and society. The shock of the neighborhood (and their own unknowing children) is detailed in the New York Times on June 28. The report also explains the struggles they went through, torn between the two worlds, with "Inceptionian" confusion creeping into their minds.

Ever since the internet enabled us to do almost everything in cyberspace (look at Facebook, MySpace or Cyworld), there are some people who live two lives, one in real space and the other in cyberspace. Avatars are created and virtual communities are formed. Even if someone dies, the cyberhome and community he or she created continue to live on until the membership is terminated by next of kin. When a married man and a married woman met online in Great Britain in 2008 and established a virtual household together, controversy erupted whether it constituted virtual adultery. Last year, the US Air Force started to weigh whether the operators of the unmanned aerial vehicles (namely drones like Predator) should qualify as "pilots," and thus be eligible to receive flight pay as with real fighter plane pilots. About two months ago, police arrested one Korean couple when they neglected to feed their real daughter while so busy raising their online daughter. The distinction between virtual life and real life gets blurry in this digital age, and to those heavily addicted, the two worlds are jumbled up.

The attack of the Cheonan in March and the following events have reminded us all how precarious and volatile the security environment is in the Korean Peninsula. What is scary is that in the face of such a national emergency the country can still remain divisive (maybe more so than before). How we will respond if a more tragic and unexpected event occur is anyone's guess. A noticeable gap exists between what transpired after the incident including China's reaction and the UN Security Council response and the initial expectations. Perhaps many of us in Korea have been living in a dream for a long time, a dream in which this level of inter-Korea military conflict is only history, in which the whole country shows unity when faced with outside aggression, in which the leadership across the Demilitarized Zone makes a rational decision, and in which all major players in the region stand supportive of us (or at least neutral) in a critical moment. Quite a sweet dream it is. Sometimes dreams do come true, but many times dreams and reality are miles apart. Over the years, dream and reality may have been mixed up in our collective minds. Like DiCaprio in *Inception*, we may have reached the point where we are forced to sort out what is real and what is fake and face the former. One silver lining of the Cheonan incident is that it may have given us a "kick" to wake up from the dream and come back to the reality.

[The Korea Herald, July 28, 2010]

2. H1N1, G-20, and Vaccines

Everybody hates this new virus. One muffled sneeze in a subway train instantly invites cold stares from all directions. People around you will scramble to find excuses to leave without hurting your feelings.

Hospitals are packed with patients and over-reactors of all sorts screaming for Tamiflu. Indeed, all of Korean society is in panic these days due to the unprecedented pace of spread of this H1N1 virus' spread. Belatedly, people lament the lack of preparation on the part of the government and a resulting shortage of vaccines, although the supply of vaccine now showing signs of improvement. Well, all I can do is keep my fingers crossed and trust the unknown effect of kimchi, which allegedly helped Koreans fight off bird flu a couple of years ago.

You won't believe this, but we need to brace ourselves for another toxic virus. This virus has been there much longer than H1N1—which has been roaming the globe since last fall. What is unique about this other virus is that it targets only states and governments, so people like you and me do not contract this disease directly.

What is further unique about this monster is that it is the people like you and me who pay the ultimate consequences of infection, not the infected states and governments themselves. This virus does not make people ill instantly, but it puts all of us slowly into a downward spiral. Adequate attention has not been paid to this disease, probably because of the slow and long-term effects. Why bother now if the effect is to be felt by my son or by me two decades later? I can guarantee, however, that although nobody has died of this virus, it is as fatal and dangerous as H1N1.

The main symptoms of the states infected with this virus include hemorrhaging vitality from the industrial vein, a short memory loss, and an increasing level of impatience with occasional signs of aggressiveness toward the neighbors. Well, this new virus is called M1Y2 (aka, "Me first, you second"), otherwise known as protectionism.

Since the financial crisis last year, quite a few states have contracted this fatal disease, and they compete among themselves to churn out protectionist measures to protect their domestic industries and markets. Many of these measures are either illegitimate or at least problematic under the existing international trade norms, but the infected states usually go ahead with them anyway. It appears that these states completely forgot about the norm (let me remind you that one of the symptoms of this disease is short memory loss). Alas, memory loss is just the beginning! The contaminated states are now exchanging barbed words and sometimes fists (remember this virus causes occasional outbursts of anger), and the whole world is holding its breath. With a vaccine still not in the sight, trade giants are now suffering the symptoms of infection. They have just ratcheted up the tension level one notch further and are now digging their heels for an all-out trade war. Other infected states will follow suit sometime soon. If left untreated, this virus will ruin the whole international community. We have vivid memories of where this protectionism-ruined international relationship led the whole world.

Actually, we knew this was coming. Korea accurately predicted this disease early on. President Lee Myung-bak warned against the spread of protectionism in the G20 summit meeting in Washington, DC, in November 2008, and proposed a "standstill" for all trade barriers. The early warning may have helped to hold down the virus for a while, but apparently it is now out from the box and on the loose. We need a vaccine for this virus real quick.

As one of the early detectors of the disease, Korea has just secured a great venue to manufacture, advertise, and distribute a vaccine for it. Korea is scheduled to host a G20 summit meeting next November. This is a precious opportunity to explain to participating states the composition of the antidote, get the authorization from the participants for the vaccine and distribute it among them. The G20 meeting next year is important not because 20 heads of states are gathering in Seoul, but because this will provide an opportunity to Korea to lead the reshaping of the post-crisis economic system in general and the vaccine for this spreading virus in particular. It is time for Korea to experiment with various formulae for the vaccine and get ready for the approval and distribution at next year's meeting.

In fact, Korea arguably possesses the trade secrets to produce this vaccine. It overcame the economic crisis 11 years ago and quickly recovered from the 2008 economic crisis as well, both thanks to robust trading. It probably knows how to deal with this particular symptom and where to get the recipe for the vaccine. If Korea is the manufacturer and seller, many states will probably be tempted to buy. So, the next year's G20 meeting is not a merely diplomatic function. It is too precious an opportunity to be wasted.

Let's not lose sight of this lurking virus and make collective efforts to cure the disease. Of course, to be able to survive until next November, we need to first curb this infectious virus lurking on the subway trains. Cover your mouth and "Gesundheit" to everyone!

[The Korea Herald, November 17, 2009]

3. Who Is Paying the Price?

When other people do not believe what you say, it really puts you on edge. When you believe (and know) that something does not exist but circumstantial pieces of information indicate that it may exist, nothing can be more frustrating. The same things also happen between states: country A argues the absence of something while country B argues otherwise, and the listening third person raises the hand of country B. Then the same feeling of frustration sinks in.

Korea knows about this awkward feeling as well. When the stories of Korea and those of foreign governments have clashed, third-party decision makers from time to time have sided with the versions presented by foreign counterparts. In particular, this has happened with respect to the nature of the relationship between the government and major banks in Seoul.

The emergency actions taken by the government in the wake of the 1997 financial crisis brought some of the government agencies in the middle of the restructuring process of the country's financial sector. Since then, the outside perception about the role of the Seoul government, whether rightly or wrongly, still persists even today—17 years after the crisis. The relationship has been mentioned by foreign governments and entities on-again, off-again, like a Whac-A-Mole game.

Now, the issue is not just about who to believe—rather, it is about the sanctions and paying hefty price as a result of such sanction. Largely unnoticed, Korea has been one of the countries that has paid and is still paying the price for the perception that financial institutions are under the control of the government. The perception turns into an official "determination" and the determination morphs into the imposition of penalty "sanctions" for the corporations and their products from Korea. Like with everything else, it is difficult to shed a perception. Knowing this, the government has gone the extra mile to ensure that it does not intervene in the financial institutions' operation other than what is called "prudential regulations" through its financial watchdog agency.

That said, the developments in the financial market during the past couple of months have been all the more puzzling. Controversies have swirled around the appointments for top positions at major banks. The unconfirmed speculation is that the government's wishes have been reflected in the selection of high-ranking officials of some banks. Of course, any sort of involvement has been flatly denied by government agencies. Here again, it is not just about whose story is true or not; it is about the lingering perception and the perception being solidified by events like this.

As before, the continuing perception or misperception comes with various costs, but these happen to be passed on to someone else. It is not the government or the banks, for that matter, that end up paying for the consequence of this perception or misperception. It is the corporations that conduct transactions with the financial institutions in Korea and participate in trade and business activities in the global market.

These days we are amazed to see how fast people in other countries get detailed information on the developments in the Korean financial market and statements made by government officials. Now, virtually all information is open and reported in real time. Visit any website of the banks and government agencies and all key information is readily available. If someone can read Korean or have someone conduct research in Korean, the webpages provide a tremendous amount of information and material. In this era of hyper-transparency, every action here is being closely monitored and followed by foreign watchers.

Perhaps, these controversies are all stemming from some misunderstandings of coincidental small events here and there. But if someone, at some point, ends up paying the hefty price in foreign markets in the form of various sanctions, it is a completely different story.

[The Korea Herald, December 17, 2014]

4. Law Enforcement beyond Borders

One of the common misunderstandings that people have about "Interpol" is that it operates secret offices at unknown places and sends out special agents all over the globe to catch the bad guys.

In many movies, agents from Interpol are sheriffs of the global village and guardians of the transnational rule of law. This is just wrong. There is no such secret office or agent. It is merely an information-gathering and sharing entity to assist national law enforcement agencies in doing their job within their territories.

The jurisdiction of the national authorities stops at their borders. A "global" law enforcement agency with jurisdiction over crimes committed on a global scale is yet to come. So, here is the dilemma: law enforcement is by nature local, but crimes are increasingly global.

The response by national authorities to this mismatch have been two-pronged. The first is an effort by them to expand their domestic criminal jurisdiction on various grounds. Key operating terms such as "territories" and "nationalities" are interpreted as broadly as possible, so that foreign nationals and activities taking place outside national boundaries are still caught by national jurisdiction for prosecution and punishment. So, global crimes can be punished one way or another. But other countries, whose nationals and their activities are covered by such broad application of one country's laws, sometimes register displeasure and even claim an illegitimate extraterritorial application of domestic law.

Another response—a more conciliatory one—is to establish and tighten the web of cooperation between individual countries' law enforcement agencies. This is to cure the fragmented nature of the authority of respective national law enforcement agencies by concluding treaties of cooperation. One country makes arrests at the request of another country and extradites those arrested. Evidence is gathered and witness arranged for another country's legal proceedings. Extradition Treaties and Mutual Legal Assistance Treaties are the two most common types of legal instruments concluded by states.

The US government's indictment of FIFA officials over the allegations of bribes and kickbacks is the most recent example portraying the global nature of crimes with a panoramic view of the two-pronged approach of law enforcement agencies.

Those indicted are mostly foreign nationals residing in foreign countries—indeed only two of 14 indicted are US nationals, and seven FIFA officials were arrested in Zurich, Switzerland. Nonetheless, their utilization of bank accounts in the United States for the alleged bribery transaction has prompted the US authorities to exercise jurisdiction. This indicates that utilization of the global financial network—which is almost inevitable for any sort of transaction these days—can invite jurisdictions of several states participating in the system, even if a criminal activity itself takes place outside the physical boundary of one country.

This exercise of jurisdiction has triggered, not surprisingly, claims of extraterritorial application of one country's domestic law. Russian President Vladimir Putin described this indictment as "yet another obvious attempt to spread (the US) jurisdiction to other states," which was echoed by Sepp Blatter, embattled FIFA president, saying arrest for US financial crimes should be made "in America and not in Zurich." This contradicts the American stance that something did happen in US territory when its financial system was used by someone, which then gives it the authority to exercise criminal jurisdiction as with any other crime happening on its soil.

Then, there is the issue of US-Swiss Extradition Treaty of 1997. This is the only legal vehicle for the US government to secure the seven officials arrested in Zurich for trial in the United States. An extradition decision takes a lengthy domestic procedure of a sending state, as we recently saw in a case between Korea and France.

So, many elements of law enforcement activities in the globalized world are being tested in the new development involving the worlds' most beloved sport. If anything, this also shows that a state with a strong financial infrastructure is better positioned to exercise national jurisdiction in this environment of fragmented, competing national jurisdictions.

[The Korea Herald, June 3, 2015]

5. Battle over Google's Search List

When it comes to an internet "search," Google is by far the most dominant player in the global market. The California-based company now handles 65 percent of search engine traffic in the United States and almost 90 percent in Europe.

As we all know, the search engine giant also provides other products, such as images, maps, Google Earth, Google Shopping, and the like. When its market dominance is combined with these other products, an anti-competition problem may arise—at least that is what worries the European Commission.

The European Commission has established a new antitrust investigation against Google. In its Statement of Objection issued to Google on April 15, 2015, the first formal step for antitrust investigation under the EU law, the European competition watchdog accused the company of abusing its dominant position in the market.

Google emerged unscathed from a similar antitrust problem in the United States in early 2013 when the Federal Trade Commission dropped the investigation, presumably in exchange for the tech giant's voluntary adjustment of its business practice.

The problem now in the EU is Google Shopping. When a customer uses the US search engine for shopping-related information, it displays its Google Shopping products at the top of search results. In other words, users see the Google Shopping products first, followed by other items related to the queries. Through this "Me First" display, so goes the contention, rival brands lose opportunities of fair competition in the EU and thus European consumers are harmed.

The issue here is not just Google's dominance in internet search. The dominance is conspicuous in the EU market, as Google enjoys a 90 percent market share in region. The issue is whether the tech giant has abused its dominance.

The EU's point in its Statement of Objection is that displaying Google's products first amounts to such an abuse of dominance. The allegation theorizes that there should be an objective sequence of products when a person uses a search engine. By changing the sequence and putting Google's products at the top of the list, has an abuse of dominance taken place?

The upcoming legal battle will determine this new question. At any rate, the notion that a search result has a predestined sequence in a particular order, the change of which would skew the competition, will galvanize interesting discussions on this novel issue.

In my case, clicking on a search engine instantly provides thousands of results, and then I randomly go through the results by looking at titles and the short key statements captured under the titles. I try to filter the information and find the most suitable site.

Oftentimes the order of the list just provides a reference guide, but not an exact order to decision making—at least in my case. Sometimes my serious reading starts from page two or three of the search results.

Perhaps an internet search, by definition, involves a high level of subjective judgment anyway. It seems difficult to imagine that there is a fixed order that should be followed all the time.

Pick any shop around us. If asked for a recommendation, a merchant's suggestion would start from their own line of products. It is then up to us to take that recommendation into consideration by also accounting for the fact that the product is their own brand and that bias may have tainted their recommendation.

But then again, the whole commonsensical discussion may not apply to Google. This is a tech giant that affects every corner of our lives with absolute market dominance. After all, its recommendation may come with tremendous—sometimes irresistible—weight.

[The Korea Herald, April 22, 2015]

6. New EU Rules to Protect Personal Data

Since about a week ago, a new batch of emails have started to fill my inbox. The senders are various entities—publishing companies, journals, academic organizations, law firms, and even airlines—in Europe and in Korea.

These emails ask for my consent to store and process my personal information such as contact details, dues payment, membership records, and the like. The senders all refer to the new regulation of the European Union called the General Data Protection Regulation that entered into force on Friday.

This new EU regulation aims to protect personal data like never before. Remember, at every turn of our online memberships and benefits, we provide our personal information. In essence, the choice is actually not ours to make. Unless all the "yes" boxes are checked, you cannot move to the next page. Many of us just check them without even bothering to read the fine print, after which, the information is saved somewhere, transferred elsewhere and shared with other entities. It disappears into cyberspace limbo and the provider loses control.

The GDPR purports to fix this problem. It requires very specific, unambiguous and informed consent from providers. Also, consenting individuals possess continuous control over the information provided. In addition, information collecting entities are required to have data protection officers in place. Noncompliance will entail harsh penalties: fines could be 20 million euros ($23 million) or 4 percent of total worldwide revenue. Given increasing concern over the provision and utilization of personal information, the direction the EU has taken is the right one.

The need for a new legal guideline to protect personal data is becoming an increasing reality. In the digital economy, such information constitutes a critical platform for production, sales, and marketing of new products and services. To stay competitive, corporations must be keen to collect and process personal information. To the contrary, individuals become more vulnerable to the information gathering drive and schemes. Therefore, the market naturally demands new legal guardrails. And Europeans have taken the initiative.

After May 25, EU corporations are all alerted, of course. Interestingly and importantly, this new regulation has also put non-EU corporations in a hurried scramble mode. In other words, those covered by the new regulation are not just the companies or entities operating in the EU that are collecting and processing personal data. Those in other countries may also be subject to the regulation if they process information collected from EU citizens or their information processing is related to EU citizens. So, foreign companies who have customers in the EU or business operations in the EU even remotely—which should be many by the way—are all subject to the GDPR.

By way of example, Korean companies with EU customers should also be directly implicated by this regulation. As a matter of fact, some new emails that I am receiving now are from Korean companies. "Extraterritorial" application of domestic law has often prompted responses from other countries whose companies and nationals are affected by the law. Given the harsh penalty provisions of the GDPR, its ultimate enforcement will probably lead to tension and clashes between Brussels and other countries.

Other countries are now all eyes and ears. Once they see how the EU regulation fares, they are likely to follow suit.

The increasing sensitivity also demands introduction of a similar legal framework in Korea to better protect personal information. As we speak, the National Assembly's special task force committee—the special committee on the "fourth industrial revolution"—just completed its pilot project to spearhead national debate on this very issue. The final report released Monday contains legislative recommendations on how personal data can be collected and utilized with proper protection measures in place and a stringent penalty in case of violation. The skeletal recommendations do not say much.

Korea is likely to be watching carefully the development of the EU's latest initiative.

[The Korea Herald, May 29, 2018]

7. Striking a Balance between Data and Privacy: A Second Try

Global trading norms have traditionally adopted a bifurcated approach: goods trade and services trade. These still constitute the two main pillars of trade agreements.

Now, a fundamental change is in the offing. The arrival of artificial intelligence and the internet of things is now blurring the conventional line between goods and services. The two are now often combined, converged and integrated in one medium or product. Goods provide services, and services in turn put more goods for sale. Consider driverless cars, smart home appliances, and medical-staff-connected medical equipment. They are goods, outwardly speaking, but they provide services that used to be provided only by human beings. Goods and services now come in the same package to give us consumers integrated benefits.

What enables this very convergence is data. Big data, as it is called. Products (or mediums) and their handlers collect data and process it for further commercial or industrial utilization. Data so processed then forms a new platform for the sale of more goods and services. So, data is the neurons and blood of the new integrated network of services and goods. No wonder the question of who stores and controls data has become critically important in terms of business.

President Moon's mention last Friday that data is to the digital economy what oil is to conventional industry is very timely and to the point. Rolling out a new data-driven economic policy, he said the government plans to invest 1 trillion won ($897 billion) in the data industry next year, and intends to build a "data expressway."

A constant concern here, though, is privacy. Hence, what is needed is a balance between the broader utilization of data and the protection of personal information.

As always, "balancing" is a tricky subject. Different countries have different approaches. Their respective balancing points slide along the scale in one direction or the other by a couple of notches. The United States favors more liberal data utilization, while the European Union is more cautious. China and Russia take even more cautious approaches, basically banning the transfer of data out of their jurisdictions.

Against this backdrop, the Aug. 31 announcement reflects Korea's efforts to strike a new balance here, a second try since the adoption of the Personal Information Protection Act in 2011. Importantly, the president's pledge signals that Korea is changing gears—adopting a new system in which personal information can be gathered and processed for commercial purposes, within the constraints of regulatory guidelines. As a counterweight, harsher penalties will be imposed for violations.

Critically, the new scheme purports to define the term "personal information" in a more detailed manner. It now features a three-layered definition: first, personal information; then, information organized into certain categories with no personal identities attached to it; third, anonymous information. The third group is not a concern as it is fully anonymous, thus protected. The first continues to be subject to full protection unless express consent is given. So, it is covered as well. The question lies with the second group. Though the person's identity is supposed to remain private, critics suggest that "identity silhouettes" may gradually appear when dozens of categories are collected and juxtaposed.

Thus, the remaining question is how to handle the information in the second group. For now, the government vows to impose harsh penalties on those who try to assemble the pieces of a puzzle based on information in this group. Interested groups and watchers will demand clearer answers when a bill to materialize the new plan is introduced at the National Assembly in the fall.

Addressing the privacy concern may also require considering the role and function of the agency in charge: the Personal Information Protection Commission. Since its establishment in 2011 to oversee the protection of personal information, the commission has made significant progress over the past seven years. But its role has been marginalized due to the lack of any clear statutory authority as a guardian or watchdog. Any prospective amendments should address this structural problem as well.

[The Korea Herald, September 4, 2018]

8. Long Overdue: Refugee Review System Overhaul

Hypothetically, visualize yourself fleeing your home country for fear of life. To make it out of the country, you would diligently throw away and destroy documents and materials relating to your identification or association. If successful, you would arrive in a foreign country, almost empty-handed and paperless. Then comes the dilemmatic part—how do you prove the circumstances that forced you to flee? The last thing you would do is contact agencies back home or consulates general abroad for issuance of missing documentation. Absence or lack of documentation would haunt you when you need it most—an application proceeding for refugee status.

According to immigration experts and lawyers, that is the most challenging, and the most determinative, obstacle for those applying for refugee status in South Korea. They pinpoint Korea's high "proof" threshold as one of the major reasons for the country's low rate of refugee application approval.

The overall approval rate in Korea stands just at 4.1 percent (839 out of 20,361 from Jan. 1994 to May 2018). This number contrasts sharply with that of other developed countries, and the global average of 38 percent. Usually at this point Japan is presented as an antithesis with an approval rate of 0.5 percent, but Korea's neighbor is a peculiar exception, whose situation is too aberrational to be taken as a benchmark.

The Oct. 17 decision of the Ministry of Justice brought these two aspects into spotlight. First, again a very low approval rate—in fact, all of the 458 applications filed by the Yemeni nationals were rejected. And the reasons given are basically the failure to prove individual circumstances and situations back home.

Notably, 339 out of the total 458 applicants were granted temporary protection status. The grounds were humanitarian consideration given the famine and poverty in the war-stricken Middle East country. So, for those 339 applicants, their refugee applications were denied but they were permitted to stay in Korea, subject to further annual reviews.

There are multiple ways to interpret the "zero" refugee approval rate together with the 74 percent rate of granting temporary protection status. One way to interpret it is an increasing awareness of the need to protect the Yemeni nationals arriving in Korea considering the unspeakable situation in the country at the moment. It is in the right direction and should be lauded.

Another way to interpret it would view the result as a stopgap measure to buy time—basically, the reflection of lack of information and time for evaluating officers to reach conclusive decisions. To agonizing officers taking a "middle way"—no refugee status recognition but permission to stay and work—may have been a tempting alternative.

Had the second scenario been a major consideration, it would hardly solve any problem. Instead, it would only exacerbate the logistical burden for future reviews. If anything, the number of applications is now skyrocketing. Ministry of Justice estimates: refugee applications this year are expected to reach 18,000 by year-end, a 132 percent increase from last year, and the upward surge will continue next year and the year after. So, what we will see is a fully flooded docket of the immigration agency. What's more, remember the temporary status is supposed to be reviewed annually. Which means a constantly increasing workload for the agency. Which in turn would mean a more likelihood of noncommittal, deferring decisions. A vicious circle is in the making.

So, the point is how to face, and hopefully fix, this structural problem now. Doing the refugee application review properly requires an effectively operating system backed by adequate resources. Only then could evaluating officers examine the merit of each application carefully and render an appropriate decision as to who to approve and who not. The present system is premised on an assumption of having just a couple hundred applications each year. As a party to the 1951 Refugee Convention, having an effective review system is a legal obligation of Korea.

There are many issues the year 2018 is to be remembered with. One of which can be an overhaul and improvement of the nation's refugee review system.

[The Korea Herald, October 30, 2018]

9. Yuan Duel Looming in Seoul

"Fair Society" has become a new term of art in Seoul. As the term spreads fast, however, people start to ask a more fundamental question: what in the world does "being fair" mean? As a matter of fact, without a clear definition and yardstick, one man's fairness could be easily criticized as another man's unfairness. Interestingly, a similar issue has long been a flashpoint of international trade. "Fair Trade" has been the mantra of the international trade regime for the past 15 years and few countries have challenged the principle, but here again the old sticky issue is, "what is fair?" And now it seems that the latest version of this "fair trade" discourse will take place in Seoul this coming November.

With the next G20 summit in Seoul only 50 days away, US Treasury Secretary Tim Geithner has recently issued a sharp warning that one of the key issues to be discussed at the meeting would be China's alleged currency manipulation. Given that this particular issue has been on the US priority list for a couple of years now with the Obama administration expecting to face a tough mid-term election just one week before the Seoul meeting, this statement is hardly surprising. What is noteworthy, however, is that this US posture may showcase the importance and timeliness of the Seoul meeting this time around. In short, the November G20 summit in Seoul could provide a perfect venue to discuss this particular issue and other similar ones.

The merit of the G20 summit as a forum to discuss economic issues lies in its flexibility. Unlike its more rigid counterparts in the WTOs and free trade areas that are about creating legal obligations and settling disputes with binding judgment, the G20 has been about discussing framework issues and building consensus to solve common problems. At the same time, this meeting has not been a mere talk shop: it has successfully positioned itself as a venue to initiate candid discussions on key global economic issues followed by reasonably prompt domestic policy adjustment by participating countries. An example can be found in the moratorium of protectionist trade barriers adopted two years ago to which the relatively quick recovery from the global economic recession since 2008 is said to be largely attributable. The Seoul meeting could provide yet another momentum by introducing a framework or guidelines to tackle various thorny issues including the US-China currency dispute.

So, as Geithner warns, if Washington raises the currency manipulation issue in Seoul and China comes back with its own counterargument as it promises it will, this would jumpstart participants' discussions on economic policies' relevance to the alleged new trade barriers. Candid discussions among participants on this very issue may lead to the prospective adoption of a framework or guidelines, in future meetings, for member countries struggling with similar issues. If materialized, this will be counted as one of the legacies of the Seoul meeting. Maybe some harsh words will be inevitable, but exchange of views is important. So, let them talk. They have been talking but probably not in a multilateral context. What the United States says and how China responds will provide important guidance and insight for the other 18 participants. So, again let them talk and let them be heard in Seoul. Indeed, in his US Senate Banking Committee testimony the other day Geithner expressed the desire to bring the attention of other participants to this issue in Seoul.

Some may doubt the wisdom of tabling contentious issues at the Seoul G20 summit that will most likely invite heated discussions between the G2. But the Sino-American trade disputes have been at the center of the global trade arena for some time now and few would be embarrassed by one more round of barbed words. Also, it is true that Korea, as the host, should try to keep all participants happy and entertained. But if the assumption is that the G20 meeting is not a mere talk shop but about getting things done, the more important consideration factor for Korea as the organizer is to focus on what legacies the Seoul gathering will leave on Nov. 12 and afterwards.

The Seoul G20 meeting has the ample potential to provide significant contribution to the global community's effort to achieve "fair trade." Well, after all, perhaps

Korea's sudden national fever for the "fair society" bodes well for the "fair trade" discussion come November.

[The Korea Herald, September 22, 2010]

10. Customs Rules behind the Times

Let's dial back to 1988. The year 1988 was the year of many changes in Korea. Nationwide preparation for the Seoul Olympics held in September of that year brought the first wave of globalization in the country.

That summer, imports of foreign cigarettes were first permitted and the first McDonald's branch opened in Seoul. It was also July of that year when mobile phone services were first introduced in Korea—the price of a mobile phone was 4 million won while a "Pony" passenger sedan was 5 million won. Nordpolitik produced its first tangible result by exchanging permanent missions with Hungary just three days before the start of the Olympic Games. Included among the many changes of 1988 was the increase of the import duty exemption to $400 (or 300,000 won at that time) from $135 set in 1979.

Notably, the $400 ceiling has not changed since, even if the actual value of $400 has changed substantially over the past 26 years. Korea has also undergone a sea change during the quarter century—by way of example, its per capita GDP in 1988 was $4,500, which now stands at $23,000. While various tax credits and exemptions were created and vanished in many categories over the years, simply no activity has been taken in this category through six administrations.

The duty-free allowance also contrasted to Japan's $2,000, the US's $800, Australia's $870, and China's $800. In fact, the average ceiling for the OECD countries stands at $720.

Actual exemption amounts in Korea, however, are somewhat higher than $400 as three categorical exemptions are also provided on top of the $400 ceiling—i.e., one bottle of alcoholic beverage, one bottle of perfume, and 200 cigarettes are also exempted from import duty payment.

The Korean Customs Service thus states that the actual exemption should be roughly about $500. Still yet, this seems to be out of touch with the drastically changed circumstances.

Since 2011, calls have been made in the National Assembly to adjust the ceiling, but then shelved largely because of the political sensitivity that only a certain select group of people stand to enjoy the benefit of any increased exemption. This concern is valid to some extent, since not all Koreans travel abroad. But at the same time, at a time when 15 million nationals exit airports in any given year, to view foreign travel as reserved for the privileged also loses persuasiveness.

The more fundamental problem of the "out-of-touch" regulation lies in its dubious effectiveness. In sample checkings conducted by the Customs Service in 2010, almost 73 percent of Korean travelers were found to possess foreign-purchased articles that exceeded the $400 ceiling. So, technically 73 percent travelers are in violation of the Customs Act. And in an ordinary situation, only 1 percent of incoming people are selected for in-depth checking by customs officials upon entry at the airport. Think about the trips you had recently. Almost all people submit their customs declarations marked as "nothing to declare," and only very few of us are check. In other words, either knowingly or unknowingly, a majority of travelers are just taking their chances.

On its part, the Customs Act imposes a substantial penalty on any violation. A failure to declare is subject to imprisonment of five years or less, payment of an extra 30 percent additional duties or confiscation of the items. As with any other import related law, this provision applies to both Korean nationals and foreign travelers. Provided the Customs Service statistics hold true, apparently the unrealistic law is now turning people—many of them innocent—into potential violators. If most people tend to do something in deviation from what is stipulated in the code book, perhaps it is either outdated or requires some serious attention.

[The Korea Herald, March 19, 2014]

11. Regulation of Foreign Exchange Market

The Korea International Trade Association's recent survey of Korean exporting companies listed the fluctuation of the won/dollar exchange rate as their No. 1 obstacle in managing their businesses. Indeed, the roller-coaster ride for the Korean won's exchange rate against the US dollar, triggered by the 2008 financial crisis, continues.

Just two weeks ago, it was heading downward with the news of the likely appreciation of China's yuan, but one week later it jumped up again when the news of tougher financial regulation in the United States emerged.

What makes Korea uncomfortable is that the roller-coaster ride is continuing despite the strong performance of the Korean exports and the Korean economy in general. The consensus is that the Korean foreign-exchange market is too exposed to foreign influence with so few safeguards in place.

It is against this backdrop that the government of Korea recently adopted a new mechanism to monitor and regulate foreign-currency transactions in Korea, including June 13 announcement of new regulations on foreign-currency forward trading, the purpose of which is to reduce fluctuations in the foreign capital flows into and out of the Korean foreign-exchange market. It appears that if the current volatile situation continues, more and more safety features will be introduced by the government in the future. Given the giddy roller-coaster rides since 2008, this attempt of the government seems both appropriate and timely. If roller coasters in the theme parks are equipped with safety harness sidebars, there is no reason for us not to have the same ones in this "green" roller coaster.

All these measures should be introduced, maintained, and explained as bona fide foreign-exchange regulation for the purpose of preserving the stability of the foreign-exchange market in Korea. The plan should not become, or be perceived as, a mechanism to drive government policies, for instance, policies to promote exports and protect domestic industries.

China has long been in the hot seat because of this particular allegation: its alleged manipulation of yuan to support its economic and trade policies. By any account, the recent measures of Korea should be considered bona fide foreign-exchange regulation considering the overall context. But there is hardly any guarantee that Korea's measures in this area in the future will be completely insulated from similar foreign accusations, whether rightly or wrongly. Previous experience and precedents counsel us to exercise care and caution in formulating future policies in order to avoid unnecessary disputes with other countries.

First of all, future attempts to introduce measures to regulate foreign-exchange market should clearly state the purpose of the prospective regulation up front. Sugarcoating of the measure might not necessarily help. Transparency and clarity are critical here and could help deter misinformed guesswork on the part of the foreign governments and investors. Even if objectives of governmental regulation are proper, when they are not clearly stated and known, governments concerned not infrequently find themselves in trouble.

The legal maxim of "in dubio pro reo" sometimes works exactly in the opposite direction in these international disputes. So, when in doubt, chances are things will get ugly for us. Once a decision is made to introduce such regulation, the process to finalize the regulation must touch all the bases for a reasonable dose of procedural transparency and fairness including public hearings, comments collection, and the like if they are necessary under the circumstances.

Foreign investors will be affected by this regulation for better or worse, so they will be dying to find any slight indication of foul play if they believe they are short-changed.

At the same time, future regulations will have to offer clear guidelines for both the regulator and entities being regulated. Foreign governments and companies have complained that certain regulations of the Korean government are overly vague and skeletal, putting ultimate decisions in the discretion of the agency concerned. It is indeed true that governmental discretion should be preserved as much as possible to address all the variations in real life. But the discretion and detailed guidelines don't have to be mutually exclusive: they can come hand in hand. Discretion without sufficient guidelines is always vulnerable to the criticism of arbitrariness.

Again, safeguards are needed to preserve the integrity and stability of the foreign-exchange market in Korea. The government's plan to introduce these safeguards is an appropriate response to the new situation. Tailored and sophisticated safeguards can ensure that unhealthy speculation does not continue. We need to switch to a cable-car ride!

[The Korea Herald, June 30, 2010]

12. Global Competition, Fragmented Disposition

Why do they always have Mr. Foreman, instead of Mr. Smith or Mr. Brown, in a jury trial? That was a small mystery in my mind following the Korean subtitles of Hollywood movies. The Korean subtitles translated "Mr. Foreman," as it appeared in a judge's famous question of "Mr. Foreman, has the jury reached the verdict?" as if it were a last name of one of the jurors. It was not until long afterwards that I realized who this Mr. Foreman was: it is a special term referring to a head juror.

Amusingly, the same mistranslations are still found in some Korean captions these days. In fact, a trial by jury would be the single most distinctive feature that many people in Korea find interesting and mystifying, although Korea recently adopted a pilot program of the jury trial with a limited scope.

The jury trial has become a mantra of the commentators in the Korean press since the verdicts of the two trials in US federal district courts were rendered lately: one in the Samsung-Apple trial in San Jose, California, and the other in the Kolon-DuPont trial in Richmond, Virginia. In both trials, the juries came back from their deliberations with adverse verdicts for the Korean companies with astronomical damages, which even affected the stock prices of these companies.

The commentaries explain how complex these patent and trade secrets issues are and yet how underequipped the jurors are in dealing with these technical issues. Some critics even depict the verdicts as a new type of trade protectionism. Well, the national frustration is understandable, but these initial reactions are either misplaced or overblown.

A jury is meant to be a group of lay people, who are supposed to have no direct knowledge of the case. Questions posed during jury selection even ask if the candidate has read newspaper articles about the case. A prospective juror with knowledge or awareness of the events at issue is thus rejected by either party. Under this system, one would be surprised if jury members include someone with high expertise in the areas of patents or technologies. So, the initial response of the Korean press misses the point.

What about the criticism that the verdicts are the reflection of the new protectionism? Well, unfortunately, it is too much of a stretch to say that protectionism underpins these decisions. Protectionism requires government action, and does not cover the flow of thinking going on in the minds of people, whether it is favoritism or patriotism. Yes, the decision is disappointing but calling it protectionism is too much. Protectionism is not a word that covers all kinds of difficulties that Korean companies may face abroad. We need to save it to condemn real protectionism.

What does raise a red flag for us, though, is an odd combination of global issues and local disposition. The issues raised here are breathtakingly global: these companies do not know boundaries and vie for the single global market. But all these global issues have been squeezed into the terminus of the local jurisdictional corridor of a country. What happens as a result is respective courts in respective countries all render different decisions on virtually the same issue. Then who coordinates these different and conflicting judgments and orders? No one does. With respect to the Samsung-Apple dispute, it may well be the case that at the end of the day we will be seeing a bunch of fragmented judgments and decisions from 30 different proceedings in nine different countries.

These trials inform us that global companies will have to struggle with this systemic loophole as market competition intensifies. This systemic mismatch is most vividly observed in IT sectors where the whole world actually operates as one single market, and yet competitors pursue judgments all torn to rags. The verdicts are indeed disappointing to the Korean companies and watchers in Korea, but the initial national reaction involving a non-expert jury and the mentioning of protectionism is largely overblown and inaccurate. An unsubstantiated misperception may only complicate the situation and blur the eyes of the corporations facing the real threat.

[The Korea Herald, September 5, 2012]

13. Calm Needed in Costco Fiasco

If people can buy a year's supply of products from Costco in a single visit, the US retail giant must have seen a year's supply of inspectors in just one single day. Last Wednesday and this past Sunday, the Seoul city government sent dozens of inspectors to Costco Wholesale's warehouses in Seoul to conduct thorough investigations into virtually all activities of the retailer in Seoul.

Wednesday's inspection is said to have detected as many as 41 violation of a plethora of city regulations: a construction ordinance, fire regulation, parking regulation, sanitary regulation, waste recycling regulation, broken guiding lights, you name it. This is a heavy-handed response from the local government to the US membership warehouse club's refusal to abide by the Seoul city ordinance requiring the closure of large supermarkets every other Sunday. The city government vows more dragnet searches if the retailer continues to remain in violation.

The Sunday ordinance has received much attention for a couple of years now, and the debates about the wisdom of the measure seem to be still going on. In any event, the ordinance has been in force and merchants operating in Seoul are bound by it: violators are subject to fines and other administrative sanctions. Costco also does not dispute its violation and accepts payment of associated fines, as stipulated.

Costco's knowing violation should be condemned and penalties have to be applied. But mobilizing all sorts of regulatory authority to give the retailer a hard time, in such a thinly veiled emotional response, is hardly a proper course of action. It only tarnishes the image of the city government and raises concerns over other (fully legitimate) regulatory measures.

Seoul city underscores that it has the legal authority to conduct these administrative inspections. That is true and there is no question about that. What is at issue here, however, is not the existence of the regulatory authority, but the way it is exercised under the circumstances. Whatever the underlying facts, a foreign corporation having a sour relationship with a government, and the government singling out the corporation with a barrage of administrative examinations is a familiar plot in international disputes.

What is further noteworthy here is the fact that the ordinance has already been found to be in violation of the enabling statute. In a challenge brought by other large supermarkets against the ordinance in June, the Seoul Administrative Court ruled the ordinance against the law, and Seoul City is planning to issue an amended ordinance as early as November. These prevailing large stores are now able to open all week long. But not Costco, because it did not participate in the June litigation and cannot enjoy the benefit from the lawsuit. So goes the rationale of the city government.

This stance is entirely correct—technically. But, one would ask, if the ordinance has already been found problematic and thus other large supermarkets are all exempt from it, what is the point of pursuing one company so relentlessly? Is it because the company did not participate in the original lawsuit against the city government? Or, perhaps, is it because this is the only company subject to the present ordinance before the amendment? It does raise the questions of why there have been inspection, and why now?

Criticism is thus raised that there is a strong appearance of the investigation of the city government being an emotional, retaliatory response. Measures consistent with domestic laws and regulations without any specific "targeting" intent are always permitted and will continue to be so in any circumstances. However, a retaliatory measure, if any, directed at a specific entity would be the last thing that a local government should consider under the current environment of a tightly knit web of treaties and agreements.

Absent a persuasive argument of why this type of action is justified, the long-term burden would outweigh any short-term catharsis. Enough is enough. Time to calm down.

[The Korea Herald, October 18, 2012]

14. In Case of Doubt, Let Competition Prevail

The digital age has complicated conventional rules of national jurisdiction. National jurisdiction under international law is drawn along the physical boundaries of a state, and looks at who or what is located inside the boundaries.

The "borderless" nature of cyber activities has made this traditional rule outdated and detached from reality. Cyber activities virtually have no relevance to national boundaries. But the law is the law, and states have to find a territorial hook to exercise jurisdiction for cyber activities.

One such hook is the location of a server. It is indeed a physical item located in one state, so fits with the conventional rules. Thus, now the location of a server dictates the national jurisdiction, including taxation issues.

Digital companies pay their corporate taxes where their servers are located. Concerns are being raised that this traditional rule creates loopholes for internet-based companies. But suggestions for new rules are still on the drawing board. Until then, conventional rules remain the standard.

One major anxiety over the perceived loophole is to do with the disadvantages for domestic digital corporations. While domestic providers are subject to a web of regulation including taxation and everything, their foreign competitors with foreign servers are basically not. So, regulatory restrictions for foreign companies are sometimes perceived (erroneously) as a counterweight to level the playing field.

Speculations have arisen whether these two practical considerations may have underpinned the debates over Google's June 1 request for a permission to transfer the digital mapping data from Korea to its foreign servers.

The data on point is 1:5,000 scale map data compiled by the National Geographic Information Institute, information in great demand for digital commercial services. The statutory deadline for a decision is Wednesday. A pan-governmental committee is scheduled to mull over the request one final time before it issues a decision.

Over the summer, it has been reported that a national security concern is the issue of contention. The digital information requested is the same information provided to Korean service providers (such as SK Telecom's T-Map), but exporting it to outside locations may let it fall into the wrong hands in terms of national security, the government cautions.

Information on the locations of key facilities is already available online from various mapping service providers and satellite image companies. People marvel at the level of resolution and graphic details of the images of structures and facilities available on the internet for free or that they can purchase. The question then is, what additional security risk does this provision reduce? There may be some, but extra efforts need to be made to explain it with all these digital images already stacked up and updated in public domain.

So, realization of this reality has fueled the said speculation. If the hidden agenda is the taxation issue for the global digital company, this may not be the best way to find a solution. The rule, for better or worse, is still based on the location of servers. Foreign corporations pay their corporate taxes when they have permanent establishments in Korea. The OECD has been contemplating introducing new rules here but they are slow in coming. Some countries are trying new rules, but there are still many things to be clarified.

If, on the other hand, the underlying reason is to somehow favor domestic service providers, it seems more problematic. Market competition through nondiscriminatory treatment is the cardinal rule countries have agreed to. Dominant Korean service providers in this sector do not provide their mapping service in English, leaving a sizable segment of people—foreign residents and tourists—outside the service coverage. Competition may help change their service model.

Again, this is just speculation raised over the summer debates, so they may not reflect the situation accurately. Obviously, there may be other valid reasons that make the government cautious and hesitant here. But at least the upcoming committee deliberation is a misplaced forum to cater to these two considerations.

[The Korea Herald, August 24, 2016]

15. Is Pandora's Box Open? The Specter of Regulatory Subsidies

Criticizing rampant subsidy programs by many governments for their domestic industries, Ronald Reagan once said, "Government does not solve problems; it subsidizes them." Perhaps subsidization for domestic industries runs in the blood of all the governments around the world. In fact, one of the core roles of a government is arguably to support its people and companies through whatever means available.

But few governments dare to provide direct monetary support to companies anymore: the WTO's Subsidies Agreement prohibits such subsidization for industries and everyone watches everyone else for instances of violation. This prohibition, however, is juxtaposed with the basic instinct of a government to mobilize all means available at its fingertips to support domestic companies and industries and help them compete in the global market. This disconnect between basic instinct and the legal norm creates a difficult situation for a government: on the one hand, they have promised not to do so. Just imagine how parents would feel if supporting their children to achieve better academic performance at school was somehow prohibited.

As fate would have it, some governments succumb to the temptation. They then try to find a way to get around the norm. An alternative path frequently explored is to formulate governmental policies that end up lending a helping hand to the companies. Governments thus introduce economic policies that indirectly support their domestic companies while requiring their foreign competitors to jump through the hoops. No money changes hands, so it is difficult to determine whether it constitutes illegitimate subsidization. Support is given, but hardly it's detectable. This is what is referred to as a "regulatory subsidy." A regulatory subsidy is invisible and amorphous. Any governmental policy or regulation can be a good candidate for this type of subsidy. Any regulatory subsidy claim is also laden with controversies between countries concerned because the alleged subsidy is invisible and amorphous.

A new round of saber-rattling has just begun concerning the regulatory subsidies. On Sept. 29, the US House of Representatives passed a bill to impose hefty extra duties on Chinese products because of the alleged provision of subsidies from Beijing government to Chinese companies through foreign exchange manipulation. This bill is the clarion call of upcoming battles on regulatory subsidies. Everyone knows who the target of the bill is, but interestingly the text does not specifically mention the country. The country-neutral nature of the bill signals that it can be applied, mutatis mutandis, to any other country as well. The US's pursuit of the regulatory subsidy enforcement will almost certainly invite other countries to play the same game. Sooner or later, all countries will be trapped in a downward spiral of illegal subsidy allegations and retaliations. Just remember that in the course of pursuing something invisible and amorphous, any governmental policy of any government could be easily implicated. No country would escape unscathed if unbridled escalation of a new breed of subsidies and related disputes rampage through the global community.

If this means that we are on the verge of opening a new Pandora's Box of regulatory subsidies, the Seoul G20 meeting is now the only opportunity to keep it shut or, if that is impossible, to have everyone wake up to the necessity to contain what is coming out of the box. Each passing day seems to notch up the stakes and importance of the upcoming event in Seoul to a new level. Korea should stay mindful to play its role as the host-mediator in this tension-filled showdown. The moment it takes side with one country or a group of countries, it would place itself at the center stage of the battle ground.

Starting from October, the media is busy presenting a series of upbeat and flashy reports about the upcoming event. Truth be told, however, this meeting in Seoul seems to be the most tension-filled international event that Korea has ever hosted. We will have to hold our breath until the final moment of the meeting.

[The Korea Herald, October 19, 2010]

16. The G-20 Summit in Seoul and Beyond

The Group of 20 summit meeting in Seoul is now over. Overall assessment of the event is largely positive. No major distraction during the event and candid discussions throughout. And finally came a joint communiqué of the participants.

As expected, the exchange rate issue was placed at the top of the agenda and leaders exchanged frank but pointy views. The leaders reached consensus not to engage in "competitive devaluation" in their future economic policies and agreed to have their finance ministers continue to tackle this issue so as to introduce by next year a new "guideline," by reflecting many economic indices such as the ratio between the GDP and current account surpluses, for respective countries' exchange rate adjustment.

In short, the consensus has been formed in Seoul but the specific framework to implement the consensus is the homework of the next year. Although it is indeed "remarkable progress to agree on detailed schedule for the discussion of guidelines" to quote President Lee Myung-bak, last week's discussions in Seoul further showed how treacherous the path to an ultimate "guideline" would be.

Candor may have led to consensus, but it is collective readiness to concede that will lead to any form of a workable "guideline." Whether such readiness to concede will still hold when it comes down to specific numbers and caps is an open question.

The additional stimulus package of $600 billion by the US Federal Reserve just one week before the Seoul meeting had put the United States on the defensive throughout the meeting. President Obama sold the measure as a necessity to facilitate US economic recovery the benefit from which would be shared by all US trading partners, but the criticism alleging it as US's own devaluation scheme apparently outsounded Washington's explanation. A meeting long considered to be supposed to be a forum of US criticism against China's foreign exchange policy instantly started to take a different tone. The surroundings of the Seoul meeting only exposed the fundamental difference in views between the United States and China regarding the exchange rates, and confirmed that the US-China trade friction would continue, at least for the time being.

In addition, the criticism directed at Washington's Quantitative Easing II apparently provided a new momentum to a group of countries that propose to reconsider the dominant role of the US dollar in international transactions. France, one of the countries in the group, is now the chair of the next year's G20 meeting, whose president just stated in Seoul that "the international monetary system is a problem and needs to be updated for the 21st century."

These countries refer to the "loose" financial regulation of the United States as a source of concern for global financial stability as evidenced just two years ago. Loose or tight, what is at least clear seems that concern and complaints about the once unquestionable dominance of the US dollar is building fast. It would be interesting to observe how Washington would react to this new development and increasing pressure. This would form yet another front for the United States in addition to the one with China.

If the international monetary regime changes, one way or another, as proposed by some countries, a new landscape will set in: the downgrading of the status of the US dollar would mean upgrading of the status of other currencies, followed by the increase of economic influence of the countries issuing these currencies. For better or worse, the polarization of the global economic hegemony would usher in a new terrain.

As a country maintaining a strong trade relationship with both the United States and China, as a country situated between the developed countries and developing ones, and, most importantly, as a country heavily dependent on the international trade, Korea's position is always precarious whenever there is a change of paradigm as a consequence of collision between the competing camps. Perhaps what we have seen so far is the exhibition films and the main feature has not started yet. This is another reason, even though the meeting is over, Korea will have to make continued efforts to be engaged in the global dialogue on these issues. It should stay tuned and stay relevant to ride out the upcoming challenges.

The G20 summit in Seoul proved the usefulness of the meeting in maintaining and improving the global economic regime. Although the meeting put off adopting a new framework and guideline for future gatherings, the contents contained in the Seoul joint communiqué may well be called a significant achievement at this stage. Hopefully, the upcoming finance ministers' meeting in Paris in February and G20 summit in Cannes in November next year will be able to tie up remaining loose ends and complete the homework. Remember that this entity came into being just two years ago. What has transpired so far since 2008 is a commendable achievement for an entity that is only two years old.

[The Korea Herald, November 17, 2010]

17. Bank Bailouts: Too Aggressive to Fail

The whole world has been in the emergency mode since last year to overcome the unprecedented financial crisis. Although there are some signs that the economic crisis is not as bad as it was originally expected, the sudden collapse of the house of cards in Dubai and the rumored national default of Greece indicate that the situation is still uncertain.

Setting the remaining uncertainty aside, the better-than-expected outcome is largely due to the reasonably good job done by many governments. They have injected an enormous amount of money to rescue their key industries, particularly the troubled financial institutions. To name a few, the US government has injected $700 billion into their financial institutions, followed by the Japan with 28 trillion yen ($310 billion) and the European Union with $260 billion. Well, with that amount of money one could even buy a new planet and build the whole financial system from scratch. Now, the signal is that existing bailouts will be extended, and more bailouts will be contemplated to make sure that the financial institutions are really back on track. In fact, US Treasury Secretary Timothy Geitner just announced that the US government would extend the financial support from TARP until October next year.

Granted, the bailout of the financial institutions has been inevitable given the abruptness and magnitude of the current economic downturn. Without it, maybe the whole economy would collapse. Under the current economic system the financial institutions (mainly banks) constitute the main bloodline of almost all economic activities of any given country. They are indeed a quarterback of the economy—they distribute much-needed credit to all industries. That is probably why all countries are so concerned about the financial health of their financial institutions and why they try to rescue them from the financial trouble.

But at the same time, we have to note that the financial institution bailouts are ironic and carry a long-term impact. First of all, they are mainly to blame for the current economic crisis. As far as one could tell, however, they have not been penalized. It is true that some of the CEOs have had difficult times one way or another since September 1998, but the financial institutions, as an entity, have not been penalized or warned. Instead, they have been given a virtual immunity for the past wrongdoing and to some extent even a reward.

The financial institutions around the globe must have figured out two things by now (or maybe they have known it for a long time): first, their governments cannot let them fail no matter what happens, and second, your over-aggressiveness is always the best tactic. The government would punish you if you made a petty mistake or violate financial laws and regulations, but the government will rescue you if your blunder is huge. When everything goes fine, you would make a lot of money by being overly aggressive in the market as proven by the financial institutions before the financial crisis. When something goes wrong, you can seek profits by being overly aggressive: the government will spend the whole national treasury to save you while your competitors are driven out of the market because they did not take enough risks to get the governmental support. So, in short, the lessons would be that aggressiveness is always rewarded and that this proposition is valid only if you are aggressive enough.

Many say that the governments have to bail the financial institutions out because they are either too big to fail or too important to fail. That is true when viewed from the governments' perspective. When viewed from the financial institutions' perspective, these bailed out financial institutions are too aggressive to fail.

Of course, financial institutions are an integral component of economic structure, so it is critical to keep them operating. But it is also critical to realize the aftershocks of the bailout. These bailouts may fundamentally change the way the financial institutions compete in the financial market and the way they regulate their own behavior. So, the remaining task is not simply about getting the repayment in full, but about introducing reliable financial regulation to guide their behavior in the future and sanction them for any unreasonable business decisions. A quarterback is important for the whole team, but he should be sanctioned or sometimes replaced if he continues to call overly aggressive moves and thus ruins the whole game. A wise head coach would not blindly stand by his quarterback all the time.

Santa Claus is supposed to make a list, check it twice and place a present under the Christmas tree only when a child is nice. Santa should not haul all his gifts for a naughty child just because he is naughty enough to wreck the holiday mood. Merry Christmas!

[The Korea Herald, December 16, 2009]

18. New Concept for Action against Genocide

Although we live in an age of abbreviation, few people will have heard of the term "R2P." I did not have any clue when I first heard it, I have to confess. R2P stands for "Responsibility to Protect." This is a new concept raised by the international community after having observed the ugly failure of the international community to take appropriate actions during genocides in Rwanda and former Yugoslavia in 1990s.

This concept sets forth a noble cause: a state has a responsibility to protect its people from grave atrocities such as genocide and, more importantly, if the state fails to implement its obligation, the international community has the obligation to step in to protect the people.

This concept was solidified when the UN Security Council endorsed it with Resolution 1674 in April 2006, followed by UN Secretary General Ban Ki-moon's blessing to the principle through the release in January 2009 of a UN report called "Implementing the Responsibility to Protect." The concept as espoused by these UN documents allows the UN Security Council to take actions to protect people from the threat of their own governments, if necessary.

The Security Council can also authorize member states to take necessary action. Some resistance to the concept has been muffled by the sanctity of the cause of protecting civilians from unspeakable atrocities and by the compatibility of the idea with the UN Charter to the extent an action is authorized or taken by the Security Council. In fact, the UN Charter allows the Security Council to take all kinds of actions including military intervention.

The current situation in Libya has become the first instance of an actual application of this concept. Angered and concerned by the Libyan leader's threat to exterminate opposition forces, last Friday the UN Security Council adopted Resolution 1973 that imposes a no-fly zone over Libya and authorizes member states to use "all necessary measures" to protect civilians in the North African country. The resolution was immediately adhered to by the United States, the United Kingdom, and France whose military assets conducted air raids against key military targets in Libya. Secretary General Ban also mentions that the UN Security Council resolution is the implementation of the R2P principle.

Perhaps no one can deny the urgency of protecting the people in Libya under the circumstances. Surprisingly, however, the international community's reaction to the military intervention last weekend was quite mixed. Russia and China, the other two permanent members in the Security Council, who abstained from voting instead of blocking the resolution with their veto power, officially expressed regret over the military action. At the same time, India, Brazil, and Germany also abstained from the voting in the Security Council. The African Union also requested that the military action be suspended as soon as possible. The League of Arab States does not seem supportive of the operation either. For his part, Moammar Gadhafi appeared on TV and pledged a long war against the foreign aggression by referring to Libya's right to self-defense under the same UN Charter.

The apparent divide among major powers in the face of the imminent threat to the civilian population in Libya describes the slippery road for the concept of R2P. Core questions raised by the critics of the R2P include who can make a decision as to whether a particular situation warrants the invocation of R2P and what are the kinds of perils against which the concept can be invoked. With respect to the first question, it is easy to say in abstract that the Security Council should make the final decision. But if a less-than-optimal level of consensus is confirmed in a specific instance despite the existence of a decision by the Security Council, a controversy seems unavoidable. Concerning the second question, when military action targets the residence of the leader, a challenge can be raised about whether the focus of the action is to change the leadership or the protection of the people. Maybe in many instances both of them are closely connected, but R2P's objective, as it stands now, is the protection of people. This is not to say that we have to turn a blind eye to a dictator, but that it is not entirely clear yet whether the R2P can be expanded to cover all these instances.

The international community committed a critical mistake by being passive spectators in Rwanda and Srebrenica. In light of this experience, R2P is the right direction for us to go. But the specific parameters of the concept will be tested through the Operation Odyssey Dawn and similar future events. As the code name itself states, maybe now is the dawn of the development of this important principle.

[The Korea Herald, March 23, 2011]

19. Laudable but Misplaced: EU's Aviation ETS Tax

The global aviation industry is still scratching its head while digesting the contents of the latest bid by Brussels to curb greenhouse gas emissions. Starting from Jan. 1, the EU included the aviation industry in its CO_2 Emission Trading System and started imposing extra taxes on airliners. Actual payments will not take place until 2013, but the system is now up and running.

A very laudable effort indeed, but here is the trick: this program of the EU applies to all foreign airlines as well, if their airplanes are heading to or leaving from airports in EU countries. And it has teeth: airline companies that ignore the law will be slapped with fines. So, Korean carriers shuttling between Incheon and all major European capitals will be required to pay the new extra taxes. According to an estimate, this means an extra payment of $3 for individual passenger per each flight. Nonetheless, the grand total of the payments for each airline may be sizable because all European airports are always bustling with travelers.

As one could imagine, many countries are concerned by this new measure. The United States, China, and Russia are all against the latest EU attempt, making it a rare occasion in which Washington and Beijing are on the same side on economic issues. Just last week, Beijing even prohibited its carriers from complying with the EU regulation. The United States is also considering a similar action. So, the level of tension is certainly ratcheting up, and the prospects would be pretty scary if all countries adopt retaliatory measures, as they threaten to.

Perhaps nobody could question the good heart of the EU in coming up with this creative idea, to save the ailing Earth from monstrous airplanes emitting tons of greenhouse gases. Good intentions, however, do not always deliver.

The fundamental reason that other countries have gone berserk about the EU measure is its nature as an extraterritorial application of a domestic law. It applies to all foreign carriers even if most of the journey takes place outside the airspace of the EU. Imagine a flight from Incheon to Paris. Only roughly one-fifth of the flights actually takes place within the EU airspace, but the EU charges the extra taxes for the entire 12-hour journey from ICN to CDG, which then forces a question of why other countries should pay one country (i.e., EU) for an activity that takes place outside the one country's jurisdiction.

A more practical drag for the measure is the fact that perhaps this noble attempt will not be as effective as it would seem. Most likely, this extra payment obligation would change no one's behavior. It certainly cannot change the behavior of the carriers because they will instantly turn around and shift the burden to their customers by raising the price of the fare. Nor will it affect the behavior of the flying customers. It is hard to imagine that someone changes his or her slight plan because of the $3 increase in an airplane ticket. Everybody knows that the airfare is anyone's guess. It is not uncommon to find out that the person sitting next to you paid just half what you paid. So, arguably, as far as carbon dioxide reduction goes, the aviation industry is different from, say, the automobile industry.

So, unlike other industries operating mainly in the domestic sphere, changing the behavior of airlines and their customers might not be achieved by this global application of the EU domestic law. Any tangible outcome would be that the money will be accumulated to be spent for some noble cause (i.e., saving the world) in the future. At this point, however, the same question comes back: how can one country claim itself to be the one?

Maybe the EU has decided to voluntarily assume the role of a caretaker having seen the slow-moving global community on this score. Some people, however, may find it difficult to enlist their sympathy for such a cause when they remember all the big airplanes that the European consortium has developed and marketed so eagerly these days. Some might even say that the level of choking inflicted upon the global community flowing from the continuing EU financial crisis far much outweighs that caused by the emission of the greenhouse gases.

The EU's spearheading effort is laudable but its direction is misplaced. A global problem can only be properly addressed by a global solution. One country's pursuit of a unilateral solution may further complicate and even undermine the efforts being made at the ICAO for this very issue.

[The Korea Herald, February 21, 2012]

20. To Make a Long Story Short

French mathematician Blaise Pascal once apologized to the recipient of his letter for its length by saying "I did not have time to write you a short letter, so I wrote you a long one." It was Mark Twain who said, "If you want me to give you a two-hour presentation, I am ready today. If you want only a five-minute speech, it will take me two weeks to prepare."

They were trying to say how difficult it is to write short but precise statements. Interestingly, this very statement of Twain was quoted by a US federal court judge who disagreed to join the majority opinion of the court and instead issued his own "concurring" opinion—meaning that he agrees to the conclusion but does not share the rationale. And it was purely about the length of the decision.

In a recent judgment rendered by the US Court of Appeals for the Eleventh Circuit in Atlanta, where it upheld a murder conviction from the district court, one judge "concurred" only, although he agrees to the final decision of the court, because he, citing Mark Twain's advice, viewed the 105-page decision of the court as unnecessarily long.

To quote some of the opinion of the judge, Judge James Edmondson:

> I—very respectfully—do not join in the majority' erudite opinion. . . . I stress that it is not because the opinion says something that I am sure is wrong or I am sure is even likely wrong. . . . But the opinion says a lot and says more than I think is absolutely needed.

He then explains why the interest of the court and the general public would not be served by unnecessarily wordy judgments which increase the possibility of inadvertent errors, cherry-picking citation by interest groups in future court proceedings and blurred core points, let alone the painful reading.

This 105-page decision would pale in comparison to the 480-page decision issued in January by Seoul Central District Court in a criminal proceeding against a CEO of a large business group. Or the 182-page decision that was rendered in January 2012 in yet another proceeding involving a well-known election bribery case.

Reading a document of this magnitude is almost the same as reading a book. Days may be needed before even the parties understand and digest the decision. An obvious trend is that the length of the judgments tends to get longer, in particular in high profile cases. Of course, this is in part because the case itself is complex and because the presiding judge is apparently touching all bases so that the judgment is not overturned on appeal. But the said Twainian advice has been getting more support, especially from younger people.

In response to this reaction, in early July the Criminal Division of the Seoul Central District Court issued an internal guideline, to be effective as of September, to screen the voluminous court decision phenomenon and foster succinct and concise judgments.

This is a move that should be welcomed by many. In fact, this is also necessary as the judgments of trial courts are going to be uploaded to the website starting from 2015, where all watchful eyes will easily scrutinize ins and outs of any decision. With the fast emergence of digital communication in Korea where all sorts of shortest expressions available are preferred, the judiciary's effort to keep up with the changing nature of the society and adjust a bit the way court judgments are formulated is indeed appropriate and important.

In fact, this is not the first time and similar efforts have been made on and off since 1991, with only few changes, if any. But the new attempt of this time is certainly getting off to a good start. It is true that sometimes legalese is necessary and lengthy discussions required. But in other times, according to the Seoul Central District Court, shorter decisions may serve the purpose.

[The Korea Herald, July 24, 2013]

21. Defining Collective Self-Defense

Although expressed in very cautious words, the US's apparent approval of the possibility of Japan's more active military involvement in the region under the name of "collective self-defense" has become a topic of much discussion in the neighboring countries.

The geopolitical implications of this development will certainly be significant in many respects. It is somewhat odd, though, to see this matter being discussed under the theme of "collective self-defense" as the situation envisioned in the pronounced plan does not seem to square with how the concept has been understood and applied in international law.

This concept of collective self-defense does not mean that one country can support its allies in terms of all sorts of military activities or conflicts.

Unlike the companion "individual self-defense," this concept basically requires and presupposes existence of an alliance treaty between or among states, although there are some rare exceptions. Once an alliance treaty is in place, the exercise of the rights is then regulated by the terms and conditions set forth in the treaty.

Enter Japan here. In its case, the alliance treaty at issue is the 1960 US-Japan Security Treaty. So, the discussion of collective self-defense in the context of the United States and Japan, to the extent Japan is concerned, is determined by the provisions of the US-Japan Security Treaty. Now, according to Article 5 of the treaty, the treaty has a very specific territorial limitation for its application. The article confines the scope of the application of the treaty to a situation of an armed attack occurring "in the territories under the administration of Japan."

In other words, for the treaty to be applicable for the purpose of collective self-defense, the attack should be the one against the United States within Japan's territory. The way it is written down, therefore, the treaty apparently does not cover a situation in which the US territory is being attacked or US warships are being attacked in high seas, or, for that matter, US armed forces in South Korea is being attacked.

So, it appears that, barring an amendment to the 1960 treaty, many emergency situations that are being discussed in the context of the present collective self-defense debates in fact do not fall under the provisions of the treaty.

Perhaps what is being discussed here is not so much related to the strict concept of collective self-defense as to a policy change to invite and permit Japan to pursue more active roles in terms of military activities in this region.

As many watchers put it, it may be the case that the United States wishes to share with Japan the increasing military burden in this part of the world, despite the concern raised by some neighboring countries whose memory is just too recent.

As stipulated in Article 51 of the UN Charter, any state possesses an inherent right of self-defense, whether individual or collective. So does Japan. There is no question about it.

The concept, however, should be interpreted and applied in a manner consistent with the established legal principles in order to allay the anxiety of the neighboring countries and to achieve the intended objectives of the scheme. If the concept is used in a way that does not exactly dovetail with the strict definition of the term itself, other countries in the region will have another reason to justify their concern.

[The Korea Herald, October 16, 2013]

22. War of Public Corporations

When first introduced in Joseon late in the 16th century, tobacco immediately became popular on the peninsula. The widespread consumption even led to a government-imposed ban on the product at one point (from 1692–1717) because of the fire risk. In the early years of tobacco consumption, Lee Ik (1681–1763), a well-known scholar of the "realist" school of Confucianism, praised it as a cure-all medicine. The revered King Jeongjo (1752–1800), also known as a heavy smoker, noted in his book *Hongjaejeonseo* that tobacco had helped him recover from fatigue and brought on sound sleep.

Tobacco was then added to the list of items that were sold through the Government Monopoly Administration in 1921 along with ginseng. The government agency became a public corporation in 1987, and was privatized in 2002 under the name of KT&G. Public corporations are established through enabling statutes and are considered government-affiliated entities under Korean law.

The decades-old governmental involvement in tobacco sales puts an interesting twist on the recent decision of the National Health Insurance Service to bring a lawsuit against tobacco manufacturers for the financial losses it has allegedly suffered as a result of tobacco-related diseases. The NHIS, a public corporation under the supervision of the Ministry of Health and Welfare, is seeking compensation for health care costs associated with such diseases. The NHIS alleges that it pays as much as 1.7 trillion won ($1.6 billion) each year for medical costs related to consumption of tobacco products.

The domestic and foreign tobacco manufacturers being targeted include KT&G, Philip Morris, British American Tobacco, and Japan Tobacco International. These manufacturers, through a joint press conference last week, dismissed the NHIS's plan as having "little legal merit" and descried the lawsuit as an attempt to disguise the organization's own budget problems. In fact, in the previous four tobacco litigations in Korea, brought about by individual smokers, the tobacco companies largely prevailed due to the difficulty of providing a direct causal relationship between smoking and the diseases and any ill intentions on the part of the manufacturers. Most likely, the same issues will be vehemently argued and tested in the NHIS case.

Besides the legal claims and defenses associated with the cigarette litigation, what is noteworthy here is that it is the NHIS, a public corporation, that plans to bring about legal action. AS mentioned, KT&G was privatized in 2002, but had been affiliated with the government until that time—as a public corporation until 2002 and as a government agency until 1987. As the NHIS data, statistics, and financial losses may well go back to before 2002, it is possible that the government may be shown to be partly responsible. The tobacco manufacturers already argue that if they are held liable the government should be held at least partially liable for any alleged damages.

No wonder the plan winds up the government. Both the Ministry of Health and Welfare and the Ministry of Strategy and Finance are reported to take a cautious approach to this complicated relationship. The NHIS might want to avoid this complication by confining the scope of its claims to post-2002, but the defendant manufacturers, multinational tobacco giants included, may have their own defense agenda.

Warning signs began to be printed on the packages of cigarettes sold in Korea in 1976. First as a government agency, then a public corporation, KR&G was adroit at managing the conflicting objectives of securing public health on the one hand and maintaining a key national monopoly business on the other. The 2002 privatization was supposed to end this, but it turns out that not all the ties may have been cut.

Whoever emerges victorious from this lawsuit, it will be an important test case that will determine the future course of the country's tobacco policy.

[The Korea Herald, February 5, 2014]

23. New Dilemma on Digital Privacy

We all know how devastating it is to lose a cellphone or tablet PC, as our daily life is entirely disrupted.

With so much personal information digitized and stored in one single device, the handheld gadget means the entire world for the owner. So, from the perspective of users, nothing would be more sensitive to their privacy than the information contained in this device.

On the contrary, for the law enforcement agencies a cellphone is an information bonanza. Make-or-break materials are stored on the device. Naturally, nothing provides sharper confrontation between national security and privacy than digital devices and cloud technologies. The digitalization cuts both ways.

As one of the most wired countries in the world, this issue is not new to Korea either. For almost two years now, law enforcement agencies and KakaoTalk, a South Korean messaging app, have been wrangling over the agencies' access to some of the tech company's messaging data. Knowing that almost 90 percent of South Koreans use the app for daily communication, the agencies have come to appreciate the value of the digital information to be mined. In the company's eyes, however, such cooperation runs the risk of compromising consumers' privacy and causing a major dent to its business image.

When the FBI retrieved an iPhone used by a terrorist in San Bernardino last December, the agency knew that the smartphone would yield critical information about the events leading to the attack. But the device was encrypted and protected by a password and someone needed to break the code to get to the information inside.

The problem was ten incorrect password entries would cause the phone to destroy all the information stored on it. A strong safety feature indeed.

In order to retrieve the information safely, the agency asked Apple to decrypt the iPhone, but the company refused to cooperate, citing the risk of such technologies leading to the invasion of privacy of its consumers. Apple's continued rejection led to a seminal legal battle over national security versus privacy in the digital age. The legal confrontation has just ended, for better or worse, as the FBI succeeded in breaking the code with the help of hired experts.

These recent examples tell us that cat-and-mouse games between law enforcement agencies and digital companies will continue, as new technologies will immediately emerge to deal with new vulnerabilities. Companies will continue to develop and apply stronger protection systems for the information of their consumers. With that, the demand from law enforcement agencies for help and cooperation to break the security walls will equally escalate. So, this issue stands to intensify over time.

Yet, reliable guidelines are yet to come that balance the state's interest for national security and individuals' interest for privacy in the new landscape of the digital age.

What applies now in this field is simply the rules developed from the days of papers and documents collected and stored by corporations, or the days of getting cooperation from phone companies for wiretapping. These conventional rules do not necessarily fit with cyber networks and devices connecting people participating in the networks. Rapid advances in technology are raising new issues in this field as well.

When confronted with this issue, people tend to have a mixed feeling. On the one hand, they release a sigh of relief because the key information has been retrieved to preserve national security. On the other, they raise their eyebrows as their messages and conversations deep inside the smartphones can be broken into and retrieved by outsiders.

We are playing both sides of this fence. Notably, to deal with this new dilemma some countries have initiated a constructive discussion between law enforcement agencies and tech companies in order to explore a new legislation. This is a new development that we need to pay our attention to.

[The Korea Herald, April 6, 2016]

24. AI Changes Everything, but How Far Can It Go?

As artificial intelligence is rippling through every corner of our lives, ethical challenges and philosophical issues are also coming our way. The most important question is: what is the outer limit of the AI technology? Recent incidents involving AI in the military sector offer some silhouette of a possible answer.

Now, AI is making an inroad into the defense industry. Autonomous weapons are becoming a reality. Taken to its technical extreme, it will not be too long before we see fully autonomous warfare machines with self-analysis and self-decision capabilities appear in future battle fields. The pace and consequences, however, raise a voice of concern. Unlike other areas of AI application, the military's use of it is in a fundamentally different league because it may well be lethal: it is feared that these "deploy and forget" types of machines can identify a target and initiate an attack on its own. Existing regulation of combat and law of war may not cover the entire spectrum of these new non-human combatants.

It is this sentiment that underlies foreign academics' concern over the Korea Advanced Institute of Science and Technology's recent plan to participate in a joint research program with a private corporation to develop, possibly, autonomous weapons. The concern was pointed at the development of autonomous weapons "lacking meaningful human control." To paraphrase: human beings must have a final say in the decision-making process of AI machines. Faced with a foreign scholars' threat of a boycott of cooperative activities, KAIST now officially denies any intention of conducting such research and the case seems to be closed.

Take another example. It has been several years since Korea deployed sentry robots or equipment along the DMZ. In response to similar concerns from foreign watchers, assurances have been given over the years that the machines remain under soldiers' control at all times.

Consider yet another one. Some of Google's employees sent a letter in early April to its management taking issue with the company's cooperation with the Department of Defense to enhance video imagery that may facilitate targeting process of drones. The concern expressed by the employees is largely similar. Both Google and the Pentagon have stated that the research would not lead to autonomous weapons that initiate an attack without human control. Here again, the key term was "human control."

This question is also related to who should be held responsible for consequences from activities of autonomous lethal machines. By having human beings in the loop, it can be ensured that final responsibility still lies in the person in charge—a strong deterrence to any misuse or abuse of new machines.

AI is taking over dangerous and difficult tasks from us. It is and will be replacing human beings in many areas and activities. What is not clear yet is who and how to supervise these autonomous machines. Recent incidents represent a compelling consensus at least in the field of military operation: regardless of the technological development or feasibility, it is critical to put AI under the control of human beings and to ensure that a final decision is only to be made by human beings. This logic may also apply to other areas where AI encounters core societal values or weighs critical ethical questions. In other words, there are tasks where human oversight can never be dispensed with.

The rise of AI and the advent of autonomous machines throw out complex legal and philosophical questions. AI in the military application brings these questions to the fore. A UN conference on this very topic is being held this week in Geneva under the auspices of the Convention on Certain Conventional Weapons. Perhaps the discussions there may lead to an adoption of legal norms that can guide the development and utilization of these autonomous lethal weapons in the future.

[The Korea Herald, April 17, 2018]

25. Rise of AI Demands Global Leaders Act Fast on Regulation

For the past few months, ChatGPT has brought to the fore the remarkable capabilities and equally worrisome side effects of artificial intelligence in our daily lives. If anything, this is just the beginning, and more surprises and concerns are on the way.

The way we think, behave and interact stands to change dramatically, as does how a government regulates people and corporations to carry out national business. The same with state-to-state interaction and competition in the global community.

It is now almost impossible to fathom our present and envisage our future without taking account of AI.

Even so, legal norms on this critical development remain largely absent. There has been legislation in various countries on some aspects of digital society—such as information gathering, privacy protection, or online fraud prevention—but none on AI in general to facilitate necessary technological development and societal permeation while also guarding against harmful consequences and attendant side effects.

The European Commission presented a draft regulation on AI in April 2021. It passed the European Parliament last month and will hopefully be adopted for implementation by the end of the year. If successful, the European Union's latest effort will mark the first attempt to introduce horizontal regulation of AI.

Given where AI stands now, domestic legislative endeavors are long overdue.

Norms are equally absent on the international plane. There is no treaty or international agreement on this issue, and neither is there any serious negotiation going on to conclude one, as far as I can tell.

What has happened of late are discussions on specific aspects of the advent of AI, such as how to regulate automated weapons, and experimental clauses inserted in conventional treaties to address particular facets of digital economy, such as cross-border data flow.

We are still waiting for a meaningful first legal stride on AI to cover its development, utilization, and regulation at the global level. This silence is rather remarkable given the fact that AI pays little heed to national borders. In the current AI debates triggered by the emergence of ChatGPT, the need for a global approach to adopt legal guard rails for AI at the international level is hardly mentioned.

Not all aspects of AI need to be addressed in this regard. A treaty setting forth basic principles of AI use and regulation will be an important stride at this juncture. For example, the responsibility and ethical parameters for developers and users of AI can be addressed in the treaty.

A treaty is critical in this case because it is this mechanism that can harmonize the domestic legislation of various states. AI use and regulation can then be guided in the right direction by reducing unexpected negative fallout as much as possible.

Look at what the Organisation for Economic Cooperation and Development has done recently. Its base erosion and profit shifting package was adopted in October 2021, and the domestic legislation of many states is set to be amended and harmonized for the taxation of large multinational corporations. This is a rare example of a global endeavor to adopt a multilateral treaty for the digital economy, and the world now needs a similar effort for AI.

It is true that a treaty will not solve all the problems AI poses at the moment.

Given the pace of its development and permeation, any treaty is likely to quickly fall out of date. Even so, it is important that a framework is introduced so we can at least begin to regulate AI for the global community in a coordinated, albeit not fully harmonious, way.

Any state that initiates this discussion could set the rules for the future. As such, this project is as important as—and perhaps even more important—other international efforts on hot-button items such as semiconductors and batteries.

These items are at the heart of the current discourse around global trade, and they also constitute some of the core items of the AI era and the digital economy. However, if semiconductors and batteries are about products, AI is about a system using those products, the latter being far more significant for the formulation of the future society, both domestic and global.

It is critical for the global community to come up with a new template as soon as possible to regulate AI. A treaty on AI use and regulation will be able to provide a reliable framework to deal with novel challenges arising from AI in a more reasonable, practical, and predictable manner.

We can neither prescribe nor contain all the details in one prospective treaty.

However, we are at least aware of the core concerns and problems surrounding this new technology. That much can and should be addressed by a treaty, by setting forth basic principles and guidelines for governments and businesses in the global community. It is time to navigate a path forward.

[South China Morning Post, July 21, 2023]

26. EU Must Rethink Carbon Border Tax to Sidestep Legal Problems

The European Union has unveiled an ambitious proposal to tackle the global climate crisis. Most notable in Brussels' forward-looking climate package is a scheme to impose, from 2026, an extra charge on imports manufactured abroad under decarbonization standards that fall below the EUs.

This Carbon Border Adjustment Mechanism is the first concrete plan to apply real trade teeth to greenhouse gas emissions.

Given the urgency of coping with global climate change, the EU's move is both timely and laudable. Climate change poses a global threat that requires swift joint action on all fronts. A trade restriction measure at the border by a major market such as the EU would be all the more effective in getting "slow" countries to fall in line.

The only thing is the legal issue: is this novel scheme compatible with trade norms, most notably the WTO agreements?

One might say that if the direction is correct, legal problems should not stand in the way. This is wrong, or at least naive. Any major legal problem may well stigmatize the project, and provide the best weapon to critics to derail it.

Knowing their trade interest would be acutely affected, many countries will have all the more reason to spot legal problems and pursue countermeasures, retaliation, and litigation. Legal discourse will devour the climate change undertaking. This is why legal tightness is a key to success for any anti-climate change scheme.

There are two fundamental issues regarding the EU proposal. For the operation of the new border scheme, Brussels will have to evaluate other countries' decarbonization systems and provide credit to the imported products for the payment made in those domestic systems. This country-specific adjustment would lead to a jagged level of charges in the EU for the same or similar products.

If imposed charges are different, even if the products are the same or can be directly substituted, then the difference will lead to discriminatory treatment, which is prohibited under a cardinal WTO principle. According to prevailing jurisprudence, policy background or good cause is not able to save otherwise existing discriminatory treatment.

The next question is whether such discriminatory treatment is nonetheless justified as an exception. Indeed, government action to preserve the environment can sometimes be shielded from a legal challenge, even if there is a violation of key principles such as nondiscrimination.

The legal bar for this exception, however, is set too high for ordinary government measures to clear. As a result, it has rarely been mobilized successfully so far.

Thus, the EU plan, while important, is embedded with structural sore spots. The plan will add yet another twist to the already battered global trade front. Ensuing trade friction will undermine the overall solidarity of the global community.

Rather than a unilateral trade measure, a specific multilateral endeavor to enhance collaboration would be more effective. Consider, for example, data collection and greenhouse gas emission calculations for industries and products.

Accurate data and calculations, when disseminated and shared, will clarify which country is failing, free-riding, or capitalizing on neighbors' decarbonization efforts. Properly enforced, it would mobilize an effective naming and shaming.

Of course, it is not sufficient, but it is probably better than multiple trade conflicts. To the extent that the EU proposal contains data collection and emission calculation formulas, it hits the nail on the head. Also, we could consider pursuing a global consensus for a new framework to take into account different carbon prices. The EU proposal also offers a good starting point for this.

In other words, except for the border charge and the way it is presented (unilateral action), the EU proposal guides us in the right direction.

Exploring all these cooperative avenues would obviously be difficult, but it would be the only proper way forward. The EU's attempt to introduce the Carbon Border Adjustment Mechanism should be reconsidered, as it is currently a recipe for a legal quagmire.

[Sunday Morning Post, September 12, 2021]

VII

CONCLUDING THOUGHTS

For a decade, I have had the honor of contributing columns to the esteemed publication, the Korea Herald. As every column represents my utmost endeavor during that period, I believe that the compilation of these columns would facilitate the dissemination of knowledge to the general public, offering a comprehensive understanding of the diverse issues encompassing Korea. The tone of these columns is distinct from my academic work due to its focus on engaging a general readership. The usage of colloquial terms is more prevalent and there is a greater inclusion of vivid idiomatic expressions. Complex concepts are elucidated using everyday language. With that being said, the substance of each column comprises the fundamental findings derived from my research as a legal scholar specializing in the field of international law. I have come to the realization that I must periodically consult my columns for reference and occasionally find myself taken aback by the realization that the subject matter explored in my scholarly articles bears a striking resemblance to the themes covered in my previous columns.

The presence of law is of paramount importance in upholding contemporary society, encompassing both domestic and international law. The extent to which the rule of law is embedded within a nation is a crucial determinant of its authentic progress, and hence the significance of legal discourse cannot be overstated. The advancement of the global community as well as Korea's economic ascent and political improvement, despite its ongoing imperfections, can largely be attributed to the bolstering of the rule of law within the UN regime and its society, respectively. Upon further reflection, it became apparent that these columns can be classified into distinct categories, such as (i) law as a critical component in domestic society; (ii) law as a critical component for the global community; (iii) international organizations; (iv) international law in the field; and (v) the outer parameters of law. Rather than merely emphasizing the importance of law, the columns also

DOI: 10.4324/9781003501749-7

highlight inherent limitations, asserting that law cannot be regarded as a definitive factor in deliberating upon such intricate social issues, as relying solely on the law for decision making can be unpredictable and imprudent.

As the international community falls into turmoil and conflicts among nations intensify, the importance of norms that regulate these issues becomes increasingly significant. We are currently facing the most severe global crisis since World War II. Wars are simultaneously unfolding in Europe and the Middle East, and the likelihood of new wars erupting elsewhere is growing. The world is entering a new Cold War era, with blocs centered around the United States, the EU, and Japan on one side, and Russia and China on the other. The conflict between developed and developing nations shows no signs of abating, and even within developing nations, divisions are widening between influential states and the least developed countries.

Climate change is accelerating global warming, leading to unprecedented natural disasters and environmental changes worldwide. The melting polar regions are presenting new opportunities and challenges, prompting heightened competition among nations. The international economic system is undergoing a phase of restructuring. Fundamental principles governing international trade and investment, previously managed under the WTO and ICSID systems, are being reevaluated. Although it has been four years since a pandemic swept the globe, its lingering effects remain. Predicting when a new pandemic might strike with similar disruptive impacts is nearly impossible. AI is rapidly permeating our lives, introducing new industries, exchanges, conflicts, societies, and even new forms of military clashes. In areas where AI operates, questions about accountability are frequently raised. Systems, not humans, are now making decisions and performing activities once carried out by individuals, inevitably leading to legal responsibility issues.

The private space industry, initiated by Elon Musk, has motivated national governments, transforming space from an object of exploration into a development target. With economic interests and national benefits at stake, competition among nations is intensifying. New combatants have emerged in armed conflicts, such as the Wagner Group of Russia, which represents a phenomenon of private military companies engaging in direct combat on behalf of or in partnership with states. Outsourcing and commercializing military power—once a core element of state sovereignty—is an unprecedented development. This raises fundamental questions about the boundaries between state and non-state actors, as well as the essence of international law, which governs state actions.

However, international norms to address these new phenomena are inadequate. Existing norms are either outdated or disconnected from reality, and in some emerging areas, norms are entirely absent. This situation is akin to introducing cars without roads or traffic laws, with vehicles accelerating without the infrastructure or regulations to manage them. This increases the likelihood of contact and collision. Despite these challenges, efforts to upgrade existing international norms or establish new ones are progressing slowly. Achieving consensus among nations is difficult, and international organizations lack the capacity to generate momentum to overcome such challenges. The limitations and problems of international organizations became evident during the pandemic (WHO), trade disputes (WTO), and armed conflicts (UN), revealing the ineffectiveness of these institutions in performing meaningful roles during crises. This situation calls for a reassessment of the rights and obligations of the 197 sovereign states that constitute the international community and the organizations they establish.

The lack of well-structured international norms has posed significant challenges for international courts and arbitration processes tasked with resolving disputes. Ambiguities in norms naturally complicate the process of deriving conclusions. Without a properly functioning legislative process, it is unsurprising that judicial procedures operate inefficiently. Recently, we have even witnessed instances where existing judicial procedures have been effectively paralyzed, while new judicial procedures are being proposed and debated. The judicial process is also undergoing re-evaluation and re-adjustment.

The international community is now facing a major crisis, and both substantive and procedural norms are encountering severe difficulties. To overcome current challenges and avoid returning to an era of large-scale armed conflict, the principle of the "rule of law" in the international community must be reaffirmed and restored across various areas. The rule of law, developed over 78 years since the establishment of the UN system, is now facing a significant challenge. Successfully addressing this challenge will demonstrate the resilience of the rule of law, strengthening trust among nations. As the saying goes, "the ground becomes firmer after the rain." Conversely, if this effort falters, the 78 years of progress may be regarded as an anomaly in human history, reinforcing the perception that the international community remains governed by the law of the jungle. In such a case, the future of the international community would be bleak.

Ironically, the current difficulties and confusion are, for this very reason, demonstrating once again the importance of international law, the importance of peaceful resolution of international disputes, and the importance of the rule of law that guides them. It is more important than ever to understand international legal norms accurately, to have a realistic understanding of their application cases, and to clearly recognize their contributions and limitations. Only by knowing the present can we compare it with the past and plan for the future. While continuing to build on the achievements of existing international legal norms, we must also identify the causes of the problems and limitations that have been identified and seek new ways to improve them. In this respect, studying international law is more necessary and important now.

This is especially true for South Korea, which has achieved growth and prosperity through multilateralism and international peace. I hope that the younger generation of Korea will recognize the importance of international law and realize that international law is a living norm that is always at work in our daily lives, and will work hard to study international law. And through this, I earnestly hope that our young generation, which has international legal skills and insight, will participate in international activities and competition in various fields.

INDEX

For Product Safety Concerns and Information please contact our EU representative GPSR@taylorandfrancis.com Taylor & Francis Verlag GmbH, Kaufingerstraße 24, 80331 München, Germany

School Social Workers in the Multicultural Environment: New Roles, Responsibilities, and Educational Enrichment

School Social Workers in the Multicultural Environment: New Roles, Responsibilities, and Educational Enrichment

Paul R. Keys
Editor

Routledge
Taylor & Francis Group
LONDON AND NEW YORK

First published 1994 by The Haworth Press, Inc.

Published 2013 by Routledge
2 Park Square, Milton Park, Abingdon, Oxfordshire OX14 4RN
711 Third Avenue, New York, NY 10017, USA

First issued in paperback 2016

Routledge is an imprint of the Taylor & Francis Group, an informa business

School Social Workers in the Multicultural Environment: New Roles, Responsibilities, and Educational Enrichment has also been published as *Journal of Multicultural Social Work*, Volume 3, Number 1 1994.

Library of Congress Cataloging-in-Publication Data

School social workers in the multicultural environment : new roles, responsibilities and educational enrichment / Paul R. Keys, editor.
p. cm.
"Has also been published as Journal of multicultural social work, volume 3, number 1, 1994"–T.p. verso.
Includes bibliographical references and index.
ISBN 1-56024-696-0 (alk. paper)
1. Social work education. 2. Multiculturalism–Study and teaching (Graduate) I. Keys, Paul R.
HV11.S3815 1994
371.2'022–dc20

94-34120
CIP

ISBN 13: 978-1-138-98137-9 (pbk)
ISBN 13: 978-1-56024-696-1 (hbk)

School Social Workers in the Multicultural Environment: New Roles, Responsibilities, and Educational Enrichment

CONTENTS

ABOUT THE EDITOR

Paul R. Keys, PhD, is Professor and Chair of the Administration Curriculum Area at Hunter College School of Social Work and a member of the City University of New York doctoral faculty. He is affiliated with the Pace University Department of Public Administration and the Edwin G. Michaelian Institute for Public Policy and Management. Dr. Keys is a member of the National Advisory Council of the National Network of Social Work Managers (NNSWM), serves as NNSWM book series editor, and co-founder of the NNSWM/NASW National Management Conference. His recent publications include *New Management in Human Service* (NASW, 1988), which he co-edited with Leon Ginsberg, and articles on public management and multiculturalism. He was a 1990/91 GARIOA/Fulbright Senior Research Scholar of the Faculty of Integrated Arts and Social Science, Department of Social Welfare, at the Japan Women's University, Tokyo. Formerly, Dr. Keys was Director of Human Services, Broward County, Florida, and Deputy Administrator for the State of Wisconsin Division of Community Services.

Foreword

Social work has been at the forefront of efforts to implement a multicultural perspective in professional education. While many other professions are still in the initial stages of introducing multicultural education, social work's accreditation standards already require that multicultural issues be given full treatment, and that content on multiculturalism be included throughout the curriculum.

However, this does not mean that social work has resolved all the issues and controversies attending the adoption of a multicultural perspective. As this collection reveals, many questions relating to multicultural education in social work still need to be answered. Indeed, many faculty still have a vague conception of what multicultural education involves, some feel uneasy about teaching this content, and others doubt its relevance to all forms of social work practice. The question of whether multicultural content can best be taught in a concentrated form within specialized courses, or whether it is most effectively communicated when infused throughout the curriculum, is still being debated. The issue of how the impact of multicultural content on the learning experiences of students can be assessed has been neglected, and there are differences of opinion about how outcomes can be measured.

School Social Workers in the Multicultural Environment: New Roles, Responsibilities and Educational Enrichment discusses these and many other aspects of multicultural education in social work. It is the first volume to consider issues of multiculturalism from the social work educator's point of view and it is wide ranging in scope. Edited by Paul Keys, who is an acknowledged leader in the field, it contains chapters by highly respected authorities on the subject. It is an important work which deserves not only to be widely read but widely used. It offers clear directions for those who seek to educate students about the realities of racism, ethnocentrism and oppression in society today. Its exposition of critical issues will inform and enlighten and, hopefully, foster the creation of a tolerant and just society.

James Midgley
Associate Vice Chancellor for Research
Louisiana State University

Introduction

This volume focuses on some vital issues involved in the teaching of multiculturalism. The Council on Social Work Education (CSWE) requires multicultural content in various Curriculum Standards. Such content includes the teaching of oppression, sensitivities to diversity, teaching about differences and similarities, content on ethnic minorities and women, and social and economic justice. What is more important is that these requirements have come about due to population changes that led to changes in the client population of contemporary human services agencies.

There are many questions regarding the teaching of multicultural content. First, there is a question of infusion. In which courses should multicultural content be taught–in specific multicultural courses, or infused throughout the curriculum? There have been many debates and still this matter is not entirely settled. A second question is whether teachers know how to teach multicultural content. If not, how will they know it? Related to this question is one of faculty development. Should schools offer courses in multicultural content to facilitate teaching?

How should a school monitor the teaching of multicultural content if it has accepted the teaching of it as a mandate? How can schools ensure that all teachers who teach courses actually incorporate the desired content? In what way should the content be evaluated–through peer evaluation, formal teaching observations, or other methods? These and many other considerations are relevant to the teaching of multiculturalism. The papers in this volume address some of these concerns.

Sharron Singleton, in the first article *Faculty Personal Comfort and the Teaching of Content on Racial Oppression*, focuses on a concern often not publicly vocalized. The issue is that of faculty uneasiness in teaching content on oppression. Many instructors are unfamiliar with the content.

Next, Dorothy Van Soest's *Social Work Education for Multicultural*

[Haworth co-indexing entry note]: "Introduction." Keys, Paul R. Co-published simultaneously in *Journal of Multicultural Social Work* (The Haworth Press, Inc.) Vol. 3, No. 1, 1994, pp. 1-3; and: *School Social Workers in the Multicultural Environment: New Roles, Responsibilities, and Educational Enrichment* (ed: Paul R. Keys) The Haworth Press, Inc., 1994, pp. 1-3. Multiple copies of this article/chapter may be purchased from The Haworth Document Delivery Center [1-800-3-HAWORTH; 9:00 a.m. - 5:00 p.m. (EST)].

Practice and Social Justice Advocacy: A Field Study of How Students Experience the Learning Process is an exploratory field study. The paper reflects on how students experience the learning process. It also examines the outcomes of a new MSW course aimed at helping students develop knowledge and awareness of cultural diversity and societal oppression. It appears that little research on student learning processes, attitudinal change, and actual student outcomes has been conducted. Professor Van Soest examines the way in which students view their role in relation to oppression. She also considers the way in which students experience the change process, and how they are influenced by interactions with others in the classroom.

John Ronnau, in *Teaching Cultural Competence: Practical Ideas for Social Work Educators*, follows upon the uneasiness in teaching and learning multicultural content identified earlier by Professor Singleton. He proposes a model that includes five classroom-tested strategies for teaching cultural competence in practice classes.

As indicated by Professor Van Soest and others, outcomes are particularly important but difficult to measure. To overcome these difficulties, Peter Manoleas, in *An Outcome Approach to Assessing the Cultural Competence of MSW Students*, introduces a series of outcome objectives for cultural competence. These are categorized by knowledge, skill, and value bases. He includes an evaluation of the model.

John Longres and Gary Seltzer take a different perspective. In *Racism: Its Implications for the Education of Minority Social Work Students*, they examine much talked about issues of retention of minority social work students. The article presents case studies describing common problems that such students experience. The paper closes with a set of broad recommendations to help social work educators retain minority group students.

Teaching diversity is equally important in field instruction and in the classroom. Many field instructors are reluctant to introduce diversity topics. Moreover, perceptions and differences of field instructors from their students greatly affect the effectiveness of teaching and learning relationships in the field. In a study of 56 urban field instructors, Professors Elaine Marshack, Carmen Ortiz Hendricks, and Muriel Gladstein examine some common elements in the successful teaching of cultural, ethnic, gender, class, and age characteristics. Their findings are presented in *The Commonality of Difference: Teaching About Diversity in Field Instruction*.

Not only are diverse field experiences needed in urban areas, but the difficulty is compounded when the setting is a rural area. *A Rock and a Hard Place: Trying to Provide Culturally-Sensitive Field Experiences in*

Rural, Homogeneous Communities by Professors Adela Beckerman and Leon Burrell, examine these concerns.

In a particular instance of rural social work, *Fieldwork Among the Navajo: Implications for Social Work Research and Practice*, Professor Susan Dawson highlights issues of research design, culture shock, working conditions, legitimation, and access. Her concern is to promote effective practice for non-American Indian social workers working among American Indians. She also highlights the critical need for admission and training of American Indian social work students.

Finally, Carol Cohen, in *What Culturally Diverse Students Say About Emotion: An Exploratory Study,* looks at student opinion from a student and a practitioner's perspective. She suggests that an examination of field interns in BSW and Associate Degree programs imply a need for continuing consideration of professional acculturation strategies.

Paul R. Keys, PhD
Editor

Faculty Personal Comfort and the Teaching of Content on Racial Oppression

Sharron M. Singleton

SUMMARY. In-depth interviews were conducted with faculty from four East Coast schools of social work. Personal comfort in the teaching of oppression content was analyzed using grounded theory methodology. Findings about the origins, nature, consequences and management of discomfort are presented.

The Council on Social Work Education (CSWE) is the agency which has responsibility for accrediting schools of social work, thereby insuring that the graduates (both BSW and MSW) possess the knowledge, values and skills pertinent to the performance of social work practice. One ongoing goal of the Council has been insuring that social work students are

---

Sharron M. Singleton, DSW, is affiliated with the School of Social Work at Barry University.

[Haworth co-indexing entry note]: "Faculty Personal Comfort and the Teaching of Content on Racial Oppression." Singleton, Sharron M. Co-published simultaneously in *Journal of Multicultural Social Work* (The Haworth Press, Inc.) Vol. 3, No. 1, 1994, pp. 5-16; and: *School Social Workers in the Multicultural Environment: New Roles, Responsibilities, and Educational Enrichment* (ed: Paul R. Keys) The Haworth Press, Inc., 1994, pp. 5-16. Multiple copies of this article/chapter may be purchased from The Haworth Document Delivery Center [1-800-3-HAWORTH; 9:00 a.m. - 5:00 p.m. (EST)].

sensitized to the presence and consequences of oppression in American society. The 1982 curriculum policy statement (CPS) was very specific in requiring that students receive "content related to oppression and to the experiences, needs and responses of people who have been subjected to institutionalized forms of oppression" (CSWE, 1982, Statement 7.4). That particular CPS further stipulated that the curriculum must have content on ethnic minorities of color and women and should also focus on other "special populations" that had been consistently affected by social, economic, and legal bias or oppression (CSWE, 1982, Statement 7.5).

In its most recent revision of the CPS the Council requires that schools of social work "provide curriculum content about the differences and similarities in the experiences, needs and beliefs of people" (CSWE, 1992, Statement 6.4). More specifically, the Council requires that programs "provide understanding of the dynamics and consequences of social and economic justice, including all forms of human oppression and discrimination" (CSWE, 1992, Statement 6.5). Oppression is a sensitive topic and can lead to highly charged feelings. This paper reports the results of exploratory research regarding the comfort level of social work faculty when teaching content specific to oppression.

Faculty comfort level can play a strategically important role in shaping the repertoire of values, knowledge and skills transmitted to students. To adequately present content related to oppression one must have valid knowledge of the subject, skills in the teaching or presentation of the content, and be guided by values which see the presentation of such material as relevant to social work education. A faculty member's comfort level with the topic of oppression will be reflected in whether the instructor sees it as a worthwhile topic to be taught, whether the instructor makes an effort to be knowledgeable about the topic, and whether the instructor is able to share this knowledge effectively with students.

RESEARCH DESIGN

The purpose of the research was not to make generalizations about the total population of social work educators or to evaluate the quality of oppression content currently being presented, but, rather, to identify and analyze, in detail, the processes through which discrete comfort and discomfort experiences arise and are managed at the individual level by the faculty as they deal with oppression topics. For these reasons, grounded theory methodology (Strauss, 1987) was utilized as being particularly suited to the open-ended, process-oriented nature of the questions.

An exploratory, cross-sectional research design was chosen. Four urban, east coast schools of social work were approached for participation in the study. All of the schools had long-standing, accredited BSW and MSW programs and prided themselves in being compliant with the Council's standards. Three of the schools were classified as being part of predominately white universities and one was classified as being part of a predominately black university. The population from which the sample was drawn was all faculty members at the four schools. Subjects were chosen based on their willingness to share personal material on this sensitive topic. A total of eleven faculty members agreed to be interviewed.

Open-ended questions were used which focused on: the decision about presenting content related to oppression, the nature of comfort and discomfort experiences, and ways of dealing with discomfort. Follow-up interviews were conducted as necessary. Interviews were tape recorded, with the respondent's permission, and the transcripts used in the data analysis. General principles which guide grounded theory (Strauss, 1987) were used to analyze the data.

Grounded theory, as developed by Glaser and Strauss (1967), is a method of qualitative analysis which recognizes the emergence of patterns of behavior, thought processes, and life experiences. This approach is based upon an avoidance of formulating hypotheses or variables prior to analyzing the data. This is done with the intent of allowing variables, and the study of relationships, particularly of process variables, as they emerge through the systematic application of grounded theory data analysis procedures. Grounded theory procedures consist of open coding, the construction of coding categories which demonstrate patterns, the constant comparative method, and the process of memo writing.

RESULTS

The eleven faculty represented more than twenty-two years of teaching experience in both predominately black and predominately white educational institutions. All had MSW degrees and most (9) had doctoral degrees. Responses reflected teaching experience at the baccalaureate, masters and doctoral levels. All respondents had taught in the professional foundation curriculum as well as the advanced curriculum. Seven were black and four were white; there were six females and five males.

A striking finding in this research was the extent to which the faculty interviewed defined oppression as racial oppression. While there were a few references to women's issues and class oppression in the interviews, there was virtually no discussion of homophobia, discrimination against the handicapped, the aged, anti-semitism, or other expressions of oppression. In fact, as the data analysis proceeded, this preoccupation with racial oppression emerged with such prominence that the results were written so as to identify the race of faculty being quoted and the racial makeup of their classroom referents.

Comfort work is defined here as those steps taken by an instructor to achieve a tolerable level of personal ease in response to experiences of discomfort in making teaching decisions relative to the presentation of oppression content. Analysis of the data revealed that a number of issues faculty grappled with in making teaching decisions and comfort work appeared to take three principle forms: (1) constructing an interpretation of one's own opinions, feelings and actions related to the oppression content, (2) constructing an interpretation of the behaviors of others (in this study, students and professional colleagues) elicited by the presentation of content on oppression, and (3) taking actions to achieve an acceptable level of comfort. In grappling with these teaching decisions, faculty made use of three decision paths: avoiding oppression terminology but presenting some minimal oppression content; definitely rejecting all content on oppression; clearly including both oppression content and terminology.

Avoiding Oppression Terminology and Minimizing Oppression Content

One route to achieving an acceptable comfort level was to avoid all mention of the word "oppression" when teaching, but to include content on diversity with either no or only little content about the phenomena that could be called oppression. For example, one white instructor in a primarily white setting reported: "We don't use the word oppression in the curriculum; we talk about dealing with people who are different." Another white instructor in a primarily white setting stated: "What I do is have guest presenters and I have those guest presenters look different from me." A black instructor in a white setting related teaching, "Not oppression directly . . . we look at the cultural biases and cultural aspects." Another white instructor speaking of her course at a predominately white institution, said: "The curriculum piece that's identified is working with racial and ethnic minorities, people of color." Avoidance of the term "oppression" often derived from the notion that oppression distinctly implies the existence of *oppressors*. As one white instructor teaching in a primarily white setting put it: "Oppression is a word that means 'different plus,' someone is oppressing and someone is being oppressed." Using *diversity* content to the exclusion of *oppression* content allows one to avoid this area of discomfort.

Definitely Rejecting All Content on Oppression

Another decision taken by faculty was to be quite definite about avoiding oppression content. A white instructor teaching in a predominantly white setting, for example, stated: "I don't specifically give focus to issues of discrimination and oppression in any particular lecture. I don't specifically address minorities or other groups who have been uniquely subjected to discrimination or prejudice . . . I don't use the word oppression at all."

Definitely Including Oppression Content and Terminology

The third decision route is to be very clear about including oppression content and using oppression terminology when teaching it. A white instructor teaching at a predominately white school, for example, said: "You can't teach those (social work) courses without talking about the isms." Similarly, a black instructor teaching at a white institution observed: "You cannot teach social work practice without talking about oppression in all of its forms."

Comfort Work Done in Regard to the Decision Paths

Comfort work done in arriving at, and living with, these types of decisions can best be discussed in terms of three areas in which interpretations and rationales for teaching decisions are constructed: (1) the instructor's knowledge and experience base regarding oppression, (2) student welfare in light of this topic, and (3) definitions of the social work profession in light of oppression.

One's knowledge and experience base. Lack of direct experience of being oppressed can be an important part of the rationale not to teach oppression content. For example, one white instructor, teaching in a predominantly white setting, who was very direct about having no oppression content, was equally clear about his motivation: "I don't bring expertise on the experience of being oppressed." Another instructor (white, teaching in a predominantly white setting) used uncertainty about her intellectual and experiential understanding of oppression to explain the modest level of oppression content in her teaching: "I am less secure and less sure about having solutions or answers once the issue (of oppression) is raised, I don't feel I can do much more than raise the issue." Alternatively, uncertainty about one's knowledge base can play an important role in stimulating one to gain new knowledge, and, in fact, to place a heavy emphasis on oppression content. For example, a white instructor at a predominantly black university who at first "experienced a great deal" of anxiety and uncertainty about teaching oppression content was motivated to "double and treble" his own studies and to achieve a high level of oppression content.

One's membership in a group that has been oppressed or has been oppressive can also be an important element in faculty interpretations of their positive stances toward oppression content. For example, a black professor teaching in a predominantly white university reflected: "I feel like I'm on a mission, this is something that has to be done and I am uniquely qualified to do it because I am black . . . I can present it from an academic and personal perspective." Another black professor observed: "This campus is one that forces a black professor to be very conscious of the need to talk about oppression . . . the campus is so white."

A white professor teaching in a predominantly black university described his initial discomfort (as a white male lecturing to his nearly all-black classes on the oppressive consequences of racism) resulted in a desire to meet the challenge with competence and spurred increased self-development efforts. In addition, an important personal factor motivating him to invest heavily in strengthening his teaching about oppression was his own personal experiences of growing up in extreme poverty and feeling an intuitive connectedness to those experiencing other forms of oppression. Similarly, a white faculty member teaching at a predominantly white university directly related her commitment to teaching oppression content to her experiences of being an outsider and having minority status during her service in the Peace Corps.

Definitions of social work as a profession. The way in which one defines the practice of social work appears to be an important factor in constructing rationales for teaching decisions. Some instructors see oppression content as intrinsic to the very definition of social work practice. A white instructor at a white university, who clearly integrated explicit oppression content, justified this in terms of the profession's relationship with clients: "There is a desire to enhance client care. All clients deserve the best services you can possibly give . . . I hope I do it [present oppression content] in a way that is not hurtful to the individual [student] but I do it." Similarly, a black instructor in a predominantly white setting said: "There is a necessity, if you are working with these kinds of [oppressed] people . . . to have something in your course outline that helps the student become sensitive to the kinds of biases that these people have to deal with." On the other hand, a white instructor at a predominantly white setting saw oppression as something extrinsic to the fundamental tasks of social work practice. He felt that practice could be generically taught in such a way that students could apply practice principles to oppression populations without specific instruction on oppression in the curriculum. As he put it: "I think that the skills, values and processes that I'm teaching hold as an underpinning to the work for whatever group of clients that these students are working with."

Concern for student welfare. Some faculty expressed concern about the resulting stressful impact on students of introducing oppression content. Faculty who expressed this concern reacted to it in different ways. For some, oppression was seen as too unsettling a topic to inflict on students. Others saw it as a potentially delicate or painful topic area but also saw it as either worth some attention in the classroom or as being absolutely essential. For instance, a white instructor spoke about his primarily white classes and his reluctance to get into issues of oppression: "I find myself hesitant to raise issues. My concern is that you will get people's prejudices out and not be able to move around them . . . you let people open up and talk about their feelings and then what do you do with those feelings?"

A white instructor talking about his primarily black classes reported high levels of oppression content in all his teaching, but identified some limits which he explained in terms of a concern for student sensitivities: "The most difficult is engaging in discussion about not just oppression but affect-laden instances of horrific oppression like the Tuskegee syphilis experiment. I've never placed it [*Bad Blood: A Study of the Tuskegee Syphilis Experiment*] on the reading list. It's intensely emotional and it would be too painful for too many students."

A black instructor in a predominantly white setting reported concern over students' pain in being exposed to certain oppression content, but is still certain of its importance to their development, and includes it: "I think it was kind of shocking to my class to learn of so many atrocities that [have been] perpetrated against minorities. I do this to make the point there has been a trend throughout history of disenfranchising blacks." A black instructor acknowledged that oppression content could be difficult for his predominantly white classes at times, but was clear that it was in the students' best interests as future social workers interacting with oppressed populations that they learn this important content: "What motivates me is . . . these people [students] are going to be working with my people and I want to get my licks in first . . . I can get in there to every student and plant some seeds . . . "

Comfort Work in the Arena of the Classroom

Faculty who chose to teach oppression content reported experiencing a variety of reactions in the classroom. Faculty described that student reactions to oppression content included: indifference, active resistance, complaints to other faculty, and receptiveness and support.

Student indifference. Obvious expressions of indifference to oppression content elicited discomforting experiences for faculty. A white discussed his astonishment at one white student's observations: "A student raised her hand in class and said, 'I'm in this program because I want to go into private practice; why do I have to study all of this stuff about poverty and black folks?'" Another white instructor described the reaction of his all white class: "Oppression was looked upon as boring or as threatening and it was very hard work to get students to take it seriously." A black professor reflected on his primarily white classes: "Here they [students] are less receptive . . . they are conditioned to think that these are special interest issues that they should have no concern in." Another black instructor reported about her almost entirely white classes: "You get students who are obviously tuned out . . . they are doing all sorts of things [while I'm teaching] . . . it's obvious that they are disinterested."

The comfort work here involved the faculty member's acknowledgment of the nature of the student reactions; acknowledgement of one's own feelings; and making a decision about a behavioral response. A black professor operating in a predominantly white setting described her feelings in the face of indifference: "My personal reaction is one of sadness . . . when they [white students] get out into the real world they are not going to be able to do a good job of social work." Another black professor in a similar setting stated: "I get angry . . . these individuals will be working with diverse groups . . . these attitudes and behaviors will obstruct the people they help." Yet another black professor, also in a predominantly white setting reported: "I try real hard to make certain the students do not see my feelings, especially my sadness [but] sometimes my anger seeps through."

Faculty often converted these feelings of anger or sadness into a heightened sense of purpose and commitment to getting the content across. A black professor reported: "What it triggers in me most is a desire to figure out a way to get the material across regardless." A white professor reported: "I struggle with not wanting students to go without examining [their] values."

Instructor's reactions included coupling perseverance with direct use of the authority of position. For example, a white instructor reflected on his actions at a predominantly white institution: "At times it felt like I was ramming it [oppression content] down their throats . . . I used the authority of my position to do it. They knew they had to learn this content to pass." A teacher described his reaction to a student who disputed the relevance of oppression content to her private practice career goals: "I looked at her and said . . . you are in a school of social work. This is what social work is about."

Active student resistance. When students moved beyond indifference to overt rejection of oppression content, a variety of discomfort experiences were invoked for faculty. Examples of resistance are illustrated in quotes from black instructors who taught in predominantly white settings and which range from the fairly mild: "One student said to me, 'well, people around here certainly raise this matter of difference'" to the intense: "One black student was very incensed with me . . . I was making her and the white students uncomfortable."

One black instructor described at length a white student's resistance to an assignment and the challenge of bringing the student to an explicit discussion of issues: "I gave an assignment . . . to do a short paper on a minority of color . . . everybody did a minority of color except one student . . . [who] did his paper on somebody [white] who was handicapped . . . I failed the paper . . . he said 'I consider the handicapped to be black, too.' I asked him what did he mean and he stated 'oh that's alright, just forget it, I'll write on somebody black.' I reminded him that he needed to write on a minority of color, not necessarily a black person and he replied 'that's okay, I'll write on a black person' . . . I still believe, although I have no way of verifying it, that he was saying to me that people who are handicapped are treated like 'niggers' and if you [the instructor] read between the lines you can see what I'm saying."

The feeling of instructors in the face of such active student resistance was overwhelmingly one of frustration. As one white instructor stated about her mostly white classes: "I've given up on giving certain kinds of essay questions [about oppression]." At the same time, this instructor also reaffirmed her commitment: "I end up feeling, well, if I can get them in touch with it [oppression] . . . that's the best you can do." The instructor who spoke of the above student who resisted the assignment topic, expressed surprise at the incident but stated: "I was not going to let him write on a [non-minority] handicapped person because that was not the assignment."

Student complaints to other faculty. Some respondents identified situations in which students engaged other faculty in their resistance to oppression content. A black instructor, speaking of primarily white classes, said: "Some of our students will run to other [white] faculty members and complain that they are being made to feel uncomfortable." Another black instructor at a white institution reported: "Students see the black instructors as projecting some of their own biases. This view tends to be reinforced by many of my white colleagues."

Student receptiveness. Not all student reactions were negative. Instructors reported experiences which were growth producing for the student and instructor. A white instructor reported: "My most uncomfortable experience was also the best. I was teaching content on oppression to a mostly black class and it elicited a positive student response where I was asked about the 'white perspective.' My reaction to that was to be uncomfortable because I'm not used to thinking about something called the 'white perspective.' But it was good . . . it really made me confront the fact that there is something to the idea of there being a white perspective, and it's so much there that it is taken for granted."

A black instructor reported about the growth of a white student: "She reported she and her 13 year-old sat around the dining room table and talked about this [oppression content]: . . . 'I can supplement his history course with what I am learning about minorities because they have cut it out of the history books.' I thought this was simply fantastic."

Another black instructor reported being surprised and pleased to learn that within her predominantly white setting: "There are some middle and upper class whites, mostly female, who are non-racists . . . and who have a genuine commitment to learning about and changing racism and oppression in American society." Other instructors talked about students who "Come back at the end of the class and say 'you really opened my eyes and got me to think hard about the values that I'm bringing with me," and identified these as very rewarding experiences.

One black instructor described in detail a particularly painful but ultimately rewarding experience with his mostly white class: "Tension [between the instructor and students] had been building up. They felt they had come week after week to hear themselves called racists. They were very confused because they liked me and they found the content excitingly presented, but it [the class] bottomed and all of a sudden, the class just came out. It was a very, very tense moment. They were really suffering, they were in agony and it came out. We talked about it . . . [we] used good social work methods and we worked through it. We went to a new level of trust after that. [Students] saw that . . . they had not trusted me before because I gave the marks. Finally, after that day they believed."

Comfort Work in the Larger Arena of the School

Moving beyond the classroom, those faculty who did present content on oppression often had comfort work to do in relating to faculty colleagues and administrators. The comfort work fell into three areas: goal discrepancy in the curriculum, collegial undermining and collegial support.

The need for comfort work was elicited by discrepancies between the formal and operating goals (Hasenfeld, 1983) schools had about teaching content on oppression. Respondents reported that faculty in some of the predominantly white schools downplayed or even shunned explicit content on oppression even when the school's curriculum materials promised it. A black instructor spoke of her predominantly white institution: "When I first came here Billingsly's *Black Families in White America* was on everyone's course outline and when I referred to the content in my class students looked at me strangely . . . it was on the course outlines and I assumed people were teaching it. I was naive. It was on the outlines for CSWE's purpose." Another black instructor in the same setting reflected: "We have a specific course on racism but you have built-in failure by hiring people who do not have the qualifications to teach it."

Some respondents in predominantly white institutions noted that negative faculty attitudes were often conveyed to the students and became a support to student resistance. A black instructor speaking of her [white] colleagues speculated: "I wonder how the information [about content on oppression] is being communicated from other white faculty [to my students]. Some faculty do have some discomfort and I think the way they deal with the content communicates that discomfort to the students." Another black instructor in a primarily white setting was more certain: "The black [instructors] become painted in their [students] minds as militant and so students can dismiss what they [black instructors] say. This view tends to be reinforced by many of my white colleagues." Another black faculty member, working at a white institution, reported: "We have a situation at the school now which is really telling . . . the white faculty are going around making denials about the existence of racism . . . it is angry lashing out and accusing people of being anti-white."

The comfort work used by instructors who found themselves in settings hostile to content on oppression involved confrontation. Confronting meant challenging the hostility and keeping the topic in the forefront of discussion. One black instructor cited: "[White] faculty know that I'm not going to let them get away with certain kinds of behavior . . . they are discomforted by it but if nobody else raises a question about it [oppression content] I'm going to raise it." A white instructor spoke of his experience at a primarily white institution: "I would always use every opportunity to push curriculum design in that direction [oppression content] but knew I was only one person with the interest . . . that made me all the more intent."

In settings where there was solid support from other faculty and administration, faculty comfort level was enhanced and the instructors described the teaching of oppression content as the norm. A black instructor reflected on his predominantly black institution: "The school encourages it [oppression content] . . . it's an integrating thread of our curriculum." In a primarily white institution a black instructor reported: "There is an expectation that there is evidence [of oppression content] on the course outline and you must show with readings and otherwise how you are going to deal with the content." A white professor spoke of the expectation of his primarily black school: "Very clearly the educational mission is the black perspective so part of the job description for teaching here is having content relevant to black Americans."

CONCLUSION

This research has established that the decision to present or not to present oppression content is not a simple one. It involves many processes and these processes are affected by overlapping influences from personal and professional values as well as life experiences, work settings and the characteristics of the student population. The processes through which social work instructors arrive at a decision regarding the presentation of oppression content can be delineated into three distinct paths: avoiding oppression terminology and minimizing oppression content, rejecting all content on oppression, and explicitly including oppression content. Two important influences on the decision-making process are the reactions of students to oppression content and the attitudes of fellow colleagues to the presentation of such content.

Further research on this topic is warranted. Survey research, built upon exploratory research such as this, could help to determine and understand the extent of the phenomena discussed here. Additional survey and qualitative research to understand students' points of view would also be helpful.

REFERENCES

Council on Social Work Education. (1982). *Curriculum policy statements for the masters degree and baccalaureate degree programs in social work education.* New York: Author.

Council on Social Work Education. (1992). *Curriculum policy statements for the masters degree and baccalaureate degree programs in social work education.* New York: Author.

Glaser, B. and Strauss, A. (1967). *The discovery of grounded theory: Strategies for qualitative research.* Chicago, IL: Aldine Publishing Company.

Hasenfeld, Y. (1983). *Human service organizations.* Englewood Cliffs, NJ: Prentice Hall, Inc.

Strauss, A. (1987). *Qualitative analysis for social scientists.* New York: Cambridge University Press.

Social Work Education for Multicultural Practice and Social Justice Advocacy: A Field Study of How Students Experience the Learning Process

Dorothy Van Soest

SUMMARY. A two-phase exploratory field study was conducted in an attempt to understand how students experienced the learning process and the outcomes of a new MSW course aimed at helping students develop knowledge and awareness of cultural diversity and societal oppression. Data were collected from a total of 97 students through a content analysis of 30 student journals in Phase I, and a questionnaire completed by 67 students in Phase II of the study. The preliminary findings are placed in the context of relevant theoretical perspectives about the concept of moral exclusion and future knowledge development and research implications.

The rapidly changing demographics of the United States place an increased demand on social work educators to help students develop

---

Dorothy Van Soest is Visiting Associate Professor, National Catholic School of Social Services, Catholic University of America.

The author expresses appreciation to Dr. Elizabeth Timberlake for her assistance in reviewing the manuscript for this article.

The author's mailing address is: 3026 Gentain Center N.E., Washington, DC 20017.

[Haworth co-indexing entry note]: "Social Work Education for Multicultural Practice and Social Justice Advocacy: A Field Study of How Students Experience the Learning Process." Van Soest, Dorothy. Co-published simultaneously in *Journal of Multicultural Social Work* (The Haworth Press, Inc.) Vol. 3, No. 1, 1994, pp. 17-28; and: *School Social Workers in the Multicultural Environment: New Roles, Responsibilities, and Educational Enrichment* (ed: Paul R. Keys) The Haworth Press, Inc., 1994, pp. 17-28. Multiple copies of this article/chapter may be purchased from The Haworth Document Delivery Center [1-800-3-HAWORTH; 9:00 a.m. - 5:00 p.m. (EST)].

knowledge and awareness of cultural diversity and oppression and to translate that theoretical understanding into practical actions designed to facilitate service delivery and social change (Nakanishi & Rittner, 1992; Jacobs & Bowles, 1988; Chau, 1992). These objectives require teaching/learning methodologies which facilitate assimilation of information that is difficult, challenge personal world view and impact personal and professional self-concept. Therefore, this paper: (1) describes an educational model designed to operationalize these objectives; (2) reports a two-phase systematic effort to discover and comprehend how students experience their self-image/identity in relation to societal oppression, the change process, and the learning environment; and, (3) discusses the exploratory findings in the context of relevant theoretical perspectives and implications for future research.

BACKGROUND

Multiculturalism and Social Justice in Social Work Education

The formulation of social work in the 1958 Curriculum Study (Boehm, 1959) identified the profession's social and interactionist focus that today provides the curriculum base for preparing students to be culturally competent practitioners. The cultural ferment of the 1960s and 1970s, along with the Council on Social Work Education's Curriculum Policy Statements (CPS), moved the profession toward an expanded concern with social responsibility and a recognition of racism and sexism (Bisno, 1984). Undergraduate and master's programs in social work have been required to include content on ethnic and racial minorities and women since the mid-1970s (Dinerman, 1984) and the 1992 CPS strengthens and expands the imperative to oppose oppression in relation to lesbians and gay men and people with disabilities as well as other populations-at-risk.

Much work has been done to develop conceptions of social work practice in relation to cultural diversity and oppression (Billingsley & Giovannoni, 1972; Blanchard, 1982; Solomon, 1976; Lum, 1986; Devore & Schlesinger, 1987; Jacobs & Bowles, 1988; Pinderhughes, 1989; Van Den Bergh & Cooper, 1986; Van Den Bergh, 1993) as well as instructional methods to meet the educational challenges (Chau, 1992; Nakanishi & Rittner, 1992; Goldstein Wicker, 1986; Latting, 1990; Fellin, 1988; Adams & Schlesinger, 1988; Echols et al., 1988; Chestang, 1988). Yet, it is contended that social work with minorities is a marginal interest for the profession, that the practice literature tends to be naive and superficial in its failure to address the social context, and that there is still a reluctance on the part of social workers to seriously examine their own "isms" and to take a stand against them at the social and political level (McMahon & Allen-Meares, 1992; Christodoulou, 1991; Moore & Isherwood, 1988).

An Educational Model for Social Justice

The ultimate goal of the educational model under consideration–an MSW course on Cultural Diversity and Societal Oppression–is to prepare students for their role in working to eliminate oppressive hierarchies, to work for equality, and to provide culturally sensitive services. Thus, the focus of the course content is on power and inequality in addition to culture (Williams, 1989). The course involves an examination of important issues on three levels: personal identity and prejudices, institutional factors, and structural causes and consequences of oppression.

The learning process begins with awareness and understanding of the student's own cultural background and its meaning and significance in interaction with others. The model is based on Pinderhughes' (1989) premise that social workers with a positive ethnic identity are better able to value their clients' identity. The course moves beyond a client-oriented approach to culturally sensitive practice to expose the pervasive influence of race, gender, ethnicity, and power on the social worker's own identity. "Beginning with where students are" involves helping them develop empathy for themselves as a first step in understanding the pervasive nature of oppression. This approach is based on the idea that one's own experience of disempowerment provides resources for developing empathy for others who have been oppressed on different grounds. The course centers around generic experiences which cross diverse populations in order to facilitate an understanding of the common elements of oppression.

A major course requirement is participation in a group presentation which focuses on the strategies used to oppress a specific population included in the course content, and the micro and macro practice implications. Students are also required to keep a weekly journal in which they are to record their thoughts, feelings, and personal connections. The journals are not graded and anonymity is assured. Students are encouraged to use a "free writing" style, with the idea being to carry on a conversation with themselves as a way to learn through writing.

STUDY OF LEARNING PROCESS AND OUTCOMES

Research Questions

Of particular interest were three exploratory questions about what happens to students as they become aware of the dynamics of oppression: (1) How do students view their own role position or identity in relation to oppression–victim, benefactor, participant? Do they experience multiple roles or identities? (2) How do students experience the change process? (3) How are students influenced by interactions with other students and the classroom environment?

Methodology

An exploratory field study was conducted that included two phases of data collection.

Phase I. In the first phase of the study, a content analysis of 453 entries from all 30 student journals from one section of the course was used to discern how often and in what manner students wrote about three themes: student self-image/social identity in relation to societal oppression content; the change process; and, the learning environment, particularly interactions with other students and the professor. Within the range of 5 to 43 journal entries per student, students averaged 15 entries of from one to ten pages in length. Student diversity included: gender–female 24 (80%) and male 6 (20%); race and ethnic identity–white 21 (70%) and persons of color 9 (30%) with 4 African Americans, 2 Hispanic Americans, 1 Native American, 1 Asian American, and 1 Hispanic-Native American; and, self-designated sexual orientation–heterosexual 16 (53.3%), homosexual 1 (3.3%), bisexual 1 (3.3%), and not indicated 12 (40%). All of the students were first year non-advanced standing MSW students.

Phase II. A year later, an anonymous questionnaire was completed at semester's end by 67 students from three sections of the course (an 89% response rate) as a follow-up to the Phase I content analysis. Student demographics in Phases 1 and 2 did not differ significantly. Narrative responses to the following three open-ended questions were subjected to a content analysis using the same three themes as in Phase I:

1. Please describe what you learned about oppression and how you personally related to oppression during the course.
2. How did interaction with other students affect your learning?
3. How did interaction with the professor affect your learning?

Phase I Results of Content Analysis

Self-image/social identity theme. There were 120 journal entries out of the total of 453 entries (27%) in which students identified themselves as either victims or benefactors of oppression. Of the 101 entries written by females, 50% addressed their role as victim and 50% addressed how they were benefactors of oppression. Of the 19 entries written by males, 14 (74%) were about their status as benefactors and 5 entries (26%) were about their role as victims. Minority students were three times as likely to write about their role as victims rather than benefactors, while Caucasian students wrote more often about their role as benefactors than as victims (3:2). Students described their experiences with multiple identities in diverse ways as illustrated by the following examples: experiencing oppression due to race (African American) and gender (female) while being in the dominant group based on sexual orientation (heterosexual); being disadvantaged based on gender (female) and ethnic heritage (Irish) while receiving privileges based on race (white) and political party membership (Republican); colluding with and benefiting from oppression due to race (white), gender (male), and class (upper class) while experiencing oppression as a recovering alcoholic.

The change process. Of the journal entries related to change, high emotional involvement of students with the issues was particularly striking with 188 entries (42%). A larger percentage of females (46%) and Caucasians (47%) wrote about their affective process compared with males (24%) and minority students (28%). The entries indicate that students often struggled on a deep level with their sense of identity in relation to oppression, as almost all of the entries were about experiencing feelings such as shock, anger, and despair.

Students discussed increased awarenesses in 132 (29%) journal entries. Of these, 53 (40%) included awareness of students' own negative attitudes and prejudices, with an equal number being disturbed about their prejudices against African Americans and homosexuals. Thirty-four (26%) of the 132 entries indicated an awareness of the oppression of groups that seemed to have been outside students' social justice consciousness previously, including lesbians and gay men (10 entries), Hispanics (9 entries), African Americans (7 entries), Asian Americans (2 entries), and Native Americans (2 entries). An additional 11 students wrote about becoming conscious of their own oppression as women or as students. A strengthened acceptance of responsibility and empowerment to advocate for social justice was indicated in 30 (23%) of the 132 entries. The following illustrates the highly emotional tone that was typical of much of the journalling:

> I have been on an emotional roller coaster since day one. Many times I wanted to return to my former role in a world that seemed so *nice*, neat, and pure. I still tend to want to do that. But I have this compelling urge to make things better. I want my children to know how devastating oppression is and how it must be beaten with social

> justice, fairness, and being able to respect every human being for being themselves; to respect self and all that each person is!

Learning environment. Interactions with students who are different from themselves were discussed as being significant in facilitating change and personal growth in 177 journal entries (39%). Forty-seven percent of those entries indicated that such interactions were difficult and even painful, even though they resulted in positive change. Fifteen different students wrote of being influenced by one particular incident in which a student came out as a lesbian to the class and shared her experiences openly, and 10 students wrote about how much they learned from another student who shared her experiences as a person with a handicapping condition. The significance of these experiences was often powerfully stated:

> It must have been quite frightening for that student to admit she was a lesbian in front of the class. What courage! She is the genesis for my taking a closer look at other cultures and climbing out of my ivory tower to smell the roses. So I guess the adage goes 'if you can save one person, then you will be successful' . . . well, I have been saved!

Fifty-eight journal entries (13% of the total) addressed issues directly related to the class environment. Of these entries, 15 (26%) expressed concerns about being politically correct as illustrated by statements such as: "I felt I wasn't angry enough to prove that I wasn't a racist"; "I was intimidated by so many women in the class and didn't want to appear sexist so I didn't say what I really felt"; and, "I feel constrained sometimes as if I have to watch every word for fear of offending someone." Another 15 entries involved comparing groups of people in terms of who is more oppressed, as illustrated by statements such as: "I'm uncomfortable when someone feels their group is more oppressed and thus entitled to more"; and, "Suffering and discrimination are not a unique [black or female or Hispanic] experience." Eighteen (31%) of the classroom environment entries were about conflict between students from different oppressed populations in the classroom, and 10 entries (17%) were related to trust issues, with 2 of those indicating a distrust of certain people in the class and 8 entries indicating that students experienced a high level of trust and openness.

Phase II Results: Preliminary Confirmation

Responses to the open-ended questionnaire completed by 67 students in three subsequent sections of the course disclosed qualitative information comparable to that obtained from the Phase I journal analysis, but used student responses as the unit of data analysis. In response to the inquiry about what students learned about oppression from the course, most often mentioned in all three sections were comments indicating that students were "amazed," "enlightened," and struck by the pervasiveness and subtleness of oppression. A significant number of students felt they learned a lot about the theory of oppression (34%) and, while 18% of the total mentioned learning about the institutional and systemic nature of oppression, 39% of the students in one section made such comments.

In response to the question about how students personally related to oppression during the course, comments were comparable to the journal entries about the change process, high emotional involvement, and self-image. Twenty-three students (34%) made comments about how they had personally changed in terms of feelings, attitudes, and behaviors or about how they used their own experiences as a member of a disadvantaged group to empathize with other oppressed people. Twenty-two students (33%) expressed feelings of guilt and shame about how they collude with or benefit from oppression.

The significance of interactions for student learning that emerged during Phase I of the study was confirmed by student responses on the questionnaire to inquiries about interactions with students and the professor. A majority of students experienced interaction with both students (84%) and professor (69%) as helpful. In a way similar to the journal entries, comments on the questionnaire indicated that hearing about other students' experiences as victims of oppression had the most impact. Professor behaviors that were reported as being most helpful included demonstrating respect for students, being supportive and available, challenging students, providing insights, being sensitive, and providing a safe environment "where feelings and views could be dealt with and discussed without judgment." Interactions with the professor that hindered learning involved students feeling intimidated by the professor's strong point of view, concerns about saying something politically incorrect, and feeling that the classroom was not open.

DISCUSSION AND IMPLICATIONS

Implications for Theory Development

Student self-image/social identity. The concept of moral exclusion (Staub, 1987) provides a framework for understanding the complex combination of multiple and sometimes contested social roles and identities that began to be uncovered by students in the present investigation. Moral exclusion occurs when persons or groups are perceived as outside the boundary in which values, rules, and considerations of fairness apply. Such persons are seen as expendable or undeserving and thus harming them appears acceptable, appropriate, or just. The process of categorizing groups into negative categories and excluding them from the realm of acceptable norms and/or values links the concept of moral exclusion with stereotypes and prejudicial attitudes related to ethnocentrism (Bar-Tal, 1989; 1990). Perpetrators and benefactors of injustice are individuals or groups that harm others, societal institutions that justify harm, and bystanders who condone harm (Opotow, 1990). Groups whose rights have been invalidated or eliminated because of their exclusion from the scope of justice include groups of particular interest to social workers, such as: women, children, aged, persons of color, homosexuals, and persons with disabilities.

Although seldom conscious of them, everyone has beliefs about which people should be treated justly, and the broadness or narrowness of one's moral boundaries is influenced by attitudes which are shaped by prevailing cultural norms. When those outside one's moral community are perceived to be inferior or deviant, harmful behaviors against them can be seen as not violating accepted principles of justice and in fact may not be perceived as a violation of rights at all (Deutsch, 1990). The exclusion of an outgroup from the norms of fairness is a cognitive, affective, and behavioral phenomenon that enables otherwise considerate people to engage in self-serving behavior or inaction in everyday situations in order to gain benefits to themselves even at injurious costs to others (Bandura, 1986). The discovery that one has excluded a group from their moral boundaries is illustrated by a student's journal entry: "It is remarkable to me that for the *first* time, I am finding that I feel empathy for homosexuals and their situation." Due to denial, self-blame, and internalizing dominant norms, victims themselves may not recognize injustice (Deutsch, 1985; Bulhan, 1985). As a Hispanic student wrote in her journal: "I had never before considered that I was 'down there' in some other people's eyes. I have become aware of the pain I experienced growing up as an immigrant. This has been quite a lesson in humility!"

The change process. Students in the present study reported considerable high emotional involvement throughout the course. Since much of the student journalling focused on aspects of loss, conceptions of the grieving process as developed by Kubler-Ross (1969) and others may provide a useful guide for future theory development and research related to student change when confronting difficult issues. Students seemed to experience loss on several levels: Some experienced a loss of self-image or social identity as they became aware of their own oppression; others experienced a psychological loss as they began to let go of their benefactor status and faced the pain and discomfort involved in giving up status and power (Pinderhughes, 1988). One student wrote of a common experience of loss in relation to identifying with one's own reference group: "I just had a very upsetting phone conversation with my father about a racial situation in my hometown. I felt so disappointed about my father's prejudiced opinions. I am faced with seeing my father as a racist and I am grieving for the perfect father who I thought was just toward all human beings."

The learning environment. In the present study, sharing by peers of their personal experiences as members of an oppressed group seemed to be a powerful influence in helping students to expand their moral boundaries. This finding is consistent with data from several studies showing that when representatives of a dominant and subordinate social group interact, the result is a more favorable attitude of the dominant group toward the subordinate group and a greater readiness to extend social justice principles about the allocation of benefits and rights to them (Cook, 1990).

It was evident from this investigation that interactions were highly significant in the learning process and that the self-concept impacts on and complicates student-student and professor-student interactions. Interactions that hindered student learning were often related to not feeling safe in the classroom environment. The ability to empathize seems to be facilitated by personal sharing, while more intellectual debates seem to result in conflictual discussions around which group is more oppressed. These findings seem consistent with studies that indicate that, when there is conflict, our scope of justice narrows and, conversely, diminished conflict offers the opportunity to enlarge moral boundaries (Opotow, 1990).

Implications for Future Theory and Research

While the current study was exploratory in nature and used a small nonrepresentative sample that is not generalizable to social work students in general, the descriptive results point to the potential for fruitful research. For example, a quasi-experimental study of a sample of MSW students from comparable colleges or universities might be used to investigate whether, as a result of exposure to course content related to societal oppression and social justice, students: (1) expand their moral boundaries, (2) undergo a change in perceptions of themselves and their identity as benefactor, perpetrator or victim of oppression; (3) change their behavior in relation to members of oppressed populations; (4) demonstrate an increased commitment to role of social justice advocate. The relationship between any changes and variables such as emotional involvement related to the issues, the nature of interactions, exposures to diversity in field placements, etc., could be explored.

The discoveries made and information gathered from the current field study, along with the theoretical implications, point to considerable potential for educational model development. A stage-conception model of the learning process that addresses how students are moved from ideas and beliefs about equality and justice to operationalizing those values, is needed. Further development of educational models that incorporate the themes of this study and that can be tested through experimental research is also indicated. The power of classroom interactions to facilitate or hinder learning makes it essential that educators pay special attention to the creation of an open and safe classroom environment that is characterized by respect, empathy, and an honoring of each student's individuality and process.

REFERENCES

Adams, A.C., & Schlesinger, E.G. (1988). Group approach to training ethnic-sensitive practitioners. In C. Jacobs & D.D. Bowles (Eds.), *Ethnicity and race: Critical concepts in social work* (pp. 204-216). Silver Spring, MD: National Association of Social Workers.

Bandura, Albert (1986). *Social foundations of thought and action: A social cognitive theory.* Englewood Cliffs, NJ: Prentice-Hall.

______ . (1990). Selective activation and disengagement of moral control. *Journal of Social Issues, 46* (1), 27-46.

Bar-Tal, Daniel (1989). Delegitimization: The extreme case of stereotyping and prejudice. In D. Bar-Tal, C. Graumann, A.W. Kruglanski, & W. Stroebe (Eds.), *Stereotyping and prejudice: Changing conceptions* (pp. 169-188). New York: Springer-Verlag.

______ . (1990). Causes and consequences of delegitimization: Models of conflict and ethnocentrism. *Journal of Social Issues, 46* (1), 65-81.

Billingsley, A., & Giovannoni, J.M. (1972). *Children of the storm.* New York: Harcourt Brace Jovanovich.

Bisno, H. (1984). Conceptualizing social work practice in social work education. In M. Dinerman & L.L Geismar (Eds.), *A Quarter-Century of Social Work Education* (pp. 47-89). Washington, DC: National Association of Social Workers.

Blanchard, E.L. (1982). Observations on social work with American Indian women. In A. Weick & S. Vandiver (Eds.), *Women, power and change* (pp. 96-103). New York: National Association of Social Workers.

Boehm, W.W. (1959). *Objectives of the social work curriculum of the future.*

Social Work Curriculum Study, Vol. 1. New York: Council on Social Work Education.

Bulhan, H.A. (1985). *Frantz Fanon and the psychology of oppression.* New York: Plenum Press.

Chau, Kenneth L. (1992). Educating for effective group work practice in multicultural environments of the 1990s. *Journal of Multicultural Social Work, 1* (4), 1-15.

Chestang, L.W. (1988). Infusion of minority content in the curriculum. In C. Jacobs & D.D. Bowles (Eds.), *Ethnicity and race: Critical concepts in social work* (pp. 230-242). Silver Spring, MD: National Association of Social Workers.

Christodoulou, Costas (1991). Racism: A challenge to social education and practice: The British experience. *Journal of Multicultural Social Work, 1* (2), 99-106.

Cook, Stuart W. (1990). Toward a psychology of improving justice: Research on extending the equality principle to victims of social injustice. *Journal of Social Issues, 46* (1), 147-161.

Deutsch, Morton (1985). *Distributive justice: A social-psychological perspective.* New Haven, CT: Yale University Press.

______ (1990). Psychological roots of moral exclusion. *Journal of Social Issues, 46* (1), 21-26.

Devore, W., & Schlesinger, E.G. (1987). *Ethnic-sensitive social work practice.* 2nd edition. Columbus, OH: Merrill Publishing Co.

Dinerman, M. (1984). The 1959 curriculum study: Contributions of Werner W. Boehm. In M. Dinerman & L.L. Geismar (Eds.), *A Quarter-Century of Social Work Education* (pp. 3-24). Washington, DC: National Association of Social Work.

Echols, I.J., Gabel, C., Landerman, D., & Reyes, M. (1988). An approach for addressing racism, ethnocentrism, and sexism in the curriculum. In C. Jacobs & D.D. Bowles (Eds.), *Ethnicity and race: Critical concepts in social work* (pp. 217-229). Silver Spring, MD: National Association of Social Workers.

Fellin, Phillip (1988). Use of ethnic minority content in teaching research. In C. Jacobs & D.D. Bowles (Eds.), *Ethnicity and race: Critical concepts in social work* (pp. 185-203). Silver Spring, MD: National Association of Social Workers.

Goldstein Wicker, Diane (1988). Combating racism in practice and in the classroom. In N. Van Den Bergh & L.B. Cooper (Eds.), *Feminist visions for social work* (pp. 29-40). Silver Spring, MD: National Association of Social Workers.

Jacobs, Carolyn, & Bowles, Dorcas D. (Eds.) (1988). *Ethnicity and race: Critical concepts in social work.* Silver Spring, MD: National Association of Social Workers.

Kubler-Ross, Elisabeth (1969). *On death and dying.* New York: Macmillan Publishing Company.

Latting, J.K. (1990). Identifying the "isms": Enabling social work students to confront their biases. *Journal of Social Work Education, 26* (1), 36-44.

Lum, Doman (1986). *Social work practice and people of color.* Monterey, CA: Brooks/Cole Publishing Co.

McMahon, A., & Allen-Meares, P. (1992). Is social work racist? A content analysis of recent literature. *Social Work, 37*(6), 533-539.

Moore, Vernon L., & Isherwood, J. Thomas (1988). Utilizing professional knowledge and values: Practice dilemmas for workers with oppressed populations. Paper presented at the Council on Social Work Education Annual Program Meeting in Atlanta, Georgia, March 1988.

Nakanishi, Manuel, & Rittner, Barbara (1992). The inclusionary cultural model. *Journal of Social Work Education, 28* (1), 27-35.

Opotow, Susan (1990). Moral exclusion and injustice: An introduction. *Journal of Social Issues, 46* (1), 1-20.

Pinderhughes, Elaine (1988). Significance of culture and power in the human behavior curriculum. In C. Jacobs & D.D. Bowles (Eds.), *Ethnicity and race: Critical concepts in social work* (pp. 152-166). Silver Spring, MD: National Association of Social Workers.

______. (1989). *Understanding race, ethnicity, and power.* New York: The Free Press, Macmillan, Inc.

Solomon, B.B. (1976). *Black empowerment: Social work in oppressed communities.* New York: Columbia University Press.

Staub, Ervin (1987, August). Moral exclusion and extreme destructiveness: Personal goal theory, differential evaluation, moral equilibration and steps along the continuum of destruction. Paper presented at the American Psychological Association Meeting, New York.

Van Den Bergh, N., & Cooper, L.B. (1986). *Feminist visions for social work.* Silver Spring, MD: National Association of Social Workers.

Van Den Bergh, N. (1993). *Feminist practice in the 21st century.* Washington, DC: National Association of Social Workers.

Williams, Fiona (1989). *Social policy: A critical introduction–Issues of race, gender and class.* New York: Basil Blackwell.

Teaching Cultural Competence: Practical Ideas for Social Work Educators

John P. Ronnau

SUMMARY. The need for inclusion of cultural competence material in Social Work curriculums is well established. There is a dramatic increase in cultural and ethnic diversity in American society. Commensurate with that increase is an alarming rise in acts of racism on college campuses. Social Work programs are required to include cultural competence material and Social Work educators need down-to-earth and practical ideas for doing so. This paper describes five strategies for teaching cultural competence which have been successfully employed in Social Work practice classes. Evaluation results are reported.

THE CASE FOR CROSS-CULTURAL CONTENT

The dramatic increase in cultural and ethnic diversity in American society is no longer a forecast but a reality, with even more dramatic changes on the horizon (Mehta, Monroe & Winbush, 1990). The alarming rise in acts of racism in American society, particularly on college campuses, cries out for response from institutions of higher education. The best place to battle willful ignorance and bigotry is in the classroom.

John P. Ronnau, PhD, ACSW, is Assistant Professor, Department of Social Work, Box 30001, Dept. 3SW, New Mexico State University, Las Cruces, NM 88003-0001.

[Haworth co-indexing entry note]: "Teaching Cultural Competence: Practical Ideas for Social Work Educators." Ronnau, John P. Co-published simultaneously in *Journal of Multicultural Social Work* (The Haworth Press, Inc.) Vol. 3, No. 1, 1994, pp. 29-42; and: *School Social Workers in the Multicultural Environment: New Roles, Responsibilities, and Educational Enrichment* (ed: Paul R. Keys) The Haworth Press, Inc., 1994, pp. 29-42. Multiple copies of this article/chapter may be purchased from The Haworth Document Delivery Center [1-800-3-HAWORTH; 9:00 a.m. - 5:00 p.m. (EST)].

"Teaching that strengthens reason over reflex, curiosity over insularity, may help improve students' behavior outside the classroom as well" (Mehta, Tifft & Woodbury, May 1990, p. 106).

"The philosophy of multicultural education suggests that ethnic diversity and cultural pluralism should be essential ingredients and unceasing characteristics of American education" (Gay, 1977, p. 95). Social Work, along with other social science disciplines, emphasizes the importance of teachers and other helping professionals being knowledgeable and attentive to cultural diversity issues (de Hoyos & de Hoyos, 1986; Hogan & Siu, 1988; Hartman, 1990; Lum, 1982; Ronnau, Lloyd, Sallee & Shannon, 1990; Sue & Sue, 1990). Cultural sensitivity is a value held by the Social Work profession and is mandated by both the Council on Social Work Education and the NASW Code of Ethics (Kantambu-Latting, 1990). Social Work curriculums must include "clearly articulated objectives, outlines, and content incorporating diverse racial, ethnic, and cultural perspectives" (Council on Social Work Education, 1987, p. 9). Whether or not attention is paid to the students' cultural background and differences can have a significant impact upon their educational experience (Hoopes & Pusch, 1979; Hoopes, 1979; Williams, 1990). "School curricula which do not include multicultural content and multiethnic perspectives in teaching are unrealistic and incapable of providing qualitative educational experiences for all American youth" (Gay, 1977, p. 96).

Many teachers, while sympathetic to the idea of helping students become aware and appreciative of cultural differences, may be hesitant to raise the subject in the classroom. Some are uncomfortable with their own lack of knowledge or are reluctant to introduce such a potentially controversial topic. Others are hesitant to put students on-the-spot by asking them to talk about their cultural and ethnic backgrounds.

Students may be similarly reluctant to discuss cultural differences or admit lack of knowledge about other cultures. While they may be very curious about other cultures, they, too, hesitate to ask questions for fear of being labeled as unknowledgeable or even racist. While understandable, this reluctance on the part of students and teachers prevents an increase in cultural awareness.

Considerable theory and research has been published regarding communication processes and the importance of cross-cultural content (Banks, 1977; Berlo, 1960; Condon & Fathi, 1975; Hall, 1963; Hoopes & Althen, 1975; Rich, 1974; Samovar & Porter, 1976; Smith, 1973); while this mostly theoretical literature is important, classroom teachers need down-to-earth practical ideas which are readily adaptable to students' needs and abilities. Five strategies are presented in this paper to meet this need.

GOAL AND OBJECTIVES

The goal of the cultural competence strategies is to encourage Social Work students to embark on the process toward becoming multi-cultural. According to Hoopes (1979)

> multiculturalism is that state in which one has mastered the knowledge and developed the skills necessary to feel comfortable and communicate effectively (1) with people of any culture encountered and (2) in any situation involving a group of people of diverse cultural backgrounds. (By comfortable we mean without the anxiety, defensiveness, and disorientation that usually accompany the initial intercultural experience.) The multicultural person is the person who has learned how to learn culture–rapidly and effectively. (p. 21)

The objectives are threefold.

1. To raise the students' awareness about the importance of being culturally competent.

The relevance of this competency is especially stressed for those entering the helping professions.

2. To create an atmosphere in which students and teachers can ask questions and share their knowledge about cultures.

By purposefully devoting time and giving permission to the class to ask questions, a non-threatening atmosphere is created; thus, setting the stage for productive dialogue and learning. "A safe, supportive atmosphere is a critical factor in the success of any support group on combating racism" (Kantambu-Latting, 1990, p. 43).

3. To increase the amount of information students have about cultures, including their own.

Presentations by their classmates from other cultures, handouts, information about community resources, and discussion provide practical and useful cross-cultural information.

The evaluation component for these strategies assessed the extent to which the goal and objectives were met.

STRATEGIES FOR TEACHING CULTURAL COMPETENCE

The five strategies for teaching cultural competence are:

1. Students are introduced to key definitions pertaining to cultural awareness and the culturally competent professional;
2. Resource papers about the cultures to be discussed are provided;
3. Students are asked to serve as cultural guides;
4. Students are informed of cultural awareness activities that are occurring on campus and in nearby communities;
5. Implications of the cultural awareness material are highlighted and discussed throughout the semester.

Defining Cultural Competence

As an introduction to the topic of cultural competence the following definition of culture is provided to students.

> Culture is the sum total of ways of living, including values, beliefs, aesthetic standards, linguistic expression, patterns of thinking, behavioral norms, and styles of communication which a group of people has developed to assure its survival in a particular physical and human environment. Culture, and the people who are part of it, interact, so that culture is not static. Culture is the response of a group of human beings to the valid and particular needs of its members. It, therefore, has an inherent logic and an essential balance between positive and negative dimensions. (Hoopes & Pusch, 1979, p. 3)

In addition to providing an entry point for the topic of cultural competence, this definition raises the students' awareness that culture is a complex, multi-faceted and personal concept having a profound, though often out of consciousness, impact upon persons (Hoopes & Pusch, 1979).

Cross-cultural awareness is the second concept which is defined. According to Hoopes and Pusch (1979)

> *Cross-cultural awareness* (sometimes "cultural awareness" or "cultural self-awareness") refers to the basic ways of learning that behav-

> ior and ways of thinking and perceiving are culturally conditioned rather than being universal aspects of human nature. In this learning, unconscious, culturally-based assumptions and values held by individuals are brought to the surface. (p. 7)

The notion of cross-cultural awareness is used to make the case that self-awareness is an important step in the process of becoming culturally competent. "As long as our way of perceiving the world–on which our communication styles and behavior patterns are based–is "out of awareness," it is not accessible to being deliberately changed, managed, understood or influenced. It will continue to contribute to misunderstanding and conflict" (Hoopes, 1979, p. 17).

Following introduction of these definitions, students are provided with a description of the culturally competent professional. Introducing this concept at the outset of the semester provides several important teaching/learning opportunities. It is an opportunity for teachers to stress that they and the Department consider cultural competence an important topic. It raises the students' awareness about the role that cultural competence plays in becoming a helping professional and opens the door for them to think and ask questions about cultural differences. This description of the culturally competent professional is borrowed from the Research and Training Center at Portland State University and appeared in their publication, *Focal Point* (Summer 1988).

First, *cultural competence requires a commitment*. Students are reminded that being a culturally competent professional is, in large part, an attitude. One which necessitates sincerely believing that all cultures are of equal worth and none are inherently superior to others (Hoopes & Pusch, 1979). This first step also requires a willingness to admit lack of knowledge about other cultures and a commitment to learn about them.

Secondly, the culturally competent professional must *become aware and accept that significant differences do exist between people of different cultures*. Students must be helped to accept the fact that ignoring or denying that differences exist is not helpful and may even be harmful. "By failing to identify and appreciate differences at the outset, they are left in the path and unrecognized so that they almost inevitably become stumbling blocks. It is the ability to appreciate cultural differences that moves us along the cultural learning continuum" (Hoopes, 1979, p. 33).

Self awareness is the third element. "To fully appreciate cultural differences, workers must recognize the influence of their own culture on how they think and act" (Focal Point, 1989). It is important that students become aware that cultural competence necessitates some introspection. They must begin to get in touch with the values, standards and messages which have been passed on to them from their families and communities. This cultural self-awareness leads to understanding "that behavior and ways of thinking and perceiving are culturally conditioned rather than being universal aspects of human nature" (Hoopes & Pusch, 1979, p. 239).

Professionals must also begin to *understand the "dynamics of difference"* which occur within cross-cultural contacts. Culturally competent professionals will develop an awareness of the different meanings that behaviors may have within different cultures. The firmness of a handshake, the directness and duration of eye contact, showing respect for elders, offering food to a visitor, inviting a visitor into the home are examples of behaviors which may take on more or less importance and be interpreted differently between cultures. "By incorporating an understanding of these dynamics and their origins into practice, workers enhance their chances for productive cross-cultural interventions" (Focal Point, 1989, p. 4).

Cultural competence requires continuous efforts to *gain more knowledge about the client's culture*. "Workers must know what symbols are meaningful, how health is defined and how primary support networks are configured" (Focal Point, 1989, p. 4). This knowledge acquisition is an ongoing process. It is unrealistic to expect workers to have comprehensive knowledge of all the cultures with which they may come in contact. "Gaining enough knowledge to identify what information is needed as well as know who to ask for information is a desirable goal" (Focal Point, 1989, p. 4).

Finally, culturally competent professionals will be able to make use of the cultural knowledge they have gained and *adapt their practice behaviors* to meet the needs of the people they are serving. The importance of mental health service providers being able to practice effectively across cultures is stressed with students (Dillard, 1987). The most effective way to make initial contact with the client, how to conduct an interview, who to include in the family session, how quickly to move in suggesting changes, and the appropriateness of interventions are examples of practice behaviors which the culturally competent professional will adapt to meet the needs of their clients from different cultures (Focal Point, 1988).

Cultural Profiles

Students are provided with resource papers which describe critical aspects of the cultural groups to be discussed. The resource papers include such topics as historical perspective, guiding principles and values, family structure, child rearing practices and beliefs and strengths (New Mexico Dept. of Human Services, 1989). They are cautioned about the limitations of cultural profiles and reminded that while they can provide valuable information about a culture, they can also perpetuate stereotypes. They are encouraged to be mindful that there are many cultures within a culture and that each person is unique (Gay, 1977). Students are also asked to critique the resource papers and point out information that does not fit their experience or knowledge.

Cultural Guides

The third strategy makes use of cultural guides (Green, 1982). Class members are asked to volunteer for the role of cultural guide to assist their classmates to learn about other cultures. Cultural guides are solicited to represent the numerically predominant cultures in the class (in this case Anglo, Afro-American, Hispanic and Native American). Students are assured that taking on this role is completely voluntary and that their grade will in no way be affected should they choose to participate. Cultural guides are asked to provide samples of food, music, art and language which are important to them and represent their culture as they view it.

Care is taken to stress that no one person can accurately represent an entire culture. All that any of us can do with any degree of accuracy is represent our own personal background; how it was in our family and community. This point helps to set realistic expectations for the cultural guides. It also introduces the knowledge that people from the same cultural background may have very different experiences and feelings.

Prior to the presentations, the class is invited to anonymously submit questions to the cultural guides through the teacher about the culture to be discussed. This invitation is extended to reinforce the notion that the sessions are learning opportunities and not confrontational or therapy sessions. Also, it is hoped that by this means students will take the opportunity to check out prejudices and biases which they might otherwise not verbalize in front of the class.

Utilizing Community Resources

Students are urged throughout the semester to attend local cultural events. They are also encouraged to announce events scheduled in their home towns. Periodically informing students of these events requires only a minute or two of class time and serves as a reminder that cultural awareness is valued, is an ongoing process, and requires active involvement.

In many communities a wide variety of cultural events occurs throughout the year. These events provide rich cultural awareness and learning opportunities. For example, in the Southwestern community where these strategies have been used within a one month period, the following events occurred: Native American dance demonstration and traditional foods, Native American Art exhibition, Ballet Folklorico, rodeo, symphony, opera, musical plays, community band concert, foreign films, "Very Special Art" with exhibits by individuals with special physical needs, Chautauqua Performance, poetry reading, a modern art symposium and a variety of sporting events (*Page One*, October 1990). All of these events provided opportunities to experience different cultures. Many of them were available at minimal or no cost to students.

Course Integration

Multicultural education cannot be achieved by means of a few classroom activities. Becoming multicultural "has to be seen as a process rather than a state of being" (Hoopes, 1979, p. 19). While providing students with new information via the components in this curriculum may heighten their cultural awareness, it is important to integrate cultural information into the curriculum by applying it to the topics presented. If students are to become culturally competent professionals, they must be provided with knowledge, values and skills (Gay, 1977). The relevance and application of cultural awareness material can be demonstrated by integrating it with topics presented throughout the course, and challenging students to identify implications for practice.

For example, building relationships with clients requires demonstrating warmth, empathy and genuineness (Perlman, 1979; Biestek, 1957); however, skills for communicating these qualities may need to be adapted depending upon the client's cultural background. An aggressive handshake may be a preferred way to show respect and warmth for some, while the same behavior may be offensive to others. Effective helping requires the skills of nonverbal communication, active listening, and questioning (Sheafor, Horejsi & Horejsi, 1988); however, the appropriate use of these skills requires cultural awareness and sensitivity (Devore, 1991; Lum, 1986; Saba, Karrer & Hardy, 1982; Tseng & Hsu, 1991). Some clients are more accustomed and comfortable with the professional helping process; with them, moving quickly in a direct manner to collecting personal data may be appropriate. With others, based upon their values and customs, much more time may need to be invested in the relationship before sensitive personal information should be requested.

EVALUATION

These five cultural competence teaching strategies have been used with both graduate and undergraduate students. Students in two first-level undergraduate social work practice classes were asked to complete a short evaluation instrument. They were told that their responses would remain anonymous and that participation was voluntary. The survey was designed to assess whether the objectives of the curriculum had been met. Table 1 describes the demographics of the forty-two students who completed the survey.

As part of the evaluation, the students were asked to rank in order of priority eight potential benefits for including cultural competence material in the curriculum. Those benefits were selected based upon a review of the cross-cultural education and communication literature (Banks, 1977; *Focal Point*, 1988; Gay, 1977; Hoopes & Althen, 1975; Rich, 1974; Samovar & Porter, 1976; Smith, 1973; Lum, 1982; Sue & Sue, 1990; Hoopes & Pusch, 1979; Hoopes, 1979; Williams, 1990). The following four benefits were ranked in the top four by over fifty percent of the students.

1. My awareness of important cultural differences between cultures has increased;
2. I am now more aware of the influences that my own culture has on how I think and act;
3. I gained new information about cultures different than my own;
4. I learned some useful practices for being a culturally competent social worker.

The amount of discussion which occurred over the semester regarding cultural competence indicates that objective two, raising the students' awareness of the importance of being culturally competent, was met. When asked to express their opinion about the usefulness of the description of the culturally competent professional, the following comments were among those made, each by a different student.

TABLE 1: Demographics of Respondents.

	Anglo	Black	Hispanic	Native American	Other	Total
Female	11	5	12	2	1	30
Male	6	0	5	1	0	12
Total	17	5	17	3	1	42

> Increased my awareness of what it means to be a culturally competent social worker;
>
> Was useful as a guide to keep me on track as a social worker;
>
> Helped clarify my role as a social worker in dealing/working with different people;
>
> Brought into perspective my responsibilities as a social worker and broadened my outlook past the personal to the professional;
>
> Made me aware of the importance that my understanding of peoples' values and beliefs will have on my relationship with them.

To further explore the extent to which objective two was met, the survey included a four-point Likert-type scale (Marlow, 1993) with an item which asked the students whether their comfort level for asking questions about cultures different than their own had increased due to the curriculum material. Ninety-one percent either agreed or strongly agreed that it had.

The survey provided reasons to believe that the third objective, increasing students' knowledge about cultures, including their own, was also achieved. When the students were asked to list five things that they learned about cultures that they did not know before, the following comments were made.

> No one culture is all good or all bad nor all right or all wrong but there is good in all cultures;
>
> Taught me to more fully understand how diverse cultures are;
>
> Learned more about the Native American cultures and their way of life;
>
> Learned more about Anglo cultures in relation to all other cultures;
>
> I learned how people in the same culture are very different;
>
> Cultural diversity is so important, not only as social workers but as individuals in our society;
>
> This was a refreshing way to look at culture. Black, white, Hispanics and their characteristics in books tend to be boring and impractical. Hands-on stuff the best!

The primary teaching methods used to implement the strategies were: (1) resource papers, (2) cultural guides, and (3) the definition of cultural competence. The students were asked to rank these methods in the order which was most useful to them for learning about cultural competence. Table 2 clearly shows the students' preference for the cultural guide presentations.

A four-point scale was used to ask students if they felt that, overall, the cultural competence material presented in class was a worthwhile use of time. Of the forty-two students surveyed, forty of them (95%) agreed or strongly agreed that it was a worthwhile use of their class time.

ADDITIONAL OBSERVATIONS

Creation of an open and trusting atmosphere is crucial to fostering cultural awareness (Kantambu-Latting, 1990). Use of this cultural competence material creates an atmosphere in which cultural differences can be explored, questions asked and uncertainties expressed. It gives students and teachers permission to admit lack of knowledge and to talk openly about sensitive subjects. One example of this openness is provided by the following student comment expressed early in the semester.

> I really feel overwhelmed. I just moved from a rural midwestern area where there were primarily Anglos. Now I'm here in the Southwest where there are so many different types of people. I don't know anything about Hispanics! How do I go about learning?

Another benefit of these teaching strategies is the extent to which students are directly involved. For example, students are encouraged to critique the resource papers, question the cultural guides, and express their uncertainties and anxieties regarding cultural differences. The role of cultural guides places the students front stage as the expert in their own

TABLE 2: Rank Order of Usefulness of Teaching Methods.

	First	Second	Third	(Rank Order)
Method 1	4	15	20	(Frequency)
Method 2	30	6	3	
Method 3	5	18	16	

culture. This format reduces the unrealistic expectation that the teacher will be the expert on all cultures and, instead, creates an atmosphere in which everyone is a learner.

The case has already been made for the importance and timeliness of this material in relation to CSWE guidelines and national priorities. But Social Work curriculums are already packed with required course content, so how can educators be expected to add yet another component? These strategies can be used all or in part and, therefore, do not necessitate a radical course restructuring. For example, a greater or lesser amount of time can be devoted to the Cultural Guide presentations. The material can be expanded to make up the subject matter for entire sessions or integrated more sparingly throughout the entire semester.

CONCLUSION

It is important that students receive clear and direct messages from their teachers that cultural competence is a critical part of their education. Effective helping professionals must be able to start where the client is and establish an effective helping relationship (Compton & Galaway, 1984; Hoffman & Sallee, in press; Sheafor, Horejsi & Horejsi, 1988). Becoming aware of and valuing cultural differences are keys to this process. This awareness becomes more and more critical to effective individual functioning as the interdependent and global nature of our collective well-being emerges (Highwater, 1981; Hoffman & Sallee, in press). "To deal with intercultural issues at home is, in a sense, to deal with them globally" (Hoopes & Pusch, 1979, p. 8). These five cultural competence teaching strategies provide practical ideas for helping students move toward the goals of multi-culturalism and cultural competence.

REFERENCES

Banks, James A. (1977). "The Implications of Multicultural Education for Teacher Education." *Pluralism and the American Teacher*, Washington, DC, American Association of Teacher Education.

Berlo, David. (1960). *The Process of Communication*. New York: Holt, Reinhart, and Winston, Inc.

Biestek, S. J. (1957). *The casework relationship*. Chicago: Loyola University Press.

Compton, B. R. and Galaway, B. (1984). *Social work processes* (3rd ed.). Chicago: Dorsey Press.

Condon, John C. and Fathi Yousef. (1975). *An Introduction to Intercultural Communication*. New York: Bobbs-Merrill.
Council on Social Work Education, Commission on Accreditation. (1987). *Handbook of accreditation standards and procedures*. Alexandria, VA: CSWE.
de Hoyos, G., de Hoyos, A. and Anderson, C. B. (1986, Jan/Feb.). Sociocultural dislocation: Beyond the dual perspective. *Social Work, 31* (1), 61-67.
Devore, W. and Schlesinger, E. G. (1991). *Ethnic-sensitive social work practice* (3rd ed.). New York: Merrill.
Dillard, J. M. (1987). *Multicultural counseling*. Chicago, IL: Nelson-Hall.
Focal Point. (1988). What does it mean to be a culturally competent professional? Portland State University, Research and Training Center, Portland, OR.
Gay, G. (1977). Curriculum design for multicultural education. In C. A. Grant (Ed.), *Multicultural education: Commitments, issues and applications*. (pp. 94-104). Washington, DC: Association for Supervision and Curriculum Development.
Gibbs, N. (1990, May 7). Bigots in the ivory tower. *Time*, pp. 104-106.
Green, J. (1982). *Cultural awareness in the human services*. Englewood Cliffs, NJ: Prentice Hall.
Hall, Edward T. (1963). *The Hidden Dimension*. Garden City, NY: Anchor Press.
Hall, Edward T. (1963). *The Silent Language*. Garden City, NY: Anchor Press
Hartman, A. (1990). Many ways of knowing (Editorial). *Social Work, 35*, 3-4.
Henry, W. A. (1990, April 9). Beyond the melting pot. *Time*, pp. 28-31.
Highwater, J. (1981). *The primal mind*. New York: Penguin.
Hoffman, K. S. and Sallee, A. L. (in press). *Social work practice: Bridges to change*. Boston: Allyn & Bacon.
Hogan, P. L. and Siu, S. F. (1988). Minority children and the child welfare system: A historical perspective. *Social Work*, 33, 6.
Hoopes, D. S. (1979). Intercultural communication concepts and the psychology of intercultural experience. In M. D. Pusch (Ed.), *Multicultural education: Cross cultural training approach*. Intercultural Network, Inc.
Hoopes, D. S. and Althen, Gary L. (1975). "Culture and Communication in Intercultural Relations." *Readings in Intercultural Communication*, D. Hoopes (ed.). Pittsburgh, PA: Intercultural Communication Network and SIETAR.
Hoopes, D. S. and Pusch, M. D. (1979). Definition of terms. In M. D. Pusch (Ed.), *Multicultural education: Cross cultural training approach*. Intercultural Network, Inc.
Kantambu-Latting, J. (1990). Identifying the "isms": Enabling social work students to confront their biases. *Journal of Social Work Education*, Winter (1), 36-44.
Lum, D. (1982). Towards a framework for social work practice with minorities. *Social Work*, 27, 3, 244-249.
Lum, D. (1986). *Social work practice and people of color: Process-stage approach*. Monterey, CA: Brooks/Cole.
Marlow, C. (1993). *Research methods*. Pacific Grove, CA: Brooks/Cole.
Mehta, N. S., Monroe, S. and Winbush, D. (1990, April 9). Beyond the melting pot. *Time*, pp. 28-31.

Mehta, N. S., Tifft, S. and Woodbury, R. (1990, May 7). Bigots in the ivory tower. *Time*, pp. 104-106.

New Mexico Department of Human Services (1989). Cultural Awareness Resources Papers. Santa Fe, NM.

Page One. (1990, October). Information Services, New Mexico State University, Las Cruces, NM.

Perlman, H. H. (1979). *Relationship*. Chicago: University of Chicago Press.

Rich, A. (1974). *Interracial Communication*. New York, NY: Harper and Row.

Ronnau, J. P., Lloyd, J. C., Sallee, A. L. and Shannon, P. J. (1990). Family preservation skills with Native Americans. in (ed.) Mannes, M. *Family preservation and Indian Child welfare*. Albuquerque, NM: American Indian Law Center.

Saba, G. W., Karrer, B. M. and Hardy, K. V. (Eds). (1990). *Minorities and family therapy*. New York: The Haworth Press, Inc.

Samovar, L. and Porter, R. (Eds.). (1976). *Intercultural Communication: A Reader*. Belmont, CA: Wadsworth Publishing Co.

Sheafor, Horejsi, C. R. and Horejsi, G. A. (1988). *Techniques and guidelines for social work practice*. Boston, MA: Allyn & Bacon, Inc.

Smith, Arthur L. (1973). *Transracial Communication*. Englewood Cliffs, NJ: Prentice-Hall, Inc.

Sue, D. W. and Sue, D. (1990). *Counseling the culturally different*. New York, NY: Wiley and Sons.

Tseng, W. and Hsu, J. (1991). *Culture and family*. New York: The Haworth Press, Inc.

Williams, L. F. (1990). The challenge of education to social work: The case of minority children. *Social Work, 35* (3), 326-330.

An Outcome Approach to Assessing the Cultural Competence of MSW Students

Peter Manoleas

SUMMARY. The past twenty years have seen a vast improvement in the cultural content of graduate social work curricula. Recently, emphasis on the affective component of education has been added to the knowledge base for cross-cultural practice. This paper takes the next step by introducing a series of outcome objectives for cultural competence categorized by knowledge, skill, and value bases. An evaluation of the model is included.

INTRODUCTION

America is, and will continue to be, more ethnically diverse than at any time in her history. Yet our nation's history of racism, oppression, and unequal access to the American dream has made it imperative that social work education give special attention to those groups classified as ethnic minorities. African-Americans, Latinos, Native Americans, and Asian-Americans have all suffered devastating colonial histories whose legacies never fail to be part of current reality for members of these groups. These

---

Peter Manoleas is affiliated with the School of Social Welfare, University of California at Berkeley.

This paper was presented at the Council on Social Work Education, Annual Program Meeting in New York City, March 1, 1993.

[Haworth co-indexing entry note]: "An Outcome Approach to Assessing the Cultural Competence of MSW Students." Manoleas, Peter. Co-published simultaneously in *Journal of Multicultural Social Work* (The Haworth Press, Inc.) Vol. 3, No. 1, 1994, pp. 43-57; and: *School Social Workers in the Multicultural Environment: New Roles, Responsibilities, and Educational Enrichment* (ed: Paul R. Keys) The Haworth Press, Inc., 1994, pp. 43-57. Multiple copies of this article/chapter may be purchased from The Haworth Document Delivery Center [1-800-3-HAWORTH; 9:00 a.m. - 5:00 p.m. (EST)].

factors, coupled with recent immigration patterns, result in trends toward the ever-increasing cultural diversity previously mentioned, and make it impossible for any social work practitioner to be thoroughly knowledgeable about all of the cultural groups they are likely to encounter. It is therefore imperative that we adopt a cultural competence approach to social work practice and training. Haynes and Singh (1992) have proposed an integrated approach in the generalist curriculum to training for ethnic sensitive social work practice. This paper attempts to take the next step by specifying outcome objectives for culturally competent practice. These objectives are grouped into knowledge, skill, and value objectives following the convention established by the Council on Social Work Education, and are intended to represent competence levels achieved by the end of the M.S.W. curriculum. For purposes of this paper, cultural competence in working with sexual minorities, as people who have been subjected to institutionalized forms of oppression, is added to that for working with ethnic minorities.

SAMENESS VERSUS DIFFERENCE

Doman Lum (1986), in *Social Work Practice and People of Color*, has documented the slow growth of the literature devoted to practice with ethnic minorities between 1970 and 1983. While this growth has accelerated since 1983, the approach has focused on the knowledge and value bases and has resulted, until very recently, in an "exotic other" approach to practice education. That is to say, social work students, both whites and minorities, have been taking "ethnic content" courses in which they studied *about* people of ethnic minority cultures. The past decade has witnessed the emergence of several practice oriented texts focusing on cultural differences which have made important contributions to the cross cultural knowledge base (Burgest, 1985; Davis, 1984; Devore & Schlesinger, 1987; Jacobs & Bowles, 1988; Jenkins, 1981; Lum, 1986; and Gibbs & Huang, 1989). This knowledge has proven to be very valuable for students, especially for those with limited exposure to persons who are culturally unlike themselves. Many graduate social work students indicate that were it not for so many required courses, they would take as many electives dealing with ethnic minority content as they could. They know what the realities of their future practice as social workers are, and who their clients are likely to be. The "use of self" nature of social work practice, however, requires that people in our profession, both students and practitioners, know themselves as thoroughly as possible as a prerequisite to effective interpersonal helping.

For decades field instructors have encouraged students to look at their "countertransference issues," but have only recently begun to ask them to think about their ethnic background and any implications that may have for practice. Such a focus is, at times, difficult but essential in developing a proficient cross-cultural skill base. Pinderhughes (1979), Nakanishi and Rittner (1992), Latting (1990), Chau (1990), and others have written about a variety of experiential teaching models which focus on ethnic differences, self-identification, cross-cultural empathy, and other interpersonal components of culturally sensitive practice. These models encourage each student to self-define prior to structuring minority-majority group interactions, and subsequently take major steps in moving beyond the "exotic other" approach.

Many studies (Chin, 1983; Gallegos, 1982; Lynch & Stein, 1987) have demonstrated that minority clients are usually best served by persons who are part of, or in tune with, their culture. Other recent findings, however, indicate that racial or ethnic similarity appears to be less important than counselor educational level or attitudinal similarity for African-Americans (Atkinson, Furlong, & Poston, 1986), Asian-Americans, and Latinos (Atkinson, Poston, Furlong, & Mercado, 1989). What does appear to be the single most important factor involved in any practitioner's ability to effectively help clients from other cultural groups is prolonged exposure to people of that group, in a variety of settings. The highly segregated and compartmentalized nature of our society makes it unlikely that many students will come to graduate training already having had these types of experiences. It is therefore important for the social work education process to structure these experiences wherever possible if we are to train culturally competent practitioners. These efforts should be made based upon an assessment of each student's needs, and is as important for students of color as well as for white students.

A WORD ABOUT "WHITE CULTURE"

Just as the term African-American reminds us that "Black" is not really a culture, neither does the term "White" help us understand the dynamics of the majority culture in this country. When we speak of the *dominant* culture in this country, we are speaking of a culture propagated by the corporate state as influenced by Euro-American values and necessitated by the grow or die imperative of our version of advanced capitalism. Strong values of youth, competitiveness, and conspicuous consumption are projected by visual, print, and electronic media. It is with this culture that individuals often feel conflict, or to which they have difficulty acculturating due to their own ethnic background and values. Even though recent world events have resulted in new waves of immigrants from all parts of Europe, the majority of professional social workers and graduate social work students continue to be what Lieberson (1985) refers to as "unhyphenated whites." These are the second or third generation progeny of immigrants who lack any clear-cut identification with, or knowledge of, specific European origins. They are usually aware of the fact that, in this sense, they may be different from other ethnic groups whose race, recent immigration, or marginalization are omnipresent reminders of their ethnic identification.

CULTURAL COMPETENCE

Ethnic culture can be conceived of as one generation's way of passing on to the next ways of seeing, experiencing, reacting, and being in this world as the former generation perceived them. Thought of in this way, culture is clearly a survival and coping mechanism and something that is dynamic and ever-changing. Terry Cross et al., in their excellent monograph entitled "Toward a Culturally Competent System of Care . . . " comment that cultural competence embraces " . . . the importance of culture, the assessment of cross-cultural relations, vigilance towards the dynamics that result from cultural differences, the expansion of cultural knowledge, and the adaptation of services to meet culturally unique needs." They also stress that becoming culturally competent is a developmental process.

For purposes of assessing cultural competence, it is useful to think in terms of factors that are universal to the human experience like birth, certain developmental milestones, social behavior, etc.; arguable universals like the need to share problems, woes, and joys; and other factors which are absolutely unique to each culture like communication styles, social structures, and family dynamics. To think in this way is to think about human sameness vs. difference. The objectives outlined subsequently in effect represent a series of universal factors within which individual cultural variation must be considered. The dimensions of cultural competence often distill themselves into the oversimplified but useful dichotomy between Eurocentric values and the values of cultures descended from the Third World, or the global periphery colonized by the ancestors of present day Europeans and Euro-Americans. This dichotomy is variously referred to as Western vs. Non-Western; European vs. Non-European; or European vs. Traditional Cultures. I will, at times, use each of these terms throughout this paper.

KNOWLEDGE BASE

Lum (1986) defines the knowledge base for practice with minority clients as involving " . . . the range of information, awareness, and understanding of the minority situational experience. It includes history, cognitive-affective-behavioral characteristics, and the societal dilemmas of people of color." It is that body of knowledge which is essential in order to contextualize, understand, and assess the behavior of minority clients, and to which the following objectives relate.

Knowledge Objective No. 1

The student will demonstrate sufficient knowledge about how culture affects basic developmental events such as: gender roles, rites of passage, sexuality development, mate selection, child-rearing practices, social networks, aging, and mourning.

Coursework on human development in the social environment appears as a part of the curriculum in all CSWE approved MSW programs. A life cycle-life events approach to development is a good and inclusive way to approach the psychosocial development of human beings. It is important to recognize, however, that current developmental models, heavily influenced by the work of Freud, Erikson, and Piaget, are Eurocentric, linear, and at times will be limited in their applicability to people and families of non-western origins. Norton (1983), for example, has challenged Piaget's notions of "irreversibility" with regard to the cognitive development of African-American children. Murillo (1976) and others have examined the role of cultural traditions in gender assignment among Mexican American males. Yu (1984) commented on the role of filial piety with aging Chinese-Americans, and its impact on senescence in that culture. Students need to be as familiar with such culturally based literature on human development as they are with the "big three" if they are to demonstrate competence in this area. Similarly, they need to recognize and acknowledge that the "coming out" process for gay and lesbian individuals is one of the most important developmental events for such people, and crucial for healthy identity formation.

Knowledge Objective No. 2

The student will demonstrate knowledge of different cultural care giving patterns within families, kinship networks, and communities. Such patterns include caring for the young, infirm, aged, and mentally ill.

Cultural competence in a person-in-environment profession like social work requires that a family and community focus be foremost in the psychosocial assessment of ethnic and sexual minorities. Lewis (1988), for example, found that African-American women, because of their ethnic group membership, have a higher probability of being part of an extended network than women from most European backgrounds. La Fromboise (1988) notes that for Native Americans, treatment goals must include drawing the individual out of isolation and integrating them back into the social life of the group. The definitions of nuclear and extended family must be flexible and adapted to each group and community. A social network analysis is a crucial part of assessing resources and supports for minorities (Attneave, 1969; Manns, 1981), and must be done prior to formulating problem statements or intervention plans. Churches and other religious networks are sources of aid in many communities where formal social agencies are less than responsive or relevant (Edwards & Edwards, 1984; Gutierrez, Ortega, & Suarez, 1990). Knowledge of certain terminology accompanies competence on this objective. The student should know what is meant, for example, if a client refers to a "compadre," or to a "play sister."

Knowledge Objective No. 3

The student will demonstrate knowledge of, and sensitivity to, non-European ways of relating to nature, metaphysical harmony, time, and spirituality.

Ethnic minorities in the United States are descended from the pre-colonial peoples of Asia, Africa, and the Americas. These non-European ancestors generally exhibited an appreciation of a spiritual quality of the universe, and tended to respect the balances, harmonies, and rhythms inherent in nature. Their preference was to learn from and adapt to the natural world rather than attempting to alter and control it. These traditions were altered in part by urbanization and modernization, but moreover by the colonial process and the forced acculturation that accompanied it. Such a spiritual nature and respect for metaphysical harmony persist among many ethnic minorities of color. Many Native American and Latino groups view mental health as directly related to the spiritual side of life and to the balances in the forces that impact their lives (Sue, D.W., 1981). Staples (1976) sees the Black church as fortifying African-Americans against the destructive force of racism. Indeed, when in a relatively powerless social position, people find comfort in spirituality. Euro-Americans, in contrast, have been characterized by their need to control, understand, and explain natural phenomena. Lefley (1990) found that Anglo-American psychiatric patients required generally higher doses of sedating medications than other patients and attributed this to their action orientation and need to control the environment. Culturally competent students need to be aware of, and sensitive to, these basically different traditions of Euro-Americans and others, and to be familiar with the fundamental beliefs of the more common organized religions.

Knowledge Objective No. 4

The student will be familiar with patterns of interdependency, mutuality, and obligation between individuals, their families, and their communities, that exist in various cultures.

This objective is essentially an elaboration of the one that urges a focus on families, social networks, and communities. The objective requires that students view critically the rugged individualist and personal ego focused approach that social casework has inherited from European psychology and psychiatry. These principles have been highly popularized in the "me first" '80s by the application to almost everything of concepts like codependence and permeable ego boundaries. These trends are culturally destructive if they do not take into consideration the patterns of reciprocal obligation found among many groups, notably Latinos, Native Americans, and Asian-Americans. Students need to understand the inherent survival value of these patterns. When possessing such competence, the practitioner will not be so quick to label as guilty an ethnic minority client who is basically feeling "*I* cannot be O.K. as long as *we* are not O.K."

SKILL BASE

The skill base for culturally competent practice has to do with "developing a helping relationship with an individual, family, group, and/or community whose distinctive physical/cultural characteristics and discriminatory experiences require approaches that are sensitive to ethnic and cultural environments" (Lum, 1986, p. 3). Interviewing and communication skills along with client and self assessment skills are included here.

Skill Objective No. 1

The student is able to assess health, illness, functional and dysfunctional behavior and psychopathology, taking into account the cultural relativity of categories and modes of expression.

Competence in this area requires that students take a culturally relative view of human functioning and behavior. That is to say, behavior must be evaluated within the cultural context, and the limitations of universalist assessment tools, like the DSM-IIIR, acknowledged. Intra-cultural definitions of deviance must be superimposed upon such universal criteria in order to arrive at useful assessments. Weibel-Orlando (1981), for example, describes a pattern of tolerance of alcohol inebriation among Native Americans that crosses tribal boundaries. The degree of community tolerance at tribal events, of persons visibly under the influence of alcohol, is directly related to the proximity of that person to sacred drum rituals. The closer to the center of the concentric circles the person is, the less the tolerance. It is unthinkable that someone would come right next to the drummers while drunk. Such behavior would clearly be deviant. Similarly, an understanding of the legacy of slavery and ongoing racism in this country is essential if students are to competently assess African-American clients. Seen in this context, a very high degree of environmental vigilance is not only understandable, but may well be abnormal by its absence. The overclassification of African-Americans as suffering from a variety of paranoid disorders has been well documented (Pinderhughes, C., 1979), and this destructive practice cannot abate or diminish without such contextual understanding. Minority clients must also be assessed holistically. In addition to the network context mentioned previously, students need to be aware that many people, notably Latinos and Asians, do not split themselves into somatic and mental spheres and that severe psychological stress is often expressed through a variety of physical complaints. Considering the cultural context for behavior, along with the use of universalist assessment tools, is the best safeguard against the over- or under-identification of problems or pathology amongst minority clients.

Skill Objective No. 2

The student will demonstrate culturally appropriate interviewing techniques which consider level of intrusiveness, directness, social distance, formality and forms of address.

The interview is the basic tool of social work practice. Effectiveness of direct or indirect practice is closely related to the worker's ability to communicate and form positive relationships. The communication of respect is especially important for clients who have experienced oppression at the hands of the system, for immigrants not used to the casualness of this country, and for others who may be inherently skeptical about social agencies. A common mistake made by students is presuming a level of familiarity with minority clients before sufficient time has elapsed. Such a mistake can make the subsequent formation of an effective professional relationship virtually impossible. A related error is overly intrusive questioning before an appropriate relationship has been established. The use of appropriate language, both in English and other languages, is an important part of conveying respect. Bilingual practitioners realize that most languages have formal and familiar forms of address. Bicultural individuals know when to use each form. Practitioners who need to work through translators should be familiar with the guidelines for doing so competently (Putsch, 1985). Culturally competent practice requires that workers know when and how to communicate these types of linguistic respect, and have a good sense of timing in presuming familiarity with clients.

Skill Objective No. 3

The student includes in psychosocial assessments an evaluation of the client/family's world view and level of acculturation or biculturality.

Lum (1986, p. 61) reminds us that, "Ethnic reality is a source of cohesion, identity, strength, strain, discordance, and strife," all at the same time. While ethnocultural factors permeate the entire interpersonal helping process, caution should be exercised not to excessively attribute psychosocial phenomena to ethnic culture. Such "cultural reification" (McGoldrick, Pearce & Giordano, 1982) cannot only result in the underidentification of diagnosable problems, but can cause students to overlook other important variables such as social class. The importance of ethnic identification to each client/family needs to be evaluated. The level of acculturation, or more properly, biculturation, of each family member needs to be determined, and the student needs to recognize the bicultural state as the most adaptive for ethnic minorities in the U.S. (DeAnda, 1984).

Skill Objective No. 4

The student is able to conduct a cultural self-assessment and make judgements about how her/his cultural amalgam complements or contrasts with client's cultural modes of expression.

This skill objective is a variant of the previous one. Here the student is asked to do the same type of assessment of acculturation that they do with clients on themselves. Awareness of one's own cultural upbringing provides a basis for appreciation of both similarities and differences with clients. Emphasis should be placed upon attitudes, beliefs, and behavioral styles that resulted from this upbringing. For example, a quiet, self-effacing style may not be effective when working with clients of certain backgrounds, while an aggressive questioning style may be inappropriate for others. Both styles can be attributed, at least in part, to cultural upbringing. The roles of supervisors and field instructors are paramount in developing this competence.

Skill Objective No. 5

The student is able to form professional relationships across cultures with the appropriate level of intimacy and with proper timing.

This objective is an elaboration of the one dealing with cross cultural interviewing skills. In addition to the issues of familiarity, intrusiveness, and timing already mentioned, professionals' relationships across cultures invariably raise issues of self-disclosure for the social work student. Positive professional relationships are most likely to form when the helping person projects qualities of "genuineness, accurate empathy, non-possessive warmth . . . and a capacity to respond flexibly to a range of possible solutions" (Cross et al., 1986, p. 35). A history of mistrust between minority communities and social agencies (Lockart, 1981; Solomon, 1976) can be partially mitigated by a degree of self-disclosure and responsiveness greater than one would use with Euro-American clients. Many African-American clients respond to a "blank screen" approach with greater mistrust. The expertise, in other areas, of the social work student may not be accessible to Latino clients if the student does not allow the client to *conocer* (know) him or her (Manoleas & Carrillo, 1991).

VALUE BASE

The value base is arguably most important in cultural competence. Students must value cultural diversity and respect its worth. They must believe that culture influences and shapes every human interaction.

Value Objective No. 1

The student acknowledges and accepts that cultural differences exist and have an impact on service delivery and utilization.

While almost intuitively obvious, this value objective is at the core of culturally competent practice and therefore bears explication. It speaks to the ever-present variation from the universalist principles of human functioning taught in psychology and social work. It reflects the acknowledgement that culture is a predominant force in shaping behaviors, values, and ways of thinking. To be competent on this objective, the student must understand the harmfulness of a "one size fits all" approach to social work practice.

Value Objective No. 2

The student believes that heterogeneity within cultures is as important as diversity between cultures.

Classification, categorization, and generalization are, of course, necessary in order to communicate and teach, yet culturally competent practice requires that we see each person as a unique individual. To do so, the student must realize, for example, that the category African-American refers to all of the African diaspora in the Americas and that enormous cultural and class differences may exist between people from the Southern United States, the Caribbean, the large cities of the north and west, and many other subcultures of African-Americans. The same is certainly true of the large group of people classified as Hispanics who may be white, black, Indian, mestizo, or any possible racial combination of these. They may have their origins in any of the Spanish speaking countries of North, Central, or South America. Similarly, at last count, the group of Asian-Americans was comprised of over two hundred distinct cultures and almost as many languages.

Value Objective No. 3

The student believes in cultural relativism; that is, there are always different ways of viewing and interpreting phenomena and that non-western and traditional views are as valid as neo-European views.

There are, at times, major differences in basic world view between members of Euro-American and non-European groups. Charles Pinderhughes has observed, for example, that "what most whites perceive as an orderly American social system, most Blacks experience as unresponsive, unremitting, dehumanized, well-rationalized, quiet, courteous, institutionalized violence not unlike colonialism." Many value differences exist between non-Western and Western peoples such as an emphasis on being rather than doing, process over product, and cooperativeness over competitiveness. Such basic differences need to be deeply understood, and their validity acknowledged in order to demonstrate competence on this objective.

Value Objective No. 4

The student recognizes that professional social work values may at times clash with, and at times complement, a client's cultural values. Most expressed social work values, like empowerment, the worth of the individual, and so forth, are consistent with minority values. A notable exception is the emphasis placed on the well-being of the individual as opposed to the group. Real conflict comes with the reality of practice and agency functioning. Budget crises, time constraints, and the missions of many services like mental health or child protective services require that information be gathered, and judgements made in short periods of time. This results in intrusion into family matters, making the private public, and aggressive information gathering, which is inevitably experienced as a culturally alien style on the part of the worker. These activities are usually mandatory parts of student field training and represent agency social control functions, particularly of oppressed groups, which have tended to be overrepresented with ethnic minority groups. An understanding of these dynamics and personal stylistic efforts to attenuate these effects will support competence in this area.

AN ASSESSMENT CONTINUUM

Rather than a pass-no pass approach to assessing performance on these objectives, we should acknowledge the developmental nature of cultural competence. Because these objectives are intended to reflect competence at the end of the M.S.W. curriculum, an evaluation system should be used which allows for partial achievement of objectives, for example, at the end of each of the first three semesters of master's level study. To do this, the author proposes using the six point cultural competence continuum developed by Cross et al. Detailed definitions of each level of competence are beyond the scope of this paper, but the continuum is reproduced here, starting with the least, and progressing to the most competent. They are: culturally destructive, culturally incapable, culturally blind, culturally pre-competent, culturally competent, and culturally proficient.

EVALUATION OF THE MODEL

An obvious criticism of this model of assessing cultural competence has to do with the irony of seeking a degree of objectivity within the subjectivity of difference. The use of such an outcome approach presumes the cultural competence of those who would be evaluating students such as classroom faculty, field faculty, supervisors, consultants, and others. For such an approach to begin to be effective, there would need to be uniform support and buy-in throughout the social work education system, that is to say, that cultural diversity be a core value of all involved, and be held in as high esteem as the model suggests. If this were to happen, much training would be needed for everyone, especially for the evaluation of skills.

Classroom based knowledge content needs to be "mainstreamed" into all courses in addition to special ethnic and sexual minority focused coursework, not just "ghettoized" within the latter. In this sense, teachers of all "universal" principles in methods, policy, and research courses need to raise questions about cultural exceptions to the principles they are teaching. Even the most empirical of our colleagues, those who seek approaches "that work," will simultaneously train students to always ask, "For whom?" All classroom and field teachers need to consult with colleagues who have specialty expertise regarding bibliography and pedagogical methods for teaching material that may be sensitive to deal with. The proposed outcome evaluation needs to be ongoing, and should be a part of self-assessment for faculty and for evaluating curriculum. Some of these objectives are applicable as outcomes for policy courses, some for research, some for methods and/or field.

CONCLUSION

This paper has been a modest attempt to specify culturally competent outcomes for M.S.W. students. It represents a synthesis of the work of many prominent thinkers in the area of cross-cultural practice, and this acknowledgement cannot be overemphasized. A recently revised projection by the U.S. Census Bureau indicates that by the year 2050, people previously aggregated as white, that is to say Euro-Americans, will comprise less than 50% of the nation's population. Stated in another way, no single ethnic group will constitute a majority of the population by the middle of the next century, or, if you will, we will all be minorities. Commitment to training culturally competent social workers needs to be the highest priority for our profession.

REFERENCES

Atkinson, D.R., Furlong, M.J., and Poston, W.C. (1986) Afro-American Preferences for Counselor Characteristics. *Journal of Counseling Psychology.* 33, 326-330.

Atkinson, D.R., Poston, W.C., Furlong, M.J., and Mercado, P. (1989) Ethnic Group Preferences for Counselor Characteristics. *Journal of Counseling Psychology.* 36, 68-72.

Attneave, C. (1969) Therapy in Tribal Settings and Urban Network Utilization. *Family Process*. 8, 192-210.

Buhrke, R. (1989) Incorporating Lesbian and Gay Issues into Counselor Training: A Resource Guide. *Journal of Counseling and Development*. Sept.-Oct., 77-80.

Burgest, D.R. (1985) *Social Casework Intervention with People of Color*. Lanham, MD.: University Press of America.

Chan, C. (1989) Issues of Identity Development Among Asian American Lesbians and Gay Men. *Journal of Counseling and Development*. Sept.-Oct., 16-20.

Chau, K. (1990) A Model for Teaching Cross-Cultural Practice in Social Work. *Journal of Social Work Education*. 26(2).

Chin, J.L. (1983) Diagnostic Considerations in Working with Asian Americans. *American Journal of Orthopsychiatry*. 53(1).

Cross, T., Bazron, B., Dennis, K., and Isaacs, M. (1989) *Towards a Culturally Competent System of Care*. Washington, D.C. CASSP Technical Assistance Center.

Davis, L.E. (1984) *Ethnicity in Social Groupwork Practice*. New York: The Haworth Press, Inc.

DeAnda, D. (1984) Bicultural Socialization: Factors Affecting the Minority Experience. *Social Work*. 29(2).

Devore, W. and Schlesinger, E.G. (1987) *Ethnic Sensitive Social Work Practice*. (2nd edition). Columbus: Merrill Publishing Co.

Dieppa, I. (1984) Trends in Social Work Education for Minorities. In: White, B. (ed.) *Color in a White Society*. Silver Spring, MD.: NASW.

Edwards, E.D. and Edwards, M.E. (1984) Groupwork Practice with American Indians. *Social Work with Groups*. 7(3).

Gallegos, J.S. (1982) Planning and Administering Services for Minority Groups. In *Handbook on Mental Health Administration: The Middle Managers Perspective*. San Francisco: Jossey-Bass.

Gibbs, J. and Huang, L. (eds.) (1990) *Children of Color: Psychological Interventions with Minority Youth*. San Francisco: Jossey-Bass.

Gutierrez, L., Ortega, R., and Suarez, Z. (1990) Self Help and the Latino Community. In: Powell, T. *Working with Self Help*. Silver Spring, MD.: NASW.

Haynes, A. and Singh, R. (1992) Ethnic Sensitive Social Work Practice: An Integrated, Ecological, and Psychodynamic Approach. *Journal of Multicultural Social Work*. Vol. 2 (2), 43-53.

Jacobs, C. and Bowles, D.D. (eds.) (1988) *Ethnicity and Race: Critical Concepts in Social Work*. Silver Spring, MD.: N.A.S.W.

Jenkins, S. (1981) *The Ethnic Dilemma in Social Services*. New York: The Free Press.

LaFromboise, T.D. (1988) American Indian Mental Health Policy. *American Psychologist*. No. 43, 365-374.

LaFromboise, T., Trimble, J., and Mohatt, G. (1990) Counseling Intervention and American Indian Tradition: An Integrative Approach. *The Counseling Psychologist*. 18(4).

Latting, J. (1990) Identifying the "isms": Enabling Social Work Students to Confront their Biases. *Journal of Social Work Education*. 26(1).
Lefley, H. (1990) Culture and Chronic Mental Illness. *Hospital and Community Psychiatry*. 41(3).
Lewis, E. (1988) Role Strengths and Strains of African American Mothers. *Journal of Primary Prevention*. 9(1&2).
Lieberson, S. (1985) Unhyphenated Whites in the United States. In Alba, R. (ed.) *Ethnicity and Race in the U.S.A.: Toward the Twenty-First Century*. London: Routledge & Kegan Paul.
Lockart, B. (1981) Historic Distrust and the Counseling of American Indians and Alaska Natives. *White Cloud Journal*. 2(3).
Lum, D. (1986) *Social Work Practice and People of Color*. Monterey, Calif.: Brooks/Cole.
Lynch, E.W. and Stein, R.C. (1987) Parent Participation by Ethnicity: A Comparison of Hispanic, Black, and Anglo Families. *Exceptional Children*. 54(2).
Manns, W. (1981) Support Systems of Significant Others in Black Families. In: McAdoo, H. (ed.) *Black Families*. Beverly Hills: Sage.
Manoleas, P. and Carrillo, E. (1991) A Culturally Syntonic Approach to the Field Education of Latino Students. *Journal of Social Work Education*. 27(2).
McGoldrick, M., Pearce, J., and Giordano, J. (1982) *Ethnicity and Family Therapy*. New York: Guilford.
Murillo, N. (1978) The Mexican American Family. In: *Hispanic Culture and Health Care: Fact, Fiction, Folklore*. St. Louis: C.V. Moseby.
Nakanishi, M. and Rittner, B. (1992) The Inclusionary Cultural Model. *Journal of Social Work Education*. 28(1).
Newman, B. (1989) Including Curriculum Content on Lesbian and Gay Issues. *Journal of Social Work Education*. 25(3).
Norton, D. (1983) Black Family Life Patterns: The Development of Self and Cognitive Development of Black Children. In: Powell, G.J. (ed.) *The Psychosocial Development of Minority Group Children*. New York: Brunner/Mazel.
Pinderhughes, C. (1973) Racism and Psychotherapy. In: Willie, C., Kramer, B., and Brown, B. (eds.) *Racism and Mental Health*. Pittsburgh: University of Pittsburgh Press.
Pinderhughes, E. (1979) Teaching Empathy in Cross Cultural Social Work. *Social Work*. July, 1979.
Putsch, R.W. (1985) Cross-Cultural Communication: The Special Case of Interpreters in Health Care. *JAMA*. 254(23).
Solomon, B.B. (1976) *Black Empowerment: Social Work in Oppressed Communities*. New York: Columbia University Press.
Staples, R. (1976) *Introduction to Black Sociology*. New York: McGraw Hill.
Sue, D.W. (1981) *Counseling the Culturally Different*. New York: Wiley and Sons.
Weibel-Orlando, J. (1981) Indian Alcohol Treatment Programs as Flawed Rites of Passage. *Medical Anthropology Quarterly*. 15(3).
Yu, C.L. (1984) Acculturation and Stress Within Chinese American Families. *Journal of Comparative Family Studies*. 15(1).

Racism: Its Implications for the Education of Minority Social Work Students

John F. Longres
Gary B. Seltzer

SUMMARY. The problem of attracting minority group students in social work is but one aspect of the larger social problem of racism. This paper therefore defines racism, its influence on the social and psychological processes associated with career identification and selection, and its influence on interpersonal relationships. As a way of illustrating the effects of racism, case studies describing common problems experienced by minority students who decide to enter social work programs are presented. The paper closes with a set of broad recommendations that should enable social work educators to retain minority group students.

INTRODUCTION

The purpose of this paper is to examine how racism affects the recruitment and retention of professionals to the field of Social Work. The problem of attracting minority group students is only one aspect of the larger

---

John F. Longres, PhD, is Professor, School of Social Work, University of Wisconsin, Madison, and Gary B. Seltzer, PhD, is Associate Professor, School of Social Work and Waisman Center, University of Wisconsin, Madison, WI.

[Haworth co-indexing entry note]: "Racism: Its Implications for the Education of Minority Social Work Students." Longres, John F., and Gary B. Seltzer. Co-published simultaneously in *Journal of Multicultural Social Work* (The Haworth Press, Inc.) Vol. 3, No. 1, 1994, pp. 59-75; and: *School Social Workers in the Multicultural Environment: New Roles, Responsibilities, and Educational Enrichment* (ed: Paul R. Keys) The Haworth Press, Inc., 1994, pp. 59-75. Multiple copies of this article/chapter may be purchased from The Haworth Document Delivery Center [1-800-3-HAWORTH; 9:00 a.m. - 5:00 p.m. (EST)].

social problem of racism; therefore, in this paper we first define racism and then examine the social and psychological processes which are associated with career identification and selection. We close with vignettes that describe the impact that racism has on the retention of minority group students in schools of social work. By exploring the underpinnings of racism and their effects on minority group students in social work, we hope to encourage reflection on the connection between the public issue of racism and the interpersonal aspects of retaining minority students. McClain (1990) underscores this point well, noting that "the successful implementation of programs to retain minority students on campus requires that both faculty and students have an understanding of the influences of their own acculturation on the interactions that occur within the classroom and within the social environment of the university."

There is little doubt that social work is in need of more racial and ethnic minority group professionals. Recent data show that the number entering the profession has been, at best, holding steady. For instance, data on African-American student enrollment (Table 1) in masters degree Social Work programs show that a rise in full time enrollment between 1969 and 1973 was followed by a slow decline from 12.1% in 1975 to 7.6% in 1987. Part-time African-American enrollment peaked around 1979 but has remained steady at around 9.25 percent since that time. The percent of full-time other (Asian, Native American, and Hispanic) minority group students has also held steady at around 6.5 percent since 1971.

The stasis in the pool of minority group persons who enter social work raises serious questions about the ability of social services to meet the needs of racially and ethnically diverse client populations. The position taken here is that the difficulty in attracting more minority group members to the field is related, in part, to racism.

DEFINITION OF RACISM

Racism operates at two levels. At the institutional level, racism refers to laws, policies, norms, and mores which give advantage to racially valued groups and disadvantage to others. It is a form of prejudice and discrimination that is not reducible to the single action of an individual but rather to processes, policies and procedures of formal and informal social systems. At the individual level, racism refers to those beliefs, feelings, behavioral intentions and behaviors which denigrate individuals on the basis of their group membership. While these generalities hold, the past twenty-five years have produced social and political changes which have

TABLE I. Masters Enrollment in Accredited U.S. Social Work Programs (1)

YEAR	TOTAL		BLACK ENROLLMENT				WHITE ENROLLMENT				OTHER ENROLLMENT (2)			
	FT	PT	Full Time		Part Time		Full Time		Part Time		Full Time		Part Time	
			#	%	#	%	#	%	#	%	#	%	#	%
1989				0		0		0		0		0		0
1988	16,239	9,024	1,429	8.8	875	9.7	13,284	81.8	7,246	80.3	1,169	7.2	758	8.4
1987	15,241	8,044	1,158	7.6	724	9.0	12,132	79.6	6,620	82.3	975	6.4	410	5.1
1986(3)	N/A	N/A	N/A	N/A	N/A	N/A	N/A	N/A	N/A	N/A	N/A	N/A	N/A	N/A
1985	14,055	7,944	1,138	8.1	755	9.5	11,652	82.9	6,768	85.2	871	6.2	302	3.8
1984	14,275	7,294	1,242	8.7	591	8.1	11,734	82.2	5,099	69.9	885	6.2	306	4.2
1983	14,265	7,225	1,255	8.8	657	9.1	11,555	81.0	6,127	84.8	899	6.3	246	3.4
1982	15,131	6,174	1,437	9.5	537	8.7	12,226	80.8	5,205	84.3	984	6.5	222	3.6
1981	16,552	5,761	1,473	8.9	536	9.3	13,424	81.1	4,897	85.0	1,142	6.9	219	3.8
1980	17,122	5,274	1,678	9.8	501	9.5	13,886	81.1	4,504	85.4	1,130	6.6	195	3.7
1979	17,397	942	1,722	9.9	103	10.9	14,039	80.7	798	84.7	1,148	6.6	29	3.1
1978	17,672	4,333	1,767	10.0	485	11.2	14,367	81.3	3,622	83.6	1,184	6.7	160	3.7
1977	17,533	3,912	1,806	10.3	391	10.0	14,237	81.2	3,278	83.8	1,157	6.6	176	4.5
1976	16,869	3,239	1,856	11.0	327	10.1	13,588	80.5	2,740	84.6	1,063	6.3	113	3.5
1975	16,676	3,203	2,026	12.1	298	9.3	13,261	79.5	2,712	84.7	1,053	6.3	114	3.6
1974(4)	16,590	2,438	2,097	12.6	224	9.2	13,049	78.7	2,103	86.3	1,087	6.6	68	2.8
1973	16,099	2,277	2,412	15.0			12,313	76.5			1,034	6.4		
1972	15,031	1,720	2,352	15.6			11,356	75.6			969	6.4		
1971	13,990	1,654	2,116	15.1			11,157	79.7			880	6.3		
1970	12,880	2,176	1,847	14.3			9,841	76.4			735	5.7		
1969	11,907	2,236	1,495	12.6			9,603	80.7			576	4.8		

COMMENTS:

1. Source: Statistics For Social Work Education in the United States (Wash DC: Council on Social Work Education, 1969-1989).
2. "OTHER ENROLLMENT" includes Asian American, Chicano, Native American, and Puerto Rican masters students.
3. 1986 edition not published.
4. 1974 total enrollment is short by 14 schools which did not report ethnicity for first year F.T. masters students and 2 schools which did not report ethnicity for second year F.T. masters students.

altered the way that racism, at both individual and institutional levels, is presently exhibited in society.

In the past, individual racism was reflected in the belief that African-American and other people of color were innately inferior. Recent evidence, however, suggests that most white Americans no longer hold such beliefs. Between 1940 and 1980, most Americans have come to accept the "principle of non-discrimination"; that is, the belief in equal opportunities to employment, housing, schools, public accommodations, social activities and marital partners (Schuman, Steele & Bobo, 1986). By 1980, only a minority of Americans could be classified as overtly racist. Yet, it would be incorrect to assume that individual racism is no longer a significant problem.

In the first place, the number of people believing in the principle of non-discrimination does not appear to have increased since 1980 (Schuman, Steeh & Bobo, 1986). Secondly, what might be referred to as symbolic racism (McConahay & Hough, 1976) still prevails. This is the belief that people of color have a number of negative learned qualities (criminality, dependence, laziness, lack of concern for education, arrogance, sexual promiscuity, or pushiness) that endanger the political, social, and economic order. Another form of symbolic racism suggests that reverse discrimination is taking place by giving undue advantage to people of color through affirmative action and other special programs. The latter form is closely related to what Katz (1976) termed tokenism; the majority group accepts limited social change to assuage guilt and protect a sense of self as egalitarian for as long as significant changes in the social order are precluded. In the past, individual racism was reinforced by government laws and policies that justified discrimination under the guise of "separate but equal."

With the advent of civil rights legislation, discrimination on the basis of ethnic and racial group appears no longer acceptable. Thus, formal legal barriers to education, employment and other opportunities for the most part no longer exist. Yet again, it would be incorrect to believe that institutional racism has disappeared. Institutional racism is still very strong with respect to the norms and mores that govern everyday life. Social norms continue to set up important barriers, especially with regard to African-Americans. Neighborhoods continue to be segregated. In addition, social mores surrounding friendships and intimate relationships still emphasize the importance of racial and ethnic group segregation. White Americans increasingly work and study with people of color, but they continue to live apart from them and do not enter into personal relationships with them. Since information about educational and employment opportunities often comes about through informal friendship processes, residential and social segregation act to inhibit the economic advancement of minorities.

THE VICTIMS OF RACISM

Not only has the face of racism been altered over the past decades, but the groups subject to it have changed as well. Up through the 1960s, racism was directed not only at "people of color" but at immigrants from southern and eastern European nations. For instance, immigration quotas were distributed on the basis of national origin with over 85% of the quotas going to northern and western Europeans. Only about 15% of the quotas went to southern and eastern Europeans, while none were allotted to Africans, Asians, South Americans and Pacific Islanders. In 1966, the "ethnocentric" immigration laws were repealed and since that time the majority of immigrants to the United States have arrived from Asia, the Pacific Islands, and South and Central America. Yet, the new immigrants are quite different from the old. Immigration laws now give special consideration to people with occupational skills considered important to American society. Thus, many among the new immigrants are likely to be educated and with a working knowledge of English. Demographers now find that new immigrants take on average only 15 years to reach economic parity with white native born Americans (Neidert & Farley, 1985).

Since World War II, displaced persons and refugees have increasingly entered the United States through special quotas aimed at helping citizens from socialist or communist regimes resettle in the United States. Cuban Americans and Asian-Americans from Indo-China are the best examples of such refugee groups. Like immigrants, many, though certainly not all, from these groups have been from families with reasonable educational background and occupational skills.

The advent of new immigrants and refugees has created problems for what might be called the "old minorities." In the first place, it is not clear that the term minority, with its connotation of oppressed and powerless group, is applicable to new immigrants and refugees. In the second place, it is not clear that new immigrants and refugees are being discriminated against to the same extent as those African, Native, Mexican and Puerto Rican Americans who have historically been subjugated to racist laws and policies. Certainly, in terms of socioeconomic well-being, the new immigrants and refugees, with some exceptions, do better than the old minorities. For instance, median family income among Cubans is significantly higher than median family income among Puerto Rican and Mexican Americans (U.S. Bureau of the Census, 1985). Finally, there is the feeling that affirmative action programs set up to right past injustices are being used to help new immigrants and refugees leapfrog over the old minorities.

The implications for the employment of students and professionals should be clear. It is not that new immigrants and refugees should not be helped to advance; all groups have the right to economic opportunities. Yet, if the intent is to resolve the problem of racism, special efforts need to be made at bringing in people from the historically disadvantaged groups.

THE LEGACY OF SOCIAL DARWINISM

The decision to become a health care professional is made within a social and developmental context. Childhood experiences, especially those in schools, set the stage. It is in schools that children begin to get a sense of their abilities, interests and above all their competence, or what Erik Erikson (1950) has referred to as "industry." In a racist society, educational opportunity, that is opportunity to experience competence, is inequitably distributed.

The effects of Social Darwinism and the Eugenics movement are still seen in the school systems today. Social Darwinism, a questionable translation of the ideas of Darwin's theory of evolution, asserted that the support of societal misfits threatened the natural order of a productive, healthy society. The idea behind the eugenic (wellborn) movement was a simple one; to create a better breed of people, people with traits that were believed desirable (Baumeister, 1970). These philosophies encourage people to believe in the idea of inferior races, people for whom no amount of social intervention was worth providing.

While these ideas are no longer promoted, they have left a legacy on our public schools. As did the eugenicists, we continue to use IQ tests as an "objective" strategy for labeling students as inferior and tracking them in programs more geared to warehousing than ensuring competence. Guthrie (1976) and Williams (1974) have argued that IQ tests are used to reinforce ideas that intelligence is a fixed, genetically inherited trait that cannot be altered. These distortions are associated with the fact that African-American children are three times as likely to be labeled as having mental retardation, are twice as likely to be suspended from school, and are twice as likely to drop out of high school before the twelfth grade as compared to white children (Denton, 1981). Similarly, Putka (1990) reports that African-Americans and Hispanics were disproportionately found in classes for "slow learners" even when they attended integrated schools. Although the prohibition of testing and tracking will not assure the academic and social achievement of minority children (MacMillan & Meyers,

1980), schools need to put greater emphasis on promoting competence than sorting out those presumed to be inferior.

RACISM AND CAREERS

Although experiences in schools are of great significance, the formation of a sense of competence, and therefore a sense that one is capable of entering a profession, must also be promoted by family and communities. From a social learning point of view, the availability of a range of models, translators and mediators, along with receipt of corrective feedback, is essential to the healthy socialization of minority group children (De Anda, 1984).

According to Chestang (1976), minority families and communities can serve as nurturant environments to protect self-esteem against the hostility from the larger society. With this in mind, people from minority communities will be the first and, perhaps, major influence in shaping career goals. Two types of influences can be distinguished. De Anda (1984) uses the term "translators" to refer to those people from the minority community who are able to share experiences, provide information, and facilitate understanding about social work and the means for becoming a social worker. "Models," on the other hand, are those minority group members who are professional social workers and whose behaviors can be directly emulated. Minority youth are more likely to consider a career as a social worker when both these types of positive influence are available.

It should not be assumed that identity formation entirely takes place within the context of family and community. Members of minority groups come into contact with the larger society through schools, clubs, religious affiliations and social services. The nature of these contacts will also be important. De Anda (1984) refers to "mediators" to describe people from the majority community who can provide concrete information and guide minority individuals into a profession. Mediators are often teachers, counselors, or social workers. Without whites demonstrating an interest in the career choices of minorities, minority group members are less likely to enter a profession they believe may not be open to them.

Translators, models, and mediators provide the more general learning context of professional identity. Behavior, that is, following through and becoming successful in achieving a professional identity, will depend on a series of trial and error experiences during which the kind of corrective feedback provided to the adolescent or young adult will play an important role. Corrective feedback serves to set and clarify expectations, and help the individual view him/herself as talented. It therefore provides the reinforcement necessary to continue in the formation of a professional identity. To the extent that feedback is given in a negative manner or that negative overwhelms positive feedback, it is unlikely that an identity as a social worker will be achieved.

Unfortunately, though, racism can shape the socialization experience so that a mediator and minority group member may never have a chance to become interpersonally involved. As noted earlier, in a racially segregated society the likelihood that minority youth will come in contact with whites who may serve as mediators is diminished. The most likely occasion for this to happen is within the context of formal roles, like that of student and advisor. Similarly, to the extent that minorities live in class-segregated communities, in poor rural areas, or in inner-city ghettos where professional and educated minority people are less likely to live, the chances that they will even come into contact with translators and models are reduced. The work of William J. Wilson (1985) would suggest that this is precisely what is occurring among underclass blacks today. He maintains that with the advent of programs to provide economic opportunity, such as Affirmative Action, there has been an increasing exodus of middle class blacks from inner city ghettoes, leaving behind an entrenched underclass. If this is the case, only special outreach efforts by committed minority and majority individuals will assure that opportunities become available for the widest number of minority youth.

RACISM AND INTERPERSONAL RELATIONS

As just described, institutional racism forms the context for understanding issues in attracting minorities to social work. It also forms the context for understanding problems in communication between majority and minority students, and between majority faculty and minority students.

Two interrelated problems in communication may be identified. The first has to do with the implications of cultural differences, differences in the beliefs and values held by people as a function of their ethnic heritage. The second has to do with the implications of status differences, differences in power and authority as a function of ethnic heritage.

As individuals are socialized, they develop a way of thinking, feeling and behaving that is unique to their particular subculture. Sometimes these differences are referred to as a world view, a cognitive map, a lifestyle, or simply as a cultural difference. Cultural differences are likely to be apparent as minority and majority come together in the helping process (e.g., in the process of resolving academic or professional issues). Majority and minority group members are likely to "talk past" each other because each will operate from a culturally-based set of assumptions about how a problem is to be identified, understood, and resolved (Greene, 1982). Robert Savard (1968), describing differences between Navajos and Anglos, gives an example of how cultural differences can get in the way of educational advancement. He posits that both believe in the ethic of hard work but the meaning of hard work differs significantly in both groups, especially as applied within an educational setting. For Anglos, educational hard work means "turning out a number of papers while carrying on regular class work, meeting deadlines, [and] not appearing harried. . . ." Anglos also have a set of explanations to support these behaviors and these are associated with the Protestant ethic "which associates hard work with salvation and assuagement of guilt" (p. 50). The Navajo, on the other hand, although they value industriousness, place a great emphasis on harmony and moderation and abhor excesses that provoke imbalance. To get ahead, that is, to work hard in order to accumulate a great amount of material goods or achieve high status, is fraught with danger and fear of group reprisal.

Problems in communication also arise from differences in social status. The United States is a racially stratified society in which whites have more relative power and authority compared to people of color. This, of course, is implicit in the meaning of racism. What is often not recognized is that differences in status create tensions which operate in those interpersonal situations when minority and majority come together. Archibald (1978) notes that people of different social status avoid each other since coming together is experienced as a threatening situation. When they must come together, as in educational and professional settings, Archibald argues that they will relate on formal terms and try to manipulate each other for their own advantage. He also suggests that a feeling of hostility will pervade the interaction although it may not be expressed openly.

Miller (1976) in a similar way describes the "dishonest communications" between dominates and subordinates (her terms for those in power versus those in minority status). She argues that this dishonest communication also affects each group's ability to understand itself. Subordinates know much more about the dominants than vice versa . . . they have to. However, the consequence for them is that they often know more about dominants than they do about themselves. Furthermore, she notes that an even more problematic effect is that too often, "subordinates absorb a large part of the untruths created by dominants; . . . this internalization of dominant beliefs is more likely to occur if there are few alternative concepts on hand" (p. 406). Some of the case study material that follows illustrates Miller's concern that minority group members internalize institutionally racist concepts into their sense of competence.

CASE STUDIES ON RACISM AND PROFESSIONAL EDUCATION

The effects of racism on social work students are reflected in a number of concrete experiences. These include poor educational preparation, economic hardship, social isolation, negative labeling, and problems relating with faculty. Each of these conditions is related to our society's maintenance of institutional racism. Although these problems are often interrelated, for heuristic purposes we will present case studies that illustrate each of these problems separately.

We are presenting these case studies in order to conclude this paper with experiential material that illustrates situations that limit the chances that students who are from minority groups will advance to careers in social work. Each case study illustrates how the types of concrete experiences of institutional racism noted above impact on a potential professional's self-perception. We feel that by providing case examples, social work educators can better confront this type of racism and thereby increase the likelihood that students from minority groups will be recruited and retained. In all case studies the names of the people involved have been changed to protect their identity.

Poor Educational Preparation

Although minorities are increasingly prepared to enter advanced educational programs, it is still the case that because of inadequate educational opportunities earlier in life, many African, Native and Hispanic American students may find themselves at a disadvantage when competing with their white counterparts. It is not surprising that they are often overwhelmed by academic expectations and have to work long and hard to do well. Social work programs should be prepared to offer non-stigmatizing educational assistance.

> Carol was a social work student who had attended a predominantly African-American elementary and high school in a mid-western city that itself was overwhelmingly African-American. During these years she had always been a model student, achieving close to a straight A grade point average. Even with that background, she found herself deficient when she entered a predominantly white university.

> She continued to do reasonably well but she acknowledged that she had to work very hard just to keep up with the academic expectations. She was always a bit disappointed in her inability to regularly achieve A's, especially considering the long hours she spent on her assignments and papers. She found it difficult to talk openly about this matter and did not want to use the special tutorial programs available to her at the university for fear of being labeled inadequate. To the outside observer, Carol appeared to be a successful student. Unfortunately, she didn't meet her own expectations and felt less competent than many of her peers. Although her internalized lack of accomplishments had root in earlier educational experiences over which she had little control, she assumed her difficulties to be intrapersonal. Because of the support of her family and her ability to form meaningful relationships with peers and faculty, she was able to share her anxieties about working "double time" learning new material which should have been taught before entering the university.

Economic Hardship

Minority students are likely to come from lower socioeconomic backgrounds. Often they will be among the first in their family to complete college or go on to an advanced degree. Financial difficulties can, therefore, be expected. However, even minorities from middle-class families are not likely to be on an economic par with their white counterparts. Landry (1987) points out that the average income of African-American middle-class men continues to be significantly below the average income of white middle-class men. In addition, he notes that African-American middle-class families are more dependent on two incomes, have less accumulated wealth, and are more dependent on credit than are white middle-class families.

The problem is no less acute for other ethnic and racial groups including minority group members who are also refugees:

> Tran was an undergraduate student in social work. He arrived as an unaccompanied adolescent refugee from Viet Nam and did very well in high school in spite of his limited knowledge of English. Throughout his education, it was necessary for him to hold part time jobs not only to support himself but to help his siblings come to the United States and help his parents survive in Viet Nam. He was very attached to his parents and wrote to them often, sending money whenever he could. He hoped that by completing his undergraduate and graduate studies he would be able to get a professional position

and truly be able to support his family, an intent that is in keeping with his cultural values. In spite of future intention to support his family, he constantly felt the present pressure to help his family financially. This pressure was compounded by the guilt that he had been able to leave while most of his family could not. Their letters to him assumed that life in the United States was financially easy, as if the "streets were lined with gold." Their letters always requested that he send more money. At one point, he received a letter from a friend informing him that his brother had drowned trying to reach Hong Kong. The friend told how he had tried to save his brother but was unable to. The friend also indicated that his own situation back in Viet Nam was difficult and requested that Tran send him money to help him out. Tran was in turmoil. One part of him felt that as a good son and friend he should leave school and take any job he could. Another part of him kept saying that if he didn't finish college his ability to help them in the long run would suffer. Although he received almost no financial assistance to help him through school, and no financial assistance to help him resettle his family, he did remain in school but only by putting aside his own basic needs.

Social Isolation

For a number of reasons, minority group students often find themselves socially isolated. In addition to economic hardship and the need to put extra effort into studying, racist social norms around dating, friendship networks, and information sharing contribute to isolation, especially in schools where minorities are disproportionately underrepresented. In many respects the isolation takes place in spite of the best intentions of white and minority group students. Not being used to social interaction, they often meet each other at a superficial level and remain more acquaintance than friend. Often minority group students stoically confront their isolation by assuring themselves that they have come to work, not to be frivolous. They are likely to treat the educational experience as a form of necessary exile from friends and family. Yet the isolation can work against the very success they so much desire.

Yolanda, a Puerto Rican student, was taking a large introduction to social work course. She didn't do as well as she had hoped on the midterm exam and came to speak with the instructor. The instructor asked if she had participated in any of the study groups the students had organized. She said no, no one had asked her. The professor on his own checked out whether any of the other minority group students in the class had participated, only to find out that none of them had. He opened the issue up to discussion by asking his class to think about friendship norms, how they were affected by race and ethnicity, and what they needed to do if they were to make friends across culture. By the final exam it was clear that the minority group students had been integrated into the study groups.

Unintended Consequences of Affirmative Action

Affirmative action has had an important impact on professional education because it has given opportunities to those who would not otherwise have had them. Yet affirmative action, as many well-intentioned reforms, has been a two-edged sword. On the one hand it opens opportunities; on the other it causes a backlash of resentment, negative labeling, and attitudes described early as symbolic racism. Whites often believe they experience reverse discrimination, complain that minorities are pushed ahead even when not qualified, or make deprecating remarks about more relaxed expectations for minorities. These resentments are confronted by minority group students in their contact with white students, faculty, professionals and staff. Under these circumstances, race may become an all-consuming experience. Minority group members can't get away from proving their worth and avoid being used as a symbol of the good will of whites (Willie, 1978).

> David was a Mexican American first year doctoral student in social work who had maintained a 4.0 grade point average throughout his academic career. He was proud of his heritage but was against the idea that he should be treated with special consideration because of it. With a great deal of hesitation he applied for financial assistance through a program aimed at recruiting and retaining minority students. When he received the award he became very troubled. He was very concerned that people would no longer treat him like everyone else and that he would become engulfed in the role of "minority person." His fears were heightened when, on the very day the award was announced, a faculty member who had previously appeared indifferent, congratulated him and added, "I didn't realize you were a minority." David was very concerned that all his efforts to maintain an excellent record would be forgotten. He was afraid that accepting the award would indicate that he only succeeded, not because he was good, but because he was from a minority group.

Difficulties with Faculty and Other Instructors

Although relationships between minority students and majority instructors are often mutually rewarding, tension and strain are not unusual. The tensions may never be expressed openly since, as discussed above, the normal tendency is for people in different social positions to avoid each other, treat each other impersonally, or manipulate each other. Unrewarding relationships may often be experienced only as a strange feeling that something is not right. The tensions may arise from differences in culturally based assumptions and expectations where instructor and student simply talk past each other. They may also arise from the fact that the white instructor and minority group student are playing out in microcosm the conflicts in race relations taking place in the larger society.

The following cases are adapted from a description of a scholarship project at the University of Texas (Frizzel, 1968). Although the incidents described herein took place awhile back, they are still very real today.

As part of a scholarship award, field instructors met weekly with minority students on the assumption that regular meetings would facilitate retention in the school. The two students who received the awards, however, failed to complete their education; both dropped out during their first year in an MSW program. Although failure may be attributed to any number of factors, the description of the case reports suggests that the necessary supportive relationship between instructor and student was never achieved. In fact, the cases, written from the instructor's point of view, reveal the inability of the instructors to openly discuss their own feelings with regard to how the minority group students made them feel. Furthermore, both cases subtly suggest that the students failed because they were unable to conform to the expectations of the educational system. No commentary is offered to suggest that the instructors also felt responsible for the failure because, as agents of the university, they were unable to accommodate to the needs of these students.

> Mr. A., aged 24, attended segregated schools through high school. He was from a large, poor family with a disabled father. His score on the Graduate Record Exam was 800, and his grade-point average was 1.6 (using a 3.0 scale). There were 15 conferences between him and the instructor. In the first, he requested help in writing papers and preparing for exams. This was the only kind of help he ever requested. In the beginning, he was unable to participate without searching frantically for his notes. He almost never volunteered information and never volunteered feelings. In the third conference, his extreme anxiety was very apparent. There was no evidence in any

> of the conferences that he was developing self-awareness. Because of his reluctance or inability to share feelings, it was difficult to know how he perceived the instructor or the conferences. Although his manner was friendly, some of his final comments indicated anger and rejection. (p. 118)
>
> Miss B., aged 31, attended integrated schools and held a B.A. in elementary education. Her parents were divorced when she was a child and the mother supported her and her sister with menial work. Her grade-point average was 2.26 and her GRE was 750. She got off to a slow start in her classes and was confused and easily discouraged. In her conferences she discussed feelings easily and used up her time discussing preparation for courses. She later discussed past difficulties with a very rigid principal, her reluctance to participate in class discussion, and her fear of being laughed at because of her accent. She often mentioned that she couldn't believe that she was really at a major university. She easily became tearful and depressed throughout the semester. She voluntarily went to a treatment center but kept only one appointment. In the field she made slow and uneven progress. Although intelligent and hard-working she was too concerned about her own performance, vacillating between recognizing her problems and denying them. (pp. 118-119)

CONCLUSIONS

This paper has focused on how racism can influence the retention of students of color. Because of differential educational opportunities, white Americans are presently more likely to enter social work programs. Past efforts succeeded in increasing the number of minorities in social work education, but for at least a decade the numbers have leveled off or declined slightly. If social work programs are to attract greater numbers of students, they will need to have a greater understanding of the processes that attract students and the stresses students are likely to experience, once in professional education. Toward this end we make the following recommendations:

1. Social workers as citizens and as members of professional associations need to be active in advocating policies that will assure educational equity. As long as opportunities for strong primary and secondary education are controlled by the socioeconomic status of neighborhoods and communities, people of color are not likely to receive a good education and be motivated to seek further education.

2. White social workers must assume responsibility for building personal friendships with a wide array of people of color. Similarly, they must consciously strive to take on the role of mediator-persons who can link potential students to opportunities in social work.

3. School social workers are in one of the primary, if not the primary, social institutions that can foster a sense of career competence or incompetence. As members of a core team that determines issues of tracking and special education, they are called upon to assess students' family backgrounds. In this role, they should also be mediators–persons who can link the students' familial and sociocultural background to culturally sensitive educational opportunities.

4. Professionals of color must consciously strive to serve as models and translators for the youth in their respective communities, both to encourage social work as a career and to explain the details of becoming a social worker.

5. Social work educators and professionals need to be sensitive and introspective when giving corrective feedback and supplying a nurturant environment to students of color as they enter and progress through educational programs. They need to appreciate that their acculturation, particularly their successful academic status, influences the interpersonal dynamics when giving corrective feedback. Nevertheless, such feedback and support is necessary to overcome potential problems of economic hardship, poor educational preparation, social isolation, and negative labeling. Said more positively, feedback and support are needed to assure economic survival, a sense of academic competence, a sense of belonging, and positive self-esteem.

REFERENCES

Archibald, P. W. (1978). *Social psychology as political economy.* Toronto: McGraw Hill.

Baumeister, A. A. (1970). The American residential institution: Its history and character. In A. A. Baumeister & E. C. Butterfield (Eds.), *Residential facilities for the mentally retarded.* Chicago: Aldine.

Chestang, L. (1976). Environmental Influences on social functioning: The Black Experience. In P. Cafferty & L. Chestang (Eds.), *The Diverse Society,* Washington, DC: National Association of Social Workers.

de Anda, D. (1984). Bicultural socialization: Factors affecting the minority experience. *Social Work, 29,* 101-107.

Denton, H. (1981, January 14). Future still bleak for black children, lobbying group's statistics show. *Los Angeles Times,* Part 1A, p. 4.

Erikson, E. (1950). *Childhood and Society* (2nd ed.). New York: W. W. Norton.

Frizzel, F. (1968). A scholarship project at the University of Texas School of Social Work. In *Educationally disadvantaged students in social work education*. New York: Council on Social Work Education.
Greene, J. W. (1982). *Cultural awareness in the Human Services*. Englewood Cliffs, NJ: Prentice Hall.
Guthrie, R. (1976). *Even the rat was white: A historical View of Psychology*. New York: Harper & Row.
Katz, P. (1976). *Towards the elimination of racism*. New York: Pergamon Press.
Landry, B. (1987). *The new black middle class*. Berkeley: University of California Press.
MacMillan, D. L., & Meyers, C. E. (1980). Larry P.: An educational interpretation. *School Psychology Review, 9*, 136-148.
McClain, J. W. (1990). *The recruitment and retention of minority trainees in University Affiliated Programs–African-Americans*. Madison, WI: University of Wisconsin-Madison.
McConahay, J. B., & Hough, J. C. (1976). Symbolic Racism. *Journal of Social Issues, 32*, 23-45.
Miller, J. B. (1976). *Toward a new psychology of women*. Boston: Beacon Press.
Neidert, L. V., & Farley, R. (1985). Assimilation in the United States: An analysis of ethnic and generational differences in status and achievement. *American Sociological Review, 50*, 840-850.
Putka, G. (1990, April 17). Tracking of minority pupils takes toll. *Wall Street Journal*, p. 3.
Savard, R. J. (1968). The basic attitudes of minorities toward opportunity for educational advancement: The American Indian. In *Educationally Disadvantaged Students in Social Work Education* (pp. 49-58). New York: Council on Social Work Education.
Schuman, H., Steeh, C., & Bobo, L. (1986). *Racial Attitudes in America: Trends and Interpretations*. Cambridge, MA: Harvard University Press.
U.S. Bureau of Census. (1982). Current Population Reports, Series p-20, No. 396, *Persons of Spanish Origins in the United States: March 1982*, Washington, DC: United States Government Printing Office.
Williams, R. (1974). The problem of match and mismatch. In L. Miller (Ed.), *The Testing of Black Children*. Englewood Cliffs, NJ: Prentice Hall.
Willie, C. V. (1978). The inclining significance of race. *Society, 15*, 5-25.
Wilson, W. J. (1985). Cycles of deprivation and the underclass debate. *Social Science Review, 59*, 550-559.

The Commonality of Difference: Teaching About Diversity in Field Instruction

Elaine F. Marshack
Carmen Ortiz Hendricks
Muriel Gladstein

SUMMARY. This paper discusses a study undertaken to determine the perceptions of new field instructors about the impact on the teaching/learning relationship of differences between them and their students. The differences and similarities arising in the tutorial relationship often parallel those in practice and provide many "teachable moments" about the significance of diversity for social workers.

In a metropolitan social work program, new field instructors representing a wide range of fields of practice responded to a question asking them to consider the impact on the educational experience of "cultural, ethnic, gender, class, and age characteristics, and the implications of these similarities and/or differences for the teacher/learner relationship." Asking the question succeeded in focussing the attention of field instructors on the significant but often unacknowledged impact of diversity in the educational encounter. A tendency for these field instructors to minimize differences may derive from their efforts to avoid stereotyping or stigmatization.

The paper presents numerous examples of field instructors' perceptions and discusses the potential effect of differences and similar-

---

Elaine F. Marshack, DSW, is Associate Professor and Director of Field Education, Carmen Ortiz Hendricks, MSW, is Lecturer, and Muriel Gladstein, MSW, is Associate Professor, all at Hunter College School of Social Work.

[Haworth co-indexing entry note]: "The Commonality of Difference: Teaching About Diversity in Field Instruction." Marshack, Elaine F., Carmen Ortiz Hendricks, and Muriel Gladstein. Co-published simultaneously in *Journal of Multicultural Social Work* (The Haworth Press, Inc.) Vol. 3, No. 1, 1994, pp. 77-89; and: *School Social Workers in the Multicultural Environment: New Roles, Responsibilities, and Educational Enrichment* (ed: Paul R. Keys) The Haworth Press, Inc., 1994, pp. 77-89. Multiple copies of this article/chapter may be purchased from The Haworth Document Delivery Center [1-800-3-HAWORTH; 9:00 a.m. - 5:00 p.m. (EST)].

ities in age, gender, ethnicity, and sexual orientation on the tutorial relationship. The study findings have implications for field teaching and performance evaluations as well as for social work advocacy around agency policies.

This paper discusses a study undertaken to determine the perceptions of new field instructors about the impact on the teaching/learning relationship of similarities and differences between themselves and their students. From the beginning of field instruction, the student and instructor have one major thing in common, their mutual uniqueness based on a number of factors including age, gender, race, ethnicity, class and sexual orientation. Diversity arising in the tutorial relationship often parallels the diversity found in actual practice. Supervisory discussions about sameness and difference provide many "teachable moments" (Kadushin, 1985) about the significance of diversity for social work practice.

Some interesting results were achieved when a varied group of field instructors were asked to respond in writing to a question about the impact on the educational experience of "cultural, ethnic, gender, class, and age characteristics and the implications of these similarities and/or differences for the teacher/learner relationship." The assumption is that by simply raising the question, the field instructors' awareness of diversity is heightened, and its saliency for field teaching is encouraged and ensured.

An earlier study in the same social work program found that unless specifically asked to do so, few field instructors will identify issues of diversity in their educational assessments of students or explicitly refer to this data in describing a student's learning style (Gladstein and Mailick, 1986). Furthermore, field instructors tend to avoid addressing a student's potential learning needs or interests when these are influenced by issues of individual or interpersonal diversity.

Asking the question did succeed in focussing the attention of field instructors on the significant but often unacknowledged issues of diversity in the educational encounter. A major finding of this study confirms the fact that field instructors do indeed achieve cognitive awareness of diversity factors in the learning situation; however, they tend to give only minimal indications of its integration into field teaching. In other words, differences and similarities are noted, and then set aside with little attention given to them in the ongoing educational experience. This is unfortunate, since the field instructor has a unique opportunity to teach students how to integrate knowledge, skills, and attitudes about age, class, ethnicity, culture, gender and sexual orientation into their learning and helping experiences.

BACKGROUND TO THE STUDY

Teaching about diversity has increasingly become an important and critical focus for social work educators today. Major shifts are taking place in the American population with increasing racial, ethnic, and linguistic diversity gaining importance in all aspects of service delivery. "Today our society is being shaken to the core by a number of complex and devastating problems and challenges, [one of which is] the demand for both differentiation and cohesion in an increasingly diverse society . . . " (Hartman, 1990, p. 44).

The powerful influences of culture, ethnicity, race, class, gender and sexual orientation affect how individuals think, feel, and behave not only in relation to clients, but in supervisory and collegial relationships. Yet few schools provide the kind of in-depth training necessary to assist social workers in acquiring the knowledge and skills essential to working effectively within a diverse society. The social, political, and economic conditions of the American society are clearly shaping the future of social work practice and the learning relationships of field instructors and students. It is also important to understand the troublesome factor of power differentials " . . . not only of the supervisor over the supervisee, but of non-minority over minority in the supervisory relationship and in the social context in which it is implemented" (Solomon, 1982, p. 28). Confronting issues of existing differences and similarities between the field instructor and student can be one of the most important contributions of the field instructor to a student's learning experience.

Historically, culture and values of the social work profession have emphasized the importance of acceptance of and respect for the uniqueness of each individual. "In our efforts to promote the melting pot myth and the notion that all individuals are equal, we tend to perpetuate the notion that to be different is to be deficient or bad" (Moore Hines et al., 1992, p. 323). Practitioners tend to think that recognizing differences is unacceptable because it may lead to generalizations or stereotypes which obscure the individuality of clients or their needs. Thus, differences based on gender, class, race, ethnicity, and sexual orientation have tended to be minimized, making it difficult for social workers to acknowledge feelings of sexism, classism, racism, ethnocentrism, or heterosexism when they occur in practice. A comparable inattentiveness characterizes the field instructors' attitudes and responses to their student supervisees.

Knowing about and dealing with diversity are two different things. Social work classroom education and field instruction tend to focus on information sharing and discussion of readings about the special characteristics which may pertain to clients. Since they cannot learn about all possible differences existing between individuals and groups, field instructors and students are often in a position to decide together what they need to know in order to best serve their client populations.

The comfort, knowledge, and skill required for effective social work practice in a diverse society involves continuous learning over time to become familiar with the populations served. Equally important is the need to develop a sensitivity to practice situations by helping students confront their attitudes, biases, and values; to respect intragroup variation; to be open to idiosyncratic behaviors of individuals and groups; and to be clear about how their own racial, ethnic, gender, class, and sexual orientation influences their practice.

Growing diversity among social work students also poses new issues in field instruction. For example, students of Asian cultures may be more comfortable with didactic teaching, and look for direction and criticism from the field instructor, whereas students of Hispanic cultures may prefer experiential learning and may experience a didactic field instructor as aloof and uncaring (Shen-Ryan and Ortiz Hendricks, 1989).

An organized curriculum on the importance of diversity has begun to emerge within social work education (White, 1984; Lister, 1987; Jacobs and Bowles, 1988; Chau, 1990). In a field unit comprised of Chicano students under the supervision of a Chicana field instructor, students are encouraged to examine and process their own ethnic identities, family history, acculturation, and racism experiences, modeling techniques that students could use in their work with clients (Zuniga, 1987). Progress is being made in the development of multicultural knowledge and skill, including the formulation of ethnic competence models for social work education (Dieppa, 1984; Gallegos, 1984; Ho, 1989, 1991), and proposals for development of ethnic-sensitive field work programs (Gladstein and Mailick, 1986). Some inroads have been made in the inclusion of content on women and sexual orientation in curricula as well. However, the transition from available knowledge to the application of this knowledge in the classroom, field instruction, supervision, and agency-based practice, is still a challenge for the profession. This paper will provide some recommendations for making issues of diversity integral components of field education and of the profession's theory and practice base.

DESIGN AND METHODOLOGY

The large northeast metropolitan area from which this study originates has a highly diverse population reflected not only among clients but also among students and field instructors. This study was carried out within the framework of a required seminar in field instruction for all new field instructors. Representing a wide range of fields of practice, instructors were a heterogeneous group as to age, race, gender, and years of experience. They were situated in agencies which varied in size, problem focus, auspice, and service delivery models. While not representative of North America as a whole, the study sample presents an intense laboratory for the study of intergroup relations.

Leaders of these seminars were generally faculty members involved in other aspects of field education. They played a critical role in the development of the field instructors' teaching and evaluation skills. They also contributed to heightening awareness of diversity as a significant factor in the teaching/learning process, and encouraging field instructors to utilize this rich content throughout the field practicum.

Ten schools of social work in three Mid-Atlantic states have a common requirement that new field instructors participate in a twelve-session Seminar in Field Instruction. Though the time commitment for the seminar may initially feel onerous to many in the seminar groups, the acquisition of knowledge and a developing sense of group support come to be perceived by most members as important contributions to the development of competence in this new role.

A written assignment in mid-first semester required by the subject school is an Educational Assessment and Plan in which a field instructor is asked to identify a student's resources in attributes and present skills, learning tasks to be accomplished, characteristic learning patterns, and the range and nature of educational opportunities in the agencies as a basis for establishing goals and methods of teaching (Lemberger and Marshack, 1990).

In order to heighten field instructors' awareness of the saliency of the educational experience of similarities and differences between them, their student supervisees, and the client populations, an item was inserted into the outline for an educational assessment asking field instructors to identify "cultural, ethnic, gender, class and age characteristics and the implications of similarities and/or differences for the teacher/learner relationship and student/client relationships." The focus of this paper is on the relationship between the field instructor and student. Variables concerning the relationships between students and clients will be addressed at a later time.

A content analysis was made of the responses of 56 field instructors in the 1990-1991 seminar in one school from this Mid-Atlantic area. This nonrepresentative sample of new field instructors was drawn from the membership of four seminar sections, each taught by a different faculty member. No directed preparation was given in the seminars for responding to this item.

FINDINGS

Of the total sample of 56 field instructors, 54 specified their student supervisees' gender and age, and 53 noted the students' race or ethnicity. Family/relationship status was cited for 39 students, and class (most often used to refer to families of origin) for 37. In reference to themselves, 51 field instructors described their race or ethnicity; 42, age; 41, gender; 32, class; and 32, marital/relationship status. The lack of self-identification by some field instructors may be due to the fact that they assumed the data was already known by their seminar leaders. Field instructors also introduced other characteristics which they perceived as contributing to feelings of difference or similarity.

Of the 56 field instructors, 13 did not discuss any implications of this diversity for field teaching. Of the remaining 43, the largest proportion (32) identified similarities in characteristics between themselves and their students which they perceived as facilitating the teaching/learning relationship. These ranged from shared ethnicity, religion, and sexual orientation to political, intellectual, and lifestyle similarities. Some sample responses follow:

> Both (student and field instructor) are Italian and share similar customs and traditions . . .
>
> (Student) was born and raised in Spanish Harlem . . . The field instructor . . . worked 4 1/2 years in Spanish Harlem.
>
> (Student) has begun to realize she comes from an 'alcoholic' family. (Field instructor) too has experience of close family members with severe substance abuse problems.
>
> We share the experience of being minority (i.e., Irish in a Hispanic community and Hispanic in an Italian community.)
>
> Both the student and the field instructor are mature, white, middle class women with adult children who are no longer living home.
>
> (Student) is an Orthodox Jewish middle aged woman whose cultural and ethnic background is quite similar to my own.

Another group of eleven field instructors noted significant differences between themselves and students. These were presented by some as obstacles to be overcome in establishing effective supervisory relationships:

> The teacher-learner relationship has been positive in nature, given cultural, gender and ethnic differences.
>
> Although from very different backgrounds, the relationship between (student) and field instructor appears excellent.
>
> Neither (student nor field instructor) felt that any of the differences in characteristics lessened our working relationship or our personal or professional respect for each other.

A small proportion of these eleven field instructors described concerns about differences between themselves and students with which they had actively struggled:

> My original concerns . . . were founded in personal bias toward upper middle or upper class 'WASPs' as I am Jewish and from a working class family. I was concerned she would not believe I had anything to offer her (but) this has not been true.
>
> An issue that has arisen between student and field instructor is gender. At times it appears that (student) has difficulty taking instruction from a female (which) appears to be a function of his traditional (Asian) history and is a subject that has been identified and continues to be discussed openly.

DISCUSSION

When specifically directed to provide information about themselves and student supervisees, most field instructors in this study provided minimal descriptions of age, race, ethnicity, and gender and then stated that either their teaching relationships were enhanced by shared characteristics (32) or that sound working relationships were achieved *despite* differences (11). Given the power differentiation between field instructors and students, and the previous "studies" cited, is it likely that the field instructor may assume that relationship(s) were achieved *despite* differences, or that the student merely did not challenge difficulties presented in the relationship? This seems to be suggested by McRoy et al. (1986). Jenkins (1981) has suggested that the social work profession seems to have inherited a predilection for accepting differences but not dealing with their consequences. This study suggests that *minimization* rather than acceptance of differences may be a more widespread dynamic in field teaching. The effect may be similar to that suggested by Jenkins–if differences are minimized, their impact on the teaching/learning relationship may not be recognized or dealt with.

"The relationship between field instructor and student is always intense, laden with realistic elements of differential power and authority and fraught with complications of transference or symbolism of past relationships, seldom thoroughly worked through" (Gladstein and Mailick, 1986, p. 47-48). Differences and similarities often trigger such reactions which can impact on the teaching/learning relationship. For example, a young student may respond to an older field instructor with feelings originally experienced toward parents and behave with dependent, rebellious, or other unrealistic responses. A field instructor, in turn, may be inappropriately protective or demanding of a younger student. Older students may have difficulty accepting the authority of younger field instructors, and will anticipate that their knowledge and skills will be devalued in this new student role, or feel undue pressure to demonstrate their competence. Younger field instructors may feel intimidated by the broader life experiences of older students, hold unrealistic expectations for them, or feel uncomfortable in exercising their authority (Marshack, 1991). Similarities in age can lead either participant to view the other as a peer, minimizing the realistic authority and power differentials.

Issues of gender can similarly provoke inappropriate responses in a supervisory relationship. Earlier studies have suggested that same-gender combinations of field instructor and student are the most comfortable (Behling, Curtis and Foster, 1982). Although gender roles are "in a state of tumultuous transition . . . " (Collins, Thomlinson, and Grinnell, 1992, p. 141), field instructors and students may bring stereotyped expectations to each other. Male instructors may expect less from female than male students or assume that women will be good with children or in need of protection. Conversely, female field instructors with male students may feel less certain of their authority and respond in either an overly authoritarian or passive manner.

The issue of sexual orientation has assumed greater importance as gay and lesbian students have increasingly communicated their specific needs to social work educators. While the atmosphere of many social work programs now makes it more comfortable for gay and lesbian students to "come out," it remains difficult to assess the receptivity of individual field instructors and agency staff to such information from a student, since they can reflect the heterosexism and homophobia which exists in the larger society. Gay students often feel isolated and self-protective if unable to acknowledge their sexual orientation, factors which may impede their receptivity to learning. Similarities in sexual orientation also present new opportunities in field instruction as one respondent in this study indicated:

> The field instructor is also gay and has stated such in supervision in response to student's self-disclosure . . .

On the other hand, a student may deprecate the competence of a gay or lesbian field instructor or an instructor may hesitate to assign same-gender clients to a gay student, assuming the student is unable to deal with problems of heterosexual relationships.

Ethnicity and race merit particular attunement in a society in which institutional bias impacts on relationships both within and across majority/minority differences. One study of cross-cultural field instruction found that both field instructors and students overwhelmingly identified more potential problems than benefits in cross-cultural supervision, but reported actual difficulties in a minority of instances (McRoy et al., 1986). Kadushin points out that some supervisors out of sympathy, guilt, fear, or negative prejudice may evaluate minority group workers differently and less confidently than white workers. He further warns that the factor of race should not be ignored nor should it be overemphasized (1985, p. 319). Prominent among potential conflicts when a white field instructor supervises a minority student are issues in trust, knowledge about cultural differences, communication patterns, and differing expectations as indicated in the following example:

> Student is a middle class black man and I am a WASP nearly 20 years his senior . . . I grew up in a small (border) town when segregation was terribly real . . . My being white must make him wary in some measure in not wanting to look anything but competent and fully knowledgeable. I presume I represent authority that so often is white, and he has said he is very sensitive to racial innuendo. That makes me strain somewhat to show a sensitivity and solidarity with him . . . and probably impedes my ability to offer criticism.

Multicultural students may differ from majority field instructors in their communication styles and cognitive, motivational, and value orientations. Even if a field instructor is knowledgeable about cultural content and effects of discrimination for one minority group, it does not mean that this knowledge is transferable to other groups (Solomon, 1982, p. 264). In their ignorance of minority students' specific cultural backgrounds, nonminority field instructors may fail to recognize students' strengths or the significance for them of dealing with white authority figures. Concerns of some non-minority field instructors around being perceived as racist or patronizing may sometimes interfere with their appropriate exercise of authority or directiveness in dealing with educational issues of students (McRoy et al., 1986).

Other issues are suggested for minority field instructors of majority students, who are in a situation in which "positional power may be in contradiction to the usual social arrangements" (McRoy et al., p. 51). It may be difficult for such field instructors to establish their role and authority, and to deal with differences in opinions, backgrounds, and life experiences (McRoy et al., p. 53).

RECOMMENDATIONS

Differences and similarities in personal characteristics often play a critical role in relationships between field instructors and social work students, as well as between students and their clients. This exploratory study suggests that field instructors tend to minimize differences between themselves and their student supervisees, emphasizing instead similarities between them on demographic or ideological bases. While attention to shared characteristics may foster a sense of engagement and identification, minimization of differences may severely limit field teaching attuned to students' strengths, educational needs, and reactions to the learning experience. This minimization may also limit field instructors' abilities to help students deal with the impact of similarity and differences on their practice relationships. Students will not have the opportunity to deal with the anxiety mobilized in interactions with others who are different; to recognize and commit themselves to the changes needed for effective cross-cultural interaction; to learn how cultural identity and issues of power and powerlessness impact on human functioning; nor to identify how their behavior affects service delivery (Pinderhughes, 1989).

Collaboration between school and field faculty to heighten mutual recognition of the saliency of this content is a necessary beginning. Administrators of field education programs have a particular role to play with agency educational coordinators and field instructors in communicating this commitment. Educational liaisons can help field instructors to apply this content in individual instances where they perceive its specific relevance.

This study is concerned with the important relationships of field instructors and student supervisees in a graduate school of social work in an urban environment. Parallels can be made to similar supervisory relationships including undergraduate field practicums in rural and suburban communities, or wherever field practicums are present, are equally intense, and where the opportunity to study and understand intergroup relations exists. Field instructors and students face the challenge of new roles and functions, a vital component of which is confronting sensitive issues of similarity and difference when they impact on the development of a productive educational environment.

As demonstrated in this study, when field instructors' attention is specifically directed to personal characteristics of field instructor, student, and agency clientele, it can stimulate recognition of these variables, but not necessarily of their implications, for the teaching/learning relationship. Some field instructors noted that preparation of educational plans had led to their first raising issues of difference and similarity with students. One white male field instructor discovered that an African-American female student had been reluctant to discuss their racial difference because they did not share the experience of personal and institutional racism.

An excellent forum for introduction of this content is seminars in field instruction or special meetings for new field instructors. The collegial group process can facilitate recognition by field instructors of their biases which may range from fears of stigmatization to racism or homophobia. For example, a field instructor shared the concerns of a gay student struggling with whether to come out in the agency as many students had done in the school. When a seminar group of field instructors was encouraged to consider this issue, they raised many relevant issues including homophobic attitudes of agency staff. They then began to appreciate the difficulty for gay students in gauging when it is appropriate to acknowledge their sexual orientation, and identified ways in which the agency's and field instructor's increased sensitivity to this issue could be helpful to students attempting to make this decision. While the leadership role in these meetings with field instructors is important in raising sensitive issues of similarities and differences, the powerful impact of a group of new field instructors can provide the strong support and encouragement to deal with the dystonic elements of intensive tutorial teaching/learning situations which often parallel the students' experiences with clients.

This paper addresses only a few of the issues of diversity confronting students and field instructors today. The increasing complexities of social work practice include working with male and female clients whose sexual orientation cannot be taken for granted and who are more racially and ethnically diverse than at any other time in social work history. Social workers also have to address the needs of clients with physical disabilities, clients who profess a wide range of religious or spiritual orientations, clients who come from almost any part of the country or the world, and who may be very poor and disenfranchised. New and experienced field instructors need the specialized knowledge, support and encouragement that special field instruction groups can provide.

As field instructors become more sensitive to the impact of differences and similarities on the teaching relationship, they model an approach for students to use in responding to a diverse environment. Further exploration is needed to better understand the complicated causes of the slow progression from the awareness of difference to its translation into teaching and learning for social work.

REFERENCES

Behling, J., Curtis, C., and Foster, S. A. 1982. Impact of sex-role combinations on student performance in field instruction. *Journal of Education for Social Work*, 18(2), 93-97.

Chau, K. 1990. A model for teaching cross-cultural practice in social work. *Journal of Social Work Education*, 26(2), 124-133.

Collins, D., Thomlinson, B., and Grinnel, R. M., Jr. 1992. *The Social Work Practicum: A Student Guide*. Itasca, IL: Peacock.

Dieppa, I. 1984. Trends in social work education for minorities. In B. W. White (Ed.), *Color in a White Society*, Silver Spring, MD: NASW, 10-21.

Gallegos, J. 1984. The ethnic competence model for social work education. In B. W. White (Ed.), *Color in a White Society*, Silver Spring, MD: NASW, 1-9.

Gladstein, M., and Mailick, M. 1986. An affirmative approach to ethnic diversity in field work. *Journal of Social Work Education*, 22(1), 41-49.

Hartman, A. 1990. Education for direct practice. *Families in Society: The Journal of Contemporary Human Services*, 71(1), 44-50.

Hines, P. M., Garcia-Preto, N., McGoldrick, M., Almeida, R., and Weltman, S. 1992. Intergenerational relationships across cultures. *Families in Society*, 73(6), 323-338.

Ho, M. K. 1989. Mainstreaming social work theory and practice with ethnic minorities. *The Americans Among Us: When the Minorities are the Majority.* Conference proceedings by the Center for Cross-Cultural Research and Social Work Practice. Department of Social Work Education, San Francisco State University, 109-122.

Ho, M. K. 1991. Use of ethnic-sensitive inventory (ESI) to enhance practitioner skills with minorities. *Journal of Multicultural Social Work*, 1(1), 57-67.

Jacobs, C., and D. Bowles (Eds.). 1988. *Ethnicity and Race: Critical Concepts in Social Work*. Silver Spring, MD: NASW.

Jenkins, S. 1981. *The Ethnic Dilemma in Social Services*. New York: Free Press.

Kadushin, A. 1985. *Supervision in Social Work*. New York: Columbia University Press.

Lemberger, J., and Marshack, E. 1991. Educational assessment in the field: An opportunity for teacher-learner mutuality. In D. Schneck, B. Grossman, and U.

Glassman (Eds.), *Field Education in Social Work: Contemporary Issues and Trends*, Dubuque, IA: Kendall/Hunt, 187-197.

Lister, L. 1987. Curriculum building in social work education: The example of ethnocultural content. *Journal of Social Work Education*, 23(1), 31-39.

Marshack, E. 1991. The older student: Social work's new majority. In D. Schneck, B. Grossman, and U. Glassman (Eds.), *Field Education in Social Work: Contemporary Issues and Trends*. Dubuque, IA: Kendall/Hunt, 295-300.

McRoy, R., Freeman, E., Logan, S., and Blackmon, B. 1986. Cross-cultural field supervision: Implications for social work education. *Journal of Social Work Education*, 22(1), 50-56.

Pinderhughes, E. 1989. *Understanding Race, Ethnicity, and Power: The Key to Efficacy in Clinical Practice*. New York, NY: Free Press.

Shen Ryan, A., and Ortiz Hendricks, C. 1989. Culture and communication: Supervising the Asian and Hispanic social worker. *Clinical Supervisor*, 7(1), 27-40.

Solomon, B. (Winter 1982-1983). Power: The troublesome factor in cross-cultural supervision. *Smith College School for Social Work Journal*, 10(1), 27-32.

White, B. W. (Ed.). 1984. *Color in a White Society*. Silver Spring, MD: NASW.

Zuniga, M. E. Fall 1987. Mexican-American clinical training: A pilot project. *Journal of Social Work Education*, 23(3), 11-20.

A Rock and a Hard Place: Trying to Provide Culturally-Sensitive Field Experiences in Rural, Homogeneous Communities

Adela Beckerman
Leon Burrell

SUMMARY. This paper discusses the importance of fieldwork in preparing students for practice with clients from diverse cultural backgrounds and the difficulties encountered in rural, culturally homogeneous settings. A survey of undergraduate fieldwork coordinators provided information about how minority content is integrated into field seminars and the fieldwork experience. The findings indicated that a variety of methods are used in the seminar and field experience. A discussion of the limitations of these methods and recommendations for alternative approaches are provided.

The extent to which institutions of higher education assume responsibility for preparing students to live and work in a multicultural society is a

Adela Beckerman, PhD, ACSW, is Program Professor and Coordinator of Practicums, Master's Programs in Child Care, Youth Care and Family Support Studies, Center for the Advancement of Education, Nova University, 3301 College Avenue, Fort Lauderdale, FL 33314. Leon Burrell, PhD, MSW, is Associate Professor/Coordinator, Undergraduate Social Work Program, Department of Social Work, University of Vermont, 499B Waterman Building, Burlington, VT 05401.

[Haworth co-indexing entry note]: "A Rock and a Hard Place: Trying to Provide Culturally-Sensitive Field Experiences in Rural, Homogenous Communities." Beckerman, Adela, and Leon Burrell. Co-published simultaneously in *Journal of Multicultural Social Work* (The Haworth Press, Inc.) Vol. 3, No. 1, 1994, pp. 91-99; and: *School Social Workers in the Multicultural Environment: New Roles, Responsibilities, and Educational Enrichment* (ed: Paul R. Keys) The Haworth Press, Inc., 1994, pp. 91-99. Multiple copies of this article/chapter may be purchased from The Haworth Document Delivery Center [1-800-3-HAWORTH; 9:00 a.m. - 5:00 p.m. (EST)].

topic that is surrounded by heated debate on college campuses today (*Chronicle*, May 1, 1991; Magner, 1991). In light of estimates that about one-third of the population will be non-Caucasian by the turn of the century, academic curricula and campus-based activities are being closely scrutinized to determine how students are being prepared for these demographic changes (Jaschik, 1991).

The importance of preparing students for practice with persons from diverse backgrounds, and the resulting educational demands, are not new to social work education (Crompton, 1974; Sanders, 1975; Proctor & Davis, 1983; Chau, 1990). The activities that social workers have historically immersed themselves in have required practice with persons from varied ethnic, economic, and racial backgrounds. In recognition, the Council on Social Work Education mandates that social work education curricula integrate material which clearly articulates "objectives, outlines, and content incorporating diverse racial, ethnic, and cultural perspectives" (Council on Social Work Education, 1990). The National Association of Social Workers also stresses the need for undergraduate, graduate, and continuing social work programs to "include relevant and meaningful content related to racial and ethnic groups of color" (*NASW News*, January 1980).

While the professional commitment to prepare students for practice with persons from culturally diverse backgrounds has long been present, the approach with which such work is viewed has changed. It was not long ago that many assumed that distinctions between ethnic or racial groups would eventually become minimal, as each group assimilated into the "melting pot" of American society (Sanders, 1975). In recent years, however, with the continuing influx of immigrants into the United States and the declining ratio of Caucasian to non-Caucasians, the pluralist nature of the population has received renewed attention, and the importance of appropriately training social work students has resurfaced. The persistence with which many communities have sustained their distinct cultural values and traditions has interfered with assimilation processes. At the same time, racial discrimination has persisted, limiting assimilation. This is underscored by the persistence of poverty and the absence of adequate health care, growing unemployment, and the number of black males in correctional facilities.

Field education plays a pivotal role in the training of students for practice with clients from racially diverse backgrounds. The field practicum augments coursework by providing opportunities for students to field-test concepts and knowledge, and master necessary practice competencies (Proctor & Davis, 1983). The integration of course content on varied cultural groups with fieldwork provides students with a value, knowledge, and skill base for effective practice with diverse client groups (Schlesinger & DeVore, 1979; Ifill, 1989). While traditional didactic teaching methods such as lectures and assigned readings are necessary, they are insufficient (Chau, 1990). Coursework and fieldwork play complementary roles, with fieldwork providing an arena for students to employ and refine the values, knowledge, and skills examined in courses. Field experiences arouse students' emotions and challenge them to examine their own values and attitudes, while witnessing cultural differences (Fox, 1983). Individually, students are expected to overcome personal biases and insensitivities, and develop an intimate understanding of the impact of institutionalized societal forces on clients.

Many social work programs are located in rural communities with little racial minority representation. In contrast to programs in urban communities where there are vast opportunities for students to provide services to a variety of clients, there is a paucity of such opportunities in rural, relatively homogeneous communities (Souflee & Schmitt, 1974; Benavides, Lynch & Velasquez, 1980). The difficulties the authors faced in developing appropriate field experiences in a rural, homogeneous community prompted an investigation of methods used by social work programs in similar communities to integrate minority content. The main focus of this paper is a discussion of the findings of the study conducted.

METHOD

A pre-tested questionnaire mailed to undergraduate field education coordinators asked for descriptions of the methods used to incorporate content on racial diversity into the field education curriculum. Coordinators in 39 undergraduate social work programs located in rural, culturally homogeneous communities received the questionnaire. Using the 1980 United States Census, the investigators identified communities with traits similar to the community in which their social work program is located. The definitions of rurality used by the Bureau of Census (1981), wherein a population cannot exceed 2,500, and the Office of Management and Budget (1975), which stipulates that the population reside outside the boundaries of a metropolitan district, were expanded for this investigation. Rurality was defined as a geographically isolated area with a population of less than 50,000. The criteria for establishing the homogeneity of a community were that the minority population not exceed two percent and that the community be relatively isolated from heterogeneous urban and suburban areas.

A cover letter explained the purpose of the study, assured confidentiality, and requested a timely response. After a follow-up telephone call urging the coordinators to complete and return the survey, 29 coordinators responded, reflecting a response rate of 74 percent.

RESULTS

The fieldwork coordinators were asked about the sites used for field placements and revealed a broad range of traditional sites. Ninety-three percent of the coordinators reported using hospitals and health facilities, while 82% place students in mental health and family counseling agencies, 85% in schools and social service agencies, and 74% in correctional facilities. More than one-half (59%) of the coordinators reported placing students in nursing homes and family planning agencies and a few (18%) said they used agencies such as women's shelters, public housing, programs for migrant children, and substance abuse agencies.

The participants were asked about non-agency based field sites. Slightly over one-third (37%) indicated that students were provided fieldwork opportunities with homeless committees, campus-based volunteer service programs, Native American groups, and internship programs in Washington, D.C.

The coordinators were also asked whether the field sites used provide services to clients from racially diverse backgrounds. Eighty-two percent of the coordinators reported that the sites used provided services to African-Americans while 67% said that agencies provided services to Hispanic-American clients and 67% to Asian-Americans. In addition, 41% revealed placements in agencies serving Native-Americans. About one-fourth of the agencies served other client groups, such as Portuguese, Franco-Americans, Jamaican, and Haitian.

In an attempt to determine whether fieldwork students received direct practice experience, the coordinators were asked about the proportion of students who work with clients from diverse backgrounds. Forty-four percent indicated that fewer than half of the students had practice experience with clients from racially diverse backgrounds. Thus, while the field sites used served a somewhat diverse client population, the volume of services in a rural community appears to be insufficient to provide all fieldwork students with direct practice experience.

Field Seminar

All of the respondents reported that students took a field seminar or course in which a variety of techniques integrated multi-cultural content.

Approximately three-fourths (78%) noted that selected reading assignments were included, and 67% incorporated an examination of real or fictitious cases. Slightly more than one-half (52%) used guest speakers who addressed topics such as "Working with the Latina Community" and "Racism–Culturally Sensitive Practice." Key national speakers such as George Bluespruce, Ron Lewis, and Wilma Mankiller, also made presentations. More than one-third (37%) of the coordinators also showed films or videotapes such as "The Trial of Standing Bear," "The Klan, A Legacy of Hate in America," and "Therapeutic Techniques with Blacks, Hispanics and Indians."

One-third (33%) of the coordinators revealed that students took field trips to visit agencies and community organizations serving minority clients in nearby communities and urban centers. One coordinator described a six-day trip to a Native American Tribal Center in conjunction with an in-depth class study unit. Another described a three-day field trip to an urban community where students participated in seminars concerning urban diversity and urban problems. These trips provided students exposure to client groups and community problems they would otherwise have only studied in class.

In response to an open-ended request to list "other ways in which minority content is included in the field seminar/class," respondents noted that they:

a. assigned papers on practice with minority clients,
b. requested student participation in campus-wide Minority Awareness Days and Black History Month events,
c. conducted class sessions devoted to practice issues concerning minority populations, barriers to communication, and the impact of value judgments when working with minority clients,
d. involved students in audio-conferences with practitioners, faculty, students, and
e. asked students to complete journals on assigned topics.

Appropriateness of Placement Sites and Seminar

The participants were asked whether they felt that the learning opportunities available in field placement sites and the field seminar adequately prepared students to work with diverse clients. Most (80%) indicated that this was not the case; they reported experiencing difficulties and frustrations, and noted the need for changes in their program. The respondents repeatedly noted the need for students to be more adequately prepared to practice with clients from diverse backgrounds. Three of the problems articulated concerned (a) the need for developing audiovisual material for field seminars, (b) the limitations of classroom discussion in the absence of minority students or faculty, and (c) the relative naivete of social work students.

Regarding the need for improved practice opportunities, the coordinators recommended that students have more "hands-on experience." Coordinators suggested that efforts be made to collaborate with social work schools already working with diverse populations for fieldwork exchanges and field trips. Because of the homogeneity of the community within which students do their field work, it was also suggested that the placement catchment area be expanded. The intent of both of these suggestions is to provide students with direct practice experience with clients different from those in their home community. Placing students in field situations dramatically different from what they are accustomed to challenges stereotypes and assumptions about practice techniques that students may have.

Many coordinators shared information about changes they had already made or anticipated making in their own programs. In addition to offering courses on practice with minority clients, respondents wrote that they were purchasing relevant videotapes on diversity issues as well as producing videotaped interviews with minority social workers. Others planned to develop workshops for field instructors on diversity and cultural pluralism, and planned to recruit minority field instructors. Also reported were efforts to offer students internship opportunities in culturally diverse rural and urban communities. One respondent wrote about the possibility of developing a student exchange program with a social work school in Puerto Rico.

DISCUSSION

Social work programs are expected to train students to provide services that are sensitive to clients' cultural frames of reference. The findings of this study clearly indicate that fieldwork programs in rural, culturally homogeneous communities need to be creative in developing methods to provide appropriate multicultural content and practice opportunities. The ability to provide experiences that prepare students for practice with racially diverse populations is limited by the geographic location of the social work program. The data suggest that rural programs face a dilemma. In the presence of limited opportunities for experiential-learning, there is much reliance on the field seminar to expose and sensitize students to the issues surrounding the provision of services to racially diverse clients. Seminars incorporate assigned readings, speakers, and audiovisual material, and encourage student participation in extracurricular activities such as field trips and involvement in special campus events as mediums for exposure and discussion.

While the assignments, discussions, and field trips that are components of the field seminar experience make an important contribution to educating students about a variety of cultural perspectives, these activities may be insufficient. A problem that persists is that such experiences cannot substitute for hours of practice experience. It is important to provide opportunities for fieldwork, so students develop competency in working with racially diverse clients. Students, upon graduation, should be able to employ interpersonal, assessment, and intervention skills sensitive to clients' cultural backgrounds. The development of a keen awareness of the presence of discrimination and oppression, and the impact that these have on individuals, families, and communities is needed.

In light of this, programs in communities with limited numbers of racially diverse members have to consider alternative means of training students. Social work programs in such communities need to reexamine the ways in which practice experiences are offered to students. The investigation findings suggest two approaches that merit serious consideration. One approach is an expansion of the catchment area within which students are placed. Students could be expected to have at least one field experience in a field site that provides services to racially diverse clients. As several respondents indicated, there are communities anywhere between 20 and 120 miles of their school that offer such opportunities. The findings indicate that several programs already encourage students to commute 75-80 miles or more to more populated and racially diverse areas or to other rural communities for work with diverse client groups such as Native-Americans, farm workers, or prisoners.

A second approach is to expand the definition of diversity. For the most part, discussions about training students to work with diverse clients refer to Hispanic, African-American, Native-American, or Asian-American clients. In rural, racially homogeneous communities, other client groups need to be identified that are also subject to discrimination, and are victims of entrenched stereotypes, low status in the community, and deeply rooted forms of oppression. Examples of these may be Franco-Americans and Portuguese groups. The significance of field experiences with clients from such groups can be that students develop competency to provide services to their clients and be trained to universalize the knowledge and skills obtained (Ifill, 1989). By the completion of their fieldwork, students would thus be able to recognize individual characteristics of racial minority groups as well as the characteristics and structural problems shared by diverse groups. Even in urban communities which offer students many opportunities to practice with clients from diverse backgrounds, there are limitations to the types of clients that any one student can meaningfully learn to work with. Every student must eventually learn to transfer the cognitive, affective, and behavioral skills learned in working with one client group to other groups that they will encounter in their practice. In field practice, emphasis is placed on training students in the transferability of acquired knowledge and skills in order to practice with any number of diverse groups. An expectation is that students be able to synthesize their practice techniques. As one respondent indicated, "This is a life-long process that is just beginning here. We expect to raise awareness and stimulate a commitment to ongoing growth."

REFERENCES

Angry Vermont Students Seize President's Office. (1991, May 1). *Chronicle of Higher Education, 37* (33), A2.

Benavides, E. L., Mary M. & Velasquez, J. S. (1980). Toward a culturally relevant fieldwork model: The community learning center project. *Journal of Social Work Education, 16* (2), 55-62.

Chau, K. L. (1990). A model for teaching cross-cultural practice in social work. *Journal of Social Work Education, 26* (2), 124-133.

Council on Social Work Education. (1990). *Curriculum Policy for the Master's Degree and Baccalaureate Degree Programs in Social Work Education*. Maryland: Council on Social Work Education.

Crompton, D. W. (1974). Minority content in social work education–Promise or pitfall? *Education for Social Work Journal, 10* (1), 9-18.

Fox, J. R. (1983). Affective learning in racism courses with an experiential component. *Journal of Education for Social Work, 19* (3), 69-76.

Ifill, D. (1989). Teaching minority practice for professional application. *Journal of Education for Social Work, 25* (1), 29-35.

Jaschik, S. (1991, May 15). Some accrediting groups may be allowed to use 'Diversity Standards'. *Chronicle of Higher Education, 37* (35), A1, A20.

Magner, D. K. (1991, May 1). Push for diversity in traditional departments raises questions about the future of ethnic studies. *Chronicle of Higher Education, 37* (33), A11-A13.

1979 Delegate Assembly Actions. (January 1980). *NASW News, 25*, 30.

Office of Management and Budget, Statistical Policy Division. (1975). *Standard Metropolitan statistical areas* (Revised edition). Washington, DC: U.S. Government Printing Office.

Proctor, E. K. & Davis, L. E. (1983). Minority content in social work education: A question of objectives. *Journal of Education for Social Work, 19* (2), 85-93.

Sanders, D. S. (1975). Dynamics of ethnic and cultural pluralism: Implications for social work education and curriculum innovation. *Journal of Education for Social Work, 11* (3), 95-100.

Schlesinger, E. G. & Devore, W. (1979). Social workers view ethnic minority teaching. *Journal of Education for Social Work, 15* (3), 20-27.

Souflee, F. & Schmitt, G. (1974). Educating for practice in the Chicano community. *Journal of Social Work Education, 10* (3), 75-84.

U.S. Department of Commerce, Bureau of the Census. (1981). *1980 Census of the population, Vol. 1, Characteristics of the population.* Washington, DC: U.S. Government Printing Office.

Fieldwork Among the Navajo: Implications for Social Work Research and Practice

Susan E. Dawson

SUMMARY. Fifty-five Navajo uranium workers and 33 key informants were interviewed concerning the psychosocial aspects of uncompensated occupational illnesses. Within this context, issues related to fieldwork among the Navajo are discussed, including research design, culture shock, working conditions, legitimation, and access. Moreover, appreciation of Navajo culture and the principle of noninterference have widespread implications for social work research and practice.

INTRODUCTION

In order to facilitate a more effective practice for non-American Indian social workers among American Indians, this paper will present a discussion of fieldwork issues related to interviewing Navajo respondents in light of American Indian traditional beliefs and culture, and fieldwork

---

Susan E. Dawson, PhD, is Assistant Professor of Social Work, Department of Sociology, Social Work and Anthropology at Utah State University, Logan, UT 84322-0730.

This article is based on a paper presentation at the Council on Social Work Education (CSWE) 38th Annual Program Meeting, February 29-March 3, 1992, Kansas City, MO.

[Haworth co-indexing entry note]: "Fieldwork Among the Navajo: Implications for Social Work Research and Practice." Dawson, Susan E. Co-published simultaneously in *Journal of Multicultural Social Work* (The Haworth Press, Inc.) Vol. 3, No. 1, 1994, pp. 101-111; and: *School Social Workers in the Multicultural Environment: New Roles, Responsibilities, and Educational Enrichment* (ed: Paul R. Keys) The Haworth Press, Inc., 1994, pp. 101-111. Multiple copies of this article/chapter may be purchased from The Haworth Document Delivery Center [1-800-3-HAWORTH; 9:00 a.m. - 5:00 p.m. (EST)].

methods and research design. By developing an understanding and appreciation of the Navajo culture as it relates to research methodology, the social work profession may facilitate strengthening of community ties and work to benefit multicultural diversity.

There is a shortage of American Indian social workers, leading to a critical need for their admission and training in the profession. Many non-American Indian social workers, as a result, are working directly or indirectly with American Indians. To illustrate, in 1992, there were 138,507 National Association of Social Work (NASW) active members in the profession. Of that group, 650 members (one half of one percent) were American Indians or Alaskan natives (personal communication, NASW, 1992). The Council on Social Work Education (CSWE) reports yearly college social work enrollments and the numbers of students graduating in schools of social work. There were 7,250 BSW undergraduates of which 80 (1%) were American Indians; of 10,063 MSW graduates, there were 50 American Indians (one half of one percent), and of 247 doctoral graduates, there was one American Indian graduate (about one half of one percent) (Spaulding, 23, 28:1990). Non-American Indian social workers working with American Indian populations may not have the necessary training or understanding of traditional Indian cultures.

An assumption is made in this paper that social work practice has been based, for the most part, in an Anglo/European tradition that has not effectively addressed the cultural aspects of American Indian traditions. This assumption leads to the idea that understanding other cultures is essential to effective practice with multicultural groups. Moreover, the researcher who understands another culture gains both personally and professionally.

METHODOLOGY

The author recently conducted a study on the Navajo Reservation and gained insights into the culture and traditions. A discussion of the methodology will be presented, followed by the issues which grew out of the study. Fifty-five Navajo households and 33 key informants were interviewed on the Navajo Reservation for an in-depth community study to determine the psychosocial impacts of uncompensated occupational illnesses among Navajo uranium workers. A triangulation of methods was employed including participant observation and interviews from a purposive sample developed through key informants. Each household had at least one family member with an occupational illness, such as lung cancer or pulmonary fibrosis, perceived to be related to the uranium mining and/or milling processes. Overall findings indicated that psychological stress and financial difficulties resulted from their illnesses.

The study was designed as a qualitative in-depth community field study and was conducted over a four-month period in 1989. The author lived with three Navajo families in Tuba City, Arizona, and Beclabito, New Mexico, throughout the study period. Interpreters were hired for the project because the majority of the cohort of elderly Navajo uranium workers, for the most part, spoke little or no English. In some cases, respondents explained they were more comfortable speaking in Navajo. Given that the researcher was from a different culture and also worked with interpreters, this increased the need to address the issue of validity. This was done by utilizing a triangulation of methods. In the present study, validity was addressed by cross-checking the interviews of Navajo-speaking respondents with English-speaking respondents as well as with key informants.

A key informants' list was developed initially through Navajo informants. The list included physicians, attorneys, politicians, engineering and environmental consultants, and community leaders. Informants also provided names for a purposive sample which snowballed as uranium miners and millworkers provided names of other workers. A random sample was not used as there is no complete sampling frame of Navajo uranium workers. However, it has been estimated by a knowledgeable informant that there were over 3,000 Navajo uranium miners who worked on the Colorado Plateau from the late 1940s through the 1970s.

Contacting respondents for interviews often required significant effort. Only five of the 55 respondents had telephones and, in some cases, the researcher had to drive to the family's home for an initial contact to arrange an interview time, and then make a second trip for the interview. In other cases, the address provided for the respondent was the family's winter home, but the respondent was actually living at the summer sheepcamp. This necessitated the identification of the new address and further travel to make the contact. The 55 families included in the study were from three areas on the reservation, including eight families from Tuba City, Arizona; nine from Blue Gap, Arizona; and 38 from the Shiprock, New Mexico, area.

The ethnographic nature of the project was designed to enable the researcher the flexibility of pursuing "leads" which emerged during the course of the research. The key informants and interpreters were essential in helping to provide access to the communities and in establishing trust and cooperation with respondents. The researcher had no prior experience working with the Navajo and, consequently, the development of ties was important. The interpreters were members of extensive family networks and provided entree and access to the respondents.

In addition to interviewing uranium workers, workers' widows and tribal members living in uranium areas were also interviewed. The interview schedule was administered in person and averaged one- to two-hours in length. Questions included both closed- and open-ended questions, including information regarding occupational and environmental history; services and programs contacted, e.g., workers' compensation and civil lawsuits; and financial and personal background information. Key informant interviews were unstandardized so that the topic area could be explored in-depth. In addition, a participant observation journal was kept and consisted of field notes over the four-month period.

FIELDWORK AND PRACTICE ISSUES

Culture Shock

One of the first issues a researcher will likely encounter, if one has neither worked nor visited an Indian reservation, is culture shock. Unless the researcher has lived in a poverty stricken area off a reservation, the initial experience of abject poverty may be one of disbelief. The first impression of the Navajo Reservation was of being in a Third World country–of no longer being in the United States. To illustrate, only 20.9 percent of homes have telephones and only 44.7 percent of homes have complete plumbing (Navajo Nation, 1988:13). While the researcher felt anger and frustration overall at the poverty level, it was pointed out by a key informant that not all Navajo feel they are living in abject poverty. This is because of their value of nonmaterialism. Many of the traditional Navajo elders do not value the same material "things" that many Anglos hold dear, e.g., telephones, microwave ovens, and compact disk players. He noted, however, that succeeding generations are struggling with the perceived lack of material goods and, consequently, feel marginal in not being able to "fit" in with either the Navajo or Anglo cultures.

In addition to the likelihood of feeling distressed at the overall economic status of the Navajo, a researcher may experience culture shock given a change of behavioral cues. Some of the cues which may prove to be different include the "Navajo handshake," which consists of lightly touching hands; pointing at people or things with your lips instead of your finger; and eye avoidance during conversation, which in Anglo culture is thought to indicate low self-esteem, shiftlessness, or lack of interest.

Besides different behavioral cues, there were physical cues identified relating to poverty, stratification, and ethnocentrism. The researcher initially took for granted, for instance, that all people have resources for buying items like stamps and stationery for writing to social service agencies, attorneys, and legislators. Also, the researcher learned quickly that gasoline and car trips were often rationed. Since the majority of Navajo do not have telephones, money must be had for payphones at trading posts or chapter houses. This brought up feelings of guilt for having greater personal resources in a situation where there was often no indoor plumbing or central heating. Yet, despite the differences in material wealth, the Navajo are gracious in terms of sharing their wealth. For example, the Navajo value the Giveaway ceremony in which they honor an event by giving gifts to relatives and friends. With this ceremony in mind, the researcher provided cans of coffee to respondents in exchange for the interview with the idea that the respondents' words held value.

Another custom which was kept throughout the interviews was waiting for the appropriate amount of time before knocking on the respondent's hogan–a traditional Navajo home. When the interview team approached a respondent's home, both sat in the car for a short time before approaching the door. Then the interpreter usually walked to the hogan, knocked on the door, and waited awhile longer until the person answered. This is a courtesy extended to the respondent so that they may ready both themselves and their home, if need be, since there is often no way to call ahead to arrange a visit.

Collecting financial information proved frustrating throughout the study and financial information was not always provided. It was explained to the researcher that anything implying bragging about one's wealth may be considered symptomatic of witchcraft and therefore a respondent may be reluctant to appear greedy or desirous of wealth (Personal communication, Barre Tolkien, 20 January 1992). Moreover, it might be considered gauche and impolite to discuss income and other financial information. Many respondents will simply respond with "Hola," meaning "I don't know," especially if they find a question to be embarrassing or inappropriate. How then does a researcher learn of financial information in such a climate? Asking questions about government assistance may prove more acceptable as it implies that the respondent is in need. Detailed information about duration, amount, and number of assistance payments, however, may simply not be known. Coded responses therefore may be designed, for example, with timespans of "approximately one year" and "monthly payments."

Legitimation and Access

As in all ethnographic research, it is paramount that acceptance by community members be established. Given that American Indians have a tradition of "being studied" by outsiders, some tribal members may be reluctant to talk with Anglo researchers. As one key informant said to the researcher, "Why should I talk with another white person?" Given the reluctance among some American Indians to talk with researchers, it is imperative that researchers and practitioners avoid doing things which may "spoil the field" for future research and practice (Punch, 1986).

One advantage to hiring interpreters is that they will "reformulate" questions which could otherwise appear absurd to respondents. Consequently, how questions are constructed is of considerable importance if interpreters are not employed. For example, a question in English such as, "Did the mushroom make you sick?" might be answered in the negative because a mushroom is not considered to cause someone to become ill. However, if worded, "Did you become sick because you were in contact with a mushroom?" the answer might be in the affirmative because it would imply responsibility of the individual for being in the area of the mushroom. As Witherspoon (1977) explains, a man may be kicked by a horse but a horse may not kick a man. Word order, then, takes on significant importance in questionnaire and interview schedule construction.

Navajo Health and Cosmology

This section is not intended to provide a full treatment of Navajo cosmology but to provide insights into the fieldworker's experiences (see Reichard, 1950; and Witherspoon, 1977). It is important to understand that, with the Navajo, health is connected to everything including Navajo religion and cosmology. The Navajo belief in "hozho" or "beauty" encompasses the idea of being in balance, in harmony.

Because everything in the world is connected, any disruption in one part of the system affects the rest of the system, so that Navajo health is not only physical but also psychological. Western medicine is beginning to incorporate this idea with the notion of holistic health. Keeping this belief in mind, it was crucial to be sensitive to Navajo belief and behavior concerning illness. There is a view held by the traditional Navajo, for instance, that one may attract a certain illness to oneself by discussing the illness with another. This is based on the Navajo belief that speaking creates reality. Witherspoon (1977:32-33) explains, "From the propositions that knowledge is the inner form of thought, language is the inner form of speech, and thought is the inner form of speech, it may be presumed that knowledge is also the inner form of language." It is as if by talking about the illness one creates the energy which attaches itself to the speaker.

In addition, there is concern about speaking of one who has died. Some traditional Navajo believe the ch'indi, or ghost/spirit, of a dead person may be invoked by speaking of the person if the deceased had not been ritually buried. In the latter instance, the spirit may become malevolent and the respondent may be reluctant to be interviewed. The researcher may have no way of knowing if the deceased person has been ritually buried but, consequently, may understand a widow or family member's reluctance. Also, given that American Indian life has become urban or semi-urban, there may be no way to prepare the deceased ritually for burial. This is anxiety-producing and problematic for the family because contact with a malevolent ch'indi may result in a number of problems including, for instance, unexplained sickness, depression, flu-like symptoms, and a sense of malaise. Overall, whether or not a Navajo will speak with someone about a deceased person depends on how recently the person has died, on whether proper rituals were undertaken, and on speaking positively about the deceased (Personal communication, Barre Tolkien, 20 January 1992).

In the study it was imperative to speak with the uranium workers' widows about their deceased husbands' occupational histories. Before the widow respondents were approached, the researcher was informed by an Anglo investigator that it would be unlikely that the widows would be interested in talking about their deceased husbands. Consequently, the researcher spoke with them using respect and reverence for the deceased. As it turned out, the widows were very cooperative.

The population interviewed consisted largely of older (median age 62) traditional Navajo men and women who, for the most part, have retained traditional beliefs concerning their culture. Cultural interpretation of radiation exposure and resulting illnesses exacerbated problems because the Navajo could not relate radiation to anything within the Navajo experience. There was no word in Navajo for radiation and the Navajo workers interviewed were generally not informed by employers that radiation was a dangerous substance. Consequently, the Navajo workers did not initially understand that the illness could be occupationally-related nor did they understand the implications of uranium mining on their land. There is concern that many Navajo on the reservation today still have not made the connection between the uranium and health problems.

In addition to uranium workers who had documented occupational illnesses, it was indicated also that there might be uranium workers who had illnesses which had not been reported. This was because either the workers did not understand the etiology of their illnesses, and therefore did not file for benefits or lawsuits, or because it was possible that some of the workers believed their illnesses were caused by natural phenomena or by witchcraft. In some cases, the respondent may have believed that a witch blew a piece of bone under the respondent's skin which then transmitted the illness. Moreover, the traditional population may believe that certain illnesses are related to their association with natural phenomena, such as being in the place where lightning strikes or by taboo-related relationships. Levy et al. (1987) note that seizure disorders are believed by some Navajo to be caused by sibling incest, thereby creating stigma, isolation and reluctance to access both traditional and modern health care treatment. The same may apply to uranium workers or others with health problems, leading to a dilemma in terms of treatment. Generally, traditional Navajo believe in the idea of personal responsibility in terms of illness and, consequently, tend not to blame someone else for the illness unless it is thought to be a case of witchcraft (Personal communication, Barre Tolkien, 20 January 1992).

Some traditional Navajo may only access medicine men/women, also known as singers or hataalii. If the medicine man/woman is not familiar with the etiology of radiation-related illnesses, there is the possibility that the worker will not know how to apply for workers' compensation and/or a lawsuit or become registered with the Navajo Nation's Office of Navajo Uranium Workers–a uranium workers' registry. The Indian Health Service hospitals practice Anglo western medicine and also provide for the services of traditional medicine upon client request. However, it is still possible for workers with occupational illnesses not to be identified in the modern health care and social service systems.

IMPLICATIONS FOR SOCIAL WORK

Non-American Indian social workers have traditionally adopted methods of intervention when working with clients. These methods refer to any professional activity assessed to be appropriate. However, when working with American Indian groups, the non-American Indian social worker may consider adopting the principle of "noninterference," particularly when working with American Indian clients. Good Tracks (1973) identified that the principle of noninterference includes a nondirective approach of respect, consideration, and etiquette for the client. He explained:

> I was visiting my cousins when one of them put on his coat and said he was going downtown. He had no car, so one could assume he was

> going to walk. I restated his intention and volunteered to drive him. The cousin showed noninterference with my activities by not asking or even suggesting that I drive him, although that is certainly what he wanted. If he had asked directly and I had not cared to drive him, I would have been put on the spot. (Good Tracks, 1973:31)

Wax and Thomas (1961) and Lewis and Ho (1975) also discuss the principle of noninterference. Lewis and Ho (1975:379) state:

> . . . the concept of "social work intervention" may be consistent with much of the white man's culture, but it diametrically opposes the native American's cultural concept of noninterference.

How do non-American Indian social workers, then, work successfully with American Indian populations, given these concerns? By understanding the culture of the American Indian tribe with whom one is working, by dispelling stereotypes of American Indians, and by using appropriate techniques and approaches, Lewis and Ho (1975) believe the non-American Indian social worker may develop a sensitive practice with American Indians. Good Tracks (1973) suggests that patience is paramount. He contends that these social workers can expect to work one year before fully gaining acceptance into the American Indian community.

In addition to the principle of noninterference, time and temporal aspects are different with American Indian groups in that time is associated with nature and natural phenomena. The non-American Indian social worker needs to be aware, too, that sharing, as compared to competition, is a prevailing value. Lewis and Ho (1975:379) explain, "If a Native American is on his way to a meeting or appointment and meets a friend, that conversation will naturally take precedence over being punctual for the appointment."

Understanding etiquette will help also to alleviate culture shock. Listening and not interrupting are social skills American Indian groups hold in high esteem, but ones that non-American Indian social workers often need to develop. It is considered rude and ill-mannered to interrupt a speaker until he/she is finished. Sometimes a listener will wait a short period to be sure that the speaker is finished with a thought. An American Indian will "withdraw his attention from a person who interferes" (Good Tracks, 1973:31-32) or interrupts, including interruption by speakers who prescribe "shoulds" or "oughts." Anglos, for example, use prescriptive behavior and advice regularly, from newspaper advice columns to discussions about buying items, e.g., "You should go to this store and buy this or that." A Navajo would likely not offer such a suggestion. Instead, he/she might discuss what has been purchased and where, but would not do so in a prescribing manner.

In sum, several issues have been raised in this paper concerning fieldwork and practice with American Indians and the Navajo in particular. The issues of culture shock, legitimation, access, and cultural understanding were presented. With an awareness of these issues, non-American Indian social workers may benefit in their practice with American Indians by understanding the concept of noninterference. An understanding of this principle may help to reduce culture shock and help the social worker in terms of access and acceptance into the community. It is important to understand traditional Navajo culture because many older people are still committed to these traditions. Many younger people, while adopting non-traditional ways, also share in the traditional aspects of American Indian culture.

The fieldwork issues described may be successfully addressed and appreciated by social work practitioners through the understanding of cultural aspects of American Indians. Patience and the appreciation of values and behavior will help alleviate distress, and will facilitate and bridge understanding and cooperation between the two cultures.

DEDICATION

This article is dedicated to William W. Vosburgh, Professor, Bryn Mawr College, The Graduate School of Social Work and Social Research, for introducing me to the rewards of research and teaching.

REFERENCES

DuBray, W. H. (1985). American Indian values: Critical factor in casework. *Social Casework: The Journal of Contemporary Social Work, 66*(1), 30-37.

Good Tracks, J. G. (1973). Native American noninterference. *Social Work, 18*(6), 30-34.

Levy, J. E., Neutra, R., & Miller, D. (1987). *Hand trembling, frenzy witchcraft, and moth madness: A study of Navajo seizure disorders*. Tucson, AZ: The University of Arizona Press.

Lewis, R. G., & Ho, M. K. (1975). Social work with Native Americans. *Social Work, 20*, 379-382.

Navajo Nation. (1988). *Navajo Nation FAX 88: A statistical abstract*. Window Rock, Navajo Nation, AZ: Navajo Nation. pregnancy.

Punch, M. (1986). *The politics and ethics of fieldwork: Qualitative research methods series 3*. Newbury Park, CA: Sage Publications, Inc.

Reichard, G. A. (1950). *Navajo religion: A study of symbolism.* New York: Bollingen Foundation.
Spaulding, E. C. (1990). *Statistics on social work education in the United States: 1990.* Alexandria, VA.
Wax, R. H., & Thomas, R. K. (1961). Anglo intervention vs. Native noninterference. *Phylon, 22,* 53-56.
Witherspoon, Gary. (1977). *Language and art in the Navajo universe.* Ann Arbor: The University of Michigan Press.

TRENDS: THE VIEW FROM THE CUSTOMER– STUDENT OPINION

What Culturally Diverse Students Say About Emotion: An Exploratory Study

Carol S. Cohen

SUMMARY. The statements of culturally diverse students suggest the need for continuing consideration of professional acculturation strategies. Formulated through agency-based work with field interns from baccalaureate and associate degree programs, this qualitative study captures students' words and offers a context for understand-

Carol S. Cohen, ACSW, 475 Warren Street, Brooklyn, NY 11217.

This study was conducted as part of the Student Internship Program of the North Brooklyn Family Center of Catholic Charities, Diocese of Brooklyn, with research related consultation by the Graduate Center of the City University of New York. This is a revised version of a paper presented at the Annual Program Meeting of the Council on Social Work Education, New Orleans, LA, March 17, 1991.

[Haworth co-indexing entry note]: "What Culturally Diverse Students Say About Emotion: An Exploratory Study." Cohen, Carol S. Co-published simultaneously in *Journal of Multicultural Social Work* (The Haworth Press, Inc.) Vol. 3, No. 1, 1994, pp. 113-124; and: *School Social Workers in the Multicultural Environment: New Roles, Responsibilities, and Educational Enrichment* (ed: Paul R. Keys) The Haworth Press, Inc., 1994, pp. 113-124. Multiple copies of this article/chapter may be purchased from The Haworth Document Delivery Center [1-800-3-HAWORTH; 9:00 a.m. - 5:00 p.m. (EST)].

ing their meaning. Findings include diverse views of professionalism, engagement, and emotional exchange. Through examination of the cultural context of the social work profession, students' reports can be linked to cultural diversity rather than simple educational naivete. In addition to identifying areas for further research, the study supports the development of multicultural consciousness in designing and evaluating student learning experiences.

INTRODUCTION

Culturally diverse students have a great deal to say about emotion. Formulated through agency-based work with over 80 field interns from baccalaureate and associate degree programs, this qualitative study captures their words and offers a context for understanding their meaning. Students' statements about experiences of emotion in their field internships call for a reconsideration of professional acculturation strategies.

The notion that social work education is a process of "tutoring the self" suggests that interns are engaged in a change experience, in which they will be transformed (with their own effort and assent) into social workers. Although students are individuals, it is assumed that they share (or will share) the same values, professional goals, and ideology. The corollary to this assumption is that clients also benefit from a defined set of values and norms for practice, including principles for emotional expression between client and worker.

However, viewing student interns merely as immature professionals can easily lead field and academic instructors to treat diversity of emotional expression as evidence of differential progress toward professionalization. This study proposes that at minimum, the range of emotional expression among students should be considered a signal to explore cultural coherence and collision. Difficulty in eliciting, hearing, and understanding cross-cultural communication of students, can run parallel to difficulty in engagement, assessment, and action between social worker and client. Acceptance of the culturally imbedded nature of social work's values and practices opens the possibility that students may not share these assumptions.

When one re-frames students' diversity of attitudes about emotion from educational naivete to cultural diversity, an entirely new picture can emerge. Although social scientists and biologists have taken up the issue of emotion, it is a crucial, yet still underdeveloped, area by social workers. This paper attempts to correct this lack of attention by exploring issues of emotional expression in social work to illuminate the norms and values of practice. Central in this effort will be the findings of a study that looked at the attitudes towards emotion and expression among a culturally diverse group of students.

EMOTIONS AND CULTURE

Catherine Lutz proposes that emotional meaning is "a social rather than an individual achievement–an emergent product of social life" (Lutz 1988, 5). In this view, emotions are integral to culture, rather than a pre-cultural, biological phenomenon. This cultural contructivist approach to emotions is widely debated in the natural and social science literature (Ekman 1983, Kemper 1981, Lynch 1990). However, it correlates extremely well with social work ideology. This theory places emotions in the social world, and supports principles of self-determination and acceptance of individual diversity.

In addition, Lutz (1986) elaborates on the inherent contradictions in the Western cultural construction of emotion, providing a context for understanding the role of emotion and expression in the social work profession. The basic Western conflict between the mind and heart, coupled with the universal need for affect, is part of social work ideology. In contrast to the larger culture and other professions, social workers place a higher value on the imperative of feeling, and incorporate the expression of emotion in every phase of work. These issues may be related to the influence of women in both the theory-building and direct practice of the social work profession.

The identification of emotions as cultural elements directs professionals to consider diversity in emotional expression on two important levels. First, emotional expression can be explored to illuminate culture as in the work of Tavris (1989) and Rosaldo (1980). Cultures are not considered unitary structures. They contain paradoxical elements, but are coherent to their members. If one can look at emotion to understand a particular culture, it seems sensible that one can also look at emotions to identify differences between and within cultures. Thus, the second level for consideration is that diversity of emotions can illuminate diversity of culture. This exploratory study relates to both levels.

Hochschild (1983) has demonstrated how the self can be effectively tutored into occupational conformity. Her study of flight attendants confirm that brainwashing, or extreme vocational acculturation, is possible. She also demonstrates the monstrous consequences of "deep acting" for individuals and their relationship to their culture of origin. Many social work student interns are members of marginalized groups; many are bi-cultural. They may be extremely sensitive to professional acculturation, since they experience a parallel process in the larger culture. As such, students can serve as "expert witnesses" to the process if encouraged appropriately. Their observations can identify the confluence of their culture and that of the social work profession.

RESEARCH METHODOLOGY

As program coordinator of student field placements, the author became conscious of students' extensive discussion about emotional exchange between themselves and clients. Terms like "professional attitude" and "emotional involvement" constantly surfaced, often with different definitions. Further, students appeared to have a variety of ways to describe their attitudes about feelings; one student said that she "was just like myself" when she saw clients, while another said that she "locked her emotions in a box" when with clients. Following two years of informal study with over 80 culturally diverse student interns, a focus group design for further research was implemented.

Three group sessions were held with students placed at each of three service sites of a community based program of a large social agency. The students worked directly with clients who requested emergency assistance and advocacy services. Held during the spring of 1990, each of these groups were comprised of 4 to 7 female students in baccalaureate and associate degree programs (total = 17) who were engaged in fieldwork at the agency for 3 to 9 months. Previous contact between participating students and the focus group leader (author) was limited to a pre-placement interview, agency orientation session, and supervision of some of their field instructors.

Participation was voluntary; no student declined. Groups were formed to include a maximum number of students at one time, without asking interns to make a special trip to the agency. Students were released from their regular assignments to participate in the group, with the full support of agency supervisors and administrators. All focus group participants were women of color, as are over 90% of the student interns in the program. Ages of participants ranged from approximately 18 to 65 years. Although not by design in composing groups, all groups were culturally mixed, although one was comprised of only Latinas (mixed only regarding country of origin). Cultures represented include: Afro-American, English Speaking Afro-Caribbean, South American, Central American, and Puerto Rican.

As the findings of a limited, exploratory study, statements made by participating students should not be considered generalizable to a cultural group. However, their words point directions for future study along these lines. The study's goal is to raise questions and suggest areas for further work.

STUDENT STATEMENTS

All students discussed the rewards of the work, including the results ("really helping someone") and the client feedback ("Oh, you were so kind, or, you were so patient, you listened to what I had to say, thanks for really listening"). Although described differentially by group and sometimes by individual, all students recognized an emotional exchange inherent in the social worker-client relationship.

Students' comments are grouped under three section headings: entering the social work profession, family and culture, and emotional exchange between student and client. The first two sections contribute to understanding why students choose this training, as well as illuminating commonalities and differences in their previous experiences. The third section explores the heart of the student-client relationship, offering students' perspectives on the emotional exchange inherent in the work.

Entering the Social Work Profession

Regardless of cultural affiliation, students consistently responded that they entered social work in order to "help people." They subsequently defined "help" differently, but all reported dedication to a humanitarian purpose. They differed on possible causes (family, cultural background, etc.). One person (English Speaking Afro-Caribbean) thought social work would be financially rewarding; others (multiple groups) mentioned that "you don't go into social work for the money."

When asked, "what becoming a 'professional' meant," students provided a range of responses. These included descriptions of emotional distancing and mastery of a body of knowledge. A cross-cultural description was one of "expert" or "old hand." A Puerto Rican student described the process and effect of taking on the "professional" mantle:

> I remember when they (clients) came and I told them I am a student, they'd say: "Well, get me somebody who is not one!–Get me a professional who knows what they are talking about." They tend to judge you in a way that, "Oh, well, you don't know because you're not finished." So there were times when I really didn't know what I was saying, but I tried to appear like I did . . . You start feeling good about yourself too–because you start trying to believe it!

For the majority of Puerto Rican and South American students, notions of professionalism were linked with personal investment.

In another context, Latina students associated the term "professional social worker" with their experiences with public assistance programs. Many identified the Latina public assistance workers as particularly hateful. The definitive emotional description of such a person was "They show no caring at all. I guess they're just doing it because they have a job to do." One Latina student described this from her previous experience as a client:

> They are the ones that treat you like you are something from the garbage. They don't respect your feelings; they don't respect that you are there because you need the service, not that you want to rely on somebody else . . .

In grappling with this issue, Latina students offered explanations for the behavior, raising the paradoxical issues involved:

> so they think that since they had a bad time they are supposed to give others a bad time–and it's not like that.

On the other hand, a Puerto Rican student credited the inhumane workers for inspiring her to set a new, and higher, professional standard for Latina social workers. Latina students were the only respondents to claim that they entered the field because of their own help-seeking experiences, as in the following:

> I think that I help myself to be self-sufficient for me and for our clients . . . I choose social work since I have problems. I wanted to make a difference in our society, the best way that I can.

Only two students (Afro-Caribbean and South American) raised issues of social justice related to the social work profession. An Afro-Caribbean student described how she marshalled her commitment to help people into a "driving force" to motivate her actions on behalf of clients. She believed this force enabled the professional social worker to work on behalf of individual clients and families, as well as to sustain a strong commitment to social justice.

Family and Culture

One Afro-American student described herself: "I'm a screamer!" In her family, she said, "They cry together, they laugh together–they're very emotional." Descriptions of families were mixed among all cultural groups, although all students described the "typical" family in their culture as the scene of "sharing," "caring," and "problem solving." A Central American student noted the differences between herself (highly emotional) and her mother (not emotional). Older students with children reflected on the warm atmosphere of their families. Afro-American and Afro-Caribbean students reported their own large families as similar to their experience as children, placing the mother at the center: "They're always coming to mommy." Three Puerto Rican students reported their own families as the antithesis of their parents', where there was a lack of emotionality and communication between parents and parents and children:

> My father was very strict, and my mother was very closed to us. I think it was the style at that time . . . At that time the mother only spent the whole time cleaning the kitchen, washing the floors, and they don't even sit down with you and even talk to you when you were crying.

Students identifying themselves as immigrants to New York City described the culture of their homeland as extremely benevolent. When given, these reports were universally rosy in their depiction of mutual aid among families and community. These immigrant students often described New York's neighborhoods in contrast, as "heartless" and "culturally lost."

Numerous students tried to explain the reason for the differences, and attributed New York City's problems to size, severity of problems, and the changing priorities of the family:

> Over there the people are closer than over here. Over here everybody's doing something else and you don't have the chance to be that close with your family or your neighbors . . . I guess we tend to be more cold–they say that over there (about New York).

However, one can question if any community could live up to the following Puerto Rican student's standard:

> But I know that in Puerto Rico, you don't even have to know the person and people are there with open arms–if they were to see someone in the street, they'll take people into their houses–they'll give them food–you know, they stay together and they really try to help them–here, there's a lot of people, they just walk by–they just don't care.

Those students who did not speak about their homeland (all Afro-American and New York born-Puerto Rican students) did not share stories of New York City as heartless and cruel.

Emotional Exchange Between Student and Client

All students reported approaching fieldwork with a degree of fear or anxiety. However, the source of worry and the strategy for dealing with it was quite diverse. Puerto Rican students expressed concerns about being naive, trusting, or too friendly in the initial stages of fieldwork. Examples include:

1. Well, at first . . . I was very sensitive to it and it affected me–I was taking it home with me–and I said "No, no, no, I can't do that" . . . and I learned that I had to read between the lines–what they were saying and not take it personally.
2. I used to be so tender a person . . . So I refuse to act with them like that, so now I am acting more professional with them . . . But I refuse to let them know my feelings.

Nearly all Latina students reported a process of "toughening." However, some also recognized and reported the inherent danger, as the following illustrates:

> you have to get personally involved with the client because if you don't then you're like a robot and you're not feeling, and this is the whole thing that you're studying in your courses–the feeling you have to have some feeling for the client in order to help the client out. You have to know where to draw the line–that's it.

"Drawing the line" was a theme among all Latina students, and was alternately described as "holding a shield" and "not getting personally involved." Many reported great satisfaction at helping clients, but the "line drawing" seems to have been attempted for three reasons. The first reason given for "not getting personally involved" was as training to protect themselves from disappointment:

> I remember seeing them (fellow students) in that situation, and they got all worked up, and they felt so good, and then, it's like a little stab. Because it actually hurts because you are let down. So I guess it is to protect you against your feeling so that you can become stronger–and you don't feel so personally hurt.

The second reason shared by many Latina students was that clients would take advantage of a student who freely displayed emotions.

> Well, inside I feel sorry for the client, and try to do the best, but I try not to let it show. I just tell them, look, I am very concerned, and things will get better, and everything will turn out all right and everything will work out. That's what I say.

The third reason reported was the need to limit emotional investment because of the intensity and impact of the client's problems on the student. Latina students' approaches to emotional control were rarely successful at blocking their feelings, and appeared to have dramatic effects:

> Sometimes you feel something emotional, but I think that it is not really good to show that feeling to the client. So you have to hide. And when you are finished with your client and the situation is really bad that you have to cry or talk, or to do something . . .

English Speaking Afro-Caribbean students took a different approach to "drawing the line." They were fairly consistent in maintaining that they presented themselves to clients "as they are," without considering the censure of emotions. Further, they did not express the same types of concerns about emotional involvement as the Latina students, suggesting that they sought an "objective" approach:

> You still have the feelings, but you tend to just take control–it's a job you're doing–it's not like this is my friend and I'll do anything to help this person. You will do it, but on a professional level.

Rather than the generally utilized view, one Afro-Caribbean student looked at "not getting personally involved" as not providing personal services to the client beyond the boundaries of the agency (such as providing clothes and other material goods).

Latina students seemed particularly attuned to the effect of their own depth of feeling on the clients. Representative is one student alternating between feeling scared and secure, and sometimes approaching a state of "halfway a professional." Another stated, "I think I am struggling with myself, because I don't want the feeling to interfere with MY emotions." English Speaking Afro-Caribbean students and Afro-American students did not seem to share the intensity of these concerns about protection from emotional involvement. However, one Afro-American student was very clear about the emotional exchange with a client:

> And then you see them maybe take what you just give them (a bag of food), and go out there and sell it–And you say, "Here, I wasted my emotion on you, and someone else could have been here–and you're just selling the food!" You know it takes you up and down, up and down!

Similarly, when faced with a client who seemed ambivalent when the student finally located the help that she had asked for, an Afro-American student stated: "I wanted to shake her! I thought she was an idiot. It seemed she had her priorities all screwed up."

Across all cultures was a feeling that women, especially mothers with small children, should be treated with more overt compassion and genuine concern. On the other hand, men should be treated in a more "business-like manner" with students prepared to "read between the lines." The comment of the following student is illustrative: "What I'm learning here is don't treat all the persons the same. You have to treat them according to the behavior and the attitude." Most students suggested that relationships between client and worker are extremely varied, and identified a need to treat clients differentially.

Representatives of all groups identified empathy as putting oneself in the client's place. Two Puerto Rican students shared their perspective:

1. I know where they're at in that situation. So since I've been there I know . . . I try to help them more, to not only help them in food, but to try to motivate them to do something else for themselves.
2. They don't think we understand, and we just mm, mm, mm . . . a lot of times they feel that you don't understand, and I just want them to know that I do understand their situation–and I am willing to help them.

In an alternate construction, an Afro-American student described empathy as "some kind of love," and continued:

> that's it–just being human; you have needs like I have needs–just being human, just being human to each other . . .

RECOMMENDATIONS AND CONCLUSION

The comments of multi-cultural students offer insights into majority and minority culture. In this study, they expressed cross-cultural similarities and differences in the areas of relationships with clients, of family and culture, and of their emerging status as social work practitioner. As already noted, more numerous and diverse student respondents are needed before the data can be used for definitive cross-cultural generalization. This analysis would additionally benefit from correlation with cross-cultural paradigms that have been related to emotional expression and worker/student/client exchange. Among these are Ryan and Hendricks' (1989) recent work with Asian and Hispanic social workers and students, and Spiegel's (1965) historical work on the cultural issues of transference and counter-transference.

Within the constraints of this exploratory study, marked patterns were found between cultural groups. When taken with the view of empathy as a complex bridge between worker and client, these patterns raise serious concerns for training students and for serving clients. On one hand, if the profession chooses to adopt unitary expectations for emotional expression, academic and field educators have a long way to go with multicultural students. If on the other hand, as this study suggests, a more flexible definition of emotional expression is adopted, issues must still be addressed.

First, one must question the effect of the worker's culturally constructed style on the client. Although students may find their own styles comfortable, this study does not ask how these styles affect clients. As examples, one must question if the "drawing a line" or "locking emotions in a box" are a factor in forming relationships with clients. Paradoxically, these findings also can shed new light on the discussion of cultural matching between workers and clients. Again, while this study found patterns among cultural groups of students, it does not suggest that these are the patterns either adopted and/or preferred by clients of the same cultural groups. In fact, some findings, such as the fear of unrestrained emotion, might identify a source of concern about client/worker matching.

Second, some of the issues raised by student respondents call for examining the range of definitions of "professionalism." It is difficult to identify students' choices of definitions as clear cultural artifacts. However, one can consider if cultural groups have experienced the professions differently, and if this has made an impact on their definitions. Research correlating students' pre-educational experiences with social workers and their views of professionalism would be valuable in this effort. From this study, it clearly appears that educators must be more conscious how commonly used words are often uncommonly defined.

Third, this study suggests that the profession take a closer look at the definitions and expectations surrounding the concept of empathy. Rather than an elementary requirement for every client encounter, the process to establish empathetic relationships with clients should be seen as a continuing and difficult struggle. This study suggests that educators acknowledge that empathy is difficult to achieve under any circumstances, particularly in multicultural settings. When empathy is framed as a skill instead of as a value, its achievement can be a triumph of cross-cultural understanding.

In raising questions about the universality of social work education and practice, these findings support the continual examination of professional ideology for ethnocentric bias. By suggesting that cultural diversity in emotional expression exists, it challenges educators and practitioners to expand knowledge and values to accommodate the multicultural world of student, practitioner, and client.

REFERENCES

Ekman, P., Levenson, R.W., & Frieson, W.V. (1983). Autonomic nervous system activity distinguishes among emotions. *Science 221*, pp. 1208-1210.

Hochschild, Arlie R. (1983). *The managed heart: Commercialization of Human Feeling*. Berkeley: University of California Press.

Kemper, T.D. (1981). Social constructivist and positivist approaches to the sociology of emotions. *American Journal of Sociology 93*, pp. 263-289.

Lutz, Catherine (1988). *Unnatural emotions: Everyday sentiments on a Micronesian atoll and their challenge to Western theory*. Chicago: University of Chicago Press.

Lutz, Catherine (1986). Emotion, thought and estrangement: Emotion as a cultural category. *Cultural Anthropology 1*, pp. 287-309.

Lynch, Owen, M. (1990). *Divine passions: The social construction of emotion in India*. Berkeley: University of California Press.

Rosaldo, Michelle Z. (1980). *Knowledge and passion: Ilongot notions of self and social life*. Cambridge: Cambridge University Press.

Ryan, Angela Shen & Hendricks, Carmen Ortiz. (1989). Culture and communication: Supervising the Asian and Hispanic social worker. *The Clinical Supervisor 7*(1), pp. 27-40.

Spiegel, John P. (1965). Some cultural aspects of transference and counter-transference. From: Zald, ed. *Social Welfare Institutions*. New York: John Wiley.

Index

Note: Page numbers followed by t indicate tables.